THE FOUNDATIONS OF MUSLIM NATIONALISM

Pathway to India's Partition

Volume I

The Foundations of Muslim Nationalism

BIMAL PRASAD

Issued under the auspices of the
Rajendra Prasad Academy, New Delhi

MANOHAR
2026

First published 1999
Reprinted 2026

ISBN 978-81-7304-247-8 (series)
ISBN 978-81-7304-248-5 (Vol. I)

Published by
Ajay Kumar Jain for
Manohar Publishers & Distributors
4753/23 Ansari Road, Daryaganj
New Delhi 110 002

Printed and bound in India

To

my wife

ASHA

but for whose keen interest

and concern

this work could not

have been completed

Contents

Preface 9

Acknowledgements 15

Introduction 19

I. The Legacy from the Past 47

II. The Economic Divide 99

III. Ideological and Emotional Environment of the Muslim Elite 135

IV. Hindu Nationalism, Ethos of Indian Nationalism and British Policy 197

Appendix I. Syed Ahmed Khan's Speech at Lucknow, 28 September 1887 261

Appendix II. *Al-Hilal*: Objectives and Political Message, by Abul Kalam Azad, 8 September 1912 273

Appendix III. Excerpts from Muhammad Iqbal's Presidential Address to the Twenty-first Session of the All India Muslim League, Allahabad, 29 December 1930 281

Appendix IV. Now or Never: Are We to Live or Perish for Ever? by Rahmat Ali and three others, 28 January 1933 289

Bibliography 295

Index 309

Preface

THE BACKGROUND of India's Partition (1947), an event of seminal importance in the history of the subcontinent, has not so far been thoroughly studied by any Indian scholar. There are, of course, a number of excellent monographs relating to aspects of this theme covering a particular period or region. Among them, mention may be made of the works by Mushirul Hasan (1916-28), Anita Inder Singh (1936-47) and two of the present author's own doctoral students at the Jawaharlal Nehru University—Uma Kaura (1928-40) and Shila Sen (Bengal, 1937-47). None of them, however, seeks to present a comprehensive view or to deal at length with the mainsprings of the movement which led to Partition or its evolution over a long span of time. Those who have cared to touch upon this theme as part of bigger studies or general essays on the history of the Indian nationalist movement have generally contented themselves with remarking in passing on the age-old conflict between Hinduism and Islam, representing two contrasting civilizations or world-views, or with holding the British policy of divide and rule, M.A. Jinnah's intransigence or Jawaharlal Nehru's ineptness as primarily responsible for it. Most of our historians have shown a marked disinclination to deal with this subject at any length and have preferred to spend their talents and energies on more agreeable themes relating to the Indian nationalist, peasant or labour movements. This is apparently due to their lurking feeling that the emergence of Pakistan represented some kind of an aberration in the evolution of the subcontinent in modern times, and was primarily the result of an artificial movement originated and sustained by British machinations and led by self-seeking persons devoid of all patriotic instincts. No wonder, whatever may be said in public or howsoever willing the Indian elite may be to recognize and deal with the reality of Pakistan today, they continue, in their heart of hearts, to treat Pakistan virtually as a false State, lacking logic or legitimacy. Due to certain obvious historical reasons, this somehow does not apply to Bangladesh which emerged out of Pakistan in 1971, signalling to the Indian elite, whether rightly or wrongly, the death of the two-nation theory which had formed the basis of the demand for the creation of Pakistan.

The discussion of responsibility for Partition has further created a serious hurdle in the way of a dispassionate study of its background, whether by an Indian or a Pakistani scholar. Partition was primarily neither the result of the mistakes or intransigence of particular leaders, belonging to the Congress or the Muslim League, nor that of the British policy of divide and rule, but of certain historical forces as well as circumstances at given points of time which shaped the policies and actions of the leaders and willy-nilly pushed them towards Partition. This is not to subscribe to the theory of inevitability in history, whose votaries present almost every major event or development as predestined and bound to take place, but only to emphasize that concentration of attention on the role of certain leaders, however important, and neglect of the historical and socio-political background or the specificities of the various stages of evolving politics will not enable us to understand how and why a certain development took place. Leaders undoubtedly play an important role in shaping events, but only within the context set by historical forces and existing circumstances. Even with this limitation, their role is quite significant and provides a fascinating field of study. In any case, it is impossible to write about any political development without examining or analysing the role of the leaders associated with it. To do so, however, at the cost of, or in lieu of the study of the relevant historical and socio-political background would make such an examination or analysis sterile and meaningless.

The Partition of India was the culmination of a powerful movement of Muslim nationalism which began in the second half of the nineteenth century, symbolized by the foundation of the Mohammedan Anglo-Oriental College at Aligarh in 1877. Hindu nationalism had been born slightly earlier, as illustrated by the emergence of the movement for the replacement of Persian by Devanagari script in the courts of the North-Western Provinces and Oudh (as UP was then called) in the 1860s. The last to be born was Indian nationalism, symbolized by the foundation in 1885 of the Indian National Congress, seeking to appeal to and represent all sections of the Indian people, regardless of their religious affiliation. After a long and arduous struggle against the forces of both Muslim nationalism and Hindu nationalism, led respectively by the All India Muslim League (founded in 1906) and the All India Hindu Mahasabha (founded in 1915), it succeeded by mid-1930s in drawing towards itself most of the vital, politically conscious elements among Hindus, but failed to do the same with regard to Muslims. It, of course, always had Muslims within its ranks, both as leaders and as ordinary workers, but the bulk of them, except during the hey-day of the Pan-Islamic movement (1912-22), kept themselves aloof from the Congress right from the time of its birth. While disorganized and divided into several small groups or parties here and there, they generally recognized the primacy of the Muslim League, except during the middle and late 1920s when the All India Muslim Conference temporarily emerged as a more powerful and representative body of Muslims. With the further growth of Muslim nationalism by mid-1930s the Muslim League was revived and, for the first time, decided to contest elections in its own name. Even though not remarkably successful in the elections to provincial legislatures held in 1937, from then onwards it moved from strength to strength and succeeded within ten years in carving out a sovereign Muslim State, comprising those areas of British India both in the east and west where Muslims constituted a majority of the population.

Neither the League's adoption of the demand for Partition (1940) nor its success in securing its fulfilment within a short span of seven years can be explained without reference to the deep historical as well as socio-political foundations of Muslim nationalism, based on a belief that Muslims, although living togther with Hindus and others on Indian soil, constituted a nation separate from the rest and had their own special interests to protect and promote. This made the bulk of the Muslim elite fiercely attached to their separate political as well as cultural identity, and predisposed them to look at almost every development primarily from the point of view of the supposed interests of their own community. It is also necessary to remember that this nationalism, based on the two-nation theory, did not burst forth all of a sudden in 1937, but had been steadily growing and acquiring strength since at least 1877. That year witnessed the foundation not only of the first significant Muslim political organization—the National Muhammadan Association in Calcutta—but also, and more importantly, that of the Mohammedan Anglo-Oriental College at Aligarh, which, under the able leadership of Syed Ahmad Khan (1817-98), soon established itself as the most powerful symbol of Muslim awakening and solidarity. Apart from the teachers at Aligarh, numerous writers and poets nurtured the two-nation theory and spread it far and wide among the Muslim elite.

The Pakistan idea, signifying the urge to set up a separate, sovereign Muslim State, though not embedded in the two-nation theory in its original form, was its natural end-product. Not surprisingly, it was born spontaneously among the Muslim youth and intelligentsia without the involvement of any particular organization at least a decade before 1937, not in UP, as has been generally imagined, but in the Punjab, and given a powerful thrust in 1933 by a Punjabi student at Cambridge. Again, contrary to the general impression that the failure of the so-called Congress-League coalition talks in UP in July 1937 triggered off the League leadership's urge for a separate Muslim State, the minds of the greatest poet-philosopher of Muslim nationalism—Mohammad Iqbal—as also of the future founder of Pakistan—Mohammad Ali Jinnah—had begun turning towards it even before the commencement of the final stage of negotiations in UP. The developments between 1937 and 1947 also require a fresh look, devoted primarily to explaining their background and significance at various stages, free from wishful thinking and pre-conceived notions and influenced neither by a search for scapegoats in one leader or another, if not in British policy, nor by a desire to defend the national leaders on either side against criticism for their role on particular occasions.

Keeping all this in mind, the author, with all his limitations, has devoted a substantial portion of his working time during more than thirty years to the task of preparing a definitive study of the background of India's Partition. This is being published now in three volumes:

I. *The Foundations of Muslim Nationalism*
II. *A Nation within a Nation, 1877-1937*
III. *The March to Pakistan, 1937-1947*

The term 'Muslim nationalism', instead of the customary 'Muslim separatism', has been used in this trilogy, after a good deal of thought, in order to underline the true nature of the movement which culminated in India's Partition and birth of Pakistan. There is no need here to go into various definitions of nationalism and nationhood, or into the question whether the Muslims of British India were a nation or not. What is relevant to our study is the fact that the bulk of the politically conscious Muslims in British India thought of themselves, whether justifiably or not, as constituting a nation right from the second half of the nineteenth century and, at a later stage, went on to demand a sovereign State for that nation. The enthusiasm and devotion generated by that demand, particularly in the last phase, was not dissimilar to that generated by the demand for India's Independence. After fifty years of both Independence and Partition, it will be indeed ridiculous, as also pathetic, if we still continue to cling on to the myth that the birth of Pakistan was primarily the result not of a powerful movement having tremendous support among the people on whose behalf the new State was being demanded, but of the British policy of divide and rule and a few chance-mistakes or intransigence or hunger for power of certain leaders, particularly between 1937 and 1947. This is not to assert either that the British policy did not play an important role in encouraging that movement, or that the leaders on either side never committed any mistake or were never intransigent or interested in securing power for themselves. It is a different matter, however, to treat any one or more of these factors as the primary cause of Partition, and remain oblivious of the strength of Muslim nationalism which really led to it.

Another term requiring explanation is 'community consciousness' as distinguished from 'communal consciousness'. Just as the concept of separate nationhood need not necessarily have led to Partition—it being open to the two supposed nations to decide to co-exist within the same State—community consciousness need not necessarily have led to communal consciousness, though, helped by the attending circumstances as well as the historical and socio-political background, it actually did so. Communal consciousness implies a tendency to view every development from the point of view of a particular community, with no regard for the rights or interests of other communities, and indeed with a feeling of hostility towards them. Community consciousness, on the other hand, signifies merely the feeling of belonging to a particular community, with certain common attitudes and interests, without being obsessed by such a feeling and without any tendency to disregard the feelings or interests of other communities or nourishing any hostility towards them.

No effort has been made to assign responsibility for Partition to any particular leader or group of leaders, including Jinnah and Nehru, who have been the usual whipping boys of historians, depending on their predilections. Value-judgements have been scrupulously avoided. Although one may feel unhappy with Partition, as a student of history one has to recognize that certain powerful historical forces and circumstances in British India favoured Partition and, in 1947, no leader could have succeeded in preventing it. While the policies pursued by various leaders have been closely scrutinized, the purpose of such scrutiny is not to praise one or blame another, regardless of the side to which he or she might belong, but to understand why a particular leader adopted a certain policy and what were its consequences. This, according to the author, is the real task of the historian.

This study may not go down well with those Indians who are prone to blame Jinnah and Nehru, either singly or together, for Partition, and also by those Pakistanis who, while extolling Jinnah's role in the creation of Pakistan, tend to blame Gandhi or Nehru and Patel for forcing him to play that role. It is, however, hoped that it will be found useful by all those who may be keen, with an open mind, to understand really why and how Partition took place and are not primarily interested in foisting responsibility for it on this or that leader. This is the need of the hour in the fiftieth year of both Indian Independence and birth of Pakistan. India, Pakistan and Bangladesh (the bulk of whose people also had played an important part in the movement which led to Partition and the emergence of Pakistan) have all to make a fresh start in living together in amity and cooperation. This is not possible until the events leading to Partition are seen in a proper, historical perspective and there emerges a situation in which the heroes of one country are not seen as villains by the citizens of another. This work represents an humble effort in that direction.

Apart from contributing to better inter-State relations in the subcontinent, such a study should also help us in India to face the truth about the background of Partition and come to terms with our recent past, which cannot leave us however much we may try to ignore it. Contrary to the thinking of many among us who even now refuse to acknowledge the rise and growth of Muslim nationalism as the chief factor behind Partition and seek refuge in British policy and the mistakes or intransigence of some of the top leaders in explaining it, facing the truth will not hamper, but actually help the task of nation-building in our country in the post-Partition scenario. For it will make us poignantly realize, in a way in which nothing else can, the immense difficulty in accomplishing such a task in a plural society, such as ours, where success is bound to elude us until all of us, whether belonging to majority or minority, learn to show due regard to each other's concerns and sensitivities. It is this faith which has sustained me in my labours during the last thirty years or so.

Rajendra Prasad Academy, New Delhi BIMAL PRASAD
3 December 1997

Acknowledgements

WHILE WORKING on this project I have incurred the debt of a number of persons and institutions. To begin with, my thanks are due to the authorities of the Indian School of International Studies (since 1970 part of the Jawaharlal Nehru University as its School of International Studies). I am grateful to late Professor A. Appadorai, then Director of the School, for inviting me to work there in 1963, and to his successor, Professor M.S. Rajan, for encouraging me to undertake this project shortly after I was offered the Chair of South Asian Studies in 1965. I must also put on record my gratitude to late Pandit H.N. Kunzru, Professor Tarachand and Professor Bisheshwar Prasad for their blessings and encouragement at that time. Subsequently, the authorities of the School and the University provided me financial support for my field trips to the United Kingdom in 1975 and 1978, and to Pakistan in 1982 for the collection of source materials for the project. I am also thankful to late Professor Nurul Hasan, then Union Minister of Education, for taking keen interest in my work and for helping me secure financial support for an extended stay in London in 1975, and to late Dr J.P. Naik, then Member Secretary of the Indian Council of Social Science Research, for providing a generous grant.

In London, I got valuable help in settling down as well as in locating materials from Dr Z.H. Zaidi of Pakistan, who was then teaching at the School of Oriental and African Studies there and is currently engaged in editing the Jinnah Papers in Islamabad. Late Professor K.N. Ballhachet, Professor of South Asian History at SOAS, invited me to the School as a Senior Fellow in South Asian History during 1976-7. This helped me immensely in my studies as well as in collecting relevant materials for my project. Late Professor P.N.S. Mansergh and his colleague, late Sir Penderel Moon, who were at that time engaged in editing the volumes relating to Transfer of Power at the India Office Library in London—the main base also for my own work in the UK—were generous with their time whenever I felt the need for a reference or discussion. Late Lord Mountbatten was most kind and generous in 1978, granting me free access to his papers and offering me his warm hospitality and answering all my questions freely and frankly while I worked on them. Professor David Dilks, then Professor of International History at the University of Leeds, invited me to work as a Visiting Professor of Modern Commonwealth History there during 1982-3. The six months spent there gave me ample time, in a congenial environment, to continue my studies and also draft some of my chapters. My warmest thanks to all of them.

It is a pleasure to thank Mr Abdul Sattar, then High Commissioner of Pakistan in India, for facilitating my trip to his country in 1982 and ensuring that I was cordially treated wherever I went. My special thanks are due to Professor Sharif-al-Mujahid, then Director of the Quaid-e-Azam Academy in Karachi, for providing me all the necessary facilities, including free access to Jinnah Papers, and to late Khalid Shamsul Hasan, then Senior Vice-President of the National Bank of Pakistan, for giving me similar access to the valuable collection of his father (Syed Shamsul Hasan, long time Secretary of the All India Muslim League), containing some extremely valuable parts of Jinnah and Muslim League Papers. Professor Mujahid was not only generous with his hospitality and time whenever I showed interest in discussing something with him, but also helped me in several other ways and arranged my meetings with some other knowledgeable persons in Karachi. Mr Hasan similarly extended many acts of courtesy and kindness, for which he will always have a cherished place in my memory.

I had to consult materials at a number of places and must put on record my debt of gratitude to the staff at these institutions, particularly Jawaharlal Nehru University Library, Library of the Indian Council of World Affairs, Zakir Husain Library at Jamia Millia Islamia, the National Archives of India, and Nehru Memorial Museum and Library (New Delhi), India Office Library and Records, Public Records Office, Library of the School of Oriental and African Studies, University of London, Cambridge University Library as also the archives of the Churchill College at Cambridge, Mountbatten Archives at Broadlands and Library of the University of Leeds (UK), and the libraries and archives of the University of Karachi and Quaid-e-Azam Academy (Pakistan). Special mention must be made of the Nehru Memorial Museum and Library, which has been the main base for my study and writing during the last twenty years or so and where the authorities as well as the staff have been most kind and courteous to me throughout.

I am thankful to my two former students, who later became colleagues at Jawaharlal Nehru University, Dr Kapileshwar Labh and

Dr Shyamali Ghosh, for valuable help in collecting materials from the National Archives of India and the Nehru Memorial Museum and Library. Mrs Sangita Mallik, also a former student and now a colleague, has helped in preparing the bibliography. Among those who have helped in typing the manuscript, special mention may be made of Sri Ramlalji, working at JNU, and Mrs Laina Anikumar, working at the Rajendra Prasad Academy. I am thankful to both of them.

I must put on record here a special debt I owe to Professor Syed Hasan Askari, one of the most revered teachers of History at the Patna College, Patna, whose lectures on politics in India in the eighteenth century during my M.A. days (1945-7) and stray remarks on contemporary political developments first kindled in me an interest in the subject matter of the present work.

I do not know how to thank my wife, Asha, but for whose constant nagging as well as encouragement and support this work would not have seen the light of the day. She neglected her own writing in order to keep me totally free from all domestic chores, thereby enabling me to devote myself to this project without any distraction. She will undoubtedly be the happiest person to see these volumes in print.

Introduction

In dealing with the foundations of Muslim nationalism, it will not do to dilate upon one or the other according to one's own predilections, but to have a comprehensive view of them in their totality. It is the conjunction of all its foundations and supports which lent strength to Muslim nationalism. While the legacy from the past, the economic divide between Hindus and Muslims, and the ideological and emotional environment of the Muslim elite constituted its main foundations, it also drew strength from Hindu nationalism, the impact of that nationalism on the ethos of Indian nationalism, and last, but not the least, British policy in dealing with the communal problem. While all the other foundations and supports have been dealt with at some length, British policy was so intertwined with the evolution of Muslim politics that its detailed working has been left to be delineated along with that evolution in the two succeeding volumes and only an outline presented here.

It may be best to begin with the legacy from the past, which has so far been generally ignored by Indian historians, except in passing. This does not mean subscribing to the theory—quite popular with a few Indian as well as most Pakistani scholars—of a clash between two contrasting civilizations or of a perpetual conflict between Hindus and Muslims in politics ever since the advent of Islam in India. If there were some points of conflict or contradiction between Hinduism and Islam as civilizations or cultures, there were also commonalities. That there were conflicts between particular Hindu and Muslim potentates cannot be denied, but such conflicts are not synonymous with a general conflict between Hindus and Muslims. Conflicts were also prevalent amongst potentates belonging to the same religious denomination. Moreover, if there were conflicts, there were also numerous instances of cooperation and intermingling between the members of the two communities in various fields.

In order to understand the historical roots of Muslim nationalism, what we need to take into account are certain aspects of the general history of Islam as well as the history of India during the later medieval period. To begin with, we must note, as several well-known authorities on Islamic history have underlined, that while laying due stress on the universal brotherhood of all human beings as all religions do, unlike most other religions, Islam succeeded, right from its birth, in inculcating among its adherents a strong sense of belonging to a community which was not merely religious but also political. In this connection, it is significant that the Muslim calendar does not commence from the date of the birth of the Prophet or that of the time when he began to receive messages from Heaven and preach the new gospel, but from the time he succeeded in establishing a nascent political community in Medina (AD 622). Due attention must be paid also to the importance given to the community of the faithful in that gospel.

As Arabs and Turks, after their conversion to Islam, expanded in various directions and established their rule over a far-flung area, encompassing territories in Asia, Africa and Europe, the Muslim elite developed a feeling that they belonged to a conquering race and had a right to rule over non-Muslims and spread Islam among them. Wars and conquests, even when really motivated by other reasons, were usually justified by reference to the need for spreading Islam. The long rule of the Turko-Afghans and Mughals over a major portion of India further strengthened the consciousness of power as well as that of community among the Muslim elite in this country.

Whatever the reasons for the emergence and continuation of a particular Muslim ruler, it was customary to emphasize his devotion to the supposed interests of Islam. This provided the moral legitimation of his rule. The role of legitimation was performed by the *ulama*, a section of whom also worked as historians. According to the latter, the ideal rule was one which was based on a partnership between the pious scholars and the pious Sultan. As Ziauddin Barni explains in *Tarikh-i-Firuzshahi* (fourteenth century), the pious Sultan was expected not merely to uphold the dignity of the *ulama* and remove hindrances to propagation of the 'true faith' by the latter, but also facilitate their task by humbling and humiliating the idolatrous Hindus, if not completely exterminating them.

It is a tribute to the sense of realism, wisdom and generosity of the Turkish Rulers of India that they did not pay heed to such outpourings, openly asserted their right to do what they considered best for their rule, regardless of the injunctions of the *Shariah* or the preachings of the *ulama*. Beginning with the fifteenth century, they also appointed Hindus to high positions in the government till a stage arrived when even the highest offices were not barred to them. Akbar is justly famous for his liberality in this respect, but, contrary to the general impression, even under Aurangzeb, known for his religious bigotry, Hindu nobles continued to occupy the highest positions in the same way as they had done earlier; if anything, their number increased as the Mughal empire incorporated more and more territories within it.

However, whether the ruler was an Akbar or an Aurangzeb, the vast majority of the nobles in the higher ranks always remained Muslim. And even though Akbar defied orthodox Muslim opinion to some extent, particularly by abolishing the *jizya*, holding discussions at the court with representatives of various religious faiths and permitting the performance of a few Hindu religious rites by his Rajput wife, he could not afford to defy it beyond a point. An exceptionally shrewd ruler, he must have been aware of the fact that, apart from belonging to the Mughal royal family, he was ruling as a Muslim and had to keep the majority of Muslims in the court and the army on his side. Besides, Muslim orthodoxy and political power were closely interrelated, and every ruler was expected to keep it in mind. While a lot of friendly intermingling undoubtedly took place, the distinction between a Hindu and a Muslim in the political as well as social fields, never ceased. It just could not, under the circumstances of the times in sixteenth and seventeenth century India.

After the disintegration of the Mughal empire, orthodoxy acquired an even stronger hold over the mind of the Muslim elite in India, who were increasingly concerned with the loss of political power and the future of Islam without it in a land where non-Muslims constituted an overwhelming majority. It began to be stressed that Islam must be cleansed of all impurities that had crept into it, largely as a result of contact with Hindus, and that Muslims must again somehow acquire supreme political power in order to preserve their civilization in India. This is best illustrated by the teachings and activities of Shah Waliullah (1703-62), generally regarded as the greatest Islamic theologian produced by the Indian subcontinent. While seeking to revive the original teachings and lost glory of Islam, he wrote to one Muslim potentate after another in the hope that the latter would restore Muslim power and thereby facilitate the preservation of the supposed Muslim way of life. Failing to secure a proper response in India, he finally wrote to Ahmad Shah Abdali, inviting him to invade India and liberate the Muslims from the rule of the non-Muslims (Marathas and Jats).

The so-called Wahhabi movement of the nineteenth century represented a continuation of the thought-process initiated by Shah Waliullah. Its leader, Sayyid Ahmad Shahid or Barelvi (1781-1831), was a disciple of the former's son and successor, Shah Abdul Aziz (1746-1824), and generally considered by his circle as the most suitable person to head the movement for the purification of Islam and revival of its political power. About the same time, there arose somewhat similar movements in Bengal, one led by Haji Shariatullah (1781-1840) and his son Dudu Miyan (1819-62), and the other by Titu Mir (1782-1831). While both these movements focused on the grievances of the peasantry and attacked Muslim as well as Hindu landlords, there is no doubt that they also based themselves on separatist Muslim sentiments and increased the susceptibility of the Muslim peasantry of Bengal to communalist propaganda later on.

The growth of community consciousness amongst the Muslim elite was paralleled by the growth of a similar consciousness amongst the Hindu elite. As mentioned earlier, while the Turkish Rulers generally followed a policy of religious toleration and appointed Hindus to the highest positions in the government, the distinction between a Hindu and a Muslim was not obliterated, and Muslims always formed an overwhelming majority among those appointed to high offices. Besides, the Turkish Rulers generally disregarded the principle of religious tolerance while attacking Hindu rulers. As was customary then, the Turkish Rulers almost invariably attacked Hindu places of worship while invading the territory of a Hindu ruler and often gave the choice of Islam or death to the vanquished Hindu soldiers. All this was bound to cause feelings of resentment and hostility amongst the Hindus. The practice of taking the daughters or sisters of the defeated Hindu rulers as wives followed by many Turkish Rulers and nobles, far from being viewed as a gesture of conciliation, must have provided further grounds for resentment, especially as the option of taking Muslim wives was not open to Hindu nobles, except on pain of death. The same was true of conversion. While Hindus could be, and were, freely converted to Islam in areas ruled over by a Muslim, a Muslim who changed his religion was punishable with death. The killing of cows by Muslims for food as well as religious sacrifice, the use of Persian as court language and the inferior status of a Hindu witness in law courts also caused resentment among Hindus. Such resentment found widespread expression in contemporary literature in various parts of India, particularly in the compositions of Hindu saints. The emphasis on religious toleration found in such voices of reconciliation as those of Nanak, Dadu and Kabir also shows the growth of mutual ill-will against which these saints felt called upon to preach. Some of the utterances of Shivaji as well as the contemporary perception of Shivaji as the saviour of Hinduism further illustrate the prevailing resentment against the Mughal (treated as Muslim) rule in the seventeenth century. There is considerable evidence to suggest that such resentment continued through the eighteenth century and the first half of the nineteenth century. Indeed, as some recent researches have shown, the mutual dislike between the Hindus and Muslims sometimes led to violent outbreaks during the period. Even when Hindus and Muslims cooperated, as for instance during the rebellion of 1857, they generally described themselves as Hindus and Muslims, and not as Indians.

While all the foundations and supports have to be kept in view while explaining the rise and growth of Muslim nationalism, there need be no doubt that the pride of place among them must be given to the historical background sketched above and discussed in Chapter I. It made the Muslim elite community conscious, and predisposed them to examine every political development primarily from the point of view of the supposed interests and rights of their own community. At the same time, while calculating those interests and rights, they never forgot that they were the progeny of those who had ruled over India for hundreds of years. This led them to develop an instinctive dislike for a system of government in which they would be outnumbered (three to one) by Hindus. The antipathy of Hindus because of the historical memories of their condition during the period of rule by Muslim kings—not hidden from Muslims—made the latter doubly averse to the prospect of being ruled over by a Hindu majority—something unavoidable in a democratic system of government in India as a whole, though in some provinces in both west and east, Muslims themselves constituted a majority. It is this factor which led the bulk of the Muslim elite to keep away from the Indian National Congress and to demand separate electorates as also weightage in the proposed legislative councils. This was done on the ground not only of Muslims being a distinct community with certain special interests of their own, but also of their supposed historical and military importance and the fact that they had not forgotten that their forefathers had ruled over this land in the not too distant past. All these points were clearly stated in the memorandum submitted to Lord Minto by the famous Simla deputation, comprising leading members of the

Muslim elite and led by the Agha Khan, in 1906. Subsequently, the Muslim elite demanded that Muslim majority in both Punjab and Bengal must be reflected in the legislative councils, regardless of the qualifications for the franchise. Side by side, the Muslim elite made it their task to ensure that the power of a democratically elected central government, if and when it was set up, must be strictly limited so as not to be able to interfere in any way with the working of similar governments in the Muslim majority provinces. It was essentially this basic idea of saving as many Muslims as possible from being ruled over by a Hindu majority that finally led to the emergence of the demand for Partition. The historical factor did not, of course, work in isolation. Rather its impact was reinforced by that of several other factors working simultaneously. Each of them requires due attention in order to understand the foundations of Muslim nationalism.

II

Just as the discussion of the historical background of Muslim nationalism has so far primarily centred round the clash of Hinduism and Islam, representing two contrasting civilizations through the ages, the economic divide between them has been generally explained by the economic and educational backwardness of Muslims as compared to the Hindus all over the country in the second half of the nineteenth and early decades of the twentieth century. This view acquired currency with the publication of W.W. Hunter's famous book, *The Indian Mussalmans* in 1871. Hunter based his conclusions mainly on the study of the situation in eastern Bengal. Though he mentioned the regional nature of his study, the style of his writing, particularly the interchangeable use of Bengal and India, led many to believe that his thesis applied to the entire subcontinent. After W.C. Smith's use of Hunter's observations to describe the condition of Muslims under British rule in *Modern Islam in India* (1946), which was for long regarded as virtually a classic, the theory of general Muslim backwardness became almost universally accepted by politicians as well as scholars. Some recent researches, however, have convincingly established that Muslims were not backward everywhere either in education or in government employment. For instance, in UP, which became the cradle of Muslim nationalism, they were much more advanced than the Hindus in these fields. What egged on the Muslim elite towards separatism was not the fact that they were backward, but the fact that Hindus were taking to modern education in large numbers and, with their overwhelming majority in the population, seemed likely to displace Muslims from their dominant position in government employment in the not too distant future, especially as, under the British dispensation, merit rather than birth was beginning to emerge as the decisive criterion governing recruitment to government positions. In India as a whole also, if we keep in mind the respective numerical strength of the two communities, the position of Muslims in government employment was not worse off than the Hindus. This fact, backed by solid statistics, has been brought to our notice by a recent study published in a reputed Pakistani research journal.

This is not to deny the economic and educational backwardness of Muslims in certain areas, particularly in Bengal and Punjab, both having a Muslim majority and occupying a crucial position in the growth of Muslim nationalism and the birth of Pakistan. In the former, the most notable point was that while Hindus formed the overwhelming majority of landlords and moneylenders, the Muslims formed a similar majority among peasants—a situation created not as a result of the permanent settlement introduced by the British in Bengal in late nineteenth century, as is widely believed, but continuing since the Mughal times. In many cases, the management of the estate was in the hands of Hindus even if the landlord was a Muslim. Hindus also occupied a dominant position in government employment and in the various professions where Muslim presence was negligible in the second half of the nineteenth century. In the Punjab, the Muslims occupied a better position than their co-religionists in Bengal, and had indeed nothing to complain about so far as ownership of land and share in government employment were concerned, but a large number of them suffered from growing indebtedness to Hindu and Sikh moneylenders and many faced the threat of being dispossessed of a part or whole of their land as a penalty for non-payment. Besides, they lagged behind the Hindus in modern education and share in the various professions like law, medicine and teaching. Thus, in both Bengal and Punjab, the economic divide between Hindus and Muslims was quite marked and this contributed significantly to the growth of Muslim nationalism there. The economic divide lay behind many apparently communal conflicts in various other parts of India also. The Mapilla rebellion in Malabar in 1921, when the Muslim peasants rose against their Hindu landlords, attacking temples and indulging in forcible conversions, presents the most glaring example of the economic divide triggering off communal conflicts. Similarly, the Hindi-Urdu controversy, which flared up in the second half of the nineteenth century and continued to adversely affect Hindu-Muslim relations ever since, had a powerful economic background, being related to the number of government jobs which might pass on from the members of one community to another.

Taking India as a whole, the most important economic factor was the small share of Muslims in the rise and growth of a middle class in India in the wake of the establishment of British rule. The ground for this also had been prepared in pre-British times. Under Mughals, for instance, while Muslims predominated in high judicial and executive positions, most of the subordinate and clerical positions in the government were held by the Hindus, who at the same time dominated the field of trade and commerce. With this background, Hindus moved forward easily to utilize the new opportunities in trade and commerce as well as the various professions in areas occupied by the British. Apart from this, they were also helped by the fact that the areas which first emerged as important centres of trade and commerce under the British were far away from the centres of Mughal power where Muslims predominated. When the British moved into these areas, the Muslims were replaced by the British in the high echelons of administration and judicial organization, but the British could not do without Indians in subordinate positions where in any case Hindus predominated since earlier times. It so happened that some of the Indian industries which suffered a decline as a result of British competition, with government backing, like, for instance, textiles and ship-building, were also the industries in which Muslims had had an upper hand. On the other hand, while some Hindu commercial classes moved to set up modern industries and banking institutions later they did not have many Muslim counterparts. All this led to a feeling among the Muslim elite that they would not get their due in the economic field unless they acquired freedom from Hindu competition. This made Pakistan quite an attractive proposition to the members of the Muslim middle class, who could look forward there to a bright economic future for themselves and their progeny unhampered by competition from the Hindus.

III

Apart from the historical barrier and the economic divide between the Hindus and Muslims, the intellectual and emotional environment of the Muslim elite also contributed significantly to the emergence and growth of Muslim nationalism in India. Since the decline of the Mughal power in the eighteenth century, the Muslim elite were gripped by a feeling of insecurity about the future of Islam in the absence of political power in their hands, especially in a situation where the original, distinctive character of the Islamic civilization had itself been blurred through contact with Hinduism in India. This feeling of insecurity was reflected in the works of the leading Muslim theologians, scholars and poets who became increasingly preoccupied with the revival and reformation of Islam in its original form, free from those elements which had crept into it as a result of contact with Hinduism during the past several centuries. This was pursued not for its own sake or in response to any fresh theological research or discovery, but as a key to the revival of Islam's lost power and glory in India. This trend is exemplified best by the writings of Shah Waliullah, whose obsession with the need for reviving Muslim political power in India in the middle of the eighteenth century has been mentioned earlier. He emphasized the utmost need for Islamic revival and reformation, and urged the Muslims to fashion their lives strictly according to the tenets of Islam as taught by Prophet Muhammad, advising them to rely primarily on the Koran and the *Hadith* (traditions of the Prophet) as their guides. His most notable achievement was the translation of the Koran from Arabic to Persian, a language then understood by almost all educated Muslims. The work begun by him was continued by his sons and successors, who translated the Koran into Urdu to make it understood by a much larger section of Muslims and also did whatever they could to revive Muslim power. As mentioned earlier, Islamic revival was the primary objective of the so-called Wahhabi rebellion, led by Sayyid Ahmad Shahid in the first half of the nineteenth century and continuing for a long time even after his death in 1831. The Muslim peasant movements in East and West Bengal in the first half of the nineteenth century, referred to earlier, were also inspired, at any rate partly, by the call of Islamic revival and reformation.

Both the movements for Islamic revival and reformation in northern India—the traditionalist, represented by the theological seminary at Deoband and the modernist, represented by the Mohammedan Anglo-Oriental College at Aligarh—claimed to be inspired by Shah Waliullah's teachings. However, while the former emphasized going back to the Koran and the traditions and sayings of the Prophet, the latter, without minimizing their importance, emphasized the need for their fresh interpretation in the context of the requirements of modern times.

The modernist school, particularly its leader, Sir Syed Ahmad Khan (1817-98), attached the highest importance to the spread of modern education among the Muslims. He also put great emphasis on maintaining the political identity of Muslims, treating them as a separate nation and, on this ground among others, advising them not to join the Indian National Congress founded in 1885, but to look towards the British Government for the advancement of their interests. That, of course, did not mean lack of attachment to India as a whole or of interest in Hindu-Muslim unity and cooperation, but a political union between Hindus and Muslims was not considered possible or desirable. The message of the Aligarh School was popularized among the educated sections of the Muslim community by several able colleagues of Syed Ahmad Khan, notably Munshi Zaka Ullah (1832-1911), Maulvi Nazir Ahmad (1836-1912) and, above all, the poet Altaf Husain Hali (1837-1914). *Musaddas-e-Hali*, first published in 1879, piognantly put into focus the past glory and contemporary decline of the Muslims and acquired tremendous popularity among educated Muslims, inculcating among them the consciousness of belonging to a community which, though in decline at the time, could proudly lay claim to a glorious heritage and revive itself again.

This consciousness was further strengthened by the writings of Syed Ameer Ali (1849-1928) based in Calcutta, for long the capital city of British India. He wrote about Islam in a more assertive tone than Syed Ahmad Khan. While the latter had taken pains to point out that there were many things in common between Islam and Christianity, thereby seeking to build a bridge between the British rulers and the Muslim elite, Ameer Ali stressed that Islam represented the last stage in the evolution of religions and the surest guide to progress in modern times. Similarly, he asserted the superiority of Prophet Muhammad over all other religious teachers in history, including Jesus Christ. As for Hinduism and Buddhism, he wondered how people could be so stupid as to adhere to them. In the political field, he founded one of the earliest Muslim organizations in modern times—the National Muhammadan Association (1877)—and refused to cooperate with the Indian National Congress founded eight years later.

Although Shibli Numani (1857-1914) differed from Syed Ahmad Khan and Ameer Ali in political as well as cultural fields and did not like the idea of Muslims keeping away from the Congress, he too, not unlike Ameer Ali, was preoccupied with the glorification of the Islamic heritage. Indeed in this respect, his contribution was more significant than Ameer Ali's for, unlike the latter who wrote in English, Numani wrote in Urdu and was more widely read. The historical novels of Abdul Halim Sharar (1860-1928), woven around the theme of the glorious past of Islam, had a similar impact. That theme was even more widely popularized by a host of lesser known writers and poets in northern India who dilated on it in innumerable pamphlets or booklets, priced moderately and couched in a language which could be followed even by those who were not highly educated. The various religious controversies raging among Muslims in northern India between modernists and traditionalists as well as between different schools of the latter, although causing divisions among Muslim ranks, also contributed significantly to the growth of Islamic consciousness among them, regardless of the school of thought to which they might adhere. Such controversies and discussions were not confined to areas like Delhi, UP and Bihar, but also extended to the Punjab and Bengal and helped to strengthen Islamic consciousness among Muslims in general. This was particularly true of Bengal which threw up a powerful movement of Islamization affecting the masses as well as the elite, and involving abstention from all forms of Hindu worship, development of a new style of Bengali, commonly called Muslim Bengali and containing a profusion of Arabic and Persian words, and the switch-over from Bengali to Arabic or Persian names for Muslims.

The rise and growth of the Pan-Islamic movement in India in the second half of the nineteenth and the first quarter of the twentieth century, itself the product of the growth of Islamic or community consciousness among Muslims, further strengthened that consciousness. Muslims in India had always been conscious of belonging to a community which was not confined to this country but was scattered over different lands, both far and near. This feeling drew sustenance from the customary pilgrimage to Mecca, which drew Muslims from various countries every year at the same time, and common allegiance to the Caliph, who was considered head of all Muslims, regardless of the place of their birth or residence. The rise and growth of the movement for Islamic revival and reformation in the second half of the nineteenth century naturally gave a fillip also to the growth of the Pan-Islamic sentiment. The generally hostile Western policy towards the Ottoman (Turkish) empire, whose head, the Sultan, was also treated as head of all Muslims as Caliph, and which acted as a great source of psychological support to the Muslim elite as a visible symbol of

Muslim power at the world stage gave an anti-imperialistic direction to the Pan-Islamic sentiment. Syed Ahmad Khan, believing that the future of Indian Muslims lay in close alliance with the British power, did not sympathize with such a sentiment and warned his co-religionists against it; but his advice, considered valuable in other fields, was not heeded in this respect. With the growth of nationalistic feelings among the Christian subjects of the Ottoman empire, the increasing Western interest in their liberation and the shrinking of that empire as also the rise of progressive movements in Persia and Turkey in the early years of the twentieth century gave a further fillip to the Pan-Islamic movement and also brought it close to the movement of Indian nationalism. This phase began around 1912 and reached its climax during the Khilafat-Non-cooperation movement in 1920-2 under Gandhi's leadership. However, as the utterances of its top leaders cited in this book will show, the driving force of Pan-Islamism was the call for Islamic revival and solidarity, and the brief association with Indian nationalism merely incidental. It is not, therefore, surprising that the collapse of the Khilafat movement in 1922, as a result of Gandhi's decision not to start civil disobedience after the Chauri-Chaura episode, and the end of the institution of Caliphate itself in 1924, as a result of a decision of the new Turkish Government, found the bulk of the politically conscious Muslims again, as in the past, arraigned against Indian nationalism and its main political arm, the Congress, with much greater ardour than ever before. Some prominent leaders of the Khilafat movement, like, for instance, M.A. Ansari and Abul Kalam Azad, continued to work with the Congress, but others joined the ranks of resurgent Muslim nationalism.

The strongest intellectual as well as emotional support for Muslim nationalism was provided by Mohammad Iqbal (1877-1938), one of the greatest poet-philosophers produced by the Indian subcontinent. He dominated Muslim elite's thinking in the first half of the twentieth century just as Syed Ahmad Khan had done in the second half of the nineteenth century. Starting as an ardent Indian nationalist, he later became an ardent Pan-Islamist, and still later an ardent champion of Indian Muslim nationalism, thereby working as a mirror of the evolution of the mind of the Muslim elite in the first half of the twentieth century. As early as 1909, he expressed the view that although the vision of a common nationhood for India was an attractive idea, it did not appear capable of fulfilment. In the same year, he wrote that Islam was not merely a creed, but also a community and a nation. His poetry played a major role in spreading and deepening Islamic consciousness among educated Muslims. At first opposed to nationalism on the ground that, for Muslims, Islam itself was a nation which could not be divided into territorial compartments, he shifted his position later in the light of the Turkish experiment in nation-building under Kamalist leadership. Although he did not agree with all that was being done in the new Turkey, he now felt that while the ideal of Islamic solidarity on a global scale remained valid as an ultimate objective, there was no immediate prospect for its fulfilment. Hence it was desirable for Muslims in various countries to build up their own strength and organize themselves on sound lines. When this process was completed, efforts might be made to give a concrete shape to the ideal of universal Islamic solidarity. Even in this phase, he emphasized again and again that while Muslims could be patriots and feel attached to the land of their birth, unlike in the West where nationalism was the moving force behind different societies, for Muslims Islam alone provided an ideal worth living and dying for. He also emphasized that the main difficulty in India in the field of nation-building lay in the fact that the Indian people were not animated by a common consciousness and did not constitute a single nation. On this ground, he demanded, in course of his presidential address to the annual session of the All India Muslim League held in December 1930 at Allahabad, the creation of 'a Muslim India within India' by the merger of the Muslim majority areas of north and north-west India into a single state.

While Iqbal, at that point of time, stopped short of demanding a separate, sovereign State for Indian Muslims, as the logical end-product of his as well as some of his illustrious predecessors' ways of thinking and writing since the second half of the nineteenth century the idea had already been born and received airing by stray individuals now and then since at least 1917. In 1927, Malcolm Hailey, then Governor of the Punjab, noted that many Muslims in the Punjab had begun thinking of a federation of their own embracing the Punjab, parts of UP, the North-West Frontier Province, Sind and Baluchistan. In 1928, a Punjabi journalist, Maulana Murtaza Ahmed Khan Maikash, wrote a series of four articles in an Urdu daily of Lahore, advocating the establishment of 'a Muslim National homeland' consisting of the Muslim majority areas of north and north-western India. One year later, in course of his address as Chairman of the Reception Committee of the All India Khilafat Conference at Lahore on 31 December 1929,

Nawab Sir Zulfiqar Ali Khan strongly supported the Two-nation theory and suggested Partition of India on that basis, for the first time including Bengal also in the proposed Muslim homeland.

The Partition idea received a great push at the hands of a Punjabi student at Cambridge, Chaudhry Rahmat Ali (1897-1951) in 1933, when he not merely demanded the creation of such a State, but also gave it its name, Pakistan (first spelled Pakstan). Circulating a four-page statement among those dealing with the Indian constitutional problem in London, 'on behalf of the thirty million Muslims of Pakstan', Rahmat Ali and his three colleagues attacked the concept of an all-India federation and demanded the setting up of a separate sovereign State consisting of the five north and north-western units of India—Punjab, North-Western Frontier Province, Kashmir, Sind and Baluchistan—on the ground that the Muslims constituted an overwhelming majority of the population in those units and had hardly anything in common with the Hindus. They made it clear that their idea was quite different from Iqbal's who had earlier suggested the consolidation of the northern and north-western areas into a single state within India. Iqbal too subsequently underlined this point. The leading Muslim members of the third session of the Round Table Conference described Rahmat Ali's scheme as merely a 'student's scheme' and 'a chimera' which did not concern them in any way.

Once born, however, the Pakistan idea, which Rahmat Ali persisted in propagating with a messianic zeal, soon caught on, at any rate in the Punjab, a fact noted by a politically perceptive Indian industrialist, G.D. Birla, in early 1936. By the middle of 1937, Iqbal too came round to supporting it in private through his letters to Jinnah, the future founder of Pakistan. While getting them published after a gap of six years, the latter mentioned that he had been in broad agreement with Iqbal's approach when he received those letters. The supreme strategist that Jinnah was, he kept his views confidential for the time being, doing all that was possible in the meanwhile to bring the politically conscious Muslims in every part of India on one platform on the basis of a vehement anti-Congress and anti-Hindu rhetoric. When finally, taking advantage of the opportunity created by the outbreak of the Second World War and the urgent British need for Muslim support in order to keep the Congress—with its demand for immediate independence—at bay, he mounted the demand for Partition in March 1940, he used a language which looked like a paraphrase of the one used by Rahmat Ali in 1933.

IV

Ironically, Muslim nationalism received considerable nourishment and sustenance from Hindu nationalism, just as the latter too derived similar nourishment and sustenance from Muslim nationalism. In this way, the two nationalisms helped each other. Again, just like Muslim nationalism, Hindu nationalism had deep historical and psychological foundations. If the Muslim elite cherished the memory of the rule over India for several centuries by their forefathers, the Hindu elite were burdened by feelings of bitterness and grievance against that rule because of religious intolerance and persecution and other disabilities to which their forefathers were supposed to have been subjected under it. The economic divide also conditioned the general Hindu attitude towards the Muslims as well as *vice versa*. Apart from this, both the communities went through a similar process of religious revival and reformation; only it began earlier among the Hindus than among the Muslims. Glorification of the community's past heritage, remorse on its contemporary condition and holding of the later accretions to the original faith as responsible for it were also common features of such revival and reformation, which in each case strengthened the community consciousness and fostered aloofness from the members of the other community. In the case of the Hindu elite, partly because they constituted a majority in the country's population and partly because they considered their forefathers as its original inhabitants, or at least resident in it since earliest times, community consciousness went hand in hand with Indian national consciousness more widely than among the Muslim elite who were conscious of their forefathers having come to India much later from Arabia, Persia and Central Asia, principally to rule over the land. However, unlike the leaders of Islamic revival and reformation, with the sole exception of Shah Waliullah, a marked antipathy towards the members of the other community was, with some exceptions, one of the basic features of the thinking of the leaders of Hindu revival and reformation, largely owing to the historical memory of the supposed misdeeds—some real and some exaggerated or purely imaginary—of Muslim rulers. It is not, therefore, surprising that right from the commencement of the era of political awakening and organization in the second half of the nineteenth century, the Muslim elite—already affected by a powerful current of community consciousness coming from various sources—became apprehensive about their future in a democratic set-up in a land dominated by the Hindu majority, which had been ruled over for centuries by Muslim kings and which carried unpleasant historical memories about conditions during the period of that rule.

The pioneer among the Hindu religious reformers was Raja Rammohun Roy (1772-1833), generally referred to in history textbooks as the father of modern India. He preached against idol-worship and pernicious social customs like *sati* (immolation of a widow on the death of her husband) and championed such causes as the freedom of the press and the spread of modern education. Even though endowed with an universalist outlook, he was mainly concerned with the revitalization of the Hindu community and believed that Muslim rule, in spite of some progressive features, was generally marked by religious intolerance and had caused severe damage to Hindu religion and culture. One of his leading disciples, Dwarakanath Tagore (1794-1846), believed that the deficiencies then noticed in the character of Hindus were not present in ancient times, but had cropped up later as a result of Muslim rule. Such views were so widely prevalent among leading Hindu families in Calcutta that even some of the non-Hindu leaders of the Bengal Renaissance like Derozio (1809-31) came to believe in them.

Antipathy towards Islam reached its high watermark in the writings of Swami Dayanand Saraswati (1824-83), the founder of the Arya Samaj (1875), which had considerable influence in northern India. He traced all the virtues, including the highest form of monotheism, to the Vedas and exhorted the Hindus to go back to them and discard all later beliefs and practices which had crept into their faith in subsequent times. Although in his famous religious treatise, *Satyartha Prakash*, he strongly attacked all faiths, including traditional Hinduism, which did not conform to his own, he used the choicest invectives for Prophet Muhammad and his teachings and opined that they could be only harbingers of harm. Such writings could not but endow his ardent followers with an anti-Muslim attitude, though all might not exhibit it, or do so to the same extent.

Swami Vivekananda (1861-1902), the most illustrious leader of Hindu revival, with the greatest impact on the mind of the Hindu elite all over India, was free from any sectarian narrowness and was endowed with a genuinely universalist outlook. He preached not merely religious toleration, but religious acceptance and argued that all religions were sound and no energy need be spent on finding out the faults of any one of them. Islam in particular, specially its message of equality among all human beings regardless of their rank or wealth, excited his admiration and led him to suggest once that the only hope for India lay in 'a junction of the two great systems, Hinduism and Islam—Vedantic brain and Islamic body'. It is extremely doubtful, however, that such a view, based on the philosophical superiority of Hindus, could be acceptable to leaders of Islamic revival simply because it conceded the superiority of Islamic social organization. There were, of course, no takers for such a view among Hindus either. In any case, this does not controvert the basic fact that Vivekananda was first and foremost a Hindu and the revitalization of Hindu society was his main concern. Naturally, after achieving eminence abroad, he spent most of his time in India extolling the virtues of Hinduism and exhorting the Hindus to arise and awake, revive their ancient glory and march forward in modern times. It is not, therefore, surprising that, however much we may justifiably eulogize Vivekananda's universalist approach in our own times, his contemporary Hindu admirers looked upon him primarily as one who had raised the position of Hindus in the eyes of the world and restored the pride of the Hindu 'nation' in its own religion and culture. He, of course, often talked of India's greatness, but this, on most occasions, was used synonymously with Hindu greatness. Similarly, when he talked of the world waiting for India's message, he actually meant the message, albeit universalist, of Hinduism. Vivekananda undoubtedly made a most valuable contribution to Indian awakening in modern times, but it would be idle to deny that his teachings also contributed to the strengthening of community consciousness among educated Hindus, though not necessarily any antipathy towards Islam or its followers.

Mahadev Govind Ranade (1842-1901), not associated with the movement for religious revival but only with that of social reform and generally known for his rational, secular outlook, also occasionally spoke in a language which made a similar contribution. Thus, he referred to Hindus and Muslims as two races, implied that Muslims were foreigners, affirmed that Hindus constituted the 'native races' of India as well as a nation, glorified the latter's religious heritage for, among other things, containing the purest form of monotheism—evolved over a period of time in a natural way and not like that in Christianity and Islam through a sudden impulse or the exertions of a single prophet or teacher—and eulogized the ancient Indian polity for its supposed liberal, democratic features in contrast to the system of despotism established in India by the Muslim rulers. Such observations would not have sounded soothing to the ears of the Muslim elite.

Hindu revivalism in the second half of the nineteenth century was widely reflected in the writings of prominent contemporary litterateurs. The most notable among them was Bankim Chandra Chatterjee (1838-94), pioneer of modern Bengali literature. Attaching the greatest importance to religion in conditioning human life, he asserted that there was no religion in the world which was as all-encompassing and full of purity and bliss as Hinduism. In his novels and essays, he generally referred to Hindus as natives and Muslims as foreigners as well as tyrannical and oppressive as rulers. His famous poem *Bandemataram*, which depicted India as a mother goddess and became the most popular national song not only in Bengal but in most parts of northern India from 1905 onwards, first appeared in his novel *Anandmath* published in 1882, describing the rebellion of Hindu religious men against tyrannical Muslim rule and expressing satisfaction with its replacement by British rule.

The pioneers of modern Hindi, Gujarati and Marathi literatures also took a broadly similar line. It is ironical that, while doing so, most of them also stressed the need for Hindus and Muslims to work together for India's progress. This can be seen in the works of Bharatendu Harishchandra (1850-85), Pratap Narain Misra (1856-94), Radha Charan Goswami (1859-1923), Balkrishna Bhatt (1844-1914) and Balmukund Gupta (1864-1907) in Hindi; Dalpatram (1820-98) and Narmadashankar (1833-86) in Gujarati; and Gopal Hari Deshmukh (1823-92), Gopal Ganesh Agarkar (1856-95), Vishnushastri Chiplunkar (1850-82), Bal Gangadhar Tilak (1856-1920), Shivarama Mahadeva Paranjape (1864-1929) and Hari Narayana Apte (1864-1919) in Marathi.

Historical writings also reflected the growing community consciousness—along with Indian national consciousness—among Hindus. The risings of Rajputs, Sikhs and Marathas against the Mughals usually provided the themes for such writings. The rise of Marathas, particularly the career and achievements of Shivaji, proved to be the most popular theme exemplifying Hindu resistance to Muslim tyranny. Even when the tone of the Hindu poets and novelists significantly changed in the context of the gathering momentum of the Indian nationalist movement in the twentieth century, most of the prominent historians continued to write in the old way eulogizing Hindu heroes who had fought against Muslim rulers. The trend was set by Mahadev Govind Ranade in his *Rise of the Maratha Power* published in 1900. He argued therein that the rise of the Marathas represented a genuine effort by a Hindu nationality to assert its independence and that Shivaji inspired not only his own, but also succeeding generations with the ideal of re-establishing Hindu power throughout the country. Jadunath Sarkar (1870-1958), one of the greatest historians of India in modern times, wrote in the fourth volume of his monumental work on Aurangzeb, published in 1919, that Shivaji proved by his example that the Hindu race could build a nation as well as found a State. In his book on Shivaji, published during the same year, he spoke of the hero in even more laudatory terms from the Hindu point of view, stressing that Shivaji had shown that the tree of Hinduism was not really dead and that it could still produce rulers of men and even a king of kings. R.C. Majumdar wrote in his introduction to V.D. Savarkar's book on Shivaji, published in 1925, that the rise of Marathas was motivated by the 'noble and inspiring ideal' of the establishment of an independent Hindu Empire. As late as 1946, G.S. Sardesai, who also occupies an honoured place among Indian historians, wrote in the first volume of his trilogy on Maratha history that the Marathas made a distinct contribution to the political evolution of India by daring to establish even though only for a brief period 'Indian self-rule throughout the country'.

The growing community consciousness of Hindus, particularly in northern India, led them to start a movement for ending the domination of Urdu in the educational and administrative fields and its replacement by Hindi on the ground that the former was really a foreign language and not understood by the majority of the people who lived in villages. That movement began in UP, then known as the North Western Provinces, as early as the sixties of the nineteenth century and was, to a great extent, responsible for Syed Ahmad Khan's feeling that Hindus and Muslims were not likely to work together in public life in the future. Except for a small number of Kayasthas and Kashmiri Pandits living in the big towns, who felt quite at home with Urdu, almost all sections of the Hindu elite supported the cause of Hindi. The strong feeling of the latter on this issue comes out clearly in the memorandum submitted to the government by Sivaprasad of Banaras in 1868. Strongly objecting to the use of the Persian script in the courts of UP and asking for its replacement by the Devanagari script, it described the former as a relic of the autocratic ways of the Muslim rulers who, unlike the British, did not ask their officers to learn the language of the people, but forced the latter to learn that of the rulers. Another memorandum submitted five years later argued that the Persian script was foreign to the country and its inherent shortcomings made it impossible for it to be used by the majority of the people, and asserted that such matters must be settled keeping the interests of the majority in view. This movement gathered greater momentum after 1881 when Hindi in Devanagari script replaced Urdu in Persian script as the language of the courts in Bihar and Central Provinces. The intensity as well as spread of the Hindi movement can be gauged by the fact that in 1882, out of a total of 145 petitions submitted to the Indian Education Commission in UP, 118 came from its protagonists, who asked for the replacement of Urdu by Hindi as the medium of instruction in primary schools. This demand was not confined to UP, but also extended to the Punjab where 46 out of a total of 96 petitions submitted to the Education Commission dealt with it. The main argument was the same as in UP, namely that Urdu was full of foreign words and the majority of the people, including Muslims who lived in the rural areas, found it difficult to handle it. Again, just as in UP, while some Hindus supported the cause of Urdu, most of them were for Hindi. Associations which had mixed membership of Hindus and Muslims failed to submit unanimous recommendations and contented themselves with summing up the views of the protagonists of each of the two languages.

If the movement for Hindi originated in UP, that for the protection of the cow originated in the Punjab and spread to UP and Bihar. The two movements were indeed interrelated. The Arya Samaj played a major role in it by organizing cow-protection societies in important towns as well as carrying on a virulent anti-Islamic propaganda as a counter-blast to the propaganda against the Arya Samaj carried on by the Muslims, particularly those belonging to the Ahmadiya sect. This naturally led to heightening of communal tension and occasionally also to violence. Pandit Lekh Ram of the Arya Samaj, who had published an anti-Islamic pamphlet in 1892, was assassinated by a Muslim five years later. The cow-protection movement similarly led to Hindu-Muslim riots on a number of occasions. Between 1833 and 1891, Punjab witnessed fifteen major riots on the issue of cow-protection and other related matters. The most severe riots of those times, however, started in the Azamgarh district of UP in 1893 and spread to several eastern districts of UP and south-western districts of Bihar. Hindu aggression in these areas was countered by Muslim aggression in western India. The final tally came to 45 riots and 107 deaths, the bulk of them in Bombay. Even Rangoon witnessed Hindu-Muslim riots. In all affected areas, the Hindus showed their determination not to allow cow-killing, especially in a demonstrative way, in a land where the Hindus constituted an overwhelming majority and revered the cow and in an era when rule by Muslim kings had come to an end. On the other hand, Muslims were equally determined to go on doing what their ancestors had done for centuries, regardless of the feelings of Hindus or the changed political circumstances. One feature of these riots worthy of notice was the participation in them on a large scale not merely of Hindus belonging to the elite or upper castes, but also by members of the Ahir or Yadav caste, though the Chamars generally kept out of them. Thus, community consciousness among the Hindu elite got transformed into a feeling of communal antagonism and also engulfed the subaltern sections of the community.

Contemporaneously, there also emerged an ideology of Hindu nationalism and efforts to provide it with organizational backing. Here the pioneering role was performed by Rajnarain Bose (1826-99), described by some as the grandfather of Indian nationalism. He founded a society in Midnapore (Bengal) in 1866, called Nationality Promotion Society, for the promotion of national feeling among the educated 'natives of Bengal', by whom he, of course, meant Hindus. His friend and colleague, Nabagopal Mitra, was at the same time bringing out a paper called *National Paper* with the same end in view. Mitra started an annual *mela* in Calcutta in 1867, which became famous as the Hindu *mela* and attracted a large number of visitors. The main items of the programme followed there included singing of patriotic songs and exhibition of gymnastic exercises of various types. In 1870, Mitra and his friends formed the *Jatiya Sabha* or National Society to carry on the responsibility of organizing the *mela*. When some critics pointed out the incongruity of calling an organization national whose membership was confined to Hindus, the *National Paper* wrote that, as Hindus formed a nation by themselves, there was no incongruity in the name. Though the Hindu *mela* ceased to meet after 1880, some Hindu nationalists in Bengal continued to advance the idea of forming an organization exclusively of Hindus in order to advance their interests. A pamphlet published in the name of 'an old Hindu' but generally supposed to have been written by Rajnarain Bose and published in Bengali in 1887 and English in 1888 forcefully championed this view, giving detailed suggestions regarding the name, aims, objectives and methods of work of the proposed organization. Special emphasis was placed on the use of patriotic songs to foster nationalistic sentiments among Hindus. It was stressed that although Hindus must become Indian nationalists, they should not forget their Hindu identity and must continue to remain Hindu nationalists also. While the type of organization envisaged by Bose did not emerge in Bengal, efforts to set up similar organizations went on elsewhere, particularly in the Punjab. A Hindu Sabha sprang up in Lahore in 1882 and, by 1906, a Hindu Sabha could be found in each district of the Punjab, all functioning under the aegis of the Punjab Hindu Sabha. The latter took the initiative to found the All India Hindu Mahasabha, which held its first session at Hardwar (UP) in 1915. Several Congress leaders continued till mid-1930s to participate also in the annual sessions of the Mahasabha and at least two of them, Lajpat Rai and Madan Mohan Malaviya, also presided over them. There was nothing unique about this as several Muslim leaders of the Congress also continued to be associated in the same way with the All India Muslim League. However, it lent credence to the general Muslim view that most of the Congress leaders sympathized with the objectives of the Hindu Mahasabha and indeed cherished similar aspirations though they might not publicly express them. This was, of course, a mistaken view, but that it existed cannot be denied.

The Hindu Mahasabha never became a powerful organization with a large following. However, during the post-Khilafat period (1924-34), when the country was swept by a communal backlash, it acquired considerable influence on the Hindu mind and this made it extremely difficult for the Congress to come to a reasonable settlement with the Muslim League on the communal issue. For the Congress could not ignore the fact that Hindus constituted an overwhelming majority of the population as well as its own membership and it dared not totally disregard the views of an organization which at that time seemed to have caught the imagination of a fairly large section of the Hindus, as illustrated by the election results of 1926, when the Congress lost several seats to candidates supported by the Hindu Mahasabha.

V

Unlike Muslim or Hindu nationalism, Indian nationalism, as represented by the Indian National Congress, was not based on appeal to any particular community but sought to encompass within its ambit all the Indian people, regardless of the religion or the community they might belong to. This was made clear by the leaders of the Congress at the time of its foundation in 1885 and remained its hallmark ever since. It had, however, to face the fact, also from the time of its birth, that the bulk of the Muslims were keeping away from it. In order to assure them of its truly national character, it decided quite early in its career not to discuss questions of social reform, recognizing that they would vary from community to community and the Congress, being a national forum, was not the right place to take them up. The Congress also realized equally early that the consciousness of the community being ingrained in the Indian society, a system of polity based on the principle of one man one vote might not lead to adequate representation for the members of the minority communities. It, therefore, adopted a resolution in 1888 stipulating that in any scheme of constitutional reform in the future seats in the legislatures should be reserved for Muslims and other minorities in accordance with their proportion in the total population of every province.

As the Indian nationalist movement gathered momentum in the wake of the anti-partition agitation in Bengal, some of its leaders, notably Bal Gangadhar Tilak (1856-1920) in Maharashtra and Aurobindo Ghosh (1872-1950) in Bengal, openly appealed to the masses and the youth in the name of the Hindu religion and constantly used its symbols with a view to broadening its base. With the emergence of Gandhi as the dominant leader of the Congress in 1920, broadly the same type of appeal continued. As the Hindus formed the overwhelming majority of the country's population as well as of the Congress membership and support-base the use of Hindu religious symbols for appealing to them had some justification in a land where those symbols provided the most effective means of communication with the elite as well as the masses. This was considered quite appropriate under the circumstances of those times and there is no evidence to suggest that any one minded it. On the contrary, Tilak played a key role in securing Congress-League understanding regarding constitutional reforms in 1916, by conceding separate electorates and weightage to Muslims, and faced no difficulty in doing so because of his use of Hindu religious symbols for instilling nationalist consciousness among the masses and the youth. Similarly, Gandhi's pronounced identification with the traditional Hindu religion—*Sanatan Dharma*, as he called it—and his deep interest in the protection of the cow, without of course, attacking any one, did not stand in the way of his securing the cooperation of so many prominent Muslim leaders, including those associated with Islamic religious institutions for the Khilafat-Non-cooperation movement during 1920-2. It cannot be denied, however, that the techniques employed by both Tilak and Gandhi were bound to, and did in fact, restrict their primary support-base largely among the members of the Hindu community. Gandhi's popularity among the Muslims during 1920-2 was purely temporary and accounted for by the fact that he had extended his whole-hearted support to the cause of the Caliphate, which was so dear to Muslim hearts.

Yet the successes of Tilak and Gandhi in securing cooperation from Muslims illustrates the fact that, regardless of their techniques of leadership and the nature of their primary support-base, so long as the Congress leadership recognized the hard reality in India, showed due regard to its political as well as cultural pluralities and sought to answer the concerns of the politically conscious Muslims, centred round the maintenance of their separate identity and assurance of adequate share in power, not necessarily circumscribed by their share in the total population of the country, it might be possible to secure their cooperation, though not merger, with the Indian nationalist movement. The problem became insoluble when, constrained by the dynamics of electoral politics in a country with a Hindu majority and having to compete with the Hindu nationalists in order to retain its support, the Congress began to oppose both separate electorates and weightage for the Muslims and insisted on all Indians being treated at par in future constitutional arrangements. This was the main cause of the failure of the Motilal Nehru Committee's Report (1928) to win acceptance by the generality of Muslims. The situation was made much worse by the assertion of the new, emerging leadership of the Congress, represented by Jawaharlal Nehru, that actually there was nothing like a communal problem in India and that the subject was kept alive by selfish and reactionary leaders to gain advantages for themselves. The main issue was economic backwardness which affected both Hindus and Muslims and also other communities in equal measure. This provided an excellent rationalization to the dominant Congress leadership—with hardly any faith in either socialism or the primacy of economic factors—for its policy in the mid-1930s of not dealing with separatist Muslim organizations in order to continue to keep the Mahasabha on the sidelines and retain its hold on the Hindu masses, which it had recently regained. Apart from this practical consideration, from the theoretical standpoint too, it was not an illogical policy for an organization wedded to Indian nationalism to pursue. It could also be argued that a different policy might add to the strength of an avowedly communal organization like the League. Whatever that might have been, neither policy had any chance of success in the India of the mid-1930s. Muslim nationalism was much too strong by that time to be wished away. The League leadership, already attracted towards the Pakistan idea, soon found a plausible ground to go to the Muslim masses with the slogan 'Islam in danger', built up the League into a powerful organization based on mass support and began to prepare the ground for demanding a separate, sovereign Muslim State consisting of those provinces of India which had a Muslim majority.

VI

Apart from Hindu nationalism and the ethos or appearance of Indian nationalism, the foundations of Muslim nationalism were considerably strengthened and reinforced from time to time by the British policy of playing off one community against the other. Though not to the same extent as Hindus, the Muslims in India too were riven by many divisions based on sect, race, language and region. The British, however, always treated them as one homogeneous community and a political community, full of antagonistic feelings towards the Hindus. In the beginning, this was not part of any policy, but simply reflected the British perception of the Indian reality. British travellers, historians and writers all contributed to its making. Almost without any exception, they saw the two communities divided by a strong wall of dislike and antagonism towards each other. Some of these writers also underlined that this could be a source of great advantage to the British in maintaining their rule. Early emphasis on Hindu-Muslim contradictions can be seen in the recollections of Sir William Henry Sleeman, published in 1844, as well as in the histories of India produced by James Mill and Sir Henry M. Elliot in 1847. While the former saw Hindu and Islamic civilizations as mutually antagonistic, the latter sought to underline the atrocities committed on Hindus by Muslim rulers during the period of their rule in India with the avowed purpose of reminding the Hindus of the advantages of British rule. The need for such reminders had indeed been stressed about two decades earlier by Bishop Heber in his account of his travels in northern India during 1824-5, published in 1828. Implicit in such writings was a deep dislike for Muslims who were suspected of nourishing a grievance against the British for supplanting their rule over India. The rebellion of 1857, for which the British generally considered the Muslims as primarily responsible, further deepened such dislike. However, knowledgeable officials soon realized that it was no more a Muslim rebellion than a Hindu rebellion, and further that nothing should be done which might again unite the two communities against the British. Canning, the Viceroy of India at the time of the rebellion, when called upon to justify his policy of clemency to his superiors in Britain, emphasized that if he followed any other policy, it would only result in such a denouement. He went on to emphasize that if a handful of Englishmen had to rule over 150 million people in India, the best policy was to leave them divided as they already were. Canning's successors did better and, whenever an opportunity presented itself, did what they could to see to it that the gulf between the Hindus and Muslims got widened more and more with the passage of time. This was a natural policy to pursue for the agents of an imperial power determined, with a limited personnel belonging to its own race, to preserve its rule as long as possible over a distant and populous country. The British did not create the divide between Hindus and Muslims—it was already there—but fully utilized it for their own purposes, in the process helping to deepen it further.

At first the British turned to the Muslim elite in the second half of the nineteenth century largely with a view to conciliating them in the wake of the rebellion of 1857 and the continuing momentum of the so-called Wahhabi rebellion, propelled by the view that it would not be wise to leave such a large portion of the Indian population totally unreconciled to their rule and in a permanent spirit of rebellion. They had sufficient ground to feel encouraged by the warm response of the rising Muslim elite, led by Syed Ahmad Khan, who for their own reasons were keen to prove that Muslims were not at all disloyal to the British and to secure a respectable position for their community under the new set-up with the latter's help. When, mainly triggered by forces unleashed by the British rule itself, such as the administrative and economic unification of the country, the growth of modern means of communication and the spread of modern education, however limited, signs of national awakening began to appear on the Indian horizon and the Hindu elite seemed particularly affected by it, the British naturally turned towards the Muslim elite with a view to creating a foil to it. The Muslim elite, again for their own reasons, were more than willing to oblige. Thus, an unwritten alliance emerged between the British authorities in India and the leaders of the Muslim elite which continued till the end of British rule in India, with only one interruption lasting about a decade (1912-22) during the hey-day of the Pan-Islamic movement in India, marked by a brief conjunction of Muslim nationalism and Indian nationalism. The early working of this alliance can be seen in the British patronage of the Mohammedan Anglo-Oriental College at Aligarh right from its foundation; the whole-hearted endorsement of the principles of separate electorates and weightage for Muslims in the legislatures by the then Viceroy, Lord Minto, immediately upon the presentation of a demand for them by the leaders of the Muslim elite in 1906 and their incorporation in the Indian Councils Act of 1909 and in all other such Acts which followed; and the effort to meet the Muslim demand for statutory majority in the legislatures of Bengal and Punjab to the extent deemed plausible under the then existing circumstances through the Communal Award of 1932.

As a part of their plan to keep the Muslims away from the Indian nationalist movement, the British also magnified the socio-cultural as well as political differences between Hindus and Muslims and consistently treated only those Muslim leaders as representatives of their community who supported that line and refused to grant representative capacity to the Muslim leaders who belonged to the Congress or worked in cooperation with it. This was the main reason for not inviting an outstanding leader like M.A. Ansari to the second session of the Round Table Conference in 1931, in spite of Gandhi's repeated pleas in this regard to Lord Irwin after the signing of the Gandhi-Irwin Pact. The nature of British policy is still more vividly illustrated by their treatment of Jinnah. He was thoroughly distrusted and abhorred and not at all treated seriously so long as, while trying to organize the Muslims, he also sought to establish a cooperative relationship between the Muslim League and the Congress. However, once he gave up his earlier predilection and began to concentrate single-mindedly on his role as the chief exponent of Muslim separatism or nationalism, he became a valuable ally in the eyes of top British officials and, even though still not much liked as a person, was treated most seriously, indeed at par with Gandhi.

CHAPTER I

The Legacy from the Past

> Men make their own history, but they do not make it just as they please; they do not make it under circumstances chosen by themselves, but under circumstances directly encountered, given and transmitted from the past. The tradition of all the dead generations weighs like a nightmare on the brain of the living.
>
> KARL MARX, *The Eighteenth Brumaire of Louis Bonaparte (1852)*[1]

ALMOST ALL historians who strive to place India's partition in a historical perspective tend to explain the emergence of Muslim nationalism by referring to a perpetual, centuries-old conflict or, at any rate, antipathy between two antagonistic cultures. Among the Pakistani historians perhaps the most forceful exponent of this view is Ishtiaq Husain Qureshi. He refers to the hope nourished by Indian nationalists that since Hindus and Muslims had lived together they would have a common desire for national unity, and that Muslims would be reconciled to the role of a religious minority and identify themselves fully with the Indian nation, and remarks: 'Such hopes were built upon the most deplorable ingorance of the psychology of the Muslim community, of the thinking of its leaders and masses, and of the history of its origins, development and integration.' As a result of this ignorance, he further adds, 'When history asserted itself and the Muslims claimed to be a nation, many were surprised and not a few even scandalised.'[2]

Elsewhere he writes that the hope of Hindus and Muslims joining together in a common nationhood was based on 'the fallacious assumption that the Muslims of the subcontinent had everything in common with the Hindus except their religion. The situation in fact was that the two peoples had little in common.'[3]

Hafeez Malik is another strong upholder of this view. He points out that although Hindus and Muslims had lived together for twelve hundred years, they had not done so by mutual consent. Nor did they share memories of a common heritage. On the contrary, they had different traditions and historical backgrounds: 'Both have independent histories of which each is proud. . . . Each nation has its own heroes who are honoured. More often than not the heroes of one are the foes of the other.'[4]

Although Khalid B. Sayeed presents a more balanced picture of the factors responsible for the creation of Pakistan and lays particular stress on their multiplicity, he goes on to affirm that perhaps a dominant or decisive cause of the emergence of Pakistan was that there had never taken place a confluence of the two civilizations—the Hindu and the Muslim—in India: 'They may have meandered towards each other here and there, but on the whole the two have flowed their separate courses—sometimes parallel and sometimes contrary to one another.'[5]

K.K. Aziz adopts a somewhat similar approach. Unlike Qureshi and Malik, he does not assert that the Muslims had been a nation in India ever since the beginning of the so-called Muslim rule here and affirms that the idea of a separate Muslim nationality in India developed much later, during the period of the Indian nationalist movement.[6] However, while discussing the cultural factor, he also characterizes the Hindu-Muslim interaction as 'the clash of two civilizations, of two peoples who had different languages, different literary roots, different ideas of education, different philosophical sources, and different concepts of art'. Asserting that this cultural gulf was enough to destroy any affinity that the two peoples might have had and defeat all efforts at forging unity among them, he further adds: 'When this cultural variance was combined with diversity in social customs and modes of livelihood the emergence of a united Indian nationalism was doomed without redemption.'[7]

Aziz Ahmad, too, sounds a dispassionate note in the preface to his book on Muslim society and culture in India during the medieval period:

> Hindu and Muslim religions, civilizations and ways of life co-existed together for well over a thousand years, undergoing alternating or simultaneous processes of mutual attraction and repulsion. Neither the attraction nor the repulsion constitutes the whole story, which is interwoven in an infinite pattern of points and counter-points.[8]

However, in the very next sentence he moves on to refer to the 'long story of divided co-existence of Hindus and Muslims in India, leading to divided existence as India and Pakistan in the twentieth century . . .'. It must be said to his credit that he sets before himself as a motto Herbert Butterfield's famous observation: 'The historian seeks to explain how the past came to be turned into the present, but there is a very real sense in which the only explanation he can give is to unfold the whole story and to reveal the complexity by telling it in detail.'[9] This he faithfully follows throughout the book and seeks to present a balanced account of Hindu-Muslim cultural interaction during the medieval period. He does not, however, hide his own view, according to which the history of India in medieval and modern times is to a very large extent 'a history of Hindu-Muslim religio-cultural tensions, interspersed with movements or individual efforts at understanding, harmony and even composite developments'.[10]

The same can be said about the views of another leading Pakistani historian, S.M. Ikram. Although he recognizes that for practical purposes, 'the gradual crystallization and realization of the idea of Pakistan' was related to the period of the British rule, he agrees with the view that 'the ground for Muslim separatism was prepared when Islam entered the subcontinent, and all efforts to provide a bridge between the Hindus and the Muslims failed'.[11] Elsewhere, he quotes an observation of a leading Indian historian to the effect that, between the Hindus and Muslims, 'the social and religious differences were so acute and fundamental that they raised a Chinese wall between the two communities' and even seven hundred years of living together, including two hundred years in common servitude, had failed to make the least crack in that solid and massive structure. Enthusiastically accepting this view, Ikram comments: 'It was this dividing wall which led, in 1947, to the partitioning of the subcontinent.'[12]

II

The Indian historian referred to by Ikram is R.C. Majumdar,[13] but before we analyse his views, we may refer to K.M. Panikkar, perhaps the first among India's leading historians to propound the theory of a clash between the two communities on the basis of differences in religion and culture. In a well-known book published in the same year which witnessed both India's Independence and Partition, he remarks:

> The main result of the introduction of Islam as a religion into India was the division of society on a vertical basis. Before the thirteenth century, Hindu society was divided horizontally, and neither Buddhism nor Jainism affected this division. They were not unassimilable elements and fitted in easily with the existing divisions. Islam, on the other hand, split Indian society into two

sections from top to bottom and what has now come to be known in the phraseology of today as two separate nations came into being from the beginning. Two parallel societies were established on the same soil. At all stages they were different and hardly any social communication or intermingling of life existed between them.[14]

An entirely different view had been presented earlier by another leading Indian historian, Tara Chand, who had analysed the nature of Hindu-Muslim interactions during the medieval period. Writing at a time when the Indian nationalist movement was engaged in propagating the theory of the existence of a composite culture in India, based largely on a positive interchange between Hindus and Muslims, he lent strong support to that theory:

The Muslims who came to India made it their home. They lived surrounded by the Hindu people and a state of perennial hostility with them was impossible. Mutual intercourse led to mutual understanding. Many who had changed their faith differed little from those whom they had left. Thus after the first shock of conquest was over, the Hindus and Muslims prepared to find a *via-media* whereby to live as neighbours. The effort to seek a new life led to the development of a new culture which was neither exclusively Hindu nor purely Muslim. It was indeed a Muslim-Hindu culture. Not only did Hindu religion, Hindu art, Hindu literature and Hindu science absorb Muslim elements, but the very spirit of Hindu culture and the very stuff of Hindu mind were also altered, and the Muslims reciprocated by responding to the change in every department of life.[15]

In the wake of India's Partition, however, the author of these lines apparently realized that they presented too romantic a view of the interaction of Hindus and Muslims during the medieval period. In an article written over a decade after Partition, he almost swings to the other side and observes:

While the Hindu mind was primarily concerned with what is true, the Muslim was exercised over what is right. The Hindu emphasized the private and personal aspect of religious experience, the Muslim its incorporation in the collective body of the faithful. The Hindu was inclined to gloss over the shortcomings of his social customs, the Muslim was annoyed with them. On the other hand, the intolerance of the Muslim and the memory of the past distressed the Hindu. The Hindu felt no kinship with the Arab past which the Muslim hugged to his bosom. The Muslim did not feel at home in Vedic India. While consciousness of group developed, and the element of territoriality was present in both, the content of the two did not quite coincide and fuse.[16]

The historian who became most famous for his opposition to the theory of the emergence of a composite Indian culture during the medieval period was, of course, R.C. Majumdar. At one place, he admits that Hindus and Muslims, living side by side for centuries, did influence each other in various ways, but asserts that this merely affected the externals and did not touch 'the essential elements of culture'. Some of the liberal religious thoughts and movements, such as those led by some Sufis or religious leaders like Nanak and Kabir were able to influence only 'a microscopic minority, less than two per cent'. The people at large remained unaffected by such religious liberalism which 'slowly ebbed away without leaving any deep impression on either community'.[17] Apparently, Majumdar considers religion as constituting the hard core of culture in medieval times and asserts that this created the main dividing line between the two communities. He observes:

> The steel frame of religion and society, which sustained the fundamental structure of medieval culture and civilization, remained unchanged both among the Hindus and the Muslims. The worship of images which formed the most cherished element in the religious beliefs of the Hindus was an anathema in the eyes of the Muslims, and the long tradition of ruthless desecration of temples by them for nearly a thousand years formed a wide gulf between the two. The method of congregational prayer among the Muslims was a thing unknown to the Hindus, and the ceremonial worship of the Hindus to the accompaniment of music, both vocal and instrumental, was not only alien to the Muslims but positively distasteful and irksome to them.[18]

Indeed, according to Majumdar, the gulf created by religion was so wide that 'the Hindus entertained a much greater degree of hostility or repugnance to Muslim than to British rule'. It is this which, according to him, explains the paradox of so little Muslim impact on Hindu culture compared to the impact created by the British on the same culture in spite of the much shorter duration of the latter's rule. The Hindus might have felt compelled to learn Arabic and Persian and adopt court dress and etiquette because of the exigencies of 'Muslim rule', but 'very little of Islamic culture that was not demanded by absolute necessity for livelihood or personal safety would appeal to them. A man does not seek to learn anything from those who are repulsive to him.'[19] And such repulsion was mutual. That is why neither the Hindus nor the Muslims imbibed, even to the slightest degree, the chief characteristic features of the other's culture which might be regarded as their greatest contribution to human civilization.

Thus, the Hindus continued to combine 'catholicity in religious outlook with bigotry in social ethics', while the Muslims continued to display 'an equal bigotry in religious ideas with catholicity in social behaviour'.[20] Even in Bengal, where Hindus and Muslims shared a common language, 'they differed in almost everything except language'.[21]

Another well-known Indian historian, Niharranjan Ray, broadly agrees with Majumdar in his analysis of Hindu-Muslim interaction during the medieval period. He argues that at certain levels of relationship Hindus were imbued with hatred against the Muslims, not because the Muslims were alien or foreign, but because in Islam the Hindus had found for the first time a religion and a way of life that admitted of no compromise, and was not only militant and aggressive in its behaviour pattern but also aimed at controlling the entire area of human activity.[22] He does not deny that at certain levels the elites of the two communities came into mutual contact, but, partly echoing Majumdar, emphasizes that at that level 'the basis of relation between the two communities was one of mutual interests dominated by political and economic, that is, pragmatic considerations, not that of any attempt at mutual understanding'. Again, like Majumdar, Ray thinks that the adaptations to each other's cultures resulting from such contacts did not touch the fundamentals of these cultures but were confined to the external aspects of life and, besides, did not have any wide impact.[23]

Needless to add, European scholars also have generally emphasized the antithetical character of Hinduism and Islam and their mutual repulsion. Thus, according to F.W. Thomas, Islam represents the 'very antithesis of Hinduism'.[24] Murray Titus writes: 'For twelve long centuries Islam has been in contact with Hinduism in India. For twelve centuries each community has been confronted by the other.'[25] Percival Spear emphasizes that in Hindu-Muslim interaction in India 'the principle of repulsion has been more obviously at work than the principle of attraction'.[26] In a more dispassionate vein, he writes:

> The two bodies remained distinct for nine centuries, yet with so much intimate contact there was bound to be some mutual influence. . . . Some of it was important but on neither side was it fundamental. . . .
>
> There was much give and take, but no fusion or synthesis. In daily life there was much day-to-day tolerance and consideration, but behind it all was a permanent tension between the two ways of life. Indo-Persian culture spread a mantle of elegance over to whole of Indian aristocratic society, but Hinduism and Islam remained apart.[27]

III

These are all eminent authorities. Yet the present author finds it difficult to accept the theory of a perpetual conflict betwen Hindus and Muslims during the medieval period because of their differences in religion and culture. Indeed, the contrary can be proved on the basis of information and analysis provided by some of the protagonists of the 'Chinese Wall' theory themelves. We propose to do so with reference to the works of one Pakistani (S.M. Ikram) and one Indian (K.M. Panikkar) historian.

To begin with Ikram, we learn from his account that Amir Khusro (*c.*1253-1325), the most distinguished writer of the early Sultanate period, famous for his Persian poetry, was also among the earliest poets of Hindi. We are further told that it were the Muslim rulers of some of the regional kingdoms who were responsible for many of the first translations of Sanskrit classics into the provincial languages. Among the examples are the translation of the *Ramayana*, the *Mahabharata* and the *Bhagavata Purana* into Bengali under the patronage of Sultan Husain Shah (*c.*1493-1518). In Kashmir, Zain-ul-Abidin (1420-70) patronized the study of Hindu literature and philosophy. It was at this time that *Rajatarangini* was translated into Persian. The state records of Golkunda and Bijapur were maintained in Marathi. The interaction in the field of music, begun at the time of the Arab conquest of Sind, continued during the period of the Sultanate and became even more fruitful with the addition of the rich heritage of Persia and Central Asia. All this resulted in the creation of a new form of music in north India, 'quite different from the traditional Indian music'. There was a parallel development in the field of architecture, the greatest artistic achievement of the Sultanate period. 'As with the musicians, the creativity of the Muslim architects was nourished by the mature styles of both the existing Islamic and Hindu traditions.'[28]

When we come to consider the interaction in the field of religious faith and practice, the task according to Ikram, becomes, more complicated, partly because of lack of evidence, for the religious movements of medieval India have left few records, and partly because of the uncertainty 'whether a pattern of behaviour and belief in both religions has a common origin in one, or if it grew up independently in both cultures'. The exact nature of relationship between the Hindu and Islamic mystical movements, for instance, is very difficult to delineate because of this factor. The same applies to an evaluation of the role of Islam in the emergence of the various *Bhakti* movements.

All the *Bhakti* movements cannot be described as sympathetic to Islam. The movement started by Chaitanya (1485-1533) in Bengal was certainly not. But this cannot be said about the movements associated with Kabir, Guru Nanak or Dadu. Kabir, whose dates are uncertain but who is generally supposed to have flourished in the middle of the fifteenth century, was probably the most influential among the religious leaders of the period covered by the Sultanate. He denounced polytheism, idolatry and caste, but was equally unspairing in his criticism of Muslim formalism and made no distinction between what he considered sane and holy in Hinduism and Islam. 'He was a true seeker of God, and did his best to break the barriers that separated Hindus from Muslims.' Similarly, Guru Nanak (1469-1539) aimed at uniting Hindus and Muslims 'through an appeal to what he considered the great central truths of both'. Dadu (1544-1603) was another important religious leader 'through whose teachings Islamic ideas found wide currency among non-Muslims'. As far as Namadeva (late fourteenth or early fifteenth century) and Tukaram (1598-1649), the two famous poet-saints of Maharashtra, are concerned, their songs clearly suggest that they were not reacting in any hostile fashion to Islam.[29]

If Islam influenced Hinduism, Hinduism too influenced Islam. This process had begun even before the establishment of the Delhi Sultanate. This is proved by the probable Hindu element in certain forms of Islamic mysticism and the intellectual interchanges that had taken place after the conquest of Sind in the seventh and eighth centuries. During the Sultanate, changes of a different order took place. While traces of Hinduism in Muslim religious practices, particularly among the lower classes, may be taken as an illustration of incomplete change from the old way of life, in social life 'Indian Islam retained certain characteristic features of Hindu society which, if not religious in themselves, certainly had been given religious sanction'. Thus, there developed among the Muslims something similar to the caste system among the Hindus. Many of the converts clung to the memory of their former status in a hierarchical society. Besides, what may be called Muslim castes developed as Indian Muslims of the upper classes classified themselves as Sayyid, Shaikh, Mughal, or Pathan. The structure of caste in the Muslim society was, of course, never as rigid as among the Hindus. Whatever that may be, this did not exhaust the Hindu impact on the social life of the Muslims. The latter, for instance, adopted from the former the custom of early marriages and objection to widow remarriage. The same was the case with certain ceremonies connected with birth, death and marriage.[30]

Nor was there a Chinese Wall between Hindus and Muslims in the economic and political fields. During the Arab occupation of Sind, Hindus had been appointed to high administrative positions. Hindus also occupied high military positions in the court of Mahmud of Ghazni, having earned a name in history as an iconoclast. During the early days of the Sultanate, the high administrative and military positions were occupied only by Turkish nobles, and Muslims of Indian origin were kept at a distance along with Hindus. As the situation became less rigid later on and Muslims of Indian origin began to secure high administrative positions, Hindu nobles also followed them. In some of the regional kingdoms, they were even appointed as ministers. Though the number of Hindus in high administrative and military positions was much smaller than that of Muslims, they generally outnumbered the latter in the lower positions. In trade and commerce, they continued to maintain their dominant position.[31] Although the Sultan was supposed to be the defender of the faith, the Delhi Sultanate was not a theocracy and the rulers took decisions on vital matters with reference to the needs of the situation and not to the principles of the *Shariah*.[32] The Hindus did have to pay *jizya*, but they were exempt from *zakat*, which the Muslims alone had to pay. Besides, the Hindus who paid *jizya* were exempt from military service.[33]

The friendly interaction between the Hindus and Muslims reached its high watermark under Akbar (1556-1605). He abolished *jizya*, imposed a ban on cow-slaughter and employed Hindu nobles to some of the highest offices in the State though, of course, Muslims continued to be employed to such positions in much larger numbers. In the fields of architecture, painting, music and literature, the close collaboration between artists and writers of the two communities continued to grow. One of Akbar's famous generals, Abdur Rahim, following in the footsteps of earlier Muslim poets of Hindi like Jayasi and Kabir, made a significant contribution to Hindi poetry and also extended his patronage to a number of Hindi poets.

The trend set by Akbar was continued by his two successors, Jehangir and Shahjahan (1605-57), and indeed reached its climax during the last years of the latter's reign when his eldest son, Dara Shikoh, the translator of the Upanishads into Persian, had the upper hand. Meanwhile, however, a reaction had set in and this reached a climax with the accession of Aurangzeb (1658-1707) famous for his championship of orthodoxy. But even during his rule, while the *jizya* was reimposed after a lapse of about a hundred years and the Hindus were subjected to discriminatory customs duties (5 per cent as against 2 per cent for Muslims), the general policy of collaboration between Hindus and Muslims in the political and cultural fields was continued. Thus, Hindus continued to be appointed to the highest positions in the State, both on the civil and the military sides. Indeed, there were more Hindu officers under Aurangzeb than under any other Mughal emperor.[34] Trade and commerce also continued to be generally in the hands of Hindu merchants.[35] It is revealing of the spirit of the times that next to Persian, which was the court language, 'the language which received the greatest patronage at court was Hindi'. Akbar began the practice of appointing a Hindi *Kavi Rai* (poet laureate) along with the Persian *Malik-ul-Saura* and this was continued even by Aurangzeb.[36]

It is doubtful whether Aurangzeb ever issued a general order calling for the destruction of all Hindu temples. Initially, such orders applied to a few specific cases. At a later stage, he did try to 'enforce strict Islamic law by ordering the destruction of newly- built Hindu temples. Still later, the procedure was adopted of closing down rather than destroying the newly-built temples in Hindu localities'. Often such orders remained unimplemented. That numerous Hindu temples were built in certain areas, e.g. in Bengal, during his rule shows that Aurangzeb's 'alleged ceaseless campaign of temple destruction obviously could have been neither thorough nor universal'.[37]

We need not dilate further on this point. What has been mentioned above, based on information supplied by Ikram, should be enough to show that while there is evidence to show occasional tension and conflict between segments of the elites of the Hindu and Muslim communities, there is no evidence of the existence of a Chinese Wall between them based on differences of religion and culture. On the other hand, there is abundant evidence of close collaboration between the two in various fields of human endeavour. Such evidence naturally affects Ikram's own conclusion. He, of course, keeps clinging to the Chinese Wall theory wherever possible and points to instances of conflict here and there between Hindus and Muslims, but he fails to produce such instances in any large number. Even so, he makes the following observation on the nature of the Hindu-Muslim interaction during the period of the Sultanate:

More striking than the amount of interaction that took place in the first three centuries of Muslim rule was the fact that there was not more. The impression one gains is that there was never a very conscious attempt to create understanding except on the part of Kabir and Nanak, and that the contacts between the two great religions were, on the whole, remarkably superficial as far as the total life of the country was concerned.[38]

Yet, as he proceeds further and surveys Indian life and culture during the Mughal period, he finds himself overwhelmed by facts which point to a contrary conclusion. It is a tribute to his integrity as a scholar that he makes no effort to resist this conclusion, although it obviously contradicts Majumdar's Chinese Wall theory which he endorses:

Any generalization about Indian history is dangerous, but the impression one gains from looking at social conditions during the Mughal period is of a society moving towards an integration of its manifold political regions, social systems, and cultural inheritances. The greatness of the Mughals consisted in part at least in the fact that the influence of their court and government permeated society, giving it a new measure of harmony.[39]

Again, in his final summing up, he emphasizes the importance of the Indian component in Islam's cultural heritage. Surveying 'the ten centuries of Muslim rule', he identifies four main strands 'that have given Indo-Islamic culture its characteristic texture': the Islamic religious inheritance, including aspects rooted in Arabic tradition; the Turkish origin of many of the rulers; the impact of Persian culture; and the indigenous environment in Afghanistan as well as India. Then he pens the final epitaph to the Chinese Wall theory in these words:

There has been a tendency to overlook this indigenous component, but its influence is deep-rooted and all-pervading. The predominantly non-Muslim environment in which Indo-Muslim culture developed, and the heritage of an ancient civilization did not leave Islam untouched. Furthermore, the vast majority of the Muslims were . . . Hindu converts, which shows not only in numerous usages and practices carried over from the ancestral Hindu society, but also in unconscious reactions and mental attitudes. The vigorous Islamic revival of later centuries has tended to overshadow the indigenous element. While the Turkish rulers and aristocracy contributed much in the sphere of government, law, dress, and food, and the Persian element was prominent in literature, fine arts, mysticism, and philosophy, essentially the two basic components which gave the civilization its peculiar flavour were the Indian and the Islamic.[40]

IV

What has been said about Ikram applies with equal force to Panikkar. Although, as shown above, he underlines the existence of two separate nations in India almost from the beginning of the thirteenth century with 'hardly any social communication or intermingling of life' between them, while actually describing the political and social conditions in India during the medieval period he writes in a different vein. Warning the reader not to take literally the accounts of the contemporary court historians, who had a vested interest in depicting the Islamic zeal of their patrons,[41] he provides profuse evidence of close contact and collaboration between the two.

Thus, he tells us that although in the period of conquest, Hindus had undoubtedly to suffer, they being deprived of political power in large areas, their religion held in contempt and their temples destroyed, after the first flush of conquest was over 'the structure of economic life in the country forced even the most zealous and fanatical of kings to moderate this policy'. Thus, the cultivating classes remained largely Hindu as the invaders had not brought cultivators with them. Nor did trade and commerce change hands to any considerable extent and the Hindu *bania* continued to occupy an important place in the social structure. Even in the field of religion, an ethos of toleration and mutual respect developed quite early. There is indeed ample evidence that 'even under the most bigoted kings, like Allauddin Khalji and Firoz Tughlaq, the Hindu religious leaders received honour and recognition'. Also the Hindus, from the very beginning of the Sultanate, provided the bulk of the lower levels of bureaucracy, though, of course, the Muslims occupied the higher positions. 'The *patwaris*, the accountants, the treasurers and others in the districts were invariably Hindu, while the governors and district officials were Muslims.'[42] Writing about the architectural achievements of the Sultanate period, Panikkar observes: 'The Indo-Muslim style is a complete harmonisation of the artistic spirit of Hinduism and Islam and nowhere does it become more clear than in the mosques at Ahmedabad and Jaunpur. The architects were no doubt Muslims but the master-builders and craftsmen continued to be Hindus.'[43] In the field of literature, he underlines the encouragement given to local talent by Muslim rulers and notes that Maladhar Basu's Bengali translation of the *Bhagavata* was undertaken at the order of Nusrat Shah and Kavindra Paramashwar's translation of the *Mahabharata* at that of Paragal Khan, a general of Hussain Shah.[44] And what could be greater evidence of

Amir Khusro's love for Hindi than his declaration that it was 'in some ways richer and more flexible than Persian'.[45] In the field of religion, we are told that Islam had a great impact upon Hinduism:

> One thing is clear. Islam had a profound effect on Hinduism during this period. Medieval Hindu theism is in some ways a reply to the attack of Islam; and the doctrines of medieval traders, by whatever names their gods are known, are essentially theistic. It is the one supreme God that is the object of the devotee's adoration and it is to His grace that we are asked to look for redemption. All Bhakti cults are, therefore, essentially monotheistic, not in the exclusive sense that other devotees cannot worship the same Supreme Being under other names, but in the affirmative sense that whether known as Siva, Krishna or Devi, they all symbolise the One and the Eternal.[46]

In his survey of the Mughal period, Panikkar naturally finds much greater contact and collaboration between Hindus and Muslims. Thus, we are told that the Mughal school of painting, famous all over the world, was 'preeminently an Indian school and Hindus and Muslims alike contributed to the artistic achievement of the period'. Out of seventeen top artists mentioned by Abul Fazal, he adds, thirteen were Hindus.[47] Fatehpur Sikri is described as 'an example of the mingling of Hindu and Muslim conceptions'. We are further told that 'the dress, social amenities, etc., which the Mughals introduced ceased to be foreign and were accepted by the higher classes everywhere'.[48] While Hindus were influenced by Muslims, they also influenced the latter:

> Kabir and Nanak, two vital figures in medieval Hindu religion, were both influenced by the rigid monotheism of Islam and in both of them there is a mingling of Sufism and Bhakti. In no one was this more remarkable than in Dara Shikoh, the unfortunate son of Shahjahan. Deeply versed in the mysteries of Sufism, Dara was an adept in yogic practices, and in the doctrines of the Hindu saints. . . . In fact, the influence of Hinduism on Indian Muslims seems to have been quite considerable. The translation of Hindu classics into Persian proceeded apace. Not a few of the leading Muslim scholars of the period seem to have known Sanskrit well, for we have Badauni's own statement that he was commissioned by Akbar to make a fresh translation of *Rajatarangini*.[49]

In the political field, the Mughal period, according to Panikkar, witnessed the emergence of a national monarchy. After noting Akbar's marriage with a Hindu princess, his appointment of his wife's nephew, Man Singh, to a high position in the State and his abolition first of the pilgrim tax and then of the poll-tax (*jizya*) in 1563, Panikkar remarks: 'The national monarchy had come into existence, and though political power was with the immediate entourage of the court with its predominantly foreign nobility, no longer could the Hindus in the empire feel that they were only the tax-payers, foreigners in their own land.' The appointment of Man Singh was followed by that of others, notably Todarmal and Birbal, who were both of middle-class origin. This policy of career open to talent converted the Mughal empire 'from a foreign government into a national State'.[50]

Though Jehangir was the candidate of the orthodox faction at the court, he generally followed his father's policy. The same was true of Shahjahan in spite of the fact that he had been responsible for the demolition of a few temples. A change came with the accession of Aurangzeb. 'To him Akbar's policy of national State seemed to be the very negation of Islamic ideas.' Even before his accession to the throne, he had shown his hostility towards the Hindus by the desecration of the Chintamani temple at Ahmedabad. In 1669, he issued his first general order 'to demolish all temples and schools of the infidels'. This marked the beginning of 'an active policy of temple demolition' and some of the most famous temples at Banaras, Mathura and Somnath 'fell to his destructive enthusiasm'. This was followed by the reimposition of the *jizya* in 1679 after the lapse of more than a hundred years. Such a policy naturally created great unrest among the Hindus. The national State now ceased to exist.[51]

Panikkar's lively imagination now leads him to the portrayal of the spirit of Hindu independence which, we are told, had not been crushed as a result of three hundred years of fight and which was embodied by the kingdom of Vijayanagar in the south, particularly after Akbar's policy in the north had deprived 'Hindu nationalism' of its hereditary leaders. However, by the middle of the seventeenth century, the central authority of the Vijayanagar kingdom had collapsed, and 'Hindu political independence' had no visible national head. 'It is to this vacant position that Shivaji, under the inspiration of Ramdas, now aspired.' But it was not only against Shivaji and the Marathas that Aurangzeb had to fight. The Rajputs and the Sikhs were also up in arms against him. 'The loyalty of the Hindu population, so sedulously built up by his three immediate predecessors, existed no longer.'[51]

We need not pause here to point out the obvious weakness of this formulation. There was never in existence any organization of, or coordination among, all or even most of the Hindu rulers and simply because a rebellious ruler was a Hindu, he could not be described as a symbol of Hindu resistance. Several rulers, who were not Hindus, but belonged to the faith of the head of the Mughal empire, were also engaged in similar endeavours. Aurangzeb's religious policy must surely have been extremely unpopular among the Hindus, but it is important to remember that the rebellions in Rajasthan and Maharashtra had already begun before the reimposition of the *jizya*. Whatever that may be, Panikkar, while contradicting himself helps us to retain a sense of perspective about the nature of political alignments and motivations in India as late as the last quarter of the eighteenth century and makes it clear that religious affiliation was not the main factor behind them.[53] The final *coup-de-grace* to the theory of two nations existing in India right from the beginning of the thirteenth century is delivered in these words:

> Before the nineteenth century, Islam in India was not separately organised. The Hindus and Muslims lived together, professing their different religions. The political power of Islam was a sufficient guarantee for the religious faith and the necessity for the Muslims to organise separately was never felt. The Muslim officers freely entered the service of the Hindu rulers and even at Panipat, where the Maratha forces met the Afghans, the Hindu side had numerous Muslim soldiers and captains, and it was Ibrahim Gardee's artillery that played the greatest havoc on the Afghan forces. The Maratha governor of Lahore in 1758 was Adam Beg. In the same way, when Babar invaded India, the Afghans allied themselves with the Hindus to resist the invaders.[54]

V

It may be added that if one were to make an effort to describe the social and cultural life of Hindus and Muslims in various parts of India as late as the nineteenth century, one would find ample evidence of a lot of sharing together by the members of the two communities. The pattern of life in the first half of that century in eastern Bengal, one of the areas where Muslims were in a majority, has been quite elaborately described by A.R. Mallick, a distinguished historian of Bangladesh, which was a part of Pakistan when he wrote his book. According to him, Hindus participated in Muslim festivals and Muslims in Hindu festivals without any hesitation and indeed with great enthusiasm.[55] Bengali Muslim writers and poets while they used Persian and Arabic words, wrote in as Sanskritized a style as their Hindu contemporaries. Besides, they adopted 'themes, modes, images and ideas' from Sanskrit in much the same way as the latter did and some even composed hymns in honour of the goddess Kali. Moreover, even when writing on Muslim themes, 'some continued to draw upon Hindu mythology'.[55]

As usual, literature reflected the social reality. As a result of long association and the liberal policy of some of the great Muslim rulers, there had evolved certain common objects of worship. This was particularly true of the common people 'who mutually applied to the deities or saints of the other community when they imagined that supplications to their own had been ineffectual'.[56] Buchanan found this practice common even among the Brahmins and Mullahs in some parts of Bengal and Bihar.[57]

Thorburn's findings in the second half of the nineteenth century in the Punjab, the next important area of preponderant Muslim population, were not very different from that of Buchanan in Bengal. In western Punjab almost the entire population consisted of Muslims and in central Punjab Muslims considerably outnumbered Hindus and Sikhs put together. In eastern Punjab Hindus outnumbered Muslims by over three to one. Here Muslims had been converted to Islam only two or three hundred years ago. According to Thorburn, they retained many of their ancient Hindu customs and superstitions and were 'very lax Mahomedans'. In central Punjab also, there was 'little active antipathy' between Muslims, Hindus and Sikhs.[58] In eastern Punjab, where the main agricultural tribes were Jats and Rajputs, we are further told, it mattered little whether they were Hindus or Muslims: 'both are socially and politically one people, ancient tribal customs and the ties of blood being stronger than the separatist teachings of a half-learnt religion'. In central Punjab, the Islamic faith of the Muslims generally was 'of a more decided type' than in the eastern districts. Thorburn adds:

> Upto the present time, however, the whole rural population of the Punjab, east of Jhelum meridian (that is in central and eastern districts) whether Hindus or Musalmans, may be regarded, for all administrative purposes, as one people. They are untainted with religious animosities. They live side by side as peaceful cultivators, in happy indifference to the petty jealousies which superior knowledge stirs up in the heads of their Hindu and Muslim brethren in the towns.[59]

Sleeman's account of his travels in the kingdom of Oudh in 1849-50, when it was still under the rule of the Nawab, presents a somewhat similar picture of relations between the Hindus and Muslims in the social and cultural field in an area where the Muslims constituted a small minority of the population, but occupied a dominant position in government and politics. Thus, Sleeman notes with surprise the fact of Hindus as well as Muslims going to a shrine at Bahraich dedicated to a Muslim general of Sultan Mahmud of Ghazni, 'whose only recorded merit consists of having sent a great many Hindoos to hell, in a wanton and unprovoked invasion of their territory'.[60] He saw the same thing at another place at the shrine of that general's father and noted: 'All our Hindoo camp followers paid as much reverence to the shrine as they passed as the Mohommedans.'[61] While passing through Bharwara, he noted how the members of a particular Rajpur tribe, though divided by religion, lived together 'in tolerable harmony; and eat together on occasions of ceremony, though not from the same dishes'.[62]

This picture must be rounded off by reference to the recent findings of Hafeez Malik, who has been earlier mentioned as one of the powerful Pakistani upholders of the 'perpetual conflict' theory regarding the relationship between Hindus and Muslims. Dilating on this relationship in Delhi during the first half of the nineteenth century, he observes:

> The relationship between the two was harmonious, while both communities maintained their cultural identity. However, the focal point of Hindu-Muslim cultural synthesis was the Red Fort, where the Mughal kings and princes liberally adopted secular Hindu mores and folkways, and the citizens of Delhi emulated the royalty. . . . On the occasions of birth, circumcision, engagement, marriage, and even death, according to the eyewitness accounts of pre-1857 Delhi Muslim culture, Hindu and Muslim women sang the same folk songs.[63]

It must also be remembered that Muslims as well as Hindus were divided among themselves socially by several barriers. The divisions among Hindus based on caste are well-known. What is not generally remembered is that this does not involve division into merely four, but innumerable castes. Besides the caste goupings and their status in society varied from area to area. A person belonging to a particular caste might mean something to people in his own area, but might be entirely meaningless in another area. But Muslims were also subject to numerous divisive factors. There was, for instance, the doctrinal division between Sunnis, who formed the bulk of the Muslim population in India, and such minority sects as the Shias and the Bohras. Besides, Muslims also were not free from the working of the caste system and the ideal of Islamic brotherhood remained an ideal only. Pakistani scholars, in spite of their interest in stressing the concept of Islamic solidarity, have also accepted this. Thus, for instance, they agree that the upper class Muslims were divided into four main groupings: Shaikhs, Syeds, Mughals and Pathans. Inter-marriages between members of different groupings were rare and this was one of the main reasons why most of the marriages took place among close relations. The four groups were regarded as constituting the *ashraf* or the respectable sections of the community. Many of them were the descendants of administrators, scholars, preachers and soldiers who had come from Central Asia, Arabia, Persia or Afghanistan. But many more claimed such descent and prepared genealogical tables as this conferred respectability. The various converts from Hindu groups like the Rajputs also maintained their own separate castes. Then there were the bulk of Muslims, converts from the so-called lower Hindu castes. They more or less continued their old social status also as Muslims, and were generally known as *azlal*. As an eminent Bangladeshi historian puts it, 'By the beginning of the nineteenth century the doctrine of caste seemed to have gained "a complete practical ascendency" over the Muslims of some parts of India and occasioned a vast number of subdivisions, the members of which did not intermarry and often did not eat in a company.'[64]

Besides, just like Hindus, Muslims living in different regions of India had developed certain marked cultural features characteristic of those regions and had indeed much more in common with the Hindus of those regions than with the Muslims living far away. Thus, for instance, the Bengali Muslim had far more in common with the Bengali Hindu than with the Punjabi or United Provinces Muslim. Art, architecture, language and literature had all been affected by this living together in different regions. Economic disparities between Muslims of different regions as, for instance, between Muslims of Bengal and those of United Provinces added another dimension to their lives. Above all, there were marked differences from the economic point of view among Muslims, just as among Hindus, living in the same region. It is, therefore, unhistorical to refer to Hindus and Muslims in the second half of the nineteenth century as monolithic communities.[65]

VI

Yet it is a fact of history that in spite of all the differences and diversities among themselves, the bulk of Muslims living in various parts of India gradually put themselves under one political umbrella and succeeded in carving out a completely separate State for themselves outside the Indian Union. Obviously, this cannot be explained by any simple formulation like the existence of two nations in India, based on differences in religion and culture, right from the time of the establishment of Turkish rule in India in the thirteenth century or the policy of divide and rule relentlessly pursued by the British, which divided a people earlier united by a composite Hindu-Muslim or Muslim-Hindu culture. The British policy, of course, did play its part but only as one of the elements in a mix of factors. This mix included also the legacy from the past and its impact on the minds of the Muslim elite.

If we are to succeed in understanding the nature of this legacy, we shall have to first go into the history of the rise and growth of Islam and take note of the fact that, unlike most other religious faiths, it succeeded right at its birth in inculcating among its followers a strong sense of belonging to a community and a community which was not merely religious but also political. Almost all authorities on Islamic history agree on this point. Thus, Montgomery Watt writes:

> Our investigations have shown one area in which Islam had great success in integrating the political life of its adherents. That was in the formation of the *ummah* or Islamic community, which, while it had a religious basis, was also a political body. The success was not merely in founding such a body, but in managing to attach to it some of the valuable attitudes which, in the case of the pre-Islamic Arabs, had been attached to the tribe. One such attitude, arising from the feeling of brotherhood between the members of a tribe, led to a strong feeling of brotherhood among the members of the Islamic community. . . .[66]

Besides, from the very beginning, Muslims began to look upon their community as a charismatic community, destined to establish the kingdom of God on earth. It is this faith in the community which lay behind the crucial role assigned to consensus (*ijma*) in the maintenance and development of the *Shariah*. Adds Watt: 'The best explanation of this recurrence of consensus seems to be that it arises out of an intense belief in the community, a belief that the community is in some way supernatural, is a divinely instituted and divinely ordered community, in brief, that it is a 'charismatic community'.[67]

The strong feeling of belonging to the community was also the main factor behind the keen Muslim interest in history, which developed quite early. As Hamilton Gibb points out:

> The historical arguments contained in the Koran, the natural pride taken in the extensive conquests and the rivalries of the Arab tribes no doubt contributed to this. But the remarkable feature that, apart from the philologists, the collectors of the historical tradition were almost exclusively theologians and *muhaddiths* suggests that a deeper reason existed. For in the theological view history was the

manifestation of a divine plan for the government of mankind; and while the historical outlook of the earlier generations might be limited to tracing it through the succession of prophets which culminated in Muhammad, all Islamic schools were agreed that it did not end there. In the Sunni doctrine, it was the Islamic community, the *ammat Allah*, with which the continuation of the divine plan on earth was bound up: consequently the study of its history was a necessary supplement to the study of the divine revelation in Koran and hadith.[68]

W.C. Smith has aptly drawn attention to the fact that the Islamic era does not begin with Muhammad's birth or with the time when he began to receive revelations but with the rise to power of the nascent Muslim community after the Prophet's shifting from Mecca to Medina (AD 622). He writes further:

> . . . for the Muslim, community and history are 'special'. For him they are, as for no other, religiously significant. The Quran, of course, is in Muslim eyes holy, or 'sacred'. One would be going only slightly too far to say that his society and its history partake of an almost sacred character also. Here is a community that has explicitly undertaken to live in accordance with God's plan. Since it has been in existence, to become a Muslim means to join that community; and to take part in the enterprise of fulfilling God's good pleasure on earth. The enterprise is hardly less important than the revelation. The privilege and duty and experience of taking part in it are central to the Muslim's faith.[69]

Both the sense of community, based on allegiance to Islam, and the sense of power, based on the assumption that Muslims must have authority to enforce *Shariah* and regulate their lives according to the injunctions of the Prophet, were reflected in the treatment prescribed for non-Muslims. They were to be treated as *Dhimmis*, to be protected as subjects by the Muslim state but not to be treated as equals. They were to pay *jizya* in order to meet the cost of protection; those who undertook or were asked to offer military service would, of course, be exempt from it.

As first Arabs and then Turks, after their conversion to Islam, expanded in various directions and established their rule over a far-flung empire, encompassing territories in both Asia and Europe, the Muslim elite acquired a faith in something like an imperial destiny and a feeling grew among them that they belonged to a conquering race and had a right to rule over the non-Muslim peoples and spread Islam among them. Wars and conquests, even when really motivated by other reasons, were justified by reference to the need for spreading Islam. This applied also to the Turks who established their rule in India. As M. Mujeeb puts it:

There was never any doubt in the minds of the Muslims of their right to spread over the earth. . . . The urge and the courage required for the conquest and occupation of alien and unknown lands cannot be the result of philosophical detachment or defeatism. Conquerors have always had some deep conviction that justified their policies. The Muslim Turks found the moral justification for their advance into India in the injunction to propagate Islam. As this could not, in the opinion of kings and warriors, be achieved without the subjugation of the non-Muslims and the occupation of their territory, the propagation of Islam became identical with war and conquest. This view is presented in the Persian chronicles with a tedious and jarring persistence as the literary embellishment of every account of the early Turkish successes, and of the wars of the Sultans of Delhi and of the Mughal emperors.[70]

VII

The long rule by the Sultans of Delhi and the Mughal emperors further strengthened the Muslim elite's pride in their community as also their faith in its destiny to rule. The Turkish rulers knew that although they had risen to power on the basis either of military prowess or hereditary right, they could rule only so long as they remained Muslims and retained the support of the court nobility which manned the higher ranks of the armed forces as well as the administration and was in the beginning exclusively and later predominantly Muslim. Besides, their identification with the interests of Islam provided the main moral prop or legitimation of their rule. The role of legitimation was performed primarily by the *ulama*, a section of whom also worked as historians. Describing the latter as 'the first Muslim communalists of India', a well-known authority on medieval Indian historiography points out with reference to the period of the Delhi Sultanate:

The ideal temporal rule of Islam which the Muslim historians of the Delhi Sultanate wished to show forth in their histories is that in which the Muslim world shall be seen to be governed by a partnership of pious scholars and pious sultans. . . . In short, the world in which 'religion and kingship are twins', the world where the continuity of the life of the Muslim community is symbolised not by the supremacy of the *Khilafat*, now in the post-Mongol period, a chimera, but by the supremacy of the *Sharia*. . . . And if history does not present a picture of obedience to Islam by the rulers of the day, then it should present a picture of the evil consequences of disobedience.[71]

The pious sultan was expected not merely to uphold the dignity of the *ulama* and remove hindrances to the propagation of the 'true faith' by the latter, but also facilitate their task by humbling and humiliating the Hindus if not completely exterminating them. The following extract from the *Tarikh-i-Firuzshahi* (fourteenth century) by Ziauddin Barani illustrates this point:

> The obligation to be the refuge of the faith cannot be fulfilled until they [the kings] have utterly destroyed infidelity and unbelief, polytheism and idolatry for the sake of God and the protection of the true religion. If they cannot wholly extirpate polytheism and infidelity because they have taken root and (exterminate) the infidels because of their large number, it will not be less meritorious if, for the sake of Islam and of affording refuge to the true faith, they use their efforts to insult and humiliate and to cause grief to and bring ridicule and shame upon the polytheistic and idolatrous Hindus, who are the bitterest enemies of God and the Prophet of God. . . . They should not, for the sake of the glory of Islam and the honour of the true faith, permit even a single unbeliever and polytheist to live as a respectable person . . . or be set in authority over a community or a group, a province or a district.[72]

Such ideas continued to be expressed in the succeeding centuries. Thus, Abd Al-Quddus Gangohi (1456-1537), a well-known Sufi divine of the first half of the sixteenth century, wrote to Babur emphasizing that in a Muslim administration and an Islamic polity, a non-Muslim (*kafir*) should not be given a government post or an assignment of revenue. He further added:

> Non-Muslims should not wield the pen in offices and they should not be commanders and tax-gatherers. In the *Sharia* the subordination of *Kafirs* is enjoined; and in accordance with it they should be humbled, subordinated and made to pay tax. *Jijya* and *zakat* upon their property should be collected according to the prescriptions of the *shar*. Kafirs should be forbidden to dress like Muslims to conceal their unbelief and they should be prohibited from practising heathen observances ostentatiously and publicly. In this manner the light of Islam will be maintained in its full glory.[73]

In the early years of the seventeenth century, a much more famous Sufi saint, Shaikh Ahmad Sirhindi (1564-1624), popularly known as *Mujaddid Alf-i-Sani* (reviver of Islam in the second millennium) and a legendary figure in the history of Islam in the Indian subcontinent, gave repeated expression to similar ideas in his letters to various nobles holding important positions in the Mughal administration during the reign of Jehangir. He sought to propagate the view that *Kufr* and Islam were opposed to each other: 'The progress of one is possible only at the expense of the other and coexistence between these two contradictory faiths is unthinkable. To honour the one amounts to insulting the other.' In one of his letters to Shaikh Farid Bukhari, he wrote:

The honour of Islam lies in insulting *Kufr* and *Kafirs*. One who respects the *Kafirs*, dishonours the Muslims. To respect them does not merely mean honouring them and assigning them a seat of honour in any assembly, but it also implies keeping company with them or showing consideration to them. They should be kept at an arm's length like dogs. . . . If some worldly business cannot be performed without them, in that case only a minimum of contact should be established with them but without taking them into confidence.[74]

The actual conditions, of course, were quite different. Barni himself, while describing conditions in India under Firoz Tughlaq, noted in *Fatawa-i-Jahandari* (Al xi), that in Delhi and other Muslim cities, the customs of 'infidelity' were openly practised and idols publicly worshipped. Indeed the Hindus adhered to their traditions 'with greater insistence than before'. The only disability they suffered was that they had to pay the *jizya*. What specially pained men of orthodox inclinations like Barni was that the Muslim kings, on ground of reasons of state, showed no interest in either suppressing Hindu religious practices or humiliating the Hindu elite. As Barni put it:

The desire for overthrowing infidels and knocking down idolators does not fill the hearts of the Muslim kings (of India). On the other hand, out of consideration for the fact that infidels and polytheists are payers of taxes and protected persons, these infidels are honoured, distinguished, favoured and made eminent: the kings bestow drums, banners, ornaments, cloaks of brocade and caparisoned horses upon them and appoint them to governorships, high posts and offices. And in their capital (Delhi). . . . Muslim kings not only allow but are pleased with the fact that infidels, polytheists, idol-worshippers build houses like palaces, wear clothes of brocade and ride Arab horses caparisoned with gold and silver ornaments.[75]

It is indeed an index of the large-heartedness as well as sense of realism and wisdom of the Turko-Afghan and Mughal rulers that they did not pay any serious attention to such outpourings, but openly asserted their right to do what they considered best in the interest of their rule, regardless of the injunctions of the *Shariah* or the rulings of the *Ulama*. Except when engaged in warfare, they generally refrained from directly interfering with the religious beliefs and practices of the Hindus and, beginning with the fifteenth century, appointed them to high positions in their governments. In due course, a stage arrived when even the highest of such posts were not barred to Hindus. Akbar's rule (1556-1605) is justly famous for this, but contrary to the general impression, even during the rule of Aurangzeb (1658-1707), notorious for his orthodoxy, nay bigotry, Hindu nobles continued to be appointed to high positions in the government in the same way as before, the only difference being that their number increased.[76]

It has also to be remembered that the voice of orthodoxy was not the only voice to be heard during the Turko-Afghan and Mughal periods. Orthodox ideologues like Quddus and Sirhindi, for instance, had their counterparts among liberals who advocated reconciliation and amity between Muslims and Hindus. 'Akbar's *Din-i-Ilahi*' aptly observes Tara Chand, 'was not an isolated freak of an autocrat . . ., but an inevitable result of the forces which were deeply surging in India's breast, and finding expression in the teachings of men like Kabir'.[77] While the latter mainly influenced the masses, there were exponents of liberal ideas among the elite too. The most notable among such men were Shaikh Mubarak and his two sons, Abul Fazl and Faizi, who wielded considerable influence at the Mughal court during the reign of Akbar in the second half of the sixteenth century. Abul Fazl, in particular, believed that all human beings belonged to one brotherhood and that there was a basic cultural commonality between the Muslims and Hindus. He, of course, recognized the existence of religious differences, but emphasized that these should not be allowed to disrupt the basic homogeneity of society.[78] In *A'in-i-Akbari*, while dealing with Akbar's religious policy, he remarks: 'But have the religious and the worldly tendencies of men no common ground? Is there not everywhere the same enrapturing beauty which beams forth from so many thousand hidden places? Broad indeed is the carpet which God has spread, and beautiful the colours which he has given it.'[79] Again, while describing the main reason behind his decision to write in detail about the religion and philosophy of the Hindus in the third part of his great work, Abul Fazl observes:

> It was indispensable in me . . . to bring into open evidence the system of philosophy, the degree of self-discipline, and the gradations of rite and usage of this race in order that hostility towards them might abate and the temporal sword be stayed a while from the shedding of blood, that dissensions within and without be turned to peace and the thornbrake of strife and enmity bloom into a garden of concord.[80]

Such thoughts, it need hardly be pointed out, were shared by large sections of the Muslim elite not merely during the reign of Abul Fazl's patron, Akbar, but also during subsequent years. For they provided the intellectual underpinning to the continuing cultural as well as political collaboration between the Muslim and Hindu elites. Yet it must also be remembered that whether the ruler was an Akbar or an Aurangzeb, Muslims always constituted the vast majority of the nobles at the court.[81] Besides, orthodoxy perforce remained their dominant ideology, though it was not fully reflected in practice. Even a ruler like Akbar was not totally free from this constraint. Although he defied orthodox Muslim opinion to a considerable extent, particularly by abolishing the *jizya*, holding discussions at the court with representatives of various religious faiths and permitting the performances of Hindu religious rites by his Rajput wife, he could not afford to defy it beyond a certain point. As Mujeeb points out, 'we must assume that Akbar was not a statesman who would deliberately undermine the basis of his own authority. He must have known that he could rule only as a Muslim, and as the leader of a minority that was in power.'[82] Further, 'the identification of Muslim orthodoxy and Muslim political power was too close and too real and they would stand or fall together'.[83]

Indeed, depending on the exigencies of the situation, even Akbar felt constrained to appeal to the orthodox Muslim sentiment in the most blatant terms. Thus, he described the fall of Chittor as the victory of Islam over infidels and issued a *fathnama* which declared:

> As directed by the word of God, we, as far as it is within our power, remain busy in *jihad* and owing to the kindness of the supreme Lord, who is the promoter of our victories, we have succeeded in occupying a number of forts and towns belonging to the infidels and have established Islam there. With the help of our bloodthirsty sword, we have erased the signs of infidelity from their minds and have destroyed temples in those places and also all over Hindustan.[84]

This is not to question the overall liberal direction of Akbar's religious policy, based on *sulh-i-kul* (peace with all), but only to underline the strength of Muslim orthodoxy even under him and the constraints under which he had to work. After his death, a reaction set in. This was spearheaded by Shaikh Ahmad Sirhindi who 'made the revival of orthodoxy something of a movement'.[85] Although the extent of this reaction has been generally exaggerated,[86] there is no doubt that 'orthodoxy gradually got the upper hand and maintained its position in spite of Dara Shikoh's liberal and mystical predilections'.[87] This trend, of course, reached its climax under Aurangzeb who reimposed *jizya* (1679) after a lapse of about a hundred years, ordered the destruction of all Hindu schools and temples (though, he also, in certain special cases, made grants for the maintenance of temples) and subjected Hindu traders to discriminatory excise duties.[88] But even if Dara Shikoh had defeated Aurangzeb and ascended the throne, it is doubtful if orthodoxy could have been effectively challenged.[89] Perhaps it was this realization about the nature of Mughal rule which accounts for the fact that in spite of marked differences in the religious outlook of the two Mughal princes, there was not much difference in the number of Hindu nobles supporting Dara Shikoh (24) and Aurangzeb (21).[90]

There is no doubt, however, about the much wider support for Aurangzeb among the Muslim nobility at the court (103 to 63 for Dara). While the contest between Dara and Aurangzeb cannot be treated as primarily a contest between a liberal and an orthodox prince and must be ascribed to their personal ambitions, the wider support for Aurangzeb among the Muslim nobility was, at any rate partly, due to the fact that orthodoxy now had a greater hold than before on the Muslim elite.[91] It is symptomatic of this trend that when, after his defeat, Dara was executed, the charge levelled against him was that he had not only deviated from Islam and practised 'infidelity and heresy', but also shown 'an inclination towards the religion of the Hindus and the institutions of those accursed ones'. The charge-sheet further added:

> He was constantly in the society of Brahmins, *Jogis* and *Sanyasis* and used to regard this crowd of prevaricators, misguided ones and worthless fellows as perfect guides and *Arif* who had reached God. He considered their books which they call as *Bed* (*Veda*) as being divine, and the word of God, revealed from heaven and the most ancient and venerable books. . . . It became manifest that if he obtained the throne and established supreme power and authority, the pillars of the exalted *Shariat*, would be in danger and the precepts of Islam would be changed for the rant of infidelity and Judaism.[92]

As mentioned earlier, the growing strength of orthodoxy among the Muslim elite is clearly revealed by Aurangzeb's decision in 1679 to reimpose *jizya* on non-Muslims, after a lapse of about a hundred years. The cause for this was certainly not his religious bigotry, as suggested by Sarkar.[93] If that were so, Aurangzeb need not have waited for twenty-two years since his ascent to the throne to order this, for his religious views were already fully formed before such ascent. It was not also due to his deference to the views of the Muslim theologians who suggested the reimposition of *jizya* or to his calculations of its advantage from the financial point of view, as suggested by Faruki.[94] It is known that Aurangzeb, just like his predecessors among the Turko-Afghan Sultans as well as the Mughal emperors, deferred to the advice of theologicians only when such advice appealed to his own reason. Besides, the financial gains from the reimposition of the *jizya* were not expected to be so large, particularly in view of the high cost of collection, as to outweigh the political discontent it was likely to create among the Hindus. In such a situation, the ground advanced by Satish Chandra alone seems convincing. According to him, the rebellions of the Rajputs and the Marathas and the continuing conflict with the (Shia) Muslim kingdoms of Bijapur and Golkunda had created a severe crisis for the empire. Aurangzeb, therefore, felt the need 'to make some striking declaration, which might rouse enthusiasm, and rally Muslim opinion behind him'.[95]

The close association of Muslim orthodoxy with political power led to the growth of a feeling among the Muslim elite that they were members of a ruling class. This feeling continued even after the disintegration of the Mughal empire. In 1844, while reporting on his travels in northern India, Sleeman noted that Muslims, by whom he obviously meant the Muslim elite, generally identified themselves as the former ruling class.[96] This self-image of the Muslim elite as the former rulers of India made it difficult for many of them, particularly those belonging to the upper strata and conscious of their descent from the court nobility of the Mughals, consisting largely of the members of the migrant families from Arabia, Persia and Central Asia, to identify themselves with the Indian nationalist movement. For that movement based itself, right from the beginning, on the democratic principle of one person, one vote and, in a land with overwhelming Hindu majority, this was bound to appear to persons imbued with a Muslim political consciousness as Hindu rule.

VIII

During the period of the decline of the Mughal empire after the passing away of Aurangzeb (1707), orthodoxy acquired even a stronger hold over the minds of the Muslim elite in India. Islam had been so closely identified in their minds with political power that its absence created a tremendous sense of insecurity in them and made them feel dubious about the future of their faith. In such a situation, it began to be said that the only way to ensure a secure future for Islam in India was to cleanse it of all impurities that had crept into it on Indian soil and to restore political power to Muslim hands. This trend of thought is best illustrated by the teachings and activities of Shah Waliullah (1703-62), justly acclaimed as 'the greatest Islamic scholar India ever produced'.[97] Although his ancestors had settled down in India as early as the thirteenth century, he wrote in his *Wasiyat Nama*: 'We are strangers. Our forefathers came to live in India from abroad. For us, Arab descent and the Arabic language are cause of pride, because these two bring us nearer to the Lord of the First and the Last, the noblest of the Prophets and Apostles.'[98] He believed that Allah's reason for creating the Islamic community had been 'mainly a political one'. It was Allah's wish that there should not exist any religion in the world which was superior to Islam. According to him, the main reason for fixing the blood-money for killing an infidel at half that for killing a Muslim was that such a distinction was necessary in order to emphasize the superiority of the latter. Besides, the slaughter of infidels also helped to diminish evil among Muslims.[99]

In the context of such ideas, it is not surprising that Shah Waliullah wrote to one Muslim ruler or nobleman after another imploring them to muster courage and start a *jihad* for the restoration of Muslim rule in India, assuring them on the basis of his intuition, that success was bound to be theirs. Thus, after the Marathas retreated from Delhi in 1737, he wrote to Nizam-ul-Mulk: 'It has become clear to my mind that the kingdom of heaven has predestined that *Kafirs* should be reduced to a state of humiliation and treated with utter contempt.'[100] In one of his writings, he reminded the Muslim kings of their duty to maintain Muslim supremacy in the land: 'Draw your swords and not put them back in their sheaths again until Allah has separated the Muslims from the polytheists and the rebellious *Kafirs*, and the sinners are made absolutely feeble and helpless.'[101] Failing to secure a satisfactory response from anyone in India and feeling more and more upset by the rising power of the Jats and the Marathas, Shah Waliullah turned his attention to the Afghan ruler, Ahmad Shah Abdali. Underlining the pitiable condition of Muslims in India since the loss of political power by them, he most earnestly implored Abdali to invade India and crush the 'infidels'. As he put it:

> In these days there is no king except Your Majesty who wields authority and power, is competent to defeat the armies of the *Kafirs*, is farsighted and expert in warfare. It is, therefore, obligatory for Your Majesty to make for India and

crush the dominance of the *Kafirs*, like the Marathas, for releasing the down-trodden Muslims who have fallen captive in their hands. If, God forbid, the grip of *Kufr* remains as such, the Muslims will forget Islam. They will soon become a people who are acquainted neither with Islam nor *Kufr*.[102]

As for Shah Waliullah's attitude towards the Hindus, this can be understood from his categorization of human beings in the ideal society of his conception. According to him, there would be three classes of men in such a society:

First, those loyal, outwardly and inwardly, to the Faith; second, those who out of compulsion would conform to the Faith and not dare oppose it; third, the humiliated Infidels, whom the Imam (the Leader) would keep so subdued and humbled that they would be kept employed in cutting the crops, threshing corn and other labours in exactly the same way as draught animals and beasts of burden.[103]

Such thoughts continued to influence certain sections of the Muslim elite during the succeeding century. Aziz Ahmad is not wrong in describing the so-called Wahhabi movement as 'the practical culmination of the religio-political thought of Shah Waliullah',[104] though, of course, it was to some extent also influenced by the movement bearing that name in contemporary Arabia, particularly in the strategy and tactics of carrying on a political struggle.[105] Its leader, Sayyid Ahmad Shahid or Barelvi (1781-1831), was a disciple of Shah Waliullah's son and successor, Shah Abdul Aziz (1746-1824), and recognized by the latter's family as the person best suited to lead the twin movements of purification of Islam and revival of its political power. It is significant that he spent a good deal of energy finding a territory that could be called *dar-al-Islam* and from where he could lead a *jihad* in strict accordance with the *Shariah*, finally settling down at a place across the north-west frontier of India.[106] He explained the nature of his mission in course of a letter to the ruler of Bukhara:

As a matter of fact the Indian territories are not *Dar-ul-Harb*, but the Kafirs of Hind and Firang have at the moment obtained dominance over it. It is, therefore, obligatory for the entire Muslim population in general and for the eminent Muslim rulers in particular that they should liberate it (from the hands of the usurpers). So far as this *faquir* is concerned, he is striving in this direction to the extent that lies within his measures.[107]

It may be noted that the 'Wahhabi' rebellion was first directed against Sikh rule in the Punjab and only later against the British rule in India though, of course, it undoubtedly had an anti-British orientation from the very beginning.[108] Its objective in either case was the establishment of an Islamic State in India.[109] It is nothing but a myth, perpetuated in the twentieth century in the context of the struggle for freedom from British rule, that Sayyid Ahmad Shahid's movement represented a war for Indian Independence and that after that was achieved, power would be left in the hands of Indian heads of states. As has been pointed out by a reputed scholar, Sayyid Ahmad would never have allowed a secular India or a united Hindu-Muslim rule where Islam or Islamic law did not predominate and where the control of the state or the sovereign authority did not vest in Islamic hands. 'Those Hindu heads of state who helped him were guaranteed their throne and a *Dhimmi* (protected subjects) status; the future for the others in the Sayyid's *dar ul-Islam* was bleak.'[110] It is also significant that the campaign for the purification of Islam, which was an important feature of the 'Wahhabi' movement, really implied freeing it from Hindu influences. As W.C. Smith observes: 'The relevant point here is that the accretions which the reformers set themselves to removing from the Muslims' religion, were mostly borrowings from Hinduism, or superstitious degradations shared with Hinduism.'[111]

Contemporaneously, there arose a somewhat similar movement in East Bengal, known as the *Faraizi* movement led by Haji Shariatullah (1781-1840) and his son, Dudu Miyan (1819-62). The movement of Muslim peasants led by Titu Mir (1782-1831) in West Bengal was more directly connected with the movement led by Sayyid Ahmad Barelvi in north India. Both those movements in Bengal aimed at focusing attention on peasants' grievances. The rebels led by them attacked Muslim as well as Hindu landlords, and the former too were generally hostile to them. Yet the fact is undeniable that they based themselves also on separatist Muslim sentiments. To quote Smith again: 'The movement made use of a religious ideology, as class struggles in pre-capitalist society have often done; but though religious, it was not simply communalist.' He further adds:

> The 'Wahhabi' movement, therefore, did not set lower-class Muslims against lower-class Hindus in open conflict, nor did it divert lower-class Muslims from economic issues to a false solidarity with their communal 'friends' but class enemies. None the less it did encourage communal attitudes especially in religious thinking, and left a considerable section of the Muslim masses more susceptible to later communalist propaganda than they might otherwise have been.[112]

IX

The community consciousness of the Muslim elite was further strengthened by their strong abhorrence for idol-worship, the most widely prevalent form of religious worship among the Hindus and the latter's social bigotry and exclusiveness which relegated all Muslims virtually to the position of the untouchables in the Hindu society. Such exclusiveness, on the other hand, was accentuated by the killing by Muslims (for food as also for religious ritual) of the cow, venerated as a mother by almost all Hindus, and the atrocities committed by the Muslim invaders in course of their wars of conquests and, in particular, their attacks on Hindu temples, and in many cases, their offer of pardon to persons defeated and/or captured in wars only in exchange for conversion to Islam. While the theory of the existence of two nations in India right from the time of the establishment of Turkish rule in India in the twelfth century must be rejected as quite unhistorical, as discussed earlier in this chapter, it will be equally unhistorical to accept the view propagated by some historians as well as leaders of the Indian nationalist movement during the period of the struggle for freedom from British rule that, as a result of living together on Indian soil, almost all significant social and cultural differences and antipathies between Hindus and Muslims had vanished and a new composite Hindu-Muslim or Muslim-Hindu culture had emerged through a synthesis or mingling of the two streams. Tara Chand's words portraying the emergence of 'Muslim-Hindu' culture have been cited earlier. Here, it may be appropriate to add the following by two nationalist intellectuals, Asoka Mehta and Achyut Patwardhan, who were also political activists and prominent socialist leaders, as a further illustration of such a view:

> Over a thousand years separate us from the first Muslim contact with India. As we review the period, we see wave upon wave of the foreigners pouring into this land of milk and honey as peaceful traders or proud conquerors. They fight and subdue the native races after prolonged and bitter conflicts. But soon the magic of the land casts its subtle spell around them. Even during the period of conflict, an unseen process of assimilation becomes discernible which like a tiny rain drop changes the harsh contours to an agreeable shape. Conflicts end in cooperation, and cooperation brings into being a new synthesis with a fine blending of the rivers and pastures of Hindustan and the arid splendour of the deserts of Central Asia. Grace and dignity become the hall-mark of this new synthesis which is the Hindu-Muslim culture.[113]

This is indeed a very attractive scenario, but it does not reflect reality. Although, there was considerable mingling and mixing between certain sections of them during the medieval period, the bulk of both the Hindus and Muslims maintained their separate cultural identities, based primarily on religious affiliation. As was true of all pre-industrial societies, religion, along with wealth and social status, was a major element in making up a person's identity in medieval India, and he naturally remained conscious of it. This was as much true of ordinary individuals as of rulers and courtiers. It is symbolic of the importance attached to the religious affiliation of a ruler that an attack on his domination was very often accompanied by an attack on the places of worship of the people belonging to his faith.[114] This was particularly true of the attacks by the Turko-Afghan invaders of India. Although the medieval Indian State was not a theocracy and the Turko-Afghan as well as Mughal rulers generally practised religious toleration within their own kingdoms, they cast this principle aside when invading other lands. As Mohammad Habib, who has taken great pains to underline the practice of religious toleration by the Turko-Afghan kings and gone to the extent of describing the medieval kingship in India as 'an essentially secular institution'[115]—which is, of course, questionable—puts it:

> . . . the tolerance of the emperor was strictly confined to the Hindus within their dominion. Once their armies crossed the imperial frontier, all tolerance, good sense and even humanity were cast aside; and the fanatical feelings forcibly kept under control at home exploded with revolutionary violence abroad. The vandalism of Sultan Mahmud in Hindustan was equalled, if not surpassed, by Malik Kafur in the Deccan. It is no use denying obvious facts. There is not a single Muslim historian of the Middle Ages who fails to record the destruction of temples, idols and monuments of inimitable art which followed in the wake of the conquering armies of Delhi. They prided themselves over these deplorable achievements and made no efforts to conceal them.[116]

The real motive behind the plundering expeditions against Hindu temples carried on by the Turko-Afghan invaders was, of course, the greed for gold and treasure and not the satisfaction of the urge for religious bigotry. Besides, there were instances also of Hindu rulers plundering the wealth of the temples. It should not, however, be difficult to imagine that the attacks on Hindu temples by Muslim invaders, regardless of their real motives, were bound to create a deep gulf between the two communities right at the start of their interaction. This was particularly so because of the significant differences between the two communities in the cultural field. Discussing the nature of these differences in his classic account of India in the eleventh century, Alberuni, who had come here with Sultan Mahmud of Ghazni, observes:

First, they [Hindus] differ from us [Muslims] in everything which other nations have in common. And here we first mention the language, although the difference of language also exists between other nations. . . . Secondly, they totally differ from us in religion, as we believe in nothing in which they believe, and *vice-versa*. On the whole, there is very little disputing about theological topics among themselves; at the utmost, they fight with words, but they will never stake their soul or body or their property on religious controversy. On the contrary, all their fanaticism is directed against those who do not belong to them—against all foreigners. They call them *mleccha*, i.e. impure, and forbid having any connection with them, be it by intermarriage or any other kind of relationship, or by sitting, eating and drinking with them, because thereby, they think, they would be polluted. . . .

In the third place, in all manners and usages they differ from us to such a degree as to frighten their children with us, with our dress, and our ways and customs, and as to declare us to be devil's breed, and our doings as the very opposite of all that is good and proper.[117]

Alberuni's description of the state of feeling among Hindus regarding Muslims in the eleventh century after the invasions of Sultan Mahmud is also worth recording:

Mahmud utterly ruined the prosperity of the country, and performed there wonderful exploits, by which the Hindus became like atoms of dust scattered in all directions, and like a tale of old in the mouth of the people. Their scattered remains cherish, of course, the most inveterate aversion towards all Muslims. This is the reason, too, why Hindu sciences have retired far away from those parts of the country conquered by us, and have fled to places which our hand cannot yet reach, to Kashmir, Benares, and other places. And there the antagonism between them and all foreigners receives more and more nourishment both from political and religious sources.[118]

As has been shown earlier, this situation did not last for ever and there was a good deal of mingling between Hindus and Muslims in various walks of life, including politics and administration and social and economic life. This was facilitated by the enlightened policy of the Turkish rulers who generally followed the principle of religious toleration within their dominions and realized the impossibility of maintaining their rule without the cooperation of Hindus who constituted the overwhelming majority among their subjects. There was no parallel to the Clarendon Code (in force in England in the seventeenth century) in medieval India and Hindus were freely employed by Muslim rulers and *vice-versa*. However, the distinction between a Hindu and a Muslim never ceased. Although few and far between and a result largely of political causes, the demolition of temples continued. Restrictions also continued to be placed on the construction of new temples, though, of course, these were not uniformly applied and sometimes even grants were made for such constructions as well as their maintenance. The continuing conversion of Hindus to Islam also must have caused considerable resentment among the Hindus. Although these conversions were largely the result of the influence of the Sufi saints and the social discrimination from which a large number of Hindus suffered, force and political and economic inducements also contributed to them. Whatever the cause, it should not be difficult for students of social psychology to imagine that in any village or town, conversion of a section of it to Islam would have caused resentment among the rest of the population, especially when it was known that a Muslim giving up his allegiance to Islam was liable to be punished by death. The imposition of the *jizya*, a tax to be paid only by non-Muslims in lieu of military service from which they were exempt, and intended to underline their inferior status, must have added to this resentment. The practice of Mughal rulers and princes, started by Akbar, of taking Hindu wives, although mistakenly considered by some historians as contributing to the process of Hindu-Muslim rapprochement, must have served further to underline the position of the Muslim elite as rulers and remind the Hindu elite of their position as subjects, for none of the latter could take a Muslim wife, and if someone dared, the punishment was again usually death. The generally inferior position of a Hindu witness in criminal cases as compared to his Muslim counterpart in a law court was another reminder of the inferior status of the Hindus in a state ruled over by a Muslim monarch. Thus, if the accused was a Muslim, he could be convicted only on the testimony of a Muslim. No such safeguard applied to a Hindu, who could be convicted on the testimony of any one.[119] The use of Persian as a court language could not have been liked by the members of the Hindu elite. The fact that many of them acquired proficiency in it for the sake of securing employment cannot be used to disprove this.

The resentment caused among certain sections of Hindus by the attacks on their religion was reflected in the literature of the times. Thus, the famous Maithili poet, Vidyapati, who flourished in the fifteenth century, writes in *Kirtilata* with reference to Muslims:

They catch a Brahman boy and place a cow's bone on his head to outrage his faith. They wipe out the sectarian mark on the forehead, tear the sacred thread and want to make them ride on horseback. They distil wine by washing a special paddy (*uridhan*), break temples and build mosques. The earth is filled with graveyards and dumps of carcasses of cows, there is no space to set feet on. To the Hindu they say, 'Go away'. The Turk, even if younger, dares assault a senior.[120]

We have the following description of the plight of Brahmans in Navadvipa, the birthplace of Chaitanya, shortly before his birth (1485) in *Chaitanya-mangla* by Jayananda:

The king seizes the Brahmanas, pollutes their caste, and even takes their lives. If a conchshell is heard to blow in any house, its owner is made to forfeit his wealth, caste and even life. The king plunders the houses of those who wear sacred threads in the shoulder and put sacred marks on the forehead. . . . He breaks the temples and uproots *Tulasi* plants, and the residents of Navadweep are in perpetual fear of their lives.[121]

Isana Nagara, a contemporary writer, describes the plight of Hindus of Bengal during the reign of Ala-ud-din Husain Shah (1493-1519) in the following words:

The wicked *mlechhas* pollute the religion of the Hindus every day. They break the images of the gods into pieces and throw away the articles of worship. They throw into fire *Srimad-Bhagavat* and other holy scriptures, forcibly take away the conchshell and bell of the Brahmanas (two necessary articles of worship), and lick the sandal paints on their bodies. They urinate like dogs on the sacred *Tulasi* plant, and deliberately pass faeces in the Hindu temples. They throw water from their mouths on the Hindus engaged in worship, and harass the Hindu saints as if they were so many lunatics at large.[122]

Vallabhacharya, one of the most prominent leaders of the *Bhakti* movement among the Hindus, which rapidly spread from south to north India during the medieval period, remarked in one of his writings in the sixteenth century: 'In a land afflicted by the *mlecchas*, made the abode of sin and full of people suffering from pain as a result of the torture of noble persons, Krishna is my only salvation.'[123] This lends some credence to the view propounded by an eminent historian of Hindi literature that the deep feeling of despondency among the Hindus because of certain oppressive actions of some of the Muslim rulers could have been partly responsible for the rapid spread of the more traditional or *sagun Bhakti* movements (i.e. those associated with the worship of the images of Lords Rama and Krishna).[124]

Eknath, the poet-saint of Maharashtra, who flourished in the second half of the sixteenth century, and preached concord and fellowship among people belonging to different religious faiths, also expressed his anguish at the doings of some of the Turkish rulers. Thus he wrote: 'Wicked kings began to rule, and they exploited their subjects like thieves. Themselves worse than shudras they converted people of all castes.'[125] In the seventeenth century, we find Ramadas, famous for his spiritual teachings as well as his contacts with Shivaji, remarking after his pilgrimage to various places:

> . . . many were those who were taken by the Muslims (*tamras*) . . . many were the good women who were abducted; many were converted to Islam . . . under the Muslim kings Muslim fairs (*urs*) are held everywhere. The holy places (of the Hindus) have been desecrated, the homes of Brahmans are destroyed, the whole earth has been shaken up, the religion (*dharma*) is lost.[126]

That the atmosphere of Hindu-Muslim antagonism enveloped not merely the elite but also the masses is borne by the compositions of the leaders of those *Bhakti* movements which preached the worship of the formless or *nirgun* God and were generally active among the poorer sections of the people. They devoted a good part of their teachings to the establishment of harmony and concord among Hindus and Muslims, and stressed their oneness. One of the foremost among them was Namadev (1270-1350), the great poet-saint of Maharashtra. Son of a shudra tailor, he attacked the religious bigotry of both the Hindus and Muslims. In one of his songs, he observes: 'The Hindu is blinded and the Muslim is cross-eyed. A saint is certainly better than both of them. The Hindu worships his temple, the Muslim worships his mosque, Namadeva will worship neither the temple nor the mosque.'[127] However, even he reflects the general Hindu resentment at the behaviour of the Muslims. Thus, at one place he remarks: 'The unclean Yavanas have become kings; sins are being committed everywhere; . . . Nama says: 'The people having found the Yavanas unendurable, are singing the praise of God; for these are ever the means of redemption.'[128]

Kabir, who carried on his mission in the fifteenth century, and was one of the most popular saint-poets of northern India, taught in the same vein as Namadev. He wrote:

> Only the one I recognise
> Those who call Him two will go to hell
> For they not know the reality.

All human beings are sustained by the same air and water, and
are illuminated by the same light;
All have been formed out by
the same dust and their creator is the same.
Wake up you fool,
The Supreme Spirit is neither Turk nor Hindu.[129]

In the sixteenth century, Dadu boldly declared: 'I am neither Hindu nor Muslim, I am not attached to any philosophical school but only to God (Rahman).'[130]

While the objective of such preachings was to put an end to the bitterness caused by religious differences between Hindus and Muslims, the strongly felt need for such preachings can be safely taken as an evidence of the persistence of such bitterness. Such evidence is also provided by the saints themselves. Thus, Kabir, in one of his famous passages, observes: 'The Hindu describes Rama as his, the Muslim Rahman; they both die fighting without knowing the reality.'[131] Dadu refers to Hindus and Muslims as 'two maddened elephants fighting each other' and observes that since he chose to follow a non-sectarian path, different from that of both the Hindus and the Muslims, both the peoples had become angry with him and were pursuing him like two 'black faced dogs'.[132] Bhai Gurdas (1551-1629), a disciple of Nanak, who strived to foster harmony and fellowship among all human beings, regardless of differences in religion during the first half of the sixteenth century, laments:

Ram and Rahim are the names of the same one God, but, in their ignorance, their followers, the Hindus and Musalmans, have taken to diverging paths.

Having forgotten the teachings of their holy book(s)—the Veda and the Quran—they have come to be beguiled to the avaricious ways of the Satanic world.

Truth has been left aside, and the Brahmans and the Maulanas are fighting among themselves.[133]

Eknath, who taught in Maharashtra in the second half of the sixteenth century and has been referred to earlier, mentions in his *Hindu-Turk Samvada* the type of religious controversies raging at that time between Hindus and Muslims. Thus the Turk describes the Hindu as a *kafir* (infidel) while the latter avoids the former's touch as it is supposed to be polluting. The Turk calls the Vedas worthless and Hindus idolators and worshippers of false gods. The Hindu in reply asserts that the Muslims too are idolators as they venerate *pirs* and offer prayers at *dargahs*. The Turk refers to the Hindu habit of treating large sections of humanity as impure and defiling in their contact. The only saving grace is that after all this argumentation the conclusion emerges that God is really one whether he is called Khuda or Allah or Rama or Krishna,[134] thus showing that in certain situations understanding and harmony could also be arrived at.

All this shows a slow but steady growth of community-consciousness among the Hindus, both at the elite and the mass levels. At first largely confined to the cultural field and revolving round religious differences *vis-a-vis* Muslims, such consciousness later on began to influence politics also. This can certainly be said about the second half of the seventeenth century when, as pointed out by an eminent authority on medieval Indian history, 'Muslim orthodoxy and militant Hinduism appear on the scene almost simultaneously'.[135] While the causes for this may be debated upon, the fact itself is beyond question. If Aurangzeb became the political symbol of Muslim orthodoxy, Shivaji became that of militant Hinduism. It is, of course, true that 'the rise of the Maratha movement was anterior to the communal policies of Aurangzeb and cannot be explained in terms of the so-called religious reaction *alone*'.[136] An undue importance need not also be attached to such symbolic gestures by Shivaji at the time of his coronation as the assumption of the title of ***haindava-dharmoddharak***, and the pledge to protect cows and Brahmins and uphold the Hindu *dharma* in his territories, such gestures having been customary among the Rajput princes during the medieval period.[137]

It would not, however, be realistic to completely ignore the rise of community consciousness among certain sections of Hindus in Maharashtra as a factor, though certainly not the only factor, behind the rise of Maratha power. There is considerable evidence to support this view. Shivaji, of course, never showed any animus towards Muslims, extended full protection to their religious places, showed great respect to Muslim divines and appointed several Muslims to important positions under him. There is, however, no doubt that he deeply resented the subjection of Hindus to Muslim rulers. We have it on the basis of the most reliable authority that while conferring with his companions and preparing for his early military adventures, Shivaji 'anxiously deliberated on the liberation of his homeland from Muslim control so as to put an end to the wanton persecution of the Hindus'.[138] Some of the sentiments expressed by Shivaji on such occasions have been thus summarized by his court historian:

Why should we remain content with what the Muslim rulers choose to give us? We are Hindus. This whole country is ours by right, and is yet occupied and held by foreigners. They desecrate our temples, break holy idols, plunder our wealth, convert us forcibly to their religion, carry away our women folk and children, slay the cows and inflict a thousand wrongs upon us. We will suffer this treatment no more.[139]

It is also significant that the rise of Shivaji was enthusiastically hailed by several of his distinguished contemporaries who interpreted it as a shield for Hinduism. On learning of his success against the Mughals, the famous Maharashtrian saint, Ramadas, burst into ecstasy and wrote a special composition, entitled *Anandavanabhuvana*, in praise of his hero:

The sinners are all lost, the land of the Hindus is now strong. The unbelievers are on the decline in this glorious land. The sinful Aurangzeb is destroyed, the *mlechhas* are destroyed, the holy places that were destroyed are now reestablished . . . and there is plenty of everything for the performance of the sacred rites.[140]

One of Shivaji's ministers, Ramchandra Nilakanth, who has left an estimate of his chief, remarks after describing his major political achievements: 'All this he did for the defence of his religion, for putting God and Brahmans in a position enabling them to have their proper functions performed without molestation.'[141]

Nor was such estimate confined to Maharashtra. Bhushan, a contemporary poet belonging to the Hindi belt and occupying a distinguished place in the history of Hindi literature, made Shivaji the hero of two of his famous poems. In one of them, *Shivabawani*, he remarks that 'but for Shivaji all art would have departed from Kashi, the whole of Mathura would have been turned into a mosque and all would have been circumcised'.[142] Continuing his laudatory description of Shivaji's achievements, he adds that the latter had 'raised the prestige of Hindus and preserved Hinduism as well as its symbols and religious scriptures'.[143]

There is some evidence too for the fact that the image of Shivaji as a protector of Hinduism against the onslaughts of Muslim religious bigotry was not confined to his Hindu contemporaries, but was also shared by others. Thus, the contemporary English merchants of Surat have left this estimate of Shivaji:

He loved his country but was not partial to anyone. He had many Muslims in his service and the head of his navy was a Muslim. But he could not tolerate the conversion of his Hindu brethren to either Islam or to Christianity. The underlying reason for his vengeance upon Aurangzeb was the religious policy of that monarch.[144]

As for Shivaji himself, although concerning himself with politics only in and around Maharashtra, he did use the phrase 'Hindawi-Swarajya' to describe his national scheme in one of his letters in 1645.[145] It is also on record that he voiced a protest against the imposition of the *jizya* by Aurangzeb on all his non-Muslim subjects in 1679. In a letter addressed to the latter in the middle of the year, Shivaji recalled Akbar's policy of *sulh-i-kul* which had brought him victory and success and stressed that Jehangir and Shahjahan also had desisted from imposing the *jizya*. 'They, too,' wrote Shivaji, 'had the power of levying of *jizya;* but they did not give place to bigotry in their hearts, as they considered all men, high and low, created by God to be [living] examples of the nature of diverse creeds and temperaments.' Admonishing Aurangzeb for departing from this policy by imposing the burden of *jizya* on people already suffering from severe economic hardships, Shivaji remarked:

> If you believe in the true Divine Book and Word of God (i.e. the Quran), you will find there [that God is styled] *Rabb-ul-alamin*, the Lord of all men, and not *Rabb-ul-musalmin,* the Lord of the Muhammadans only. Verily, Islam and Hinduism are terms of contrast. They are [diverse pigments] used by the true Divine Painter for blending the colours and filling in the outlines [of His picture of the entire human species]. If it be a mosque, the call to prayer is chanted in remembrance of Him. If it be a temple, the bell is rung in yearning for Him only. To show bigotry for any man's own creed and practices is equivalent to altering the words of the Holy Book. . . .[146]

X

It will not, of course, be sound to treat this letter as the expression of a fully developed, pan-Indian Hindu political consciousness, but it does indicate the extension of the growing community-consciousness among at least a section of the Hindu elite to the political field. Just like the Muslim rulers, some Hindu rulers too were now beginning to show interest in matters affecting their co-religionists and perhaps also to realize the value of stressing their religious identity to buttress their legitimacy and expand their support-base. This trend got further strengthened in the eighteenth century and the first half of the nineteenth century. Several studies currently in progress as well as recently completed, bear this out. Thus C.A. Bayly has drawn attention to the fact that Madhav Rao Peshwa (1761-72) was keen to drive the Muslim rulers from Malwa and Gujarat in order to free the Hindu holy places there from Muslim control. Similarly, his will of 1772 sought to impress upon his successor the duty of freeing the holy places of Prayag and Kashi from Muslim control. Note has also to be taken of the fact that wherever a Hindu or a Sikh ruler gained control over a territory, he made it a point to ban cow-slaughter there. Even Ranjit Singh, the Sikh ruler of the Punjab during the early years of the nineteenth century, who generally allowed freedom of worship to Muslims and appointed them to high positions in the state, followed this policy. He also put a ban on the public call to prayer by the Muslims in the Sikh holy city of Amritsar.[147]

Some earlier examples from the history of Mughal-Sikh relations show deep animosities based on religious affiliation. Thus, when the Sikhs captured Sirhind in 1769, they tried to destroy every building there, including mosques, as a vengeance for the execution of Guru Teg Bahadur and the killing of the wife of Guru Govind Singh during Aurangzeb's reign. When the Sikhs captured Delhi in 1783, they did not follow such a policy. Perhaps such a course was not practicable. They did, however, succeed in demolishing a mosque at Rakabganj, near the place where Guru Teg Bahadur had been cremated, and in replacing it with a gurudwara. At Sisganj, where the Guru had been executed, the mosque was not demolished, but a gurudwara was built in its compound.[148]

Besides, localized communal conflicts erupted also in the rural areas as a result of dispute over possession of land. Thus, Hindu and Sikh zamindars in UP and the Punjab sometimes violently reacted against extension into their areas of revenue-free (*madad-i-maash*) tenures held by the Muslim gentry and the religious divines. While these conflicts were primarily caused by the clash of economic interests, particularly relating to ownership of land, in several cases 'the vocabulary of religious conflict was freely used'. Besides, they had a general tendency 'to take on the lineaments of communal conflict and to assimilate religious symbols'.[149]

This is amply substantiated by some recent researches of Muzaffar Alam into agrarian relations in UP and the Punjab during the first half of eighteenth century. For example, in June 1713, over five hundred Rajputs of a neighbouring village attacked Ahrora, a *madad-i-maash* village of Saiyids in pargana Husampur in Awadh, and killed a number of Saiyids and burnt their houses, libraries and other properties. 'Five of their women were burnt alive, and the surviving women and children of this community were driven out bare-footed.' Simultaneously, four other neighbouring villages falling within the domain of the Saiyids were also attacked and 'completely devastated, and the graveyards of their ancestors, the mosques and the *madrasas* were levelled to ground'.[150] Needless to add, all such conflicts did not assume the colouring of a Hindu-Muslim conflict or involve attacks on mosques and graveyards. In some of them, Muslim zamindars joined with Hindu zamindars in clashes with the Saiyids, while in others some Hindu zamindars came to the rescue of the Saiyids.[151]

Something similar happened in the Punjab around this time in course of the Sikh rebellion spearheaded by Banda Bahadur. Here also the *madad-i-maash* holders were the special targets of attack by the Sikh peasantry during 1710-12. 'In almost all the towns which fell into their possession', says Alam, 'the Muslim *Shurafa* [gentry] and their mosques and the graveyards were the chief targets of the Sikh atrocities'.[152] It is not surprising that some of the leading Sunnis who later organized the defence of Lahore, described it as a '*jihad* against the Sikhs'.[153] Needless to add, just like in Awadh, the clashes in the Punjab too did not have a uniform character and at many places Hindus and even Khatri Sikhs joined the Muslims against the Sikh (Jat) peasantry, and Banda's efforts to impart to his struggle the character of a *dharma-yuddha* for the defence of Hindu interests against Muslim tyranny did not succeed.[154]

A similar clash of economic interests led to communal conflicts in some urban areas also, particularly in the sea-port towns, between groups of Hindus and Muslims. We have accounts of such groupings and riots in places as far apart as Calcutta and Surat where certain Hindu *bania* families had amassed wealth due to their close connections with the British commercial interests and excited the jealousies of their Muslim rivals, who secured wide support from their poor co-religionists. In a riot in Calcutta in 1789, the houses of rich *banias* were the main targets of attack by a number of Muslims. 'Deliberate sacrilege' went hand in hand with 'straightforward plundering',[155] which was much more in evidence than in some other communal riots. The new rich among the Hindus, apart from exciting jealousy among their Muslim brethren, had also contributed to a worsening of the situation by conspicuous displays of Goddess Durga's images through Muslim quarters. Something similar happened in Surat in

1795, when the poor sections of the Muslim population attacked the shops and houses of the Hindu *banias* 'looting grain, demolishing the images of their gods and tearing up their account books'.[156]

Sometimes riots broke out on the issue of cow-killing. Ahmedabad was the scene of such a riot in 1714. The account of the happenings on that occasion is quite similar to the accounts of many riots which took place in India towards the end of the nineteenth century and later. When a Muslim family slaughtered a cow to celebrate Prophet Muhammad's birthday, a group of Hindus attacked it and killed one of its young members. Local Muslims were joined by Afghan soldiers in the rioting which lasted three days. Hindu-Muslim riots also took place in some other parts of India in subsequent years on seemingly minor issues. Athar Abbas Rizvi has given details of such riots during the first half of the eighteenth century in Kashmir and Delhi as well as Ahmedabad.[157]

Hindu and Muslim festivals falling on the same day often provided occasions for communal riots in the eighteenth century and first half of the nineteenth century, just as in later years. The Calcutta riots of 1789, mentioned earlier, had been occasioned by the Muharram and Durga Puja being celebrated at the same time. In northern India, Muharram and Holi sometimes came together and became the occasion for considerable tension between the members of the two communities. Allahabad became the scene of such tension in the forties of the nineteenth century. Again, a contemporary eye-witness account of what happened on that occasion vividly reminds us of what happened on a much wider scale later. We are told that on the approach of Muharram some of the leading Muslims requested the local judge that 'the Hindus, who were about to perform some of their idolatrous worship, should not be permitted to blow their trumpets, and beat their drums, and bring their heathenish devices in contact with the sad and holy solemnity. . . .' The Hindus, on their part, 'were equally tenacious in upholding their rights, and it became necessary to draw out the troops for the prevention of bloodshed'.[158]

Such tensions and riots naturally fostered a strong community consciousness among both Hindus and Muslims. Some of the researches of Gyanendra Pandey clearly bring this out with reference to eastern UP during the first decade of the nineteenth century. He has unearthed petitions submitted by sections of Hindus and Muslims which speak of the woes of their respective communities, not merely in a religious, but also in a socio-political sense. Thus, following a Hindu-Muslim riot in Banaras in October 1809, groups of Hindus and Muslims submitted separate petitions to the British authorities couched in a language which shows signs of a fairly developed community-based socio-political consciousness. The Hindu petitioners observed:

> We, all the Brahmins, Chuttries and persons of the Byse and Sooder cast, beg to lay before the English a representation . . . in order that . . . our existence as a people (may be) preserved. . . . After the destruction of the power of the Hindoo Rajahs, a Mahomedan Government ruled for several centuries. . . . [But] None of the Mussulman Emperors interfered with our places of worship till the reign of Aurangzeb Alymgeer. The Mussulmans have now violated our religion. . . .

The petitioners went on to add that such violation, which had not taken place even under 'the administration of the Mahomedan Emperors', had occurred under the rule of the English. Faced with such a situation, the Hindus, 'overwhelmed with grief, distracted with astonishment, and pained to the quick', had deliberated among themselves, gone from house to house and cried out: 'Oh Hindoos, in this way have the Mussulmans been beforehand in oppression.'

The Muslim petitioners, responding through the 'humble memorial of the whole body of Mussulmans' of Banaras, spoke in a similar vein. 'The country of Hindostan', they observed, 'has for many centuries been the seat of the true faith. The city of Benares, a small spot thereof, was held sacred by the Hindoos . . . and true to their sovereign, they met with tolerance.' As for the practice of killing cows, which had been one of the issues in the communal clash in Banaras in 1809, the petitioners asserted that this had been prevalent in Banaras ever since the arrival of Muslims at Banaras who had not been hindered or prohibited even though the province of Banaras had been 'held and governed by Hindoo chiefs'.

A petition submitted by the Muslim weavers of Mubarakpur (an important centre of cloth-manufacturing in the district of Azamgarh, not far from Banaras) in 1813 after the occurrence of a bloody riot there, echoed the tone and temper of the petitioners of Banaras in 1809. 'Upto now', affirmed the petitioners, 'all over Hindustan, Hindus and Muslims lived together—in amity—practising their respective religions and rituals freely. . . . But since the Hindus have gained *amaldari* [i.e. become *amils* or important state officials], since then the killing of Muslims has begun.'

Even when there was no clash, and the Hindus and Muslims were working together, it was apparently becoming customary for the Indian people to refer to themselves as groupings of Hindus and Muslims. This is illustrated by a petition submitted in 1810 when, forgetting the clash of 1809, the people of Banaras waged a united struggle against the introduction of a house-tax, and resorted to *hartal* in the city. This petition was described by its signatories as 'the petition of Hindoos and Mussulmans of all classes from Saurung Panee', the place where they had assembled in great strength and composed the petition. Another petition submitted a little later, in course of the same agitation, urged the preservation of 'the rules contained in the Shera and Shaster [Sharia and Shastra] together with the customs of Hindostan . . . (and) the rights of the Government as they were exercised in the times of the Mohammedan and Hindoo princes'.[159]

The same consciousness of Hindus and Muslims constituting two separate communities, even when cooperating among themselves, is revealed by the famous Azamgarh Proclamation of 25 August 1857, issued by a grandson of the Mughal emperor, Bahadur Shah, during the great revolt of that year. It declared:

> It is well known to all, that in this age the people of Hindoostan, both Hindoos and Mohammedans, are being ruined under the tyranny and oppression of the infidel and treachrous English. . . . I, . . . the grandson of Abul Muzuffer Serajuddin Bahadur Shah Ghazee, king of India . . . have . . . erected the standard of Mohammed, and persuaded the orthodox Hindoos who have been subject to my ancestors . . . to raise the standard of Mahavir. . . .[160]

XI

The growth of community consciousness among Hindus as well as Muslims up to the middle of the nineteenth century need not, of course, be exaggerated. The same applied to the existence of various differences among the two communities, each divided within itself into various segments and not at all homogeneous or monolithic in any sense. If they sometimes collided against each other in some areas, the members of each more often collided among themselves in much wider areas. Besides, Hindus and Muslims continued to collaborate among themselves in numerous fields. They certainly did not yet consider themselves as members of two distinct nations. Indeed the very concept of nationhood was beyond their intellectual horizon.

It would not, however, contribute to our understanding of the nature of Hindu-Muslim differences in modern times if we completely ignore the existence of such differences during the pre-British period and their impact on the people's minds, particularly the minds of the elites of the two communities, and treat them as solely the result of conditions created under British rule. It has already been shown that it is not possible to prove the existence of a 'Chinese wall' between the two communities as they emerged out of the medieval period. It is, however, equally impossible to prove that there was no wall between them at all. The wall was, of course, neither very high nor very strong and had also been breached and even demolished at some points, but it did exist and was indeed being reinforced at some other points. The views of one of our most perceptive historians of modern times, Sushobhan Sarkar, can be taken as a safe guide on this subject. While decrying the view that 'the Muslim rule was essentially a foreign government over us like the British' and refuting the theory of 'a permanent unbridgeable cleavage' between Hindus and Muslims, he at the same time remarks:

> Some well-meaning thinkers go to the other extreme of denying Hindu-Muslim differences. This surely is a wrong reading of the situation. The differences are real enough, and have persisted through centuries. They have often led to clashes, and it is puerile to attribute such [differences] in modern times to British intrigues alone. Tagore was right to point out that even Satan cannot obtain a foothold unless there is already an opening, a chink in the body-politic.[161]

These differences, together with the slow but steady growth of community consciousness among both Muslims and Hindus to which they contributed, and the memories of the rise and growth of Islam as a political force as well as of the so-called Muslim rule over India for several centuries, constituted the historical roots of Muslim nationalism. To point to these roots, however, is not to assert that they, solely by themselves, brought about the emergence of that nationalism and increasingly provided nourishment to it. That was made possible by their conjunction with a number of other factors: the economic divide between sections of the two communities, the intellectual and emotional environment of the Muslim elite in the second half of the nineteenth century and early decades of the twentieth century, the rising tide of Hindu revivalism and nationalism during the same period, the ethos of Indian nationalism, and last, but not the least important, the British policy of playing off one community against the other. To them we now turn.

NOTES

1. Karl Marx and Frederick Engels, *Selected Works* (Mascow, 1970), p. 96.
2. Ishtiaq Husain Qureshi, *The Muslim Community of the Indo-Pakistan Subcontinent, 610-1947* (The Hague, 1962), p. 6.
3. Ishtiaq Hussain Qureshi, *The Struggle for Pakistan* (Karachi, 1969), p. 10.
4. Hafeez Malik, *Moslem Nationalism in India and Pakistan* (Washington D.C., 1963), p. 294.
5. Khalid B. Sayeed, *Pakistan: The Formative Phase* (London, 1968, 2nd edn), pp. 11-12.
6. K.K. Aziz, *The Making of Pakistan: A Study in Nationalism* (London, 1967), p. 209.
7. Ibid., p. 143.
8. Aziz Ahmad, *Studies in Islamic Culture in the Indian Environment* (Oxford, 1964), VIII.
9. Ibid.
10. Ibid., p. 73. See also the same author's *Islamic Modernism in India and Pakistan*, 1857-1964 (London, 1967).
11. S.M. Ikram, *Modern Muslim India and the Birth of Pakistan* (1858-1951) (Lahore, 1965, 2nd edn, 1st pub. 1950), p. 1.
12. S.M. Ikram, *Muslim Civilisation in India*, ed. by Ainslie T. Embree (New York, 1965, 2nd edn), p. 294.
13. See R.C. Majumdar, in R.C. Majumdar, ed., *The Delhi Sultanate*, Vol. VI of *The History and Culture of the Indian People* (Bombay, 1960), p. 624. See also the same author's *Glimpses of Bengal in the Nineteenth Century* (Calcutta, 1960), p. 48.
14. K.M. Panikkar, *A Survey of Indian History* (London, 1971, 1st pub. 1947), pp. 143-4.
15. Tara Chand, *Influence of Islam on Indian Culture* (Allahabad, 1963, 1st pub. 1936), p. 137.
16. Tara Chand, 'India and the West', in Humayun Kabir, ed., *Abul Kalam Azad* (Bombay, 1959), p. 238.
17. R.C. Majumdar, 'Impact of Islam on Hinduism', in Horst Kruger, ed., *Kanwar Mohammad Ashraf* (Delhi, 1969), pp. 266-7.
18. Ibid., p. 267.
19. Ibid., pp. 268-9.
20. R.C. Majumdar in R.C. Majumdar, ed., *The Delhi Sultanate,* n. 13, pp. 616-17.
21. R.C. Majumdar, 'The National Movement 1833-1905', in N.K. Sinha, ed., *The History of Bengal, 1757-1905* (Calcutta, 1967), p. 189.
22. Niharranjan Ray, *Nationalism in India* (Aligarh, 1973), p. 53.
23. Ibid., pp. 55-6.
24. F.W. Thomas, *Mutual Influence of Muhammedans and Hindus in India* (Cambridge, 1892), p. 12.
25. Murray Titus, *Indian Islam* (London, 1930), p. 176.
26. Percival Spear, *India, Pakistan and the West* (London, 1958), p. 88.
27. Percival Spear, *India: A Modern History* (Ann Arbor, 1961), p. 10.
28. Ikram, n. 12, pp. 116-21.

29. Ibid., pp. 123-30.
30. Ibid., pp. 130-1.
31. Ibid., pp. 97-109.
32. Ibid., p. 88.
33. Ibid., pp. 95-6.
34. Ibid., p. 199.
35. Ibid., p. 226.
36. Ibid., p. 243.
37. Ibid., pp. 198-9, 232.
38. Ibid., p. 131.
39. Ibid., p. 237.
40. Ibid., p. 295.
41. Panikkar, n. 14, p. 139.
42. Ibid., pp. 139-40.
43. Ibid., p. 137.
44. Ibid., p. 138.
45. Ibid., p. 145.
46. Ibid., pp. 144-5.
47. Ibid., p. 184.
48. Ibid., p. 187.
49. Ibid., p. 188.
50. Ibid., pp. 168-9.
51. Ibid., pp. 171-5.
52. Ibid., pp. 176-81.
53. Ibid., pp. 206-7.
54. Ibid., p. 248.
55. Azizur Rahman Mallick, *British Policy and the Muslims in Bengal, 1757-1856* (Dacca, 1961), pp. 4-5.
56. Ibid., p. 21.
57. Ibid.
58. S.S. Thorburn, *Mussalmans and Money-Lenders in the Punjab* (Edinburgh, 1886), p. 2.
59. Ibid., pp. 13-14.
60. P.D. Reeves, ed., *Sleeman in Oudh* (Cambridge, 1971), p. 69.
61. Ibid., p. 288.
62. Ibid., p. 240.
63. Hafeez Malik, *Sir Sayyid Ahmad Khan and Muslim Modernism in India and Pakistan* (New York, 1980), p. 25.
64. Mallick, n. 55, pp. 22-3.
65. See Anil Seal, *The Emergence of Indian Nationalism* (Cambridge, 1968), pp. 338-40.
66. W. Montgomery Watt, *Islam and the Integration of Society* (London, 1970, 4th edn), pp. 174-5. How the strong attachment to the community conditioned Indian Muslims' attitude towards politics is very well brought out in Farzana Shaikh, 'Muslims and Political Representation in Colonial India: The Making of Pakistan', *Modern Asian Studies,* Vol. XX, No. 3, 1986, pp. 539-57.
67. Watt, n. 66, p. 204. See also Farzana Shaikh, *Community and Consensus in*

Islam: Muslim Representation in Colonial India, 1860-1947 (Combridge, 1989).

68. H.A.R. Gibb, *Studies in the Civilization of Islam* (London, 1962), p. 115.
69. W.C. Smith, *Islam in Modern History* (Princeton, 1957), pp. 15-16.
70. M. Mujeeb, *The Indian Muslims* (London, 1967), pp. 67-8.
71. P. Hardy, 'The Muslim Historians of the Delhi Sultanate: Is What They Say Really What They Mean'?, *Journal of the Asiatic Society of Pakistan* (Dacca), Vol. IX, No. 11, June 1964. See also the same author's *Historians of Medieval India* (London, 1960).
72. Cited in Mujeeb, n. 70, p. 68.
73. Simon Digby, 'Abd Al-Quddus Gangohi (1456-1537 AD): The Personality and Attitudes of a Medieval Indian Sufi', *Medieval India—A Miscellany*, ed. by S. Nurul Hasan, III (1975), pp. 33-4. See also Iqtidar Alam Khan 'Shaikh Abdul Quddus Gangohi's Relations with Political Authorities: A Reappraisal', ibid., IV (1977), p. 83.
74. Saiyid Athar Abbas Rizvi, *Muslim Revivalist Movements in North India in the Sixteenth and Seventeenth Centuries* (Agra, 1965), p. 248.
75. Cited in Mohammad Habib's 'Introduction' in Khaliq Ahmad Nizami, *Some Aspects of Religion and Politics in India during the Thirteenth Century* (Delhi, 1974), pp. xxi-xxii.
76. M. Athar Ali, *The Mughal Nobility under Aurangzeb* (Bombay, 1966), p. 32.
77. Tara Chand, n. 15, p. 165.
78. Azra Nijami, 'Socio-Religious Outlook of Abul Fazl', *Medieval India. A Miscellany*, n. 73, II (1972), p. 121.
79. Ibid., pp. 127-8.
80. Abul-Fazl Allami, *The A'in-i-Akbari*, trans. and ed. by H.S. Jarrett, III (Calcutta, 1978), p. 2.
81. The proportion of Hindu *Mansabdars* of the rank of 500 and above to the total number of *Mansabdars* was 22.5 under Akbar, 22.4 under Shahjahan and 21.6 to 31.6 under Aurangzeb, Athar Ali, n. 76, p. 31.
82. Mujeeb, n. 70, p. 258.
83. Ibid., p. 264.
84. Cited in Iqtidar Alam Khan, 'The Nobility under Akbar and the Development of His Religious Policy, 1560-80', *Journal of the Royal Asiatic Society*, 1968. See also the same author's 'A Note on the Conception of Akbar's Religious Policy', Debiprasad Chattopadhyaya, ed., *History and Society* (Calcutta, 1978), pp. 455-66.
85. Mujeeb, n. 70, p. 243. For details see Ikram, n. 12, pp. 167-74; and Aziz Ahmad, n. 8, pp. 182-89. See also W.C. Smith, 'The Crystallization of Religious Communities in Mughal India', in the same author's *On Understanding Islam: Selected Studies* (The Hague, 1981), pp. 177-96.
86. Irfan M. Habib, 'The Political Role of Shaikh Ahmad Sirhindi and Shah Waliullah', *Enquiry*, No. 5, 1961, pp. 36-50. See also Rizvi, n. 74, pp. 421-7; and Yohanan Friedmann, *Shaikh Ahmad Sirhindi: An Outline of His Thought and a Study of His Image in the Eyes of Posterity* (MacGill, 1971), pp. 113-14.
87. Mujeeb, n. 70, p. 247. See also S.R. Sharma, *The Religious Policy of the Mughal Emperors* (Bombay, 1972), pp. 81-126.

88. Ibid., pp. 127-213.
89. Mujeeb, n. 70, p. 363.
90. M. Athar Ali, n. 76, p. 96.
91. Smith, n. 85, p. 190.
92. Saiyid Athar Abbas, n. 74, pp. 362-3.
93. Jadunath Sarkar, *A Short History of Aurangzeb* (Calcutta, 1962), pp. 149-50.
94. Zahiruddin Faruki, *Aurangzeb and His Times* (Delhi, 1972), p. 150.
95. Satish Chandra, 'Jizyah and the State in India during the 17th Century', *Journal of the Economic and Social History of the Orient*, 1968, p. 336.
96. W.H. Sleeman, *Rambles and Reflections of an Indian Official* (London, 1844), I, p. 254.
97. Ikram, n. 12, p. 263. According to Shibli Numani, Shah Waliullah occupies a higher place than such world-renowned scholars as Ibn-i-Taimiyya, Ibn-i-Rashid, Imam Ghazali and Imam Razi; see Khaliq Ahamad Nizami, 'Shah Waliullah Dehlawi and Indian Politics in the Eighteenth Century', *Islamic Culture*, 1951, p. 133.
98. Saiyid Athar Abbas Rizvi, 'Ideological Background of the Wahhabi Movement in India in the 18th and 19th Centuries' in Bisheshwar Prasad, ed., *Ideas in History* (Bombay, 1968), p. 96.
99. Saiyid Athar Abbas Rizvi, *Shah Wali-Allah and His Times* (Canberra, 1980), pp. 294-5.
100. Ibid., pp. 295-6.
101. Ibid., p. 299.
102. Cited in A.D. Muztar, *Shah Wali Allah* (Islamabad, 1979), p. 154. See also Khaliq Ahmad Nizami, ed., *Shah Waliullah ke Sayasi Maktubaat* (Delhi, 1969), pp. 42, 79-98.
103. Cited in Irfan Habib, n. 86, p. 53.
104. Aziz Ahmad, n. 8, p. 210.
105. K.A. Nizami, 'Socio-Religious Movements in Indian Islam', in S.T. Lokhandwalla, ed., *India and Contemporary Islam* (Simla, 1971), pp. 103-4.
106. Mujeeb, n. 70, p. 395.
107. Saiyid Athar Abbas, n. 98, p. 98.
108. See Qeyamuddin Ahmad, *The Wahabi Movement in India* (Calcutta, 1966), pp. 326-7.
109. See Smith, n. 69, p. 52. Also Mujeeb Ashraf, *Muslim Attitudes towards British Rule and Western Culture in India in the First Half of the Nineteenth Century* (Delhi, 1982), p. 119.
110. Saiyid Athar Abbas Rizvi, *Shah Abd Al-Aziz: Puritanism, Sectarian Polemics and Jihad* (Canberra, 1982), p. 535.
111. W.C. Smith, *Modern Islam in India* (Lahore, 1969; 1st pub., 1943), pp. 191-2.
112. Ibid., pp. 192-3. It is noteworthy that the followers of Titu Mir, while attacking a village owned by a Hindu landlord, killed a cow in a public place and smeared the temple there with its blood. See Muinuddin Khan, *The Faraidi Movement* (Karachi, 1965), p. lxvi.
113. Asoka Mehta and Achyut Patwardhan, *The Communal Triangle in India* (Allahabad, 1942; 2nd edn), p.. 10. For a detailed exposition of this view see *A History of the Hindu-Muslim Problem in India, Being the Report of the Committee Appointed by the Indian National Congress (Karachi Session, 1931)*

to Enquire into the Cawnpore Riots of March 1931 (Allahabad, 1933), pp. 77-110. Reproduced in N. Gerald Barrier, ed., *Roots of Communal Politics* (New Delhi, 1976), pp. 125-58.

114. It is, of course, a fact that sometimes a Hindu ruler when attacking another Hindu ruler's dominion also attacked and plundered the temples therein, but it should be obvious that this would not have created any bitterness based on religious distinction. Nor could these instances have prevented the growth of such bitterness when the invader belonged to a different faith.
115. Mohammad Habib, *Politics and Society During the Early Medieval Period: Collected Works*, ed. by K.A. Nizami, I (New Delhi, 1974), p. 16. See also Iqtidar Alam Khan, 'The Secular State in India: Historical Perspective', in *Essays in Honour of Professor S.C. Sarkar* (New Delhi, 1976), pp. 165-80; and 'Medieval Indian Notions of Secular Statecraft in Retrospect', in *Social Scientist*, No. 152, January 1986, pp. 3-15.
116. Habib, n. 115, p. 20.
117. Edward C. Sachau, ed., *Alberuni's India* (Delhi, 1964), I, pp. 19-20.
118. Ibid., p. 22.
119. See B.B. Misra, *The Central Administration of the East India Company* (Manchester, 1959), pp. 301-7.
120. Jagdish Narayan Sarkar, *Hindu-Muslim Relations in Bengal* (*Medieval Period*) (Delhi, 1985), p. 12.
121. Majumdar, n. 20, p. 632.
122. Ibid., p. 633.
123. Harishchandra Verma and Ram Niwas Gupta, *Hindi Sahitya ka Itihas* (Rohtak, 1982), p. 79.
124. See Ram Chandra Shukla, *Hindi Sahitya ka Itihas* (Banaras, n.d.) p. 44. Shukla's thesis has, however, been contested by another eminent historian of Hindi literature who holds the view that the policies of the Muslim rulers had had nothing to do with the rise and growth of the *Bhakti* movement in northern India. See *Hazari Prasad Dwivedi Granthawali* (New Delhi, 1981), III, p. 307.
125. S.R. Sharma, *The Founding of Maratha Freedom* (Bombay, 1964), p. 130.
126. Balkrishna Govind Gokhale, 'Hindu Responses to the Muslim Presence in Maharashtra', in Yohanan Friedmann, ed., *Islam in Asia, I: South Asia* (Boulder, Colorado, 1984), p. 157.
127. Bhalchandra Nemade, 'The Revolt of the Under-privileged', in Jayant Lele, ed., *Tradition and Modernity in Bhakti Movement* (Leiden, 1981), p. 117.
128. Sharma, n. 125, p. 112.
129. Savitri Chandra Shobha, *Social Life and Concepts in Medieval Hindi Bhakti Poetry: A Socio-Cultural Study* (Meerut, 1983), pp. 48-9.
130. Ibid., p. 41.
131. *Dwivedi Granthawali*, n. 124, IV, p. 452.
132. Shobha, n. 129, p. 42.
133. Ganda Singh, 'Development of Sikh thought upto the End of the Eighteenth Century', in Prasad, n. 98, p. 12.
134. Gokhale, n. 126, pp. 15-16.
135. See Satish Chandra, *Medieval India* (New Delhi, 1982), p. 101.
136. Ibid., p. 103.
137. Ibid., pp. 139-40.

138. G.S. Sardesai, 'Shivaji', in R.C. Majumdar, ed., *The Mughal Empire,* Vol. VII of *The History and Culture of the Indian People* (Bombay, 1974), p. 251.
139. Cited in ibid., pp. 251-2.
140. Gokhale, n. 126, p. 157.
141. Govind Sakharam Sardesai, *New History of the Marathas*, I (Bombay, 1957), p. 273.
142. *Bhushan Granthawali*, ed. by Brajratna Das (Allahabad, 1950), p. 80.
143. Ibid., pp. 86-7.
144. Sardesai, n. 141, p. 296.
145. Ibid., p. 277.
146. Jadunath Sarkar, *Shivaji and His Times* (Calcutta, 1961), pp. 320-3. Also the same author's *History of Aurangzeb,* III (Calcutta, 1972), pp. 190-2.
147. See C.A. Bayly, 'The Pre-History of 'Communalism'? Religious Conflict in India, 1700-1860', *Modern Asian Studies*, 19, 2 (1985), pp. 187-8.
148. Ibid., p. 188.
149. Ibid., pp. 190-3.
150. Muzaffar Alam, *The Crisis of Empire in Mughal North India: Awadh and the Punjab, 1707-1748* (Delhi, 1986), pp. 115-16.
151. Ibid., p. 116.
152. Ibid., p. 141.
153. Ibid.
154. Ibid., pp. 142-3.
155. Bayly, n. 147, pp. 199-200.
156. Lakshmi Subramanian, 'Capital and Crowd in a Declining Asian Port City: The Anglo-Bania Order and the Surat Riots of 1795', *Modern Asian Studies,* 19, 2 (1985), p. 205.
157. Saiyid Athar Abbas, n. 99, pp. 197-202.
158. Ketaki Kushari Dyson, *A Various Universe: A Study of the Journals and Memoirs of British Men and Women in the Indian Subcontinent, 1765-1856* (Delhi, 1978), p. 53.
159. Gyanendra Pandey, *Notes on the Construction of the Hindu Community in 19th Century North India,* handwritten notes which formed the basis for an oral presentation to the seminar on 'The Historical and Contemporary Character of Hinduism' held at the Nehru Memorial Museum and Library (New Delhi) in May 1986. I am indebted to Professor Pandey for making these notes available to me and for permitting use of them here. For some more examples of Hindu-Muslim riots in early nineteenth century, see C.A. Bayly, *Rulers, Townsmen and Bazars: North Indian Society in the Age of British Expansion, 1770-1870* (Cambridge, 1983), pp. 335-8.
160. For the full text of the Proclamation see Rudrangshu Mukherjee, 'The Azamgarh Proclamation and Some Questions on the Revolt of 1857 in the North-Western Provinces', in *Essays in Honour of Professor S.C. Sarkar* (New Delhi, 1976), pp. 495-8. Also Charles Ball, *The History of the Indian Mutiny* (New Delhi, 1981; 1st Indian rpt.), II, pp. 630-2.
161. Susobhan Sarkar, 'General President's Address', *Indian History Congress: Proceedings of the Thirty-Third Session*, Muzaffarpur, 1972 (New Delhi, 1973), pp. 10-11.

CHAPTER II

The Economic Divide

WHILE DEALING with the economic divide between Hindus and Muslims scholars tend to exaggerate the backwardness of Muslims in modern education, government employment and other avenues of making a living in comparison to Hindus. They contend that the British had deliberately kept the Muslims away from all positions of profit and privilege bacause of their supposed leadership of the rebellion of 1857 and encouraged the Hindus who were considered docile and long used to living under foreign rule. Thus, a big lag developed between the two communities and this became a major factor behind the growth of separatism among the Muslims. With a few notable exceptions, this has so far been the standard economic explanation for the rise and growth of Muslim nationalism or separatism.

This theory owes its origin to a British civilian, W.W. Hunter. Called upon to investigate the causes of widespread disaffection among Muslims, as reflected in the continued popularity of the so-called Wahhabi movement Hunter produced a book published in 1871 under the title *The Indian Musalmans*. Here he made it clear that he was best acquainted only with the conditions under which Muslims lived in eastern Bengal and added that he would be sorry if the readers got the impression that what he had written applied to the condition of Muslims in India as a whole.[1] However, the title of Hunter's book as well as the way in which he wrote its fourth chapter, entitled 'The Wrongs of the Muhammedans under British Rule', conveyed exactly the belief he had warned against. For he often used Bengal and India as interchangeable terms, sometimes using the one and sometimes the other. Sometimes, as in the following lines, on the basis of study of the condition of the Muslims of Bengal, he generalized about the condition of Indian Muslims in general and gave expression to the dominant feeling at that time in British ruling circles in India, worried by the spread of the Wahhabi influence and seeking means of pacifying the Muslim population:

. . . from the highest official to the lowest . . . there is now a firm conviction that we have failed in our duty to the Muhammedan subjects of the Queen. A great section of the Indian population, some thirty millions in number, finds itself decaying under British rule. They complain that they, who but yesterday were the conquerors and Governors of the land, can find no subsistence in it today. Any answar based on their own degeneracy is a *petito principii*, for their degeneracy is but one of the results of our political ignorance and neglect. Before the country passed under our rule, the Musalman(s) professed the same faith, ate the same food, and in all essentials lived the same lives, as they do now. To this day they exhibit at intervals their old intense feeling of nationality and capability of warlike enterprise; but in all other respects they are a race ruined under British rule.[2]

Hunter proceeded to contrast the position of Muslims to that of Hindus who seemed to be forging ahead with the help of modern education: 'The truth is that our system of public instruction, which has awakened the Hindus from the sleep of centuries and quickened their inert masses with some of the noble impulses of a nation, is opposed to the traditions, unsuited to the requirements, and hateful to the religion, of the Musalmans.'[3]

This theory was avidly seized upon by the British publicists as a justification for certain special measures which the Government was then undertaking in order to pacify the Muslim elite and keep them away from the emerging movement of Indian nationalism. The Muslim elite, smarting under the effects of the change of political order and feeling more and more gloomy about the future, were happy to lap this theory, for it not merely provided a vindication of their own belief, but also a potent means for winning concessions from the British as well as adherents to the cause of Muslim nationalism from both the professional classes and the masses. Indeed the theory became so respectable that even the leaders of the Indian nationalist movement began to believe in it.[4] It became equally acceptable in scholarly circles, particularly since the publication of W.C. Smith's *Modern Islam in India* in 1946. Referring to Hunter's presentation as 'a fairly full and very convincing indictment of the Government policy', and quoting with approval the latter's remark that the Muslims had been shut out alike from official employment and recognized professions, Smith observes:

The repression of the Muslims that is indicated above—keeping them out of the administration and of the medical, legal and other such professions, and in general not educating them—was clearly a policy affecting the upper and the potentially middle classes. It was at this time that the clerical and professional classes among the Hindus were developing, and beginning to wield some power. The India Office was afraid to allow that same power to the Muslims, whose upper classes, as the Mutiny supposedly showed, already wielded more power than was comfortable for the foreigner. More especially, it was afraid to allow that power to both groups at the same time.[5]

This view has continued to prevail right up to the present-day.[6] According to P.C. Joshi, for instance, what explains Hindu-Muslim antagonism 'is not just the fact of *lag* in social and economic development between the two communities. It is the fact that for the major part of British rule and in the key areas of the Indian subcontinent, the Muslim upper class steadily *lost ground* to the Hindus.'[7]

Some recent studies, however, have created doubt about the validity of such analysis and convincingly shown that the picture of Muslim backwardness in education and employment has generally been overdrawn. Calling for a 're-examination and regional redefinition' of the time-lag theory, Aparna Basu, for instance, has shown on the basis of official statistics that Muslims were not educationally backward, as compared to Hindus, everywhere. In Bengal and the Punjab, where the bulk of Muslims were agriculturists, they were, of course, backward, but this was not the case in areas like Madras, Bombay and UP. Thus in Madras between 1871-2 and 1881-2, while the number of Hindu boys going to school doubled, that of Muslim boys quadrupled. In 1885-6, one out of every 64 Muslim boys and one out of every 76 Hindu boys were in school. According to the 1901 Census, Muslims constituted 6.5 per cent of the population of the Madras Presidency, but Muslim pupils constituted 9.7 per cent of the school-going population. Muslims were, of course, backward in higher education, but the same was true of all Hindus except Brahmins in the Bombay Presidency. Except in Sind, where the Muslims were mainly agriculturists and quite backward in education, the percentage of Muslim pupils was higher than the percentage of Muslim population. Thus in 1881, Muslims formed only 10 per cent of the population in Gujarat but over 12 per cent of the pupils. Similarly, in the Deccan, they formed only 5.4 per cent of the population, but 6.5 per cent of the pupils. Again, except for Sind, literacy among Muslims was more widespread than among Hindus. In UP, Muslims were ahead of Hindus at all stages of education, including higher education.[8]

It is, of course, true that when Hunter wrote his book, the Muslims in British India, as a whole, to some extent lagged behind Hindus in sending their children to schools imparting education on modern lines. This is borne out by Table 2.1

TABLE 2.1
PERCENTAGE OF MUSLIMS IN POPULATION AND PERCENTAGE OF MUSLIM BOYS IN SCHOOLS IN SIX PROVINCES OF BRITISH INDIA IN 1870-1

Provinces	Total			At School		
	Population	Muhammedans	Percentage	Total	Muhammedans	Percentage
Madras	31,281,177	1,872,214	6.00	123,689	5,531	4.4
Bombay	16,349,206	2,528,344	15.40	190,153	15,684	8.2
Bengal and Assam	60,467,724	19,553,420	32.3	196,086	28,411	14.4
North-Western Provinces	30,781,204	4,188,751	13.5	162,619	28,990	17.8
Oudh	11,220,232	1,111,290	9.9	48,929	12,417	25.3
Punjab	17,611,498	9,102,488	51.6	68,144	23,783	34.9
Total	167,711,041	38,356,507	22.8	789,620	114,816	14.5

SOURCE: *Report of the Indian Education Commission* (Calcutta, 1883).

However, the gap between the proportion of Muslim boys to the total school population and that of the Muslim population to the total population of the country was not as wide as is implied by the myth, popularized by Hunter, that impelled by a pride of race, the memory of their bygone superiority and religious fears Muslims generally stayed away from government schools.

Indeed the Education Commission of 1882-3, presided over by Hunter himself, admitted that 'the enquiries made in 1871-2 went to prove that, except in the matter of the higher education, there had been a tendency to exaggerate the backwardness of the Muhammedans'.[9] Besides, as a result partly of Government's encouragement since 1871,[10] and more particularly since 1883,[11] and partly because of efforts by the advanced sections of the Muslim community itself, the gap between the Hindus and Muslims in the matter of education, except at the University level, did not last long.

Indeed, instead of steadily losing ground to Hindus, Muslims steadily improved their position in the field of education. This is brone out by Table 2.2.

TABLE 2.2
PERCENTAGE OF MUSLIM PUPILS AND THE PERCENTAGE OF MUSLIMS IN THE COUNTRY

Year	Percentage of Muslim pupils to total number of pupil in schools	Percentage of Muslims to total population of British India
1881-2	17.8	19.1
1886-7	22.6	19.1
1891-2	23.0	21.8
1896-7	22.2	21.8
1901-2	21.6	22.6
1906-7	21.8	22.6
1911-12	22.9	23.5
1916-17	23.2	23.5
1921-2	23.5	24.1
1926-7	25.3	24.1
1931-2	26.7	24.7

SOURCE: Computed from Table 193 in *Progress of Education in India, 1912-17*, Vol. II, p. 193; and Table CXXIV in *Progress of Education in India, 1927-32*, Vol. 1, p. 239.

This progress was evenly distributed throughout the country and not concentrated in any particular region (see Table 2.3).

This progress in education, however, had one serious limitation: at the college and university levels, the Muslim representation always remained quite low. In 1871, Muslim students constituted only 3.65 per cent of the total student population in colleges.[12] By 1931-2 this percentage had gone up to only 13.6, while Muslims at that time constituted 24.7 per cent of India's population. Indeed the higher one went, the rarer were the Muslims. Thus in 1931-2 while they constituted 30.5 of the total student population in class I, they formed only 25.3 per cent in class II, 19.4 per cent in class V, 18.2 per cent in middle school, 15 per cent in secondary schools and 13.6 per cent in colleges.[13]

II

What has been said about education also applied to government employment. Quite a wrong impression has been created by imagining that what Hunter said about Bengal in this respect was more or less true of the whole country. It is true that most British officials believed in the theory that Muslims had played a leading role in the revolt

TABLE 2.3
MUSLIM POPULATION AND MUSLIM PUPILS IN THE DIFFERENT PROVINCES OF BRITISH INDIA IN 1931-2

Provinces	Muslim population	Muslim pupils	Percentage of Muslim population to total population	Percentage of Muslim pupils to total pupils
Madras	3,305,937	319,506	7.1	10.9
Bombay	4,456,897	259,003	24.4	19.4
Bengal	27,497,624	1,437,978	54.9	51.7
Bihar and Orissa	4,265,035	148,141	11.3	13.5
UP	7,181,927	282,782	14.8	18.6
Punjab	13,332,460	675,061	56.5	50.6
CP and Berar	682,854	49,249	4.4	10.7
Assam	2,755,914	108,802	32.0	29.2
NWFP	2,227,303	64,158	91.8	72.5
Coorg	13,777	366	8.4	3.5
Delhi	206,960	13,328	32.5	30.0
Ajmer and Marwar	97,133	5,034	17.3	20.9
Baluchistan	405,309	6,225	87.4	60.9
Bangalore	28,625	2,457	21.3	14.6
Other Administered Areas (excluding Administered Areas in Hyderabad)	25,613	4,237	21.8	18.9

SOURCE: *Progress of Education in India, 1927-32*, Vol. II, Table 99 (B).

of 1857 and for quite sometime did not look upon their employment in government with favour, but this certainly did not mean total exclusion of Muslims from all positions in the government. This is borne out by the detailed researches of Thomas R. Metcalf. He, of course, acknowledges that the British displayed 'the most bitter and widespread hostility' towards the Muslim community whom they generally considered as 'fomentors of the revolt and its chief beneficiaries'. Though not firmly grounded, this hostility left its mark on government policy for several decades. According to Metcalf, however, this mark consisted not in the total exclusion of the Muslims from the various services but, except in Bengal, only in the limitation of their number roughly to their proportion in the total population of the country. Moreover, with the passage of time, British hostility was gradually effaced and the Muslims were able 'to regain the favour they had enjoyed in the early days of British rule'.[14]

TABLE 2.4

NUMBER OF HINDUS AND MUSLIMS APPOINTED TO HIGHER POSITIONS IN GOVERNMENT SERVICE (I.E. POSITIONS CARRYING A SALARY OF NOT LESS THAN RS.150 PER MONTH) IN THE DIFFERENT PARTS OF BRITISH INDIA IN 1871

Areas	Number of Hindus	Number of Muslim	Muslim percentage of total appointments
Bengal	88	11	11
Bombay	51	5	9
Sind	3	1	25
Madras	70	1	1
North-Western Provinces	30	16	35
Punjab	51	31	38
Oudh	6	5	45
Central Provinces	4	2	33
Total	300	72	24

SOURCE: Great Britain, *Parliamentary Papers*, Vol. LIV (*Accounts and Papers*), *63*, 1875, cited in Islam and Jansen, n. 15, pp. 88-9.

The subject of Muslim share in government employment has been dealt with more thoroughly in an article by Zafarul Islam and Raymond L. Jansen, published in a reputed journal in Pakistan. They categorically state that 'the Muslims fared far better than has been alleged. That the Muslims 'were nearly excluded from "Civil Employ" is obviously untrue'.[15] This is borne out clearly by Table 2.4. The situation, of course, varied from province to province—while Muslims were under-represented in most provinces, they were also over-represented in some. Considering India as a whole, however, the Muslim representation in government service was 'quite equitable' (see Table 2.5).

The position was not much different a decade or so later when the Public Service Commision (1886-7), popularly known as the Aitchison Commission, looked into this matter.

The figures in Table 2.6 clearly indicate that while the percentage of Hindus employed in the executive and judicial services in the eighties of the nineteenth century was greatly in excess of their population proportion in Bengal and Assam, it fell greatly short of it in the North-Western Provinces and Oudh and in the Hyderabad Assigned Districts. On the other hand, the percentage of Muslims so employed was largely in excess of their population proportion in the North-Western Provinces and Oudh, the Central Provinces and the Hyderabad Assigned Districts, but fell greatly short of it in Bengal,

TABLE 2.5
MUSLIM REPRESENTATION IN GOVERNMENT SERVICE PROVINCEWISE

Area	Total population	Muslim population	Per cent Muslims population	Per cent Muslims Appointed
Bengal	60,467,724	19,553,420	32	11
Bombay	16,349,206	2,528,344	15	9
Madras	31,282,177	1,872,214	6	1
North-Western Provinces	30,781,204	4,188,751	14	35
Oudh	11,220,232	1,111,290	10	45
Punjab	17,611,498	9,102,488	52	38
Total	167,712,041	38,356,507	23	24

SOURCE: Islam and Jansen on the basis of the *Report of the Indian Education Commission, 1882-83*, p. 404 and computation from Table 2.4.

Assam and Bombay, and to some extent also in Madras and the Punjab.

When, over a quarter of a century later, another detailed investigation into the state of the public service took place, the situation was not much different. This should be clear from Table 2.7.

Thus, on population basis the Muslims were under-represented in Assam, Bengal, Bombay and the Punjab, but over-represented in Bihar and Orissa, the Central Provinces and Berar, Madras and the United Provinces. While there was a slight deterioration in the overall proportion of Muslim representation, in absolute numbers Muslim representation had steadily increased. Thus, the number of Muslims holding positions in government service carrying a monthly salary of Rs. 200 or more was 408 in 1887, 533 in 1897, 577 in 1903 and 711 in 1913.[16] The slight deterioration in the proportion of Muslim representation was largely caused by the much greater growth of Muslim population as compared to Hindu population. Thus, according to the census report of 1911, between 1881 and 1911, while the Hindu population in India increased by 15.1 per cent, the Muslim population increased by 26.4 per cent.[17]

In both education and employment, therefore, what is pertinent is not that the Muslims in British India were on the whole weaker or backward as compared to the Hindus, but that the Muslim elite felt that they were so. And this feeling was further strengthened because

TABLE 2.6

PROPORTION OF APPOINTMENT HELD BY HINDUS AND MUSLIMS RESPECTIVELY IN PROPORTION TO POPULATION IN THE PROVINCES IN 1885

Provinces	Hindus: Percentage of total population	Hindus: Percentage of total number of persons employed in the Executive Service and in the Judicial Service of the Service Provinces			Muslims: Percentage of total population	Muslims: Percentage of total number of persons employed in the Executive Service and the Judicial Service of the Service Provinces		
Madras	91.4	Executive Service Judicial Service	82.8 91.4	86.0	6.2	Executive Service Judicial Service	5.4 1.6	4.0
Bombay and Sind	79.6	Executive Service Judicial Service	82.7 91.4	85.4	18.3	Executive Service Judicial Service	7.4 0.8	5.4
Bengal	65.3	Executive Service Judicial Service	73.4 96.1	83.7	31.2	Executive Service Judicial Service	12.9 3.1	8.5
North-Western Provinces and Oudh	86.2	Executive Service Judicial Service	49.4 52.5	50.2	13.4	Executive Service Judicial Service	44.8 45.9	45.1
Punjab	40.7	Executive Service Judicial Service	48.1 53.4	49.8	51.3	Executive Service Judicial Service	41.8 33.6	39.3
Central Provinces	75.3	Executive Service Judicial Service		75.2	2.4	Executive Service Judicial Service		18.1
Hyderabad Assigned Districts	90.7	Executive Service Judicial Service		69.0	7.0	Executive Service Judicial Service		16.6
Assam	62.7	Executive Service Judicial Service	83.6 90.9	84.8	26.9	Executive Service Judicial Service	0.9 0.9	9.0

SOURCE: *Report of the Public Service Commission, 1886-87* (Calcutta, 1888), p. 38.

TABLE 2.7
PROPORTION OF MUSLIM REPRESENTATION IN THE PUBLIC SERVICES CONCERNING POSITIONS CARRYING A MONTHLY SALARY OF RS. 200 OR MORE IN 1913

Area	Percentage of Muslims in the total population	Percentage of positions held by Muslims of all positions	Percentage of positions held by Muslims of all positions held by Indians
Assam	28.1	7	16.8
Bengal	52.7	8	12.2
Bihar and Orissa	10.6	12	20.9
Bombay	20.5	4	7.2
Central Provinces and Berar	4.1	8	18.3
Madras	6.6	4	7.2
Punjab	54.9	16	39.3
United Provinces	14.1	16	33.5
Whole of India	23.5	7	16.9

SOURCE: *Ishington Commission Report, 1913* (Calcutta, 1913), p. 128.

of the growing competition for government employment which became particularly fierce during the 1920s and 1930s, when there was a considerable expansion of education in the country. Between 1917 and 1937, the number of pupils in schools and colleges rose from 7 million to 14 million and the number of graduates from 4,000 to 20,000. The number of Muslim pupils was growing faster than that of members of other communities. Thus, between 1917 and 1927, the number of Muslim pupils in British India rose from one and half million to two and a half million. While the percentage of pupils of all communities put together to the total population of the country rose from 3.1 to 4.3, the percentage of Muslim pupils to the total Muslim population rose from 3.2 to 4.7. This educational expansion, however, was not accompanied by a corresponding enlargement of economic opportunities. On the contrary, there was decline in production, both in the agricultural and industrial sectors, and a reduction in public expenditure.[18] This meant fewer jobs and more intensified competition among those qualified to hold them. The worldwide economic depression further aggravated the problem. While all suffered alike in a situation of rising expectations and limited opportunities, the tendency among the members of one community to blame those of the other for the difficulties faced by them became stronger and communal animosity increased.[19] The idea of a separate Muslim State was bound to appear attractive to educated young Muslims in such a situation.

III

That the Muslims were not backward either educationally or economically everywhere is best illustrated by their position in UP, a leading centre of Muslim nationalism in both the nineteenth and twentieth centuries.[20] With the help of a rich collection of data, Paul R. Brass has conclusively proved that during the second half of the nineteenth century and at least the first three decades of the twentieth century, the Muslims of UP were not significantly behind the Hindus and were, in fact, ahead of them in various fields. Thus, the Muslims were far more urbanized than the Hindus. In 1931, 29 per cent of Muslims in UP lived in towns campared to only 8 per cent among Hindus. Besides, Muslims constituted more than 38 per cent of the total urban population of the province. Though Muslims constituted only 13 per cent of the total population of the province, they constituted more than 50 per cent of the population in twenty-one towns, and between one-third and a half in thirty-one other towns. According to official statistics, in 1871-2, Muslims were proportionately over-represented as compared to Hindus in both schools and colleges. Again, it was reported by the provincial government in 1883 that the proportion of Muslim boys in schools to their total population was 2.18 while that of Hindu boys to the total Hindu population was only 1.3. Muslims were behind Hindus in general male literacy in 1881, but they gradually closed the gap and went ahead of Hindus by 1911. In male English literacy, Muslims were consistently ahead of Hindus throughout between 1891 and 1931. Besides, Muslims went on improving their condition, and by 1931 they constituted more than 15 per cent of the literate population of the province, nearly 20 per cent of the English educated population, more than 28 per cent of the urban literate population, and more than 22 per cent of 'that tiny, but politically crucial political segment, the urban English educated class'. The same was true of employment. Thus, in 1882, out of 54,130 Indian officials holding government employment, Hindus constituted 65.22 per cent and Muslims 34.78 per cent as against 86.75 and 13.25 in the general population. During the succeeding years, Muslims not merely maintained their lead, but also increased it. Thus, in 1911 and 1921, they held respectively 41.94 and 47.67 per cent of government jobs.[21]

Francis Robinson has similarly shown that the Muslims held the leading position in UP also as landlords, holding 20 per cent of its land. They held particularly large areas of land around several important towns of UP, including such centres of British power as Allahabad and Lucknow, and this gave them a tremendous influence in government and politics, out of all proportion to their numbers. This was particularly true of Awadh which was dominated by large *taluqdars,* many of whom were Muslims.[22]

In commerce and industry also, the Muslims of UP occupied a leading position. Thus, in 1911, there were only 3,974 Hindus engaged in industrial occupations as compared to 5,990 Muslims. Apart from dominating cotton textiles and tailoring industries, they also contributed to several other industries, such as other textiles, wood, metals and food. Besides, as mentioned earlier, Muslims resided far more in towns than Hindus and though all industries were not located in towns, a large proportion of the urban population was engaged in industrial occupations. Among Hindus 75.6 per cent were cultivators, including 10 per cent who were agricultural labourers, and only 22 per cent followed occupations which were not agricultural or closely connected with agriculture. Out of them, nearly 10 per cent were engaged in industries and 4 per cent in trade. On the other hand, only 50 per cent of Muslims followed agricultural or pastoral pursuits, including 4 per cent who worked as agricultural labourers; 25 per cent of Muslims were engaged in industries and nearly 7 per cent in trade.[23]

The comparatively better position *vis-a-vis* Hindus, which Muslims in UP held in education and employment, however, far from keeping them aloof from Muslim nationalism, really made them the pioneers and leaders of that nationalism in India. This was because they became growingly concerned with threats to their privileged position as education spread among Hindus and more and more of them secured government employment. Besides, the British, in the immediate aftermath of 1857, were welcoming the increase in the number of Hindus in government offices. Thus, though Muslim share in government service, compared to the size of their population, remained higher than that of Hindus on a similar basis, in absolute terms their number was going down, as compared to Hindus, at least in the higher ranks of that service.

Besides, although not backward as compared to Hindus, in education *per se,* Muslims did lag behind Hindus, for sometime, in going to government schools and colleges. As Robinson points out, 'it was not until the late 1860s that the proportion of Muslim students in government primary and secondary schools was as large as their proportion of the population, and it was not until the 1890s that they achieved this in higher education'.[24] Since a large number of Muslims in UP were town-dwellers and had traditionally held a far higher position than Hindus in both education and government employment, this situation filled some of them, most notably Syed Ahmad Khan (1817-98), with the fear that unless serious efforts were undertaken to encourage Muslims to take to modern education, their future was doomed. This concern with Muslim position in government employment became one of the foundations of Muslim nationalism.

Another cause for worry to the Muslim elite in UP arose from the earlier start of English education in Bengal consequent to the earlier establishment of British rule there. The members of the Hindu upper castes in Bengal generally known as the *bhadralok*, who took advantage of that education, had not merely secured a dominant position amongst Indians in government service and the various professions in Bengal, but also seemed poised to occupy a similar position in other parts of northern India. The Brahmins in Madras and the Brahmins and Parsis in Bombay were also placed in a similar situation in their respective areas. The scions of upper class Muslim families did not relish the gowing influence of the upper caste Hindus in British India as a whole and felt seriously concerned regarding their future. With education spreading among Hindus and the increasing demand for recruitment to the higher ranks of government service on the basis of a competitive examination, they did not feel sure that they would be able to maintain their earstwhile dominant position even in UP. This feeling particularly became strong during the period of Congress rule in UP (1937-9), which saw the end of the traditional pattern of recruitment to the public services, based on a special concern for maintaining Muslim representation at a fairly high level.[25]

IV

While UP was unboubtedly a leading centre of Muslim nationalism, it was by no means the only centre. By basing our conclusions on the origins and nature of Muslim nationalism in British India mainly on the basis of our study of the situation in UP, we shall be committing the same mistake which many earlier scholars committed by basing theirs mainly on a study of the situation in Bengal. Muslim nationalism became such a powerful force and finally won because, with minor exceptions here and there, it was a pan-Indian phenomenon and finally entrenched itself, particularly in Bengal and the Punjab, even at the mass level. But for the strength of that ideology in these two provinces, there would have been no partition and no Pakistan. Even in the nineteenth century, there were counterparts of Syed Ahmad Khan in several other parts of India. Indeed, the first *significant* political organization of Indian Muslims in modern times, the National Muhammedan Association, was founded in 1877, not by Syed Ahmad Khan in UP, but by Syed Ameer Ali (1849-1928) in Calcutta.[26] Besides, as pointed out by a noted authority on the history of the Punjab in modern times, 'during the latter half of the nineteenth century, Hindu-Muslim antagonism was probably more intense in the Punjab than in Bengal and the United Provinces'.[27] It is time, therefore, to turn to the economic background of Muslim nationalism in Bengal and the Punjab.

As far as Bengal is concerned, the first thing worthy of attention is the fact that while most of the landlords were Hindus, the majority of the peasants consisted of Muslims. Thus, in the second half of the eighteenth century, there were only two Muslims among the fifteen biggest landlords in Bengal.[28] According to the census of 1881, while the cultivators among the Hindus were only 49.28 per cent, the ratio of cultivators among the Muslims was 62.81 per cent. Besides, among the Muslim cultivators, the ratio of tenants was much larger than among the Hindu cultivators. According to the census of 1901, landowners among Muslim cultivators totalled only 170 in 10,000 as against 217 Hindu landowners in the same number. In some of the districts of eastern Bengal where Muslims constituted the majority, the situation was even more glaring. In the Bogra district, according to the census of 1901, Muslims constituted over 80 per cent of the population, but the zamindars were mostly Hindus, there being only five Muslim zamindars of any importance. In Rajshahi, according to the census of 1911, the Muslims constituted 78 per cent of the population, but could boast of only two zamindars of any importance. In Mymensingh district, again the Muslims constituted 75 per cent of the population, but the landlords belonged mainly to Hindu Brahmin and Kayastha families.[29]

Even where the zamindars were Muslims, the actual managers of the estates were mostly Hindus. Thus, in the second half of the eighteenth century, only one-tenth of such managers in eastern Bengal were Muslims.[30] In 1911, though there were 5400 Muslim landlords in eastern Bengal (less than half of all landlords in that area, though the Muslims constituted two-thirds of the population) only 7500 Muslims were engaged in estate management, either in a superior or a subordinate position.[31] This further strengthened the image of upper caste Hindus or the *bhadralok* as landlords and rent-collectors. This may partly account for the fact that even in areas where the number of Muslims subsisting mainly, though not wholly, on rent from land was not much smaller than that of Hindus, as in the northern and eastern parts of Bengal, according to the census of 1911, these persons were treated as peasants and not as exploiters or oppressors.[32] Generally known as *jotedars*, these substantial cultivators had risen from the ranks of common peasantry and often joined in the cultivation of the portion of their land not let out to others. Though economically well off, they were socially and culturally part of the Muslim peasant community and shared the same communal bond along with the rest of its members. It is these substantial cultivators who provided leadership to the Muslim peasantry in Bengal and became a bridge between them and the provincial Muslim leadership.[33]

The preponderance of Hindus among landlords in Bengal has been generally ascribed to the Permanent Settlement of Lord Cornwallis (1793) and the resumption proceedings which followed from 1828 onwards.[34] This view has, however, been recently proved erroneous by N.K. Sinha, a leading authority on the economic history of Bengal, who has pointed out that Hindus had held a preponderant position among landlords in Bengal even during pre-British times. Thus, under Murshid Quli Khan, who was Nawab of Bengal from 1700 to 1727, most of the collectors of revenue had been Hindus and 90 per cent of the zamindaris in Bengal had been held by them.[35] Whatever the cause, the existence of the Hindu landlord-Muslim tenant syndrom was a fact of life in Bengal, and this not merely influenced the attitudes of the members of the two communities towards each other in the countryside, but also the thinking of their leading members in the metropolitan towns. This is illustrated by what happened at the time of the consideration of the Bengal Tenancy Bill which became an Act in 1885 and whose purpose was to provide some security of tenure to tenants and regulate the power of landlords to enhance rents. Among the landlords who assembled at the Calcutta Town Hall on 29 December 1883 to protest against the bill, a large majority belonged to the Hindu community with only three Muslims from Bengal proper (most of the Muslims present had come from Bihar).[36] More significantly, when the matter was being discussed in the Governor General's Council, Syed Ameer Ali, dissociated himself from the two Hindu members, who had supported the cause of the landlords, and warmly championed the cause of the tenants. He justified his stand on the ground that most of the tenants were Muslims and as a Muslim it was his duty to support them. He observed:

> As far as I am concerned, it was a labour of love, for I cannot help taking a keen interest in the measure. The bulk of the peasantry in Eastern Bengal, numbering seven million of souls, belong to my faith, and naturally have claim upon the Muhammedan member for the time being in your Excellency's Council. In Eastern Bengal, the agrarian troubles are aggravated by religious differences and the fact that many of the zamindars are new comers. The new landlords, generally speaking, have little or no sympathy with their peasantry, most of whom are Mussalmans. If the law gives them power, say, of enhancement or ejectment, it is worked without compunction and without mercy. I say this advisedly.[37]

This set a pattern which continued to be followed in Bengal politics in subsequent years. Thus, in 1928 at the time of amendment to the Bengal Tenancy Act, almost all the Hindu members of the Bengal Legislative Council, including those belonging to the Congress, voted in favour of the rights of landlords while most of the Muslim members supported the rights of the tenants.[38] The same division occurred ten years later at the time of the enactment of the Bengal Tenancy (Amendment) Act, 1938.[39]

The peasants had to pay to the landlords not only the legally fixed land revenue, but a number of illegal cesses of various types, including contributions towards celebrations of important Hindu festivals, like *Durga puja*. This led to large-scale indebtedness among them. As usury was prohibited among Muslims, most of the moneylenders were Hindus. So were the traders and shopkeepers. This added another dimension to Hindu-Muslim relations in Bengal and accentuated conflict. It was stated in evidence before the Indian Famine Commission of 1880 that the rates at which money or foodgrain was advanced was 'simply exorbitant'. The result often was that not only were all the peasants' savings swept into the moneylenders' coffers, but the adverse balance went on increasing, and the client was fortunate if he was not eventually ruined 'by being compelled to part with his plough, cattle and homestead'.[40] It is not, therefore, surprising that the Hindu-Muslim riots which took place in eastern Bengal in 1906-7 in the wake of the Swadeshi movement were 'communal in form, very largely agrarian in content'.[41] The main lesson of these riots, from the Muslim point of view, was that 'communalism to be really effective in Bengal must have an agrarian base'.[42]

There was no radical change in the situation in subsequent years. According to the report of the Bengal Banking Enquiry Commission, 1929-30, the rate of interest on loans in Dacca ranged from 12 per cent to 192 per cent, and in Mymensingh from 24 per cent to 225 per cent. These two districts belonged to the jute growing area of Bengal and peasants there were particularly hard up because of recurrent fluctuations in jute prices. This landed them more and more in debt, at exorbitant rates of interest, and accounts for the fact that, in the twenties of the present century, 'snatching of debt bonds constituted the single most important element in rural rioting'.[43] Indeed, the background of some of the riots in Bengal in the twenties and thirties was so heavily dominated by this economic factor that they have been considered by some, justifiably, as embodiments not of communal, but of basically economic conflicts. This is illustrated by the comment of the District Magistrate of Mymensingh on the disturbances in the Kishoreganj sub-division of that district in 1930. According to him, they were 'primarily economic with a necessary communal tinge'. This was so because more than 90 per cent of the peasants and debtors in the affected areas were Muslims while the majority of the money-lenders were Hindus. He added that as far as he knew, there had been no case of serious attack on any one except moneylenders; nor had any attempt been made to attack Hindus as Hindus.[44]

However, it must also be noted that only Hindus figured in all the reported instances of attacks on the moneylenders. Further, all attacks on the houses or shops of these moneylenders were carried on in day-time. It was said in the court on behalf of some of the raiders that to go out at night amounted to committing theft which was against the *shariah*; on the other hand, it was 'a brave and laudable action to commit loot and plunder at day time'.[45] It seems that, for whatever reason, the District Magistrate of Mymensingh was deliberately seeking to minimize the role of communalism. The reports from some of his subordinates definitely indicated that, while economic factors certainly predominated, communal passions also played their part and many Hindus, who were neither landlords nor moneylenders, were attacked by Muslims. The SDO of Kishoreganj, for instance, reported that all the Namasudra houses at Jaitra, evidently not belonging to the rich, had been looted and damaged. According to the Assistant Superintendent of Police, Mymensingh, Muslims had attacked about 70 Hindu houses at Bahadia 'including many huts of poor people'. Similarly, the Superintendent of Police noted about the market centres of Pulerghat and Kaliachhapra that 'loot was the object and since only Hindu shops were looted, Muhammedan shops being exempted, a certain amount of communal bias was evident'.[46] All this shows how the economic and communal motivations got meshed together.

Men like Syed Ameer Ali were even more incensed by the abysmally small representation of the Muslims of Bengal in higher echelons of government service. With the establishment of British rule, the higher positions in the army were all held by Britons and both Hindus and Muslims were excluded. Under the changes introduced by Cornwallis in the eighteenth century, Muslims were also edged out from top positions in revenue administration which were now given to Englishmen. For sometime, they continued to occupy important positions in the judiciary, but the replacement of Persian by English or the local vernacular as the court language in Bengal in 1837 and the requirement of English education as an essential qualification for holding senior offices in the administration seriously affected their position and their number in various services further declined. Here Hunter's testimony can be safely relied upon. According to his computation in 1871, in the highest grade among the gazetted officers of government, there was one Muslim to three Hindus; in the second grade, one Muslim to ten Hindus; in the third grade three Muslims to a total of twenty-seven Hindus and Englishmen; in the lower ranks, four Muslims among a total of thirty-nine; and among probationers, not a single Muslim. In the less conspicuous departments, the position was even worse. Thus, in 1869, in the three grades of assistant engineers there were fourteen Hindus and not one Muslim; among the apprentices four Hindus, two Englishmen and not one Muslim; among the sub-engineers and supervisors of the Public Works Department, twenty-four Hindus and one Muslim; among the overseers, sixty-three Hindus and two Muslims; in the office of Accounts, fifty Hindus and not one Muslim; and in the Upper Subordinate Department, twenty-two Hindus and not one Muslim. On the basis of this data, Hunter estimates that the proportion of Muslims to Hindus in the services in Bengal was less than one-seventh; that of Hindus to Europeans more than one-half; and that of Muslims to Europeans less than one-fourteenth. He further adds:

The proportion of the race, which a century ago had the monopoly of Government, has now fallen to less than one-twenty-third of the whole administrative body. This too, in the gazetted appointments, where the distribution of patronage is closely watched. In the less conspicuous office establishments in the Presidency Town, the exclusion of Mussalmans is even more complete. In one extensive Department the other day it was discovered that there was not a single *employee* who could read the Mussalman dialect; and, in fact, there is now scarcely a Government office in Calcutta in which a Muhammeden can hope for any post above the rank of porter, messenger, filler of ink-pots and mender of pens.[47]

While Hunter's data need not be questioned, the impression created by the tone of his writing requires to be moderated. The Muslims in Bengal had near monopoly of office in pre-British times only in the higher ranks of the army and a few civil departments, and not in all branches of administration as implied by him. As has been pointed out in a recent study: 'Even in the heyday of Muslim rule most of the well-to-do and literate inhabitants of east Bengal were not Muslims, but Hindus of the higher castes; the imposition of British rule strengthened, and did not create, their hold upon administration and the land.'[48] There is, however, no doubt that Muslim representation in the services in Bengal was going down in the second half of the nineteenth century. Thus, in 1867 Muslims formed 11.7 per cent of the Indians who held government jobs; twenty years later, they formed only 7 per cent. In 1871, they held about 12 per cent of the gazetted appointments; a decade later, they held only just over 8 per cent of these appointments.[49]

This downward trend was most marked in the legal profession. Among the judges of the High Court in Bengal, there were two Hindus, but no Muslim. Among the Law Officers of the Crown, there were four Englishmen, two Hindus and not one Muslim. Among the twenty-one senior officers of the High Court, there were seven Hindus but not one Muslim. Among Barristers-at-Law, there were three Hindus, but not one Muslim. The list of pleaders told a similar tale. Up to 1851 the number of Muslim pleaders was equal to the combined total of Hindu and British pleaders. Among the pleaders admitted to the rolls of the High Court between 1852 and 1868, however, there were two hundred and thirty-nine Hindus and only one Muslim. Among the attorneys, proctors and solicitors of the High Court, there were in 1869 twenty-seven Hindus and not one Muslim. Again, among the articled clerks, there were twenty-six Hindus and not one Muslim. 'It matters not to what department of the Profession I turn,' remarks

Hunter, 'the result is the same'.[50] In the profession of modern medicine, the situation was even worse. In 1869, the Calcutta University produced four graduates of medicine. Of these, three were Hindus, and one an Englishman. Out of eleven Bachelors of Medicine, ten were Hindus and one an Englishman. Among the hundred and four Licentiates in medicine, ninety-eight were Hindus, five Englishman and only one Muslim.[51]

The economic backwardness of the Muslims in Bengal went hand in hand with their backwardness in the field of modern education. This is testified by the fact that in 1874-5 while they constituted 48.8 per cent of the total population in Bengal proper (excluding Darjeeling and Jalpaiguri) Muslim students constituted only 29 per cent of the number of pupils in the schools therein.

The Muslim position in higher education was much worse than that indicated by these figures. As Rafiuddin Ahmed has remarked: 'The higher the education the rarer were the Muslims.' Thus, in 1875, Muslims constituted only 5.4 per cent of the total college enrolment in Bengal in contrast to Hindus who constituted 93.9 per cent. The situation was not very different at the secondary school level. It was only at the primary school level that the percentage of Muslim pupils approximated and in some cases even exceeded the general Muslim percentage in the population.[52]

The view popularized by Hunter, however, that Muslims in Bengal kept aloof from modern educational institutions, partly because for a long time they remained brooding in isolation over their lost glory and partly because the instruction imparted in such institutions was opposed to their tradition and culture, can no longer be considered tenable. Such a view is invalidated by the progress of modern education among Muslims in other parts of India, who were the inheritors of the same tradition and culture. As was pointed out by Lieutenant-Governor A.R. Thompson as early as 1885, the low education percentage of Muslims was generally confined to those areas where they occupied a comparatively low position in the social scale, the situation being reverse in those areas of the country where they were comparatively better off. This shows that the traditional explanation is not valid, and that it was poverty and not prejudice which accounted for the backward condition of Muslims in the field of education in Bengal.[53] Besides, facilities for English education were not equally available in all parts of Bengal. 'The upper class Muslims of Bengal', aptly observes Aparna Basu, 'were . . . not so much prejudiced against receiving English education, as they were limited in their opportunities of receiving it.' In support of this view, she points out that Calcutta, where Hindus predominated, saw the foundation of new schools and colleges. On the other hand, the eastern districts of Bengal, where Muslims predominated in the population, caught the attention of educational authorities much later. Besides, the majority of Muslims in eastern and northern Bengal were peasants, converts from low-caste Hindus, and their condition was not much different from the latter. Among the Hindus, it was mostly the members of the upper castes or the *bhadralok* who went to schools in large numbers. So did the Saiyads and Sheikhs among the Muslims. It is misleading to compare Hindus and Muslims as monolithic entities in this respect. 'In the three predominantly Muslim areas of East Bengal, West Punjab and Sind, the majority of the Muslims were illiterate, not so much because of pride of race, religious fears or memories of bygone superiority, but because they were cultivators to whom English education was neither useful nor necessary.'[54]

Whatever the cause, the fact cannot be denied that Muslims in Bengal were on the whole backward in modern education as compared to Hindus in the second half of the nineteenth century. Though the gap between the two communities in this field was gradually narrowed down, except at the university level, over a period of time, this coupled with the poor share of Muslims in government employment in Bengal contributed significantly to the building up of the myth, started by Hunter, that Muslims of India everywhere were lagging behind Hindus in the race of life and needed, on the one hand, serious efforts on the part of the Muslim community and, on the other, special consideration on the part of the government to rectify the balance. It was also this supposed Muslim backwardness in India everywhere which was used by Muslim leaders as the main ground for opposing recruitment to the various services through competitive examinations.

In Bengal, the gap between Hindus and Muslims, in terms of economic opportunities began to appear more and more glaring as Muslims became politically conscious and in spite of efforts to reduce this gap it continued to exist. Thus, as late as 1921, Muslims in Bengal were almost double the number of Hindus among ordinary cultivators, but only about one-third among landlords and middlemen. Besides, nearly all the big landlords were Hindus. Although Muslims outnumbered Hindus in some non-agriculturist occupations, like furniture and building industries, cartering, inland steamer and boat traffic, service on seafaring vessels, tailoring and butchering, and trade in means of transport, they were outnumbered by Hindus three to one in trade generally, by two to one in the police force, three to one in public administration, and nearly five to one in the professions and liberal arts.[55] When, with the rise of Muslims to power in the twenties and thirties, efforts were made to narrow this gap, there was stiff opposition from Hindus. This further strengthened the economic foundations of Muslim nationalism in Bengal.

V

Turning to the Punjab, we find that in the second half of the nineteenth century the majority of Muslims in the province were cultivators and hence quite backward in education compared to Hindus. Thus between 1858 and 1878, only 57 out of 3,155 graduates in the province were Muslims.[56] This was partly reflected in their share in government employment. Although constituting a majority of the population in Punjab (56 per cent), they had a smaller share in government employment compared to Hindus in 1871. This is clear from Table 2.8.

The disparity between Muslims and Hindus was explained by the provincial government in terms of the educational attainments of the members of the two communities. For appointment as extra assistant commissioners, *tahsildars* and *munsifs*, no examination test was required and this made the entry of many Muslims to these cadres possible, but they did not do equally well in securing appointment to those jobs which required special and technical education.[57] Like in Bengal, this situation gave substance to the widespread Muslim feeling that they were lagging behind Hindus in education and government employment, and therefore needed special protection against competition with the latter in these fields.

Another factor which had a great role in conditioning Hindu-Muslim relations in the Punjab was the ever present animosity between the Muslim peasants, on the one hand, and Hindu and Sikh moneylenders, on the other. Of course, all peasants were not Muslims, but since Muslims constituted a majority of the peasantry as well as of the population and most of the moneylenders were Hindus or Sikhs, relationship between the two had a tendency to exacerbate communal animosities. This was particularly true of the last quarter of the nineteenth century when peasants were being increasingly forced to part with their land because of their inability to pay off their debts.

TABLE 2.8

COMPARATIVE POSITION OF MUSLIMS AND HINDUS IN HIGHER GOVERNMENT APPOINTMENTS IN THE PUNJAB IN 1871-2

Appointments	Muslims	Hindus
Extra Assistant Commissioners	54	38
Tahsildars	50	72
Munsifs	28	46
Superintendents of Settlement	9	15
Total Administrative and Judicial Appointments	141	171
Executive and Asst. Engineers, Public Works Department	2	18
Assistant Surgeons	13	52
Professors and Headmasters Education Department	4	22
Forest Rangers, Forest Department	8	9
Grand Total	168	272

SOURCE: *Report of the Indian Education Commission* (1883), p. 503.

The magnitude of the problem can be imagined from the fact that by 1878, 7 per cent of the total agricultural land in the province was under mortgage. At about the same time, there were 798 mortgages in Amritsar as against only twenty-three recorded before 1865; and in Jullunder mortgages accounted for Rs. 14 lakhs as against only Rs. 40 thousand in the fifties. Taking the province as a whole, while mortgages had averaged only 15,000 a year in the early seventies, twenty years later (1888-93) they averaged over 50,000. In ten years between 1875-8 and 1884-8, the annual increase in the area under mortgage had risen from 165,000 to 385,000 acres.[58] As Malcolm Darling Lyall points out, Muslims, forming 56 per cent of the rural population of the Punjab, had 'necessarily to bear the major part of its debt'. What made the position worse was that this debt was almost entirely owed to Hindus and Sikhs, a fact not calculated to contribute towards the improvement of the relationship of Muslims with them.[59] This was particularly noticeable in Western Punjab where Muslims constituted an overwhelming majority. Referring to the situation there, Thorburn remarks in his pioneering study of this problem:

Throughout Eastern Europe the Jews are hated and persecuted rather because they are successful aliens and professors of an old-world faith than because they are successful. So with the *Bunniahs* of the Western Punjab. They offend not only because they thrive on the misfortunes of monotheistic agriculturists, but because they are interlopers and polytheists, if not idolators.[60]

This situation was further aggravated by the fact that the proportion of debtors amongst the Muslim peasantry was much larger than that among their Hindu counterparts. The settlement officer of Muzaffargarh (where there were 5 Muslims to 1 Hindu) reported in 1879 that 70 per cent of the Muslim proprietors, but only 30 per cent of the Hindu proprietors were in debt. Similarly, 40 per cent of Muslim tenants as against 20 per cent of Hindu tenants were in debt. Dealing with the causes of this difference in indebtedness among the members of the two communities, the settlement officer observed:

> Mohammedans are mostly spend thrift and improvident: the Hindus are the reverse. Mohammedans are nearly always uneducated: Hindus are always more or less educated. Hindus usually avoid acts that would bring them within the reach of the criminal law, while Mohammedans supply almost the whole criminal population, and so incur the expenses which follow from being suspected by the police and by being prosecuted. Mohammedans have only one source of income, viz., agriculture. Hindus, who own and cultivate land, almost always combine money-lending and trade with agriculture. Hindus acquire land as payment for debts. Mohammedans generally borrow money to buy land.[61]

While commenting on the settlement report of a part of that district, J.B. Lyall, Settlement Commissioner, commented: 'These *kirars* (as the Hindu moneylenders were popularly called) are the Jews of the country, and have special natural aptitude for earning and saving money.'[62] How the clash of interests caused by the juxtaposition of Muslim peasants and Hindu moneylenders influenced the minds of a section of Muslims and strengthened in them the image of an educated Hindu as a moneylender is illustrated by the following extract from the English translation of an Urdu poem, read by one Mohammad Shams-ud-Din at an anti-Congress meeting in the Punjab and published in 1889:

> There is a lust for starting a War
> A war between the mountain and the mustard seed.
> We will comment on this for welfare of all
> Moneylenders should listen to the truth.
> The bravery of the Congress is tormenting.
> The decision is made to confront imperialism

All this is but a sign of self-destruction
Listen, moneylenders, we speak for your own good.[63]

When the Government sought to help the peasants by putting restrictions on the transfer of land from agriculturist to non-agriculturist hands through the Punjab Alienation of Land Act (1901), which banned such transfer, except with the approval of the District Officer, opinion among the educated people in the Punjab was polarised largely on communal lines, Muslims generally supporting the measure and Hindus opposing it. This was not a passing phase but represented a continuing strand in the politics of the Punjab with urban Hindus feeling that the Act represented an unfair deal for them.[64]

The problem of peasant indebtedness was, of course, not solved by the Act. Its only result was that instead of the non-agriculturist moneylender, the field was soon occupied by the agriculturist moneylender. Agriculturists having a large holding or those able to supplement their income from agriculture by earnings in the army had a certain amount of surplus cash which they found very profitable to invest in moneylending at high rates of interest. Such agriculturist moneylenders included some Muslims also, who were able to overcome Islam's injunction against usury, but most of them consisted of Sikh and Hindu Jats. So the old problem of a clash of interests between Muslim debtors and Hindu and Sikh moneylenders remained in a new form, with this change that the plight of the former became more difficult than before. As Malcolm Darling Lyall describes the situation:

> The *sahukar* will occasionally forego part of his interest, but, as a villager in Ludhiana remarked, 'a Jat foregoes nothing—not even a pebble (*giti*)'. The Jat, too, being an agriculturist, knows how the cow can be milked, and is able to squeeze the last drop out of his client. Moreover, the *sahukar*, being timid by nature, can sometimes be intimidated, but 'the Jat seizes you by the throat and knocks you down'. As a zamindar said to the writer, if the Land Alienation Act has rescued the sheep from the wolf, it has only been to hand him over to the butcher.[65]

The Muslims' consciousness of their economic backwardness in contrast to the various advantages enjoyed by the Hindus and Sikhs was heightened by the fact that the latter not only constituted the bulk of moneylenders, but also that of traders. Thus, in 1881, Hindu and Sikh traders (numbering 73,000) combined numbered 6,10,000 in contrast to only 30,000 Muslim traders.[66] This situation continued up to the twentieth century. 'Of the occupations', declared a memorandum prepared by the Punjab Government in 1928, 'in which Hindus display a predominance out of proportion to their numbers, the most important is trade'. Thus out of about 1,750,000 persons supported by trade, Hindus accounted for 1,110,000, being 13 per cent of their population, as compared to 419,000 Muslims, less than 4 per cent of their population. Among the people engaged in banking, from the village moneylender to the city banking establishment, there were 128,000 Hindus as compared to 11,000 Muslims, the latter being surpassed even by Sikhs who came second with 16,000. Trade in foodstuffs supported 624,000 Hindus to 191,000 Muslims and 80,000 Sikhs. If those forms of trade in which Muslims generally specialized, like those of sellers of milk, petty hawkers, dealers in horses, cattle, sheep and goats, are excluded, the Hindu preponderance was even more marked and it became greater where Muslims predominated in the general population. 'Broadly speaking', the memorandum went on, 'it is not unfair to say that the peasant whenever he requires to borrow money to finance his crop, or to sell the crop when he has grown it and with the proceeds to purchase the necessaries and luxuries which he does not produce himself, has to turn to a Hindu for the purpose'.[67]

VI

The working of the economic factor behind apparently communal conflicts was really not confined to any particular area, but could be discerned in varying shapes and forms in several parts of India. A good example is provided by the Mappila or Moplah rebellion in 1921, when the poor Muslim peasants of Malabar (at that time in the Madras Presidency) rose in revolt against their Hindu landlords. The Bombay riots of 1928 really represented a clash between the striking workers of the Oil Installations at Sewri and the Pathan blacklegs who had been employed to break the strike; some of these Pathans had also been lending money to the workers at usurious rates of interest. Behind the Kanpur riots of 1931, which flared up on the occasion of a *hartal* as a mark of protest against the execution of Bhagat Singh, Sukhdeo and Rajguru, lurked the rivalry between Hindu shopkeepers and traders and their Muslim counterparts, the former resenting the latter's refusal to close their shops. In all these cases, 'the real economic causes were masked by religious causes'.[68]

Similarly, behind the Hindi-Urdu controversy, which flared up in northern India in the second half of the nineteenth century and continued right up to the eve of Partition, and carried on largely on cultural grounds, lurked the question of share in government jobs. Hindus pressed for the replacement of Urdu written in Persian characters by Hindi written in Devanagari script in courts and schools primarily because they thought it would end the special advantage enjoyed by Muslims in the matter of recruitment to government employment and enable Hindus to increase their share in it. And this was precisely the reason why Muslims opposed the introduction of Hindi. The following extract from a memorial on behalf of supporters of Urdu, submitted to the Indian Education Commission (1882-3) in the Punjab bears this out:

> At some other place the Hindu memorialists say that their learned pandits pine away in neglect because of the Persian characters. But this constitutes no sufficient reason why the majority of poor Muhammedans should be discarded from the offices and posts of Government and deprived of the means of earning their livelihood in order to make way for Hindi-writing Hindus, which no doubt is the ultimate end aimed at by the Hindi clamourers.[69]

The Hindi movement succeeded in Bihar in 1881 when the use of Persian characters in courts was replaced by that of Devanagari or Kaithi. This was followed by a decision in 1900 in UP providing for the use of Devanagari along with the Persian script in courts. The Muslim elite vehemently opposed that order. They particularly objected to part three of the Government resolution which provided that no person would be selected for any ministerial appointment, except in a purely English office, unless he could read and write both the Nagari and Persian characters fluently. Later this was modified by providing that the order would come into force after one year and any one appointed in the interval who knew one of the two languages but not the other would be required to qualify in the latter within one year of his appointment. Muslim fears were frankly expressed by Hamid Ali Khan, a barrister and member of the Indian National Congress, who wrote in his brochure on this subject that the above-mentioned rule would place the Muslims of UP, who were generally not acquainted with the Nagari characters, under 'unnecessary disadvantage', in respect of certain types of public appointments and would 'at least for a time deprive them of such appointments altogether'.[70] *The Muslim Chronicle*, published from Calcutta, in course of a leading article remarked in May 1900 that the Urdu issue affected 'the most vital interests' of the Muslim community and in that connection recalled what had happened to Bengali Muslims in the wake of the removal of Persian from courts in 1837 and the gradual introduction of Bengali.[71]

At the all-India level, the economic factor which contributed most to the rise and growth of separatism among the Muslim elite was, of course, the fact underlined by W.C. Smith that the share of Muslims in 'middle class development' was relatively weak as compared to that of the Hindus.[72] Communalism or separatism, according to him, was 'the nationalist ideology, adopted by the emergent and precarious Muslim middle class in its struggle against domination within India by the much more developed Hindu middle class'.[73] Smith ascribes the comparative weakness of the Muslim middle-class largely to the fact that while the Turko-Afghans and Mughals spread their rule by land from the north, the British extended their sway from the sea-coasts in the east, south and west. From this arose a situation in which generally 'the areas most affected by the Muslims, the areas where they established themselves most successfully as the upper class, were the areas least or last affected by the British'. The earliest centres of British power—Calcutta, Bombay and Madras—were all quite remote from the areas dominated by the Muslim upper class.[74]

Actually the relatively weak position of the Muslim middle class was not entirely a new development taking place in the wake of the establishment of British rule. Even under Mughal rule, while the Muslim upper class held a dominant share in high judicial, executive and military appointments, Hindus continued to dominate the fields of commerce, finance, and banking.[75] The exceptions to this were certain areas like western India where the Khojas, Memons and Bohras had an important share in commercial activity.[76] Hindus also dominated the lower sections of the administrative hierarchy, including the clerical positions. With the establishment of British rule the disparity between the two communities in the field of trade and industry became more marked. The Hindu trading and commerical classes, especially in the new cities of Calcutta, Bombay and Madras, took full advantage of the new opportunities in the field of commerce and expanded their operations. On the other hand, some of the trading and industrial activities in which the Muslims had a predominant share, like cotton textiles, other handicrafts and shipping, suffered a decline. The story of the decline of Indian textile industry is too well-known to require any recounting here. It will suffice to recall that the artisans engaged in this industry had been largely Muslims. The same was true of most of the other handicrafts which too suffered a decline with the establishment of British rule. Ashin Das Gupta has shown how the process of the establishment of that rule resulted in wholly wiping out the Muslim shipowners of Surat, Calicut, Musulipatam and Hugli. 'As the obviously wealthy element, they attracted the attention of the desperate, local officials, and as the obvious competitors, they stood no chance of collaboration with the English. Thus much of Muslim trade disappeared along with Muslim administration in the 18th century India. . . .'[77]

There is also no doubt that in the new commercial and industrial activities which developed after the establishment of British rule, Muslims generally had very little share. The jute industry centred in Bengal was mainly owned by Englishmen. The cotton textile industry was the first modern industry to be developed in India by Indians. But most of the 56 Indian owned cotton mills, which had sprung up in Bombay by 1880, were owned by Parsis and Bhatias and not one mill of any significance by a Muslim. The only cotton mill of any significance owned by a Muslim, the Curimbhai Cotton Mills, was projected in 1886. In modern banking and insurance, it was the same story. Between 1881 and 1906, as many as 176 new banking concerns had been founded, but Muslims had no significant share in this development. Of the many insurance companies established up to 1906, Muslims had a predominant share in only two: the Bombay Mutual Life Assurance Society and the Oriental Government Security Life Insurance Company. The Hindus dominated the share market everywhere. The comparatively small Muslim share in the commercial and industrial life of India under British rule is also illustrated by the decline in the nineteenth century of cities like Dacca, Murshidabad, Lucknow, Tanjore and Madurai in which Muslims predominated, and the rise of new cities like Calcutta, Bombay, Cawnpore and Ahmedabad in each one of which Hindus constituted an overwhelming majority of the population.[78] This is borne out by Table 2.9.

There was no appreciable change in the position of Muslims in the commercial and industrial field in the twentieth century. Table 2.10 illustrates the small Muslim share in the control of Indian industries in 1911 and 1931.

The situation might have been different if in addition to the Khojas, Memons and Bohras of western India, who had been participating in trade and commerce, the Muslim landlords of the Punjab and UP had also entered the field. But that was not to be. Apart from the fact that there was no tradition of trade and industry in their families, they

TABLE 2.9
COMPARATIVE FIGURES OF HINDU AND MUSLIM POPULATIONS IN THE NEW CITIES IN SECOND HALF OF THE NINETEENTH CENTURY

City	Hindus	Muslims	Total Population
Calcutta	553,271	249,939	847,796
Bombay	508,608	155,747	776,006
Madras	410,648	57,331	509,346
Cawnpore	144,013	47,949	197,170
Ahmedabad	129,505	38,159	185,889

SOURCE: *Census of India, 1901*, Vol. I.

were also hemmed in by the fact that most of them were in debt. And this debt, in most cases, was owed to Hindu moneylenders. Reference has been made earlier to the situation in the Punjab where a natural antipathy had developed between agriculturists and moneylenders. The situation in this respect was not very different in UP. This is borne out by the Report of the United Provinces Provincial Banking Enquiry Committee of 1929-30. A Muslim witness before the Committee, for instance, explained the growing indebtedness among Muslims in the province by referring to the high cost of living among Muslims as compared to others. The Muslims, according to him, had not adjusted to the changed circumstances and still followed the habits and ways which characterized them during the period of decadence

TABLE 2.10
INDUSTRIAL CONTROL BY COMMUNITY

	Number of Companies		Number of Directors	
	1911	1931	1911	1931
British	282	416	652	1,335
Parsis	15	25	96	261
Gujaratis	3	11	71	166
Jews	5	9	17	13
Muslims	—	10	24	70
Bengalis	8	5	48	170
Marwaris	—	6	6	146
Mixed	28	28	102	181
Total	341	510	1,016	2,342

SOURCE: M.M. Mehta, *Structure of Indian Industries* (Bombay, 1955), p. 352.

of Mughal rule. Their standard of living was generally more expensive than that of Hindus. Their economic position was also affected by the Muslim law of inheritance. In a Hindu joint family, widows got merely a life interest, daughters got nothing and the estate was managed by a *karta* or agent. Among Muslims, on the other hand, when the head of a family passed away, the division of property into innumerable shares was inevitable. Besides, a Muslim generally had a greater tendency to be involved in litigation than a Hindu. Family pride prevented him from taking to trade or commerce, unless he happened to be born into some trade, and even then he found it difficult to make both ends meet. The natural result of all this was that the Muslims fell into debt much more than the Hindus. The report of the Enquiry Committee added that because of indebtedness, much land was passing from Muslim and Rajput hands to moneylenders belonging to Brahmin, Kurmi, Jat or Vaish castes.[79] When it is remembered that the Muslim middle class emerged largely from Muslim landowning families,[80] the significance of Muslim landowner-Hindu moneylender syndrom in shaping the attitude of that class can be easily imagined.

Dealings with Hindu moneylenders also affected the attitude of the lower sections of the Muslim middle class, a portion of whom had emerged from the surviving Muslim artisans in towns. As D.R. Gadgil points out, in the twenties and thirties, all artisan industry, whether owned by Hindus or Muslims, suffered from lack of finance and of direct contact with sources of raw materials and markets, when they were not local. 'The result was complete dependence on moneylenders and trader intermediaries, high costs and low earnings.'[81]

The lack of a substantial Muslim share in modern commerce, industry and banking was further highlighted by the absence of modern industries in those areas of north India, both in the east and the west, where Muslims predominated in the population. This was in spite of their being exceptionally rich in natural resources such as jute in Eastern Bengal and cotton in the Punjab and Sind, constituting 'the most important raw material base of the two biggest manufacturing industries of undivided India'.[82] On the eve of partition, out of a total production of one million bales of high quality, long staple cotton in West Punjab and Sind, 80 per cent was consumed by mills located in territories that remained in India and the rest exported. Similarly, while East Bengal produced 73.4 per cent of the total jute produced in the country, the jute mills were all located around Calcutta in West Bengal.[83] As Rehman Sobhan observes, this turned the areas which were to form Pakistan into 'the rural hinterland of India'.[84] It naturally provided invaluable support to the argument of the protagonists of Pakistan that Muslims could look forward to a secure economic future only in a separate State of their own, free from Hindu domination.

NOTES

1. W.W. Hunter, *The Indian Mussalmans* (Lahore, 1968, rpt. from the 1871 edn), p. 133.
2. Ibid., pp. 127-8.
3. Ibid., p. 151.
4. See, for instance, Asoka Mehta and Achyut Patwardhan, *The Communal Triangle in India* (Allahabad, 1942), pp. 80-103; *Jawaharlal Nehru: An Autobiography* (London, 1936), p. 460, and *The Discovery of India* (Calcutta, 1946), pp. 362-3; and Rajendra Prasad, *India Divided* (Bombay, 1947, 3rd edn), p. 95.
5. Wilfred Cantwell Smith, *Modern Islam in India* (London, 1946), p. 163.
6. See, for instance, A.R. Desai, *Social Background of Indian Nationalism* (Bombay, 1957), p. 362; Ram Gopal, *Indian Muslims: A Political History, 1858-1947* (Bombay, 1959), pp. 26-9; and Rafiq Zakaria, *Rise of Muslims in Indian Politics* (Bombay, 1970), pp. 5-25.
7. P.C. Joshi, 'The Economic Background of Communalism in India', in B.R. Nanda, ed., *Essays in Modern Indian History* (Delhi, 1980), p. 172 (Emphasis in the original).
8. Aparna Basu, *Education and Political Development in India, 1898-1920* (Delhi, 1974), pp. 147-50.
9. *Report of the Indian Education Commission* (Calcutta, 1883), p. 484.
10. The Government of India, in its Resolution no. 300, dated Simla, 7 August 1871, advised the various provincial Governments to provide encouragement to the teaching of the classical and vernacular languages of Muslims, provide more Muslim teachers of English in schools and facilitate the starting of their own schools by Muslims. See *Report of Indian Education Commission* (1883), p. 484.
11. The Indian Education Commission, 1882-3, made seventeen recommendations for encouragement of modern education among Muslims, including, among other things, provision of special scholarships and freeships for Muslims, appointment of Muslim teachers and inspectors, and special consideration for educated Muslims in the distribution of Government's patronage. Ibid., pp. 505-7. Most of these recommendations were accepted by the government.
12. *Report of the Indian Education Commission* (1883), p. 275.
13. *Progress of Education in India, 1927-32*, Vol. I, p. 241.
14. Thomas R. Metacalf, *The Aftermath of Revolt: India, 1857-1870* (Princeton, 1964), pp. 298-302.
15. See Zafarul Islam and Raymond L. Jansen, 'Indian Muslims and the Public Service', *Journal of the Asiatic Society of Pakistan* (Dacca), Vol. IX, No. I, June 1965, pp. 85-149. The lines quoted occur on p. 148.

16. *Islington Commission Report*, 1913 (Calcutta, 1914), pp. 509-10.
17. *Census of India*, 1911, Vol. I, pt. I, p. 129.
18. Aparna Basu, 'Growth of Education and Muslims Separatism, 1919-1939', in Nanda, n. 7, pp. 228-9.
19. For a detailed elucidation of this point see Bipan Chandra, *Communalism in Modern India* (New Delhi, 1984), pp. 34-5.
20. See Francis Robinson, *Separatism Among Indian Muslims: The Politics of the United Provinces Muslims*, 1860-1923 (Cambridge, 1974), pp. 3-5.
21. Paul R. Brass, 'Muslim Separatism in the United Provinces: The Social Context and Political Strategy of the Muslim Minority Before Partition', in his *Language, Religion and Politics and North India* (Cambridge, 1974), pp. 141-56.
22. Robinson, n. 20, pp. 15-20.
23. *Census of India, 1911*, Vol. XV, *United Provinces of Agra and Oudh*, pt. I, pp. 411-12.
24. Robinson, n. 20, p. 38.
25. See Lance Brennan, 'The Illusion of Security: The Background to Muslim Separatism in the United Provinces', *Modern Asian Studies*, Vol. XVIII, No. 1 (1984), pp. 237-76.
26. This was by no means the first political organization of Indian Muslims in modern times, but the one that was, 'Anjuman-i-Islamia' or 'Muhammedan Association' was also founded in Calcutta in 1855; it, of course, did not last long, see S.R. Mehrotra, *The Emergence of the Indian National Congress* (New Delhi, 1971), p. 212.
27. N.G. Barrier, 'The Punjab Government and Communal Politics, 1870-1908', *Journal of Asian Studies*, Vol. XXVII, No. 3, 1968.
28. A.H.M. Nooruzzaman, 'Rise of the Muslim Middle Classes as a Political Factor in India and Pakistan, 1858-1947' (unpublished Ph.D. Thesis, University of London, 1964), p. 42.
29. Sufia Ahmed, *Muslim Community in Bengal, 1884-1912* (Dacca, 1974), pp. 99-103. See also Amalendu De, *Roots of Separatism in Nineteenth Century Bengal* (Calcutta, 1974), pp. 15-18.
30. A.K.N. Karim, 'The Modern Muslim Political Elite in Bengal' (Unpublished Ph.D. Thesis, University of London, 1964), p. 272.
31. *Census of India*, 1911, Vol. V, pt. 1, p. 553.
32. Partha Chatterjee, 'Agrarian Relations and Communalism in Bengal', in Ranajit Guha, ed., *Subaltern Studies* (Delhi 1982), pp. 10-11.
33. Partha Chatterjee, 'Bengal Politics and the Muslim Masses, 1920-1945', in *The Journal of Commonwealth and Comparative Politics,* Vol. XX, No. 1, March 1982, pp. 31-2.
34. See, for instance, Azizur Rahman Mallick, *British Policy and the Muslims in Bengal* (Dacca, 1977; 2nd edn), pp. 38-9.
35. N.K. Sinha, *The Economic History of Bengal from Plassey to the Permanent Settlement*, II (Calcutta, 1962), p. 229. See also A.F. Salahuddin Ahmad, 'Muslim Thought and Leadership in Bengal in the Nineteenth Century', in *Essays in Honour of Professor S.C. Sarkar* (New Delhi, 1976), pp. 633-5.
36. Sufia Ahmed, n. 29, pp. 110-11.
37. Ibid., pp. 111-12.

38. See Partha Chatterjee, 'Agrarian Relations and Politics in Bengal: Some Considerations on the Making of the Tenancy Act Amendment 1928', *Occasional Paper No. 30,* Centre for Studies in Social Sciences, Calcutta (September, 1980). See also the same author's *Bengal 1920-1947,* Vol. I. *The Land Question* (Calcutta, 1984), pp. 81-4.
39. For details see *Bengal Legislative Assembly Proceedings,* 1937, Vol. II, No. 4, pp. 1319-403, 2274-315. For a summary of the benefits conferred by this measure on the peasantry, see Shila Sen, *Muslim Politics in Bengal, 1937-1947* (New Delhi, 1976), p. 102.
40. Sufia Ahmed, n. 29, p. 113.
41. Sumit Sarkar, *The Swadeshi Movement in Bengal* (New Delhi, 1973), p. 441.
42. Ibid., p. 462.
43. Tanika Sarkar, 'Communal Riots in Bengal', in Mushirul Hasan, ed., *Communal and Pan-Islamic Trends in Colonial India* (New Delhi, 1981), p. 293.
44. Cited in Partha Chatterjee, n. 32, p. 30.
45. Ibid., p. 31.
46. See Sugata Bose, 'The Roots of Communal Violence in Rural Bengal: A Study of the Kishoreganj Riots of 1930', *Modern Asian Studies,* Vol. XVI, No. 3 (1982), p. 485 and the same author's *Agrarian Bengal: Economy, Social Structure and Politics, 1919-1947* (Cambridge, 1986), pp. 181-232; also Tanika Sarkar, *Bengal, 1928-1934: The Politics of Protest* (Delhi, 1987), pp. 38-124. For a somewhat different view of the Kishoreganj riots of 1930 (i.e. emphasis on their class character), see Suranjan Das, *Communal Riots in Bengal 1905-1947* (Delhi, 1991), pp. 131-2.
47. Hunter, n. 1, pp. 142-5.
48. Anil Seal, *The Emergence of Indian Nationalism* (Cambridge, 1971), p. 301.
49. Ibid., p. 302.
50. Hunter, n. 1, pp. 146-7.
51. Ibid., pp. 148-9.
52. Rafiuddin Ahmed, *The Bengal Muslims, 1871-1906* (Delhi, 1981), p. 135.
53. Shila Sen, n. 39, p. 6.
54. Aparna Basu, n. 8, pp. 152-5.
55. *Census of India,* 1921, Vol. V, pt. I, pp. 413-14.
56. Mushirul Hasan, *Nationalism and Communal Politics in India* (New Delhi, 1979), p. 17.
57. *Report of the Indian Education Commission* (1883), pp. 503-4.
58. Malcolm Lyall Darling, *The Punjab Peasant in Prosperity and Debt* (London, 1925), pp. 208-9.
59. Ibid., p. xvi.
60. S.S. Thorburn, *Mussalmans and Money-Lenders in the Punjab* (Edinburgh, 1886), p. 1.
61. Ibid., p. 85.
62. Ibid.
63. Cited in N. Gerald Barrier, *The Punjab Alienation of Land Bill of 1900* (Duke University, 1965), pp. 60-9. See also Satya M. Rai, *Partition of the Punjab* (Bombay, 1965), pp. 28-9; and P.H.M. van den Dungen, *The Punjab Tradition* (London, 1972), pp. 264-5, 285-6.
64. For an example of continued urban Hindu hostility to the Act, see Raja

Narendranath, 'Punjab Agrarian Laws and their Economic and Constitutional Bearing', *Modern Review*, Vol. LVX, No. 1, January 1939, p. 20.

65. Darling, n. 58, p. 230.
66. Thorburn, n. 60, p. 35.
67. *Memorandum Prepared for the Use of the Simon Commission by the Government of the Punjab* (Lahore, 1928), Vol. I, pt. I, p. 8.
68. K.B. Krishna, *The Problem of Minorities* (London, 1939), pp. 265-92. In this connection, it is significant that the Mappila reprisals against landlords were characterized more by destruction of records and plunder of property than by physical violence or forcible conversion to Islam; see K.N. Panikkar, *Against Lord and State: Religion and Peasant Uprisings in Malabar, 1836-1921* (Delhi, 1989), pp. 169-87. Also Robert L. Hardgrave, J.R., 'The Mapilla Rebellion, 1921: Peasant Revolt in Malabar', *Modern Asian Studies*, Vol. XI, No. 1 (1977), pp. 57-100. Gyanendra Pandey has shown a similar situation in Azamgarh district in eastern UP during the communal riots there in 1813 and 1842: the Muslim weavers while defiling the Hindu temple also attacked the houses and account-books of some of the big Hindu traders and moneylenders; see Gyanendra Pandey, *The Construction of Communalism in Colonial North India* (Delhi, 1990), p. 179.
69. Education Commission, *Report of the Punjab Provincial Committee* (Calcutta, 1884), p. 574.
70. Hamid Ali Khan, *The Vernacular Controversy* (n.d., n.p., but perhaps published in 1900; presented by the author to the British Museum on 8 February 1902), pp. 9-11, 28.
71. Ibid., p. 53.
72. Smith, n. 5, p. 163.
73. Ibid., p. 180.
74. Ibid., p. 164.
75. D.H. Buchanan, *Development of Capitalistic Enterprise in India* (Cambridge, 1934), pp. 147-8.
76. B.B. Misra, *The Indian Middle Classes* (London, 1961), p. 248.
77. Ashin Das Gupta, 'Trade and Politics in 18th Century India', in D.S. Richards, ed., *Islam and the Trade of Asia: A Colloquium* (Oxford, 1970), p. 207. See also Ratna Naidu, *The Communal Edge to Plural Societies: India and Malayasia* (Sahibabad, 1980), pp. 27-8.
78. Rafiq Zakaria, n. 6, pp. 266-72. See also Radhe Shyam Rungta, *The Rise of Business Corporations in India, 1851-1900* (Cambridge, 1970), pp. 164-241.
79. *Report of the United Provinces Banking Enquiry Committee, 1929-30*, Vol. I, (Allahabad, 1930), pp. 41, 125-7, cited in P.C. Joshi, n. 7, pp. 175-6.
80. See Z.V. Gankovsky and L.R. Gordon-Polonskaya, *A History of Pakistan* (Moscow, 1964), p. 15.
81. D.R. Gadgil, *The Industrial Evolution of India in Recent Times 1860-1939* (London, 1971; 5th edn.), p. 334. See also Gyanendra Pandey, n. 68, pp. 72-9.
82. Amiya Kumar Bagchi, *Private Investment in India, 1900-1939* Cambridge, 1972), pp. 432-3. See also Penderel Moon, *Divide and Quit* (London, 1961), p. 288.
83. C.N. Vakil, *Economic Consequences of the Partition* (Bombay, 1948), pp. 17,

40. See also Akhlaqur Rahman, ***Partition, Integration and Economic Growth and Inter-Regional Trade, 1948-1959*** (Dacca, 1963).

84. Rehman Sobhan, 'Political Dimensions of South Asian Cooperation: The Perspective for Bangladesh', V. Kanesalingam, ed., ***Political Dimensions of South Asian Cooperation*** (Delhi, 1991), p. 35.

CHAPTER III

Ideological and Emotional Environment of the Muslim Elite

THE INTELLECTUAL and emotional environment of the Muslim elite in the nineteenth and twentieth centuries was dominated by Islamic revival and reformation, a situation similar to that of the Hindu elite whose intellectual environment was dominated by Hindu revival and reformation. At times the roles of the revivalists and reformers overlapped in both the communities because both were primarily concerned with their all-round regeneration. They emphasized religious revival and reformation not so much because they were deeply interested in religion *per se*, but because they considered religion as holding the key to the regeneration of the community. The challenge posed by the Christian missionary propaganda also necessitated, in their view, an emphasis on religion in order to ensure that modernization did not result in conversion to Christianity, and educated Hindus and Muslims were able to hold their heads high and make the required changes without losing faith in their own religions. With a few exceptions, the leaders of such movements in one community were not hostile to the other community or its religion, but the very nature of their task ordained an exclusive attention to or emphasis upon the problems of only one community. Such attention or emphasis, in its turn, was bound to foster only a Hindu consciousness or a Muslim consciousness and hamper the growth of an all-inclusive, Indian consciousness.

The movement for Islamic revival and reformation in India in the colonial period owed a good deal to the pioneering efforts of Shah Waliullah who flourished in the eighteenth century (1703-62). According to Muhammad Iqbal (1875-1938), himself one of the greatest leaders of Islamic revival and reformation in India, Shah Waliullah was the first Indian Muslim 'who felt the urge of the new spirit in him'.[1] Hafeez Malik has described him as 'the founder of modern Islam in India'.[2] According to Aziz Ahmad, he 'forms the bridge between medieval and modern Islam in India'.[3] M. Mujeeb does not see 'all the modernism that has been read into his works',[4] and asserts that there is no evidence to show that he made any effort at the reinterpretation of the sources of religion, or even at a change in emphasis.[5] However, Mujeeb accepts that Shah Waliullah 'did stimulate thought' and 'struck out a new path'.[6]

Shah Waliullah did not face the problem of propaganda by Christian missionaries, but he was extremely worried by the decay in Muslim society in the wake of the disintegration of the Mughal empire after the passing away of Aurangzeb (AD 1707). The fundamental remedy for it, according to him, lay in the revitalization of Islam both as a system of faith and as a social order. For this, he laid great stress on freeing Islam from the crusts or accretions which had accumulated around it through the centuries, and restoring to it the austere simplicity and vitality it had possessed during the days of Prophet Muhammad and the first two Caliphs. He attacked *taqlid* (imitation) and championed *ijtihad* (reasoned reconstruction). 'Time has come', he wrote in *Hujjat Allah Al-baligha*, his greatest work, 'that the religious law of Islam should be brought into the open fully dressed in reason and argument.'[7] He tried to end dissensions among Muslims through an integration (*tatbiq*), on the one hand, of the four main systems of law which were generally followed by Muslim scholars, selecting the best elements of each in the context of the teachings of the Prophet and the first two Caliphs, and, on the other, the reconciliation of the remnants of various Sufi disciplines with orthodox Islam. This integration or reconciliation did not include within its scope the tenets of the Shia faith,[8] but in other ways he tried to end the bitter hostility between the Sunnis and the Shias, and, unlike other Sunni divines, refused to condemn them as infidels or heretics.[9] On the other hand, he exhorted Muslims to free themselves from the practices and customs of the Hindus which had crept into them through long association between the two on Indian soil. His greatest emphasis was on the study of the Koran and *Hadith* (traditions of the Prophet), and he was very keen to spread their knowledge among Muslims. With this end in view, he translated the Koran into Persian, the language almost every educated Indian Muslim understood, so that it could be more widely read. He was widely attacked for this by the *ulama*, but he did not care.[10] In his *Wasiyat Nama* he exhorted Muslims to hold firmly to the Koran and the *Sunnah* (the example of the Prophet), follow what was enjoined therein and eschew what was forbidden and avoid any relationship with those who might be indifferent in these respects.[11] His efforts at the revival of Muslim rule in India and his views regarding the position of Hindus under such a rule have already been referred to in the first chapter.

After the passing away of Shah Waliullah, his mantle fell on his eldest son, Shah Abdul Aziz (1746-1824), who continued to teach at the school set up by his father and applied himself in other ways to spreading the latter's message. His three younger brothers fully cooperated with him, two of them making a significant contribution to the movement of Islamic revival by translating the Koran, for the first time, into Urdu, thus making it possible for a much larger number of Muslims than before to read that sacred book. Shah Rafi-al-Din's translation, a literal rendering, was the first to appear. This was followed by Shah Abd al-Qadir's which had been prepared in idiomatic Urdu and was much more readable. It has generally been assumed that by signing a *fatwa* describing India under British rule to be *dar-ul-harb* (land of the enemy), Shah Abdul Aziz sanctioned a *jihad,* or holy war, against it and blessed the movement of the *mujahidin* (holy warriors) or the *tahriq-i-muhammadiya*, led by Syed Ahmad Shahid of Rai Bareilly (1786-1831),[12] which has for long been wrongly decribed as the Wahhabi movement because of certain common features which it shared with the contemporaneons movement of that name in Arabia.

Sayyid Ahmad Shahid valiantly carried forward the mission initiated by Shah Waliullah and continued by Shah Abdul Aziz. His exertions in organizing an army, carrying on a bitter struggle against the Sikhs in the Punjab, and his ultimate objective of ending the British rule in India with a view to re-establishing Muslim rule and turning India from *dar-ul-harb* to *dar-ul-Islam* (land of peace) need not be discussed here. It will suffice for our purpose to note that because of his exertions, Shah Waliullah's message no longer remained confined to the Muslim elite, but also reached the Muslim masses from the north-west frontier to Bengal. The essentials of that message, as propagated by Sayyid Ahmad Shahid, did not change in any way. The emphasis, as before, continued to be on firm adherence to the Koran and the *Sunnah*, and rejection of all accretions, particularly those from Hindu beliefs and practices. The attitude of the *mujahidin* movement towards Hindu religion itself, however, was marked by tolerance. This comes out clearly in the writings of Shah Ismail Shahid (1781-1831), a grandson of Shah Waliullah and a close associate of Sayyid Ahmad Shahid.[13]

After the defeat and death of Sayyid Ahmad Shahid at Balakot (1831) at the hands of the Sikhs, his disciples continued his work. Some of them participated in the revolt of 1857 and continued their activities even after the suppression of that revolt. It was only in the 1860s that the British were able to suppress them finally. Even after this, Sayyid Ahmad Shahid's religious teachings continued to be preached for a long time. This was so particularly in Bengal and Bihar where a number of his disciples remained active for a long time. The most famous among them were the Patna Caliphs, Maulvi Wilayat Ali (1791-1835) and Maulana Ianayat Ali (1794-1858). Karamat Ali (1800-74) who, in 1867, broke away from the movement associated with Sayyid Ahmad Shahid and his disciples and founded a separate movement called *Taiyuni*, also did a lot to spread the teachings of Islam in rural Bengal.

In the meanwhile, a contemporary of Sayyid Ahmad Shahid, but drawing inspiration from the Wahhabi movement in Arabia, where he had spent about eighteen years of his life, Haji Shariatullah (1781-1840) had started a powerful movement of Islamic revival and reform in eastern Bengal, generally known as the *Faraizi* movement (because of his insistence on *Faraiz*, i.e. the obligation to carry on the duties imposed by God and His Prophet). He not merely declared India to be *Dar-ul-harb*, but even forbade the holding of the customary Friday prayers on this account. His son and successor, Dudu Miyan (1819-62), organized his followers more systematically and gave his movement a greater social and political orientation, calling upon the Muslim peasants to resist the illegal levies imposed upon them by the landlords, most of whom were Hindus. Western Bengal became the scene of another movement of Muslim peasantry under the leadership of Titu Mir (1782-1831), inspired by the teachings of Sayyid Ahmad Shahid. Both these movements, apart from championing the cause of the peasantry, emphasized the urgent need for Muslims to return to the austere faith enshrined in the Koran and the teachings of the Prophet, and give up the 'pernicious' customs and beliefs acquired from contact with the Hindus. Sometimes the peasant struggles led by them resulted in attacks on Hindu temples along with those on Hindu landlords, though Muslim landlords, who oppressed their tenants, were also not spared. The political significance of these movements has already been briefly discussed earlier. It would suffice to emphasize that they not merely preached religious reform, but spread social and political awakening among the Muslim masses of rural Bengal and thus 'helped to transform a people into a community'.[14] Besides, they also provided a living link between Bengal and the movements of Islamic renewal and revitalization in other parts of northern India.[15]

II

The movements for Islamic revival and reformation, which arose in the second half of the nineteenth century may broadly be divided into two streams: traditionalist and modernist. Both claimed to be inspired by the teachings of Shah Waliullah, but while the former emphasized going back to the Koran, the *Hadith* and the *Sunnah*, the latter, without detracting in any way from the value of these, emphasized *Ijtihad* and called for a reinterpretation of Islam with the help of reason and argument, keeping in view the requirements of the present-day world. Deoband became the main centre of the former, and Aligarh of the latter.[16]

The religious seminary at Deoband (near Delhi) was founded in 1867 by a group of *ulama* led by Muhammad Qasim Nanautovi and Rashid Ahmad Gangohi, both disciples of Imdadullah, a famous divine of the Waliullah school. All three of them are generally reputed to have taken an active part in the revolt of 1857; after its collapse Imdadullah, migrated to Mecca and the other two were let off without any severe punishment by the British for lack of evidence.[17] The seminary began in a modest way, but gradually established itself as the leading centre of learning in the field of Islamic theology in India and second only to the seminary at Al Azhar (Cairo) in the entire Muslim world. It drew scholars not merely from all parts of India, but also from a number of foreign countries. Its syllabus followed the traditional path and included such subjects as Arabic and Persian grammar, prosody and literature, history of Islam, logic, *hadis*, etc. Modern science was not included. In the beginning, the course extended up to ten years but was later restricted to six. The main emphasis was on training scholars in Islamic theology so that they might be able to provide religious guidance to Muslims in regulating their lives according to the tenets of Islam. In this, it was highly successful and its products were to be found all over India providing religious guidance to the Muslim population.

The views of Deoband's eminent leaders were increasingly sought by members of the *ulama* on various social and political issues and these were given in the form of *fatwas*. Indeed so many *fatwas* had to be issued that in due course Deoband came to have a separate department for it. The leaders and products of Deoband took active interest in the religious controversies of the day and engaged in frequent disputations with the champions of Hindu revival and reformation as well as with Christian missionaries. They laid particular emphasis on preserving and strengthening the separate religious and social identity of Muslims. Some of the *fatwas* issued by Rashid Ahmad Gangohi in the 1880s, for instance, discouraged too much social contact with Hindus, called for the removal of Hindu beliefs and practices and the avoidance of any similarity with them in appearance 'whether in dress, hair style, or the use of brass instead of copper vessels'.[18]

The Deobandis, of course, treated the teachings of Syed Ahmad Khan (1817-98) as nothing short of poison in religious matters. In political matters also they refused to support his view that Muslims must remain aloof from the Indian National Congress. When around 1889 this question was posed before Gangohi, he observed that Muslims should not join Syed Ahmad Khan, who administered 'sweet poison', but they could join Hindus, provided such association did not lead them to do anything against the teachings of their religion, or cause degradation or humiliation of Muslims or 'even assist the progress of Hindus'.[19]

III

In political matters in late nineteenth century, however, what was of crucial importance was not the views of the *ulama*, but those of the Muslims of the middle-class, educated in modern educational institutions and seeking positions for themselves in the new dispensation established by the British. It is they who were going to shape the future and, by and large, they followed the lead of Syed Ahmad Khan and Aligarh. A scion of the Mughal nobility, Syed Ahmad Khan had realized quite early that the days of Mughal glory were over and had taken up service under the East India Company's government in a low, clerical position. Rising from that position by dint of hard work, character and personality he had become a judicial officer of medium rank (subordinate judge) and was serving in that position at Bijnor in UP when the revolt of 1857 broke out. He loyally served the British and helped them out of a critical situation there.[20] But far from seeking to reap a reward for himself for such activity after the British success in suppressing that revolt, as most others who had sided with the British on that occasion did, he was filled with utmost remorse at the sad plight of his countrymen, particularly Muslims, whom the British generally considered to have been primarily responsible for the revolt. Muslim families in Delhi, where Syed Ahmad's own family also lived, had particularly been subjected to unspeakable sufferings and hardships. Many who did not die at the hands of the British soldiers perished as a result of shock and privation later. Among such persons were several of Syed Ahmad Khan's close kinsmen and relatives, including his mother and uncle. His feeling of remorse must have been deepened by the thought that in that conflict he had been on the side of the British and against his own people. Indeed, he felt so miserable that he contemplated leaving India and settling in Egypt. He, however, rejected that step as being cowardly and self-centred and decided instead to remain in India and dedicate himself to the service of his community. That would be his atonement. He had, of course, even before 1857 written a number of books in Urdu, which not merely show his abilities as a writer, but also his concern for purification of certain Islamic practices, not unnatural for a person associated in his formative years with the descendants and disciples of Shah Waliullah.[21] It can, however, be legitimately said that it is only after 1857 that his career of dedicated public service began. Thus, the trauma of 1857 proved a turning point in his life and launched him on the road to leadership.[22]

As Syed Ahmad Khan surveyed the plight of Muslims in India after the revolt of 1857, he came to the conclusion that they could have a future only if they were prepared to come to terms with the then existing reality around them. That reality was represented by the British power in India which was there to stay, if not for ever, for a very very long time. He, of course, never lost consciousness of the fact that not long ago Muslims had been the ruling power in India, but emphasized that it was not a time for brooding, but for action to build up the community afresh in order to secure for it a position of prestige and power commensurate with its past. This would require not only cooperation with the British, but also an appreciation of the strong points of the modern civilization which they represented and an adoption of that civilization without giving up the fundamentals of the Muslims' own faith. He, in short, became for the Muslims what Rammohun Roy (1772-1833) had earlier been for the Hindus—the herald of a new age and the founder of their modern consciousness. His path was full of difficulties, for the majority of the Muslim elite still clung uncritically and broodingly to their past and bitterly opposed him. But if he had opponents, he also had followers and supporters. The latter belonged to 'the incipient Muslim bourgeoisie, created by and developing under the bureaucratic and industrial imperialism of the British, as it more and more reached the northern, Muslim parts of India'.[23] Mainly landlords and government servants, they were keen to progress under the r ew dispensation without having to give up their past cultural heritage. Syed Ahmad Khan became their messiah.

The first major task which he set before himself was, on the one hand, to turn the mind of his co-religionists from brooding and opposition to the British to their willing acceptance of and active participation in the advantages and responsibilities accruing from it and, on the other, to turn the mind of the British rulers from distrust and hostility towards Muslims to understanding and sympathy. With a view to influencing the latter, he wrote, mainly for the perusal of high British officials, a treatise (in Urdu) on the *Causes of Indian Revolt* (1859) showing therein that the revolt had been caused not by a so-called Muslim conspiracy, but by the mistakes committed by the British rulers, their lack of understanding of the feelings of the ruled as a consequence of the absence of any Indian members in the legislative councils, and their disregard for the sentiments and interests of the Indian people. In order to disabuse the British of their distrust of the Muslims, he went so far as to criticize the British for having kept Hindu and Muslim soldiers in the same regiments and to argue that if this had not been done, the latter might not have joined the revolt at all. As he put it:

> When Nadir Shah conquered Khorassan, and became master of the two kingdoms of Persia and Afghanistan, he invariably kept the two armies at equal strength. . . . When the Persian army attempted to rise, the Afghan army was at hand to quell the rebellion, and *vice-versa*. The English did not follow this precedent in India. . . .
>
> Government certainly did put the two antagonistic races into the same regiment, but constant intercourse had done its work, and the two races in regiment had almost become one. It was but natural and to be expected that a feeling of friendship and brotherhood must spring up between the men of a regiment, constantly brought together as they were. . . .
>
> If a portion of the regiment engaged in anything, all the rest joined. If separate regiments of Hindus and separate regiments of Mohammedans had been raised, this feeling of brotherhood could not have arisen, and, in my opinion, the Mohammedan regiment, would not have refused to receive the new cartridges.[24]

Syed Ahmad Khan followed this up by a serial publication, entitled *The Loyal Mohammedans of India* (1860) with a view to apprising both the British officials and the Indian people of the 'eminent services' rendered by Muslims during the revolt of 1857-8 and the reward received by them. Here he asserted that 'if in Hindustan there was one class of people above another who, from the principles of their religion, from habits and associations, and from kindred disposition, were fast bound with Christians, in their dread hour of trial and danger, in the bonds of amity and friendship, those people were the Mohammedans. . . '. He further pointed out that during the days of the revolt he did not see that 'any class besides the Mohammedans displayed so much single-minded and earnest devotion to the interests of government, or so willingly sacrificed reputation and status, life and prosperity, in its cause'. The Muslims did so because, in his view, it was their religious duty 'to identify themselves heartily with the Christians and to espouse their cause', for the Christians, like the Muslims, had been favoured with a revelation from heaven, believed in the prophets and held sacred the word of God in His holy book.[25] In 1862, he published a commentary on the Bible, the first such book to be written by a Muslim anywhere in the world. Here he underplayed the differences between Islam and Christianity and tried to focus on the similarities between the two faiths.[26] Indeed, almost on every page he seemed to be saying to his co-religionists: 'Look, what similarities there are between our faith and Christianity, the creed of the English.'[27]

When in 1871, W.W. Hunter published his famous book on Indian Muslims and asserted therein that Muslims were naturally prone to rebel against the British rulers because of their religion and dilated upon the seriousness of the threat to British power posed by the so-called Wahhabi movement, Syed Ahmad Khan wrote a detailed review of the book (1872) pointing out its shortcomings. He asserted that Hunter was wrong in his assumption that all Wahhabis were rebels and that religious reformation preached by them was bound to foster rebellious tendencies among Muslims. According to him, religious reformation among Muslims was perfectly compatible with loyalty to the Government. He indeed laboured to show that the Wahhabi movement had been directed solely against the Sikhs and never against the English. Quoting from the Koran, he pointed out that 'as long as Musalmans can preach the unity of God in perfect peace, no Musalman can, according to his religion, wage war against the rulers of that country, of whatever creed they be'. Muslims in India, he stressed, had 'every sort of religious liberty'. They were able to discharge the duties of their faith 'with perfect freedom', they could preach their religion as freely as Christians and even convert the latter to Islam 'without fear or prohibition'. In such a situation, there could be no religious ground at all for rebellion against British rule.[28]

In the beginning, Syed Ahmad Khan had been quite pro-Turkish and, in 1870, complimented Sultan Abdul-Aziz for gracing and defending 'the throne of the Caliph'. He had also popularized the Turkish cap (*fez*) in India and shown keen interest in the campaign for reforms and the adoption of European dress in Turkey. 'In fact everything was perfect as long as the British, to whom he had pledged his own and his community's loyalty, and the Turks, towards whom his community felt an emotional attachment, were on good terms.'[29] But when in 1877-8, on the occasion of the Russo-Turkish war and the Congress of Berlin, he found that the widely prevalent Pan-Islamic and pro-Turkish sentiments among Indian Muslims were likely to tamper with their loyalty to the British who were considered quite cool, if not hostile, towards Turkey, he raised his voice against such sentiments. Reminding his co-religionists that they were 'devoted and loyal subjects' of the British and not those of the Turkish Sultan, he asserted that the latter as Caliph had, or could have, no spiritual jurisdiction over Indian Muslims. His title of *Khalifa* was effective 'only in his own land and only over the Muslims under his sway'.[30] He was so determined not to let his loyalty be found wanting in any way that he even described Lytton's Vernacular Press Act (1878), enacted to curb Indian newspapers and periodicals, as a very liberal measure.[31] Sometimes he was even more loyal than the Government. For even though the latter itself had introduced the famous Ilbert Bill (1883), empowering Indian judges to try Englishmen, he advised Muslims not to join the general agitation in its favour as Englishmen in India were opposed to it.[32]

According to Syed Ahmad Khan, the need of the hour was a thoroughgoing social and religious reformation among the Muslims. He particularly became convinced of its need after his stay in England during 1869-70. In one of his letters from London, written on 15 October 1869, he observed: 'Without flattering the English, I can truly say that the natives of India, high and low, merchants and petty shopkeepers, educated and illiterate when contrasted with the English in education, manners and uprightness, are as like them as a dirty animal is to an able and handsome man.' Indians, however did not need to despair. If they were prepared to change, they could also become equals of Englishmen, if not their superiors. Syed Ahmad Khan was happy that his Bengali and Parsi brethren had begun 'to promote civilization', but felt that their pace was so fast that there was danger of their falling. He felt distressed by the fact that the Muslim community in India was covered by 'the fatal shroud of complacent self-esteem; they remember the old tale of their ancestors, and think that there are none like themselves'.[33] The main thing to do was to fight against this attitude and persuade the Muslims to look around and introduce changes in their life where necessary. He did not find anything wrong in the essential teachings of Islam. Indeed, if anything, his faith in those teachings became stronger than before. As he wrote in a letter from London on 10 September 1869, his 'faith in the fundamental principles of Islam was strengthened more by exposure to the conditions of Europe and by gaining the knowledge of (European) scholars' views rather than by going on a pilgrimage to Mecca . . . '.[34] But he became more and more convinced of the necessity of change, without giving up the essentials of the Islamic faith. It is important to remember that he looked upon this issue not so much from the religious as from the secular point of view. As has been pointed out by Mujeeb, he had basically a secular mind, or rather one dominated by common sense. 'He desired a position of honour for the Muslims in India, and he felt, quite correctly and genuinely, that the traditional view of Islam was a real hindrance to progress.'[35]

In order to carry out his programme of social and religious reformation, one of the first things Syed Ahmad Khan did after his return from England was to bring out a periodical in Urdu called *Tahzib-al-Akhlaq*, patterned after the English periodicals *The Tatler* and *The Spectator*. In course of an article published in its first issue dated 24 December 1870, he indicated that its main objective was 'to make the Muslims of India desirous of the best kind of civilization, so that it shall remove the contempt with which civilized people regard the Muslims . . .'.[36] This was to be achieved by turning Muslims towards modern civilization, showing Islam as a stimulus to progress, making natural sciences popular among the Muslims, eradicating from Muslim society the folkways and superstitions of Hindus, Jews and Roman Catholics, bringing about a reform in the manners of Muslims and raising the standard of Urdu.[37] The writings of Syed Ahmad Khan in *Tahzib-al-Akhlaq* attacking the various outmoded customs and beliefs of Muslims raised a hornet's nest and resulted in their author being attacked as a *kafir* and an atheist or a Christian.

This controversy created 'a deep stir in the still waters of the Muslim community',[38] but failed to deter Syed Ahmad Khan from his chosen path.

Apart from his writings in *Tahzib-al-Akhlaq*, Syed Ahmad Khan expressed his religious views in his book called *Essays on the Life of Mohammed* (1870) which he published mainly as a reply to Sir William Muir's attack on Islam contained in his biography of Muhammad (1858), which had been written with a view to showing the superiority of Christianity over Islam. Syed Ahmad Khan also wrote detailed commentaries on the Koran towards the end of his life between 1880 and 1895. The basic task that he set before himself in these writings was to reconcile the teachings of Islam with modern knowledge based on reasoning and scientific investigation. This, according to him, was the only way to make Islam attractive to those who were receiving modern education. Basing himself on Shah Waliullah's dictum that the time had come to present Islam fully dressed with reason and argument, he presented a fresh interpretation of Islam in the light of his own reason, always guided by the underlying principles and not by the minutiae of details accumulated through centuries of traditional interpretations. He again and again asserted that Islam could not but be in harmony with nature, for there could not be a conflict between the word of God (Islam) and the work of God (nature). On this ground, he rejected the existence of miracles and supernatural beings like angels and devils and asserted that the references to them in the Koran had to be interpreted not literally but symbolically. For saying so, his critics nicknamed him Naturist, but he did not care. He took particular pains to explain those practices in Islam which were being used by Christian missionaries to attack it. He, for instance, affirmed that *jihad* only meant defensive warfare and did not sanction aggression, and argued that the Prophet had, in fact, fought against slavery and polygamy. On the latter, he quoted the following verse from the Koran in support of his interpretation, on the assumption, of course, that no one is capable of loving more than one woman equally at any given point of time:

> If your fear that you will not act justly towards the orphans, marry such women as seem good to you, two, three, four; but if you fear you will not be equitable, then only one, or what your right hands own; so it is likelier you will not be partial.[39]

Similarly, Syed Ahmad Khan refused to accept *rajm* (stoning to death) as punishment for adultery or the payment of ransom money for murder (*dit*) to the family of the deceased, describing them as merely customs prevailing in Arabia during the days of the Prophet and not having the sanction of religion.[40] In putting forward these assertions, he based himself on his own interpretation of the Koran. He regarded the latter as the only infallible source of Muslim law. He did not put much reliance on *Hadith* (the traditions of the Prophet) as a major portion of it was either based on hearsay or imagination and related only to conditions in the lifetime of the Prophet. He also rejected the validity of *Ijtihad* (consensus among the *ulama*) as a source of Islamic law. He, however, attached great value to *Izma* (individual reasoning) and thought this could be utilized to bring Islamic theology in line with the requirements of the modern age. Very few even among Syed Ahmad Khan's supporters accepted his strictly rational approach to Islamic theology, but this became the foundation of all subsequent modernistic movements in Indian Islam.[41]

Syed Ahmad Khan himself attached the greatest importance to, and spent most of his energy upon, his educational work. This, he thought was the panacea for the regeneration of his community. According to Graham, his motto was: 'Educate, educate, educate.' He once told Graham: 'All the socio-political diseases of India may be cured by this treatment. Cure the root and the tree will flourish.'[42] It will be noticed that here Syed Ahmad Khan talks of India and not the Muslim community which became the sole object of his attention later. This revealed his true position in the earlier phase of his public work when, while primarily concerned with the welfare of the Muslim community, he did not exclude the Hindu community from the domain of his activities and really worked in the interest of what has been rightly termed as the Urdu-speaking elite, including Hindus as well as Muslims.[43]

Syed Ahmad Khan believed that the regeneration of India required a complete overhaul of its educational system and its reorganization on modern lines, but he moved cautiously in this direction. His first educational experiment was the foundation in 1859 of a primary school at Moradabad (UP), where he was posted at that time in course of his official career. It was very much a traditional Persian school with some modern elements grafted on to it, the most important of them being the inclusion of an introduction to modern history in the syllabus. The school was managed by a local committee of notables including both Hindus amd Muslims.[44] In 1864, he proceeded to a higher stage and, again with the help of a local committee of notables, including both Hindus and Muslims, and a local Hindu landlord as its patron, he helped found an English Secondary School at Ghazipur (where he had been transferred) which became known later as the Victoria High School. Here the curriculum was fully modern with emphasis on the teaching of modern arts and science subjects. Provision was made for the teaching of Arabic, Persian, Sanskrit, Urdu and English (but not Hindi).[45]

The same pattern of joint Muslim-Hindu endeavour, on the basis of common attachment to Urdu, is noticeable in other major activities of Syed Ahmad Khan about this time. Thus, the Scientific Society, founded in 1864, with Syed Ahmad Khan as its moving spirit and honorary secretary, worked for the translation of standard works, mainly on political economy and history, into Urdu, in order to make them available to a wider circle. By 1875, twenty-seven such works had been translated. The Scientific Society also organized occasional lectures on important topics. It took particular interest in the development of modern agriculture and set up a model farm. In 1866, the Scientific Society was housed in its own building called the Aligarh Institute, and began to publish a weekly newspaper named the *Aligarh Institute Gazette*, with articles both in English and Urdu, many of them by Syed Ahmad himself. In the same year, he founded another organization with a much wider purpose. This was called The British Indian Association of the North Western Provinces and Oudh (as UP was then called). Its object was 'to improve the efficiency of the British Indian Government and to promote its best interests'. With this end in view, the Association would draw the attention of the government to redress and amend such existing measures as appeared likely to prove injurious to the interests of the country, or to adopt such other measures as might be calculated to promote those interests. Both the Scientific Society and the British Indian Association had Hindus as well as Muslims as their members. In 1869 when the British Indian Association submitted a petition to the government asking for the setting up of a separate vernacular University for the North Western Provinces, it was signed by four Hindus and six Muslims, including Syed Ahmad Khan.[46]

After sometime, Syed Ahmad Khan's interest in joint Muslim-Hindu endeavour in public life began to wither. This was caused primarily by the rise in 1860s of a pro-Hindi movement in UP. Some Hindus began to say that if a vernacular university was to be established, its medium should not be Urdu but Hindi, which was spoken by a much larger number of people. Indeed they began to argue that the use of Urdu instead of Hindi in the courts was hampering the growth of primary education where emphasis continued to be laid on Urdu, which was alien to the overwhelming majority of the people and, on this ground, to ask for the replacement of Urdu by Hindi, written in Devanagari script, as the court language. This was the burden of the memorandum published by Sivaprasad of Banaras in 1868.[47] Syed Ahmad Khan, who had been taking both Hindus and Muslims along with him in his public work so far, now realized that that might not be possible any longer. He felt that Hindus were likely to become more and more interested in Hindi. On the other hand, he was not prepared to see the replacement of Urdu by Hindi and presumed that other Muslims would feel the same way. He himself described his premonitions during those days to his biographer Hali in the following words:

> During those days when Hindi-Urdu controversy was going on in Banaras, one day I met Mr. Shakespeare who was posted there as the Divisional Commissioner. I was saying something about the education of the Muslims, and Mr. Shakespeare was listening with an expression of amazement, when, at length he said, 'This is the first occasion when I have heard you speak about the progress of the Muslims alone. Before this you were always keen about the welfare of your countrymen in general'. I said, 'Now I am convinced that both these communities will not join whole-heartedly in anything. At present, there is no open hostility between the two communities, but on account of the so-called educated people, it will increase immensely in future. He, who lives, will see.'
>
> Mr. Shakespeare, thereupon, said, 'I would be sorry if your prophecy were to prove true'. I said, 'I am also extremely sorry, but I am convinced about the accuracy of this prophecy.'[48]

This feeling of Syed Ahmad Khan became stronger during his stay in England in 1869-70, when he heard that the Hindu members of the Scientific Society had begun to demand the use of Hindi in its work. In a letter to Nawab Mohsin-ul-Mulk, dated 29 April 1870, he observed:

> I have learnt another news which has caused me so much grief and anxiety. At Babu Shiva Prasad's instigation, Hindus have generally resolved to do away with the Urdu language and Persian script, which is *a memento of the Muslim rule in this country*. I have heard that they have moved the Hindu members of the Scientific Society to see that Hindi should replace Urdu in the newspapers

as well as books published by the Society. This is a proposal which will make Hindu-Muslim unity impossible. Muslims will never agree to Hindi, and if Hindus also, following the new move, insist on Hindi, they also will not agree to Urdu. The result will be that the Hindus and Muslims will be completely separated.[49]

It was against this background that the plans for a college for imparting higher education on modern lines to the sons of the leading Muslim families began to mature in Syed Ahmad Khan's mind and took final shape during his stay in England in 1869-70. Himself belonging to one of the aristocratic families associated with the Mughal court, he was most deeply interested in their future, which in his eyes was identical with the future of the entire Muslim community. He was convinced that without taking enthusiastically to modern education these families faced utter ruin. Yet they were keeping away from such education partly out of being engrossed in the memory of their past greatness, but mainly out of fear of losing their religion if they joined modern educational institutions. Syed Ahmad Khan, therefore, devised a scheme under which children of the Muslim elite would receive the best modern education available in India together with instructions in the tenets of their religion. His own rational approach to Islam was suspect in the eyes of most Muslim families. He was so obsessed with the urgent need of imparting modern education to the sons of the Muslim elite that he announced that the instruction of Islam in the college would be on orthodox lines and managed by orthodox scholars, and his own views on Islamic theology would play no part in such instruction. This was perhaps the greatest sacrifice which he made for the college. In every respect, the Mohammedan Anglo-Oriental College at Aligarh was his handiwork. He formed a committee to collect funds and was able to secure donations not only from Muslims, but also from Hindus and Sikhs. Government also came forward with generous assistance. School classes began functioning in 1875. The Viceroy, Lord Lytton, laid the foundation stone of the college in 1877. Upon his retirement from government service in 1876, Syed Ahmad Khan took residence at Aligarh and till his death in 1898, remained mainly preoccupied with the foundation and development of the college. The main contribution of the college at Aligarh did not lie in its producing a large number of Muslim graduates—out of 1184 Muslims to graduate between 1882 and 1892, it produced merely 220[50]—but in endowing its graduates with a new outlook. Although its doors always remained open to people of other religious faiths from the very beginning, it became famous not merely as a seat of modern learning, but also, and indeed much more so, as a symbol of Muslim awakening and solidarity and the determination of the Muslim elite to revive their lost glory within the context of Muslim-British friendship and loyalty to British rule. Direct indoctrination as well as the extra-curricular activities and the informal social milieu of the college contributed to the growth of this consciousness of solidarity. Besides, the British principals of the college as well as its founder went on reiterating to successive batches of students the core of their message, namely that 'Indian Muslims, the former rulers of the country, had declined, and that the only hope for their regeneration was to mobilize them under the aegis of Aligarh'.[51]

In 1886, Syed Ahmad Khan founded the All India Muhammedan Educational Congress (changed to Conference in 1890) which held its annual sessions in different parts of the country and spread the message of Aligarh far and wide. With its departments of elementary and secondary education, female education, development of the Urdu language, business administration and technical education, and general education, including adult literacy, it sought to promote awareness of modern educational needs and problems among the Muslim elite.[52] Its programme of work as decided upon at its first session in 1886 included dissemination of European science and literature and promotion of higher education among Muslims, research on the past academic achievements of Muslims, publication of biographies of renowned Muslim scholars, location and publication of rare works by Muslim authors, collection and publication of proclamations, orders and decrees issued by Muslim emperors; arranging for religious instruction in Muslim English schools; and improvement of the standard of traditional Muslim educational institutions. While primarily concerned with the educational problems of Muslims, it had a wider, though unstated objective and sought to 'combine the functions of articulation and aggregation of the Muslims' educational, political and economic interests . . . '.[53] Indeed, before the foundation of the All India Muslim League in 1906, it functioned as an informal 'political mouthpiece' of the Muslim elite.[54] It is significant that Syed Ahmad's first major speech opposing the Indian National Congress was delivered on the occasion of the second annual session of the Muhammedan Educational Congress (1887) and its annual session of 1906 at Dacca provided the occasion for the foundaion of the All India Muslim League, whose office, in its early years, remained located at Aligarh.

IV

The point whether Syed Ahmad Khan believed in a Muslim nation or in an all-inclusive Indian nation has been debated for a long time.[55] Extracts from his speeches and writings can be, and have been, cited on both sides. The confusion is made worse confounded by his use of the Urdu word ***kaum***, which can mean both community and nation, sometimes only for Muslims and sometimes for all persons residing in India. This controversy need not detain us long. It should suffice to point out that he opposed the Congress not only on the ground that its demands, if accepted, would harm Muslim interests, but also because he thought it premature to start such an organization at that stage and considered its activities harmful to the interests of India as a whole. At the same time, it is also true that his main grounds for opposition always remained the former and he used rather strong language while appealing to Muslim sentiments in that connection. In the beginning, he founded an organization consisting of Hindus as well as Muslims (United India Patriotic Association 1888) to oppose the Congress. It was only at a later stage, in the wake of the widespread movement against cow-killing and the Hindu-Muslim riots in India, that he founded a purely Muslim organization (Muhammedan Defence Association, 1893). On the other hand, it is also true that he had spoken of Muslims as a nation much earlier and indeed called his journal *Tahzib-al-Akhlaq* which he had founded in 1870, on return from England, as *Muslim National Reformer* in English. Both the names were used together.[56] From then onward, though he always remained a strong supporter of Hindu-Muslim cooperation and friendship, to the extent possible, the central objective of his public activity was to safeguard the future of the Muslim elite in India. He strongly believed that their interests would not be served by joining the Congress and working for elected legislatures and competitive examinations for recruitment to the higher ranks of government service, the two main political demands of the Congress in its early years. The former would result in the swamping of the Muslims by the Hindu majority and the latter in increased preponderance by young men belonging to the Hindu upper castes in the three maritime provinces of Bengal, Bombay and Madras, whose families had had an earlier start with English education. Therefore, the best thing for the Muslims, according to Syed Ahmad Khan, was to concentrate on English education and rely on the British to safeguard their future.

We cannot, of course, ignore the fact that Syed Ahmad Khan had, in several speeches, specifically emphasized the fact that Hindus and Muslims together constituted a nation, even though he had referred to them separately also as nations. This is, for instance, what he said in course of a speech at Patna in 1883:

> Gentlemen, just as many reputed people professing Hindu faith came to this country, so we also came here. . . . Thus India is the home of both of us. We both breathe the air of India and take the water of the holy Ganges and the Jamuna. We both consume the products of the Indian soil. We are living and dying together. By living so long in India, the blood of both have changed. Thus if we ignore that aspect of ours which we owe to God, both of us, on the basis of being common inhabitants of India, actually constitute one nation; and the progress of this country and that of both of us is possible through mutual cooperation, sympathy and love. . . . My friends, I have repeatedly said and say it again that India is like a bride which has got two beautiful and lustrous eyes—Hindus and Mussulmans. If they quarrel against each other that beautiful bride will become ugly and if one destroys the other, she will lose one eye.[57]

This was not a solitary speech of its kind. During his tour of the Punjab in 1883 and 1884, Syed Ahmad Khan repeatedly spoke in this vein.[58]

Such exhortation on Syed Ahmad Khan's part, however, went hand in hand with his understanding that in reality the situation was quite different and that the different sections of the Indian people did not yet feel that they belonged to the same nation. Indeed, he strongly felt that this reality should be kept in mind while laying down the framework for the emerging self-governing institutions in the country. This is clearly borne out by his speech in the Indian Legislative Council on 12 January 1883, in which he supported the Government's decision while introducing local self-government in India to retain the power of nominating a portion of their members and not to go in for a system of election 'pure and simple' on the ground that such a system could work satisfactorily only in a society which consisted of one homogeneous people.[59]

This strand in the thinking of Syed Ahmad Khan became much stronger after the foundation of the Congress in 1885. Although he continued to advocate Hindu-Muslim cooperation in educational and cultural fields, he now completely stopped talking about Hindus and Muslims constituting one nation. On the contrary, he again and again asserted the separate nationhood of the Muslims and completely ruled out the possibility of the Hindus and Muslims cooperating together to run the country harmoniously if the British ceased to rule over it. Thus, speaking before a gathering of Muslim gentry and government officials at Lucknow on 28 December 1887, he emphasized that as the Muslims were in a minority in India and also educationally backward as well as economically weaker as compared to Hindus, their interests would not be served by joining the Congress and agitating for the setting up of elective legislatures (where they would be outnumbered four to one by the Hindus) and recruitment to the higher services through competitive examinations.[60]

When Badruddin Tyabji, a fellow-Muslim from Bombay, who had only a day before delivered the presidential address to the third session of the Congress held at Madras, wrote to Syed Ahmad Khan expressing his inability to understand how the latter justified his stand in asking the Muslims to keep away from the Congress,[61] Syed Ahmad Khan said in his reply that as India was not the home of one nation it could not have an organization like a national congress.[62] To Tyabji's argument that there were certain matters which touched the interests of all the communities living in India and the interests of Muslims would be served better by joining the Congress rather than keeping out of it,[63] Khan replied that Hindus and Muslims belonged to two different nations, and could never cooperate politically.[64]

In his rejoinder to Tyabji in the *Pioneer* in April 1888, Syed Ahmad Khan did acknowledge that there were certain questions on which Hindus and Muslims could, and indeed should, unite, but explained that these were purely social questions. Thus, he pointed out, both Hindus and Muslims desired that there should be peace in the country, that the two nations should improve their social condition, live in a brotherly manner, help and sympathize with one another, see to it that religious quarrels did not arise between them and try to end the animosity 'everyday increasing between the two communities'. If the Congress had been formed to deal with such social questions, affirmed Syed Ahmad Khan, he himself would have presided over it and relieved his friend, Tyabji, of the burden. But the Congress, he emphasized, was a political organization and there was not one of its fundamental principles, and 'especially that one for which it was in reality founded', to which the Muslims were not opposed. Implying that the Congress had been founded in reality to put Muslims under Hindu rule, he solemnly affirmed: 'We may be right or we may be wrong: but there is no Mohammedan, from the shoemaker to the *Rais*, who would like that the ring of slavery should be put on us by that other nation with whom we live.'[65]

In the light of such assertions, it is not possible to agree with the view advanced by some scholars in India that the confusion regarding Syed Ahmad Khan's position on Indian *versus* Muslim nationhood has been created by his use of the Urdu word *Kaum* which, as has been mentioned earlier, means both community and nation, and that every time he used this word for Muslims, he only meant a community, and only when he used it for all Indians, including both Hindus and Muslims, did he mean a nation.[66] On the contrary, one feels compelled to accept the view of the noted Pakistani historian, S.M. Ikram, that Syed Ahmad Khan was the 'Father of Modern Muslim India' and 'the first prophet of their new nationhood'.[67]

On the other hand, we must guard against going to the other extreme, in the company of such Pakistani historians as I.H. Qureshi, who brush aside Syed Ahmad Khan's pre-1885 assertions of Hindus and Muslims together constituting a nation as of no particular significance and comparable to his repetition of the Koranic credo that all human beings belong to the same nation.[68] Even after 1885, he never fought shy of advocating Hindu-Muslim cooperation even though only in the educational and cultural fields. He, of course, looked upon Muslims as a nation, but always placed them within the wider entity of India. Indeed, whatever the logical implications of his ideas, once the prospect of British rule coming to an end appeared on the horizon—and opinions on this can vary—he himself never contemplated any future for Indian Muslims outside India. One can, therefore, legitimately say that for him Muslims were 'a nation within a nation'. He was deeply attached to the interests of the Muslim elite and worked untiringly for bringing about their awakening and solidarity, but he was also attached to India and regarded it as the common habitat of both Hindus and Muslims. He did not see any contradiction in his position. Few in the India of his time, and indeed of much later times too, did. The categorization in either/or terms did not obtain in those days. People were fond of using the words race and nation for all kinds of groupings. Syed Ahmad Khan himself, in the same speech in which he emphasized that Hindus and Muslims living together all over India constituted a nation, also referred to Bengalis (meaning of course educated Bengalis belonging to the Hindu upper castes) as well as Hindus and Muslims separately as nations.[69] Such was the prevailing mode of expression that even some Kayasthas of

UP, an educationally advanced but numerically quite small Hindu caste, in a conference in 1886, described themselves as a distinct race and adopted a resolution emphasizing the urgency of taking suitable measures to protect their interests in the 'competition among nations' then going on in India.[70] Syed Ahmad Khan's contribution to India's future political development, therefore, lay not so much in his characterization of Muslims as a nation, as in his stand that there could be no political union between Hindus and Muslims and his advice to the latter to keep away from the Congress and work for the advancement of their interests through alliance with the British.

V

The same dual attachment to the community and the country marked the attitude of some of the close collaborators and disciples of Syed Ahmad Khan. Mention may first be made of Munshi Zaka Ullah (1832-1911), a great educationist and a member of the Board of Trustees of the M.A.O. College at Aligarh. He attached great importance to education through the mother tongue and worked hard to spread new learning among Muslims by writing and translating textbooks on various subjects in Urdu for use in schools. He differed from Syed Ahmad Khan about the emphasis on education through the English medium which became the hallmark of Aligarh, but was too devoted to the latter and his mission to make an issue of it and fully cooperated with him. Indeed, of all the modern intellectual movements in India, Aligarh was 'the one that was nearest to his heart'.[71] He was deeply attached to the Indian soil and did not at all like the tendency of some Muslims whose forefathers had come to India from abroad and settled here generations ago to regard themselves as foreigners and make a distinction between their interests and those of India. He once told C.F. Andrews, 'with impassioned accents':

> India is our own mother country, the country which gave us birth. We have made our homes here, married here, begotten children here; and here on this soil of India we have buried our sacred dead. India, therefore, must needs be dearer to us than any other country upon earth. We should love this very soil of India, which is mingled with the dust of our ancestors. For a thousand years, our own religion of Islam has been intimately bound up with India, and in India, Islam has won some of the greatest triumphs for its own peculiar form of civilization. We should love, therefore, the history and government of India, which have been shaped by such great monarchs as Akbar the Great and his successors. I cannot bear to hear Indian Mussulmans speaking without

reverence and affection for India. It is a new fashion, unfortunately springing up, which did not exist in my younger days.[72]

He had absolutely no ill-will against the Hindu community and had several close friends among it. He also ardently hoped that relations between Hindus and Muslims would gradually improve, particularly as a result of the spread of modern education among them. However, he could not visualize this improvement to reach the level of a permanent union between the two and considered the presence of the British in India, as a neutral, mediating power, absolutely essential. When Andrews expressed doubt about the permanent need for the British in India because of Hindu-Muslim differences, Zaka Ullah observed:

> As you are aware, I love India with the love of a son for his own mother. I know also my own people. I know the Mussalman community. At the same time, I have close friends, as you are aware, among the Hindus, and I respect them as my fellow countrymen. But I am sure of one thing, and have become more certain of it the longer I have lived: the difference between Hindu and Mussalman is too great for any permanent union; and we shall always have the need of a balancing power. That is why, in God's providence, the English had to come in as rulers when the Mughal power declined.[73]

Just like Syed Ahmad Khan, Zaka Ullah was preoccupied with the plight of the Muslim elite, as compared to their Hindu counterparts, since the decline of Mughal power. He realized that thanks to the leadership provided by Syed Ahmad Khan, there was no longer any opposition to modern education and sons of the Muslim noble families were going in for it in increasing numbers. However, he still felt during the closing years of his life that 'the deficiency to be made good, the leeway to be recovered, was enormous'. For compared with the advance made by the Hindus in modern education, Muslim education 'could scarcely be said to have begun. The community, as a whole, was so backward'.[74] This must have appeared especially galling in view of Zaka Ullah's high estimation of Muslims' contribution to civilization in the past.

Zaka Ullah's history of India in Urdu in ten volumes, published in the closing decade of the nineteenth century, is typical of the outlook of the Aligarh school. Though called History of India (*Tarikh-i-Hindusthan*), it is actually a history of the so-called Muslim rule in India, beginning with the Arab conquest of Sind and ending with the suppression of the rebellion of 1857 and the exile of the last Mughal emperor from India. There is no criticism of any conqueror or ruler.

Far from showing any disgust for the cruelties of Timur, for instance, he seeks to paint his 'civilised, efficient and just administration'. He shows unconcealed sympathy for Aurangzeb and lays stress on his 'courage, devotion to duty, justice, and, of course, on his respect for the Islamic *Sharia*'. He specially mentions that not one Hindu was ever forced to accept Islam by Aurangzeb, and the only criticism he has to offer for Aurangzeb is that he 'foolishly imposed the *jizya*, broke a few temples and issued the ineffective order to dismiss Hindu employees'. In the final chapter of his history, while discussing the benefits conferred on India by Muslim rule, he asserts that 'in administration, law, manner and customs, in arts, in literature, the Hindus had nothing worth mentioning—at least nothing that could be compared with those of the Muslims whose rule, therefore, brought civilization to India'.[75] To quote his own words, 'Of all the laws of the world, Hindu law is the worst; Hindu law-makers were utterly brainless people, in Hindu rule there was no order in Government.' Further, 'Muslim manners are superior to those of the Hindus; Persian poetry is better than Hindu poetry; the *Mahabharata* is childish; in music, sculpture and painting, Muslims, Hindus and Chinese were equal'.[76]

Maulvi Nazir Ahmad (1836-1912), who was born in the district of Bijnor in UP and educated at the Delhi College, and rose to be a high government official, was another distinguished disciple of Syed Ahmad. Considered as the father of the Urdu novel, he used his novels to spread the message of the Aligarh School, particularly its emphasis on education and social reform. Thus, the theme of one of his most famous novels, *Taubat-un-Nasuh*, is the importance of female education. Another novel, *Fasana-e-Mubtata*, focuses attention on the evils of polygamy. Nazir Ahmad was not for a cheap imitation of the West and *Ibn-ul-Vaqt* presents a satire on those who were inclined towards such imitation.[77] Some consider it a satire on Syed Ahmad Khan himself,[78] but this is doubtful in view of his deep devotion to the work of the master. He, of course, did not agree entirely with all of Syed Ahmad Khan's theological views. In his writings in this field, he took a somewhat conservative position and did not think it prudent or necessary to go as far as the latter in the direction of a modernistic interpretation of Islam.[79] But he most ardently believed in the great value of the educational work started at Aligarh and also shared Syed Ahmad Khan's strong opposition to Indian nationalism as symbolized by the Congress. Thus, in course of a speech at an anti-Congress meeting in Delhi on 15 October 1888, Nazir Ahmad observed:

The Indian National Congress continually brags about itself, but any student a little familiar with the history and geography of India will pick his ears and say, 'Where is this India and where is this nationality?'! There is no country on this globe as this India. India is in fact a diversity of faiths, rituals, habits and nations. Thus it is an utter delusion to unite these diversified factions and consider them as one nation. There is nothing objectionable as long as Indians think Hindu and Muslims are different nations, but how can that be when Indians vow the two into one nation and will themselves 'Indian nationalists'? *The rivers Ganges and Sind can unite, but union is not possible between a Hindu and a Muslim as long as they are Hindus and Muslims (Cheers).*[80]

At the same time, just like Syed Ahmad Khan, Nazir Ahmad also, while strongly opposed to Hindu-Muslim union for political purposes, continued to believe in the desirability of Hindu-Muslim friendship. This should be clear from the following lines written by him shortly before his death:

Today in India it is a common place which is very often repeated, that there exists below the surface an inseparable link between Hindus and Mussalmans which is so strong that the one cannot exist without the other; and the British Government keeps peace between them.

But ignorant and short-sighted people, who belong to either of these two religions, have often caused endless disputes to arise in the past, especially through the North of India, by exaggerating the differences between them and by laying undue and mistaken emphasis upon various kinds of daily ceremonial observances in each religion. This is done mainly out of ignorance and prejudice. Nevertheless, I do not consider this state of things to be lasting.[81]

The man who made the most significant contribution to the spread of the message of Muslim awakening and solidarity, symbolized by Aligarh, was the biographer of Syed Ahmad Khan and one of the greatest poets of Urdu literature, Altaf Husain Hali (1837-1914). Born at Panipat (then a part of the Punjab, now in Haryana in India), he had spent the formative years of his life at Lahore before moving on to Delhi and coming in contact with Syed Ahmad Khan. *Musaddas-e-Hali* (1879) is his most important work and his chief passport to fame. As has been aptly observed, 'What gave the *Mussaddas* its enormous vogue, was not its style, admirable as it is, but its subject-matter.'[82] It presents a moving account of the rise and fall of Islam, draws attention to the sad plight of Muslims in India in the second half of the nineteenth century and emphasizes the urgent need for their awakening and revival through the path shown by Syed Ahmad Khan. It was indeed at the latter's instance that Hali had undertaken this work and he duly mentioned it in his preface. Referring to it, Syed Ahmad Khan remarked that he was so proud of the fact that when asked on the Day of Judgement to give an account of the good deeds performed by him, he would say: 'Nothing except that I got Hali to write his *Musaddas*.'[83] This tribute was richly deserved. The *Musaddas* ran into several editions, and its stanzas were recited with deep emotion at innumerable cultural functions of Muslims. Indeed, it became the most potent instrument for the spread of the message of the Aligarh movement among the Muslim intelligentsia and youth and has been rightly described as its Bible.[84] The main appeal of the poem lay in its depiction of the glorious past of Islam and its tragic fall. Lines like the following reminded the readers of the former:

From the mountains of Mecca arose a storm
Its fame resounded in all four corners
Its thunder and lightning rang in the spheres
It roared on Taigus,* it rained on Ganges
It ignored neither creatures of land nor of sea
To emerald it turned all of Allah's gardens.

Unlettered men englightened the world
The word of Islam was trumpeted from heights
From Arabia and Iran were banished the idols
And every sinking ship was set right
World resounded with the creed of One Allah
Each house rang with the name Allah Allah.

Ripples of good arose in hearts of scoundrels
Edifices of infidels were with tremours rocked
Fires were extinguished in sacred fireplaces
Dust swirled around and settled over temples
Kaaba became the hub and dens were ruined
Abandoning all places all gathered at one spot.[85]

The lines depicting the fallen state of the Muslims in India were equally moving and underlined their all-round decline:

The millat whose foot rested upon heavens
At every post whose flag was hoisted high
The community which by the skies was revered
The Ummah which was titled 'Highest of Ummahs'

*A river in Spain.

There's only one mark which remains of it here
That we numerate ourselves 'Muslims'—no more.

Otherwise neither in our veins nor blood
In our aspirations nor yet in our quests
In our hearts, on our tongues or in speech
Our temperament, habit, nature and manner
Not a grain of nobility is now to be found
If any exists—it is by accident profound.[86]

While laying stress on the decline in the character of Muslims Hali did not forget to refer to their sad economic plight:

O Quom of Muslims it is cause for shame
That progeny of kings beg door to door
Anyone you see is with penury strapped
Anyone you hear is afflicted and dumb
Who earns a living? Not one perhaps
But many are here just begging for scraps.[87]

According to Hali, the most important factor behind the decline of Muslims was the disappearance of the feeling of solidarity and brotherhood from their ranks:

If we hadn't forgotten the word of the Prophet
That All Muslims are each others' brothers
Until such time that a brother is a brother's friend
Allah is himself his helper
Then our ship would not have foundered
We would have ruled even in our destitution.[88]

Yet all was not lost. The Muslims could still rise and secure their rightful place in the world:

Our nation is like a sick young man whom weakness has so reduced that he despairs of life. He cannot leave his bed nor move from his place, and the signs of impending death are plain to all. His every ailment looks as though it were chronic; but in fact no fatal illness is upon him.

His senses are sound, his faculties in order. He feels the appetite for food and drink. His heart and mind, his eyes and ears perform their functions. The pride and verve of youth are unimpaired. And if one attends upon him with full care, he will in all likelihood find him yet numbered among the living.[89]

The hope of recovery lay through the path shown by Syed Ahmad Khan. Obviously referring to him and the band of devoted leaders and workers he had collected, Hali concluded:

True it is that there is a dearth of men in our nation, yet not all men in a nation are alike, and if the fragments of broken vessels are piled high, yet among them lie fragments of jewels concealed. Hidden among the gravel there are pearls to be found; and mingled in the sand are particles of gold.

Among those devoid of feeling are men of feeling too. Among the callous there are men of sympathy. Amongst these heedless sleepers, some are awake. In the taverns are some who are still sober. There are men who are like the rest of their group. Among the worthless are still some men of worth.[90]

Although in the *Musaddas* the emphasis throughout is on the past glory and contemporary decline of Muslims and they are referred to as a nation, the book is free from any expression of hostile feelings towards Hindus. This was not accidental. Before writing *Musaddas,* Hali had written a poem called 'Patriotism' which contains the following lines:

If you desire the good of your country,
Then do not consider any compatriot of yours as a stranger,
Be he a Muslim or a Hindu
Be he a Buddhist, or a Brahmo,
Look on them all with the eyes of friendship
Consider them like the pupils of your eyes.[91]

Yet the same Hali wrote another moving poem, *Shikwa-i-Hind* (1887), whose opening lines declared: 'Farewell, *Hindusthan*, land of eternal spring, for long have we, as foreign guests, stayed here and enjoyed your hospitality.'[92] The poet bemoans the contemporary decline of Muslims in India and asks:

Whither has gone the superiority of the Muslims,
In wealth, wisdom and learning?
Whither has gone that fixity of purpose,
That knew no barrier of land or sea?
Whither has gone that vigour and where are those sturdy
arms?

Obviously implying that they had all disappeared as a result of Muslims living on the Indian soil, the poet observes:

Just as the army of Alexander marched back after reaching
your border,
I wish we also had returned unsuccessful from your gates![93]

Another poem by Hali was in the form of an appeal to the Prophet 'to heed the sad plight of his followers, who had once emerged from their home in so much glory but were now in a miserable condition in a strange land'.[94]

VI

Islamic revival received a great boost also from the writings of Syed Ameer Ali (1849-1928), the most prominent among those who were working for Muslim awakening in the second half of the nineteenth century in Calcutta and one of the leading figures in the history of Muslim renaissance in India in modern times. Through his extensive writings in English, the most famous and influential among which were *Short History of Saracens* (first published 1889) and *The Spirit of Islam* (first published 1891), both running into several editions, he sought to instil among the educated Muslims a pride in their religion and culture and to secure for them respectful and sympathetic treatment at the hands of the British. Shedding the defensive or apologetic tone adopted by Syed Ahmad Khan, he adopted an assertive, almost aggressive tone *vis-a-vis* Christianity. He had absolutely no doubt about Islam providing the surest guide to progress in modern times. While Syed Ahmad Khan emphasized that Islam was not inimical to progress, Ameer Ali emphasized that Islam itself represented progress.[95] He analysed and interpreted Islam's teachings on such topics of contemporary discussion as war, religious tolerance, position of women, slavery, rationalism and democracy in a way as to show not merely that it was not opposed to trends in contemporary liberal thought, but that it was 'the first religion to proclaim all the virtues'.[96] He was, of course, not a fundamentalist and, like Syed Ahmad Khan, believed that some of the teachings of the Prophet were valid only for his own times, but he had absolutely no doubt about either the supremacy of Prophet Muhammad among all religious teachers in history, including Jesus Christ, or Islam representing the last stage in the evolution of religion. He took particular care to compare Prophet Muhammad with Jesus Christ wherever possible in order to show the superiority of the former.[97] Although he said at one place in *The Spirit of Islam* that 'excepting for the conception of the sonship of Jesus, there is no fundamental difference between Christianity and Islam', this idea did not animate the whole work and he did not leave any opportunity unutilized to establish the superiority of Islam over Christianity. His attitude to other religions, including Buddhism and Hinduism, was more critical. Indeed he wondered how people could be so stupid as to follow these religions.[98] In the political field Ameer Ali founded a separate Muslim political organization and refused to cooperate with the Indian National Congress.

Glorification of the Islamic past also marked the works of Shibli Numani (1857-1914), a great historian, essayist, poet and theologian. Born and brought up in eastern UP, he taught Arabic at the M.A.O. College, Aligarh for sixteen years, came into close contact with Syed Ahmad Khan and became a supporter of the Aligarh movement, but after the passing away of the latter, charted a path of his own. He adopted a middle position between orthodoxy and modernism, and showed interest in both Pan-Islamism and Indian nationalism. He wrote in Urdu and had a much greater impact on the Muslim mind than Ameer Ali. Even during his Aligarh days, he developed his own approach to the study of Islam which was quite different from that of Syed Ahmad Khan. As has been aptly observed, 'Sir Sayyid approached Islam from the values of the modern West; Shibli approached Western values from the viewpoint of Islam. His programme was not to reform Islam with some new criterion, but to revive it from within. . . .'[99]

Shibli sought to bring about this revival mainly by drawing attention to the great cultural and intellectual achievements of the Islamic peoples in the past and published a number of scholarly biographies of selected heroes of Islam, basing his methodology on 'a synthesis of the traditional Islamic disciplines of chronicles and hagiography and the western discipline of objective analysis'.[100] The first three books in this series were *Al-Mamun* (1887), a biography of Mamun-ul-Rashid; *Sirat-ul-Numan*, a biography of Abu Hanifa; and *Al-Faruq*, a biography of Umar, the second Caliph of Islam. He later wrote two more biographies, one of Imam Ghazali and the other of Maulana Rumi. His most ambitious project was a multi-volume biography of Prophet Muhammad, entitled, *Sirat-un-Nabi*, but he was able to complete only one volume. Among his other books, mention may be made of *Shir-ul-Azam*, (1908-18), a history of Persian poetry in five volumes, and *Ilm-ul-Kalam* (1903). His essays and short stories were brought together during his lifetime in a volume called *Risail-i-Shibli* (1898). After his death, an eight volume collection was published in India under the title *Maqalat-i-Shibli* under the editorship of Syed Suleman Nadvi. Another collection has been published in Pakistan under the title *Baqiyat-i-Shibli*, including certain articles omitted from the former.[101]

Among Shibli's early poems, one of the most famous is *Subh-i-Ummeed* or *The Dawn of Hope* (1887), which is 'the best versified account of the Aligarh movement and contains, perhaps, the warmest tribute ever paid to Syed Ahmad Khan'.[102] After sometime, however, Shibli's enthusiasm for the Aligarh movement gradually waned and he began to feel that a system of education with major emphasis on producing candidates for government employment would not be able to bring about a regeneration of the Indian society. According to him, what was needed was not a complete elimination of the old system of education, but 'a mingling of the old and new'. The establishment of an organization of the *ulama* (religious scholars) in Lucknow, called *Nadvat-ul-Ulama* in 1894 inspired him with a new hope and he thought that he could turn it into the ideal educational institution of his conception. In 1898, he resigned from the Aligarh College to devote all his time to *Nadvat-ul-Ulama,* but had to take up service for a few years in the Hyderabad state due to certain financial and other constraints. When he finally joined it as the head of its educational wing, the *Dar-ul-Uloom*, he introduced a number of changes in its syllabus, including the teaching of English, but he could not last there long and had to resign in 1913. However, before his death, he founded another institution, in 1913, named the *Dar-ul-Musannifin* (Academy of Authors) at Azamgarh, the town near which he had been born. This continues to this day.

During his post-Aligarh days, Shibli wrote several articles and poems criticizing the work at Aligarh and describing the M.A.O. College as 'An Institute for Training in Slavery'. He also criticized the policy being followed by the Muslim League and exhorted the Muslims to join hands with the forces of Indian nationalism. The main factor drawing him towards Indian nationalism, however, was Pan-Islamism which was creating a spell over the minds of a growing number of Muslims in India, both educated and uneducated, in the wake of the decline of the Turkish empire, the most powerful Muslim political entity still extant, the unsympathetic British attitude towards it, and the reform movements going on not only in Turkey but also in Persia. This naturally led to much greater emphasis on the Islamic heritage than ever before. Unlike Syed Ahmad Khan who, though working for

Muslim regeneration, wanted religion and politics to be kept apart, Shibli believed that religion would be a more potent factor in bringing about such regeneration than mere emphasis on political and economic issues. In one of his speeches at the *Nadvat-ul-Ulama*, he observed with reference to the work of the Aligarh School:

> For the last thirty years, efforts have been made to uplift the Muslims in the name of nationhood, but the failure of these efforts is only too obvious. The followers of the Prophet do not respond to the call of nationhood. Appeal to them in the name of religion, and you will see what a splendid response you get.[103]

Such an approach naturally led not only to greater emphasis on the role of the Muslim religious scholars in politics, but also to an over-emphasis on the Islamic heritage even though simultaneously an effort was being made to promote Hindu-Muslim cooperation in politics against British imperialism, the common enemy. Shibli felt almost the same way as Zaka Ullah regarding the civilizing role of Muslims in India. He apparently felt that even Aurangzeb had to be eulogized in order to foster among Muslims a pride in their past history. Thus, in spite of his anxiety to avoid issues which might contribute to internal discord, we find Shibli in his monograph on Aurangzeb (*Aurangzeb Alamgir par ek Nazar*, 1912) putting up a strong defence of that ruler and his policies. As has been pointed out by a knowledgeable scholar, 'Aurangzeb's adherence to theological rules in matters of state, his deliberate reversion of Akbar's policy of Indianization, his suppression of Dara Shikoh's religious eclecticism, all find warm support, and the Emperor is commended as a Muslim rather than evaluated as an Indian king'.[104]

The historical novel also played its part in the glorification of the Islamic past. Abdul Halim Sharar (1860-1928), made a notable contribution in this field. A prolific writer and journalist, he made his name and his place in history largely through his historical romances. His range was quite wide and covered the entire Islamic world from India to Spain. He particularly selected those episodes and themes which he thought would endow his fellow Muslims with a keen desire to revive the glories of their past. In his note on one of his famous historical novels, *Malik-ul-Aziz Varjana*, he observes: 'This novel depicts those splendid achievements of Muslims which can revive their drooping spirits and dead aspirations. Every sentence of it moves one with a sense of national pride. . . .'[105]

VII

The glorification of Islam contained in the works of persons like Ameer Ali, Shibli and Sharar were spread among the middle and lower middle class Muslims in the last decade of the nineteenth and the first two decades of the twentieth century by innumerable known and unknown writers through 'thousands of small pamphlets, each with a small circulation, through little lectures by little men, through local editorials, neighbourhood gatherings, small clubs and societies, through articles and discussion groups'.[106] The most important ideas emphasized by these publications and lectures were the great civilizing role of Islam and the unique personality of Prophet Muhammad. Particular care was taken to highlight the patronage of art and learning by the rulers belonging to Islam, and the maintenance of large libraries and the famous universities of Basrah, Kufah, Baghdad, Cairo and Cordoba. The contribution made by the Arabs to the advancement of science was emphasized again and again. Almost all scientific advances in medieval and modern times were ascribed to the efforts of the Islamic pioneers. It was further claimed that the Islamic rulers had set a unique example of religious tolerance, and Islamic societies had treated their poor and destitute with great sympathy and compassion. The advances made by early Islam in art, science and social organization were contrasted with the backward conditions then prevailing in Europe, and it was claimed that it was only by borrowing from Islam that Europe finally became civilized. One writer indeed claimed that whatever progress the world had made in learning and civilization from the seventh century to the present-day had been the result, directly and indirectly, of 'the mind of the Founder of Islam'. That Islam was superior to Christianity, of course, went without question and was emphasized in several writings. Surprisingly, the contribution made by Islamic culture to India was less often glorified. As for Prophet Muhammad, it was repeatedly asserted that he was the embodiment of all virtues that one could think of. 'To whatever traits of virtue we look', observed one writer, 'we find that the Prophet Muhammad possessed all of them in the highest degree and was the most ideal figure that the world had produced.' Usually the virtues attributed to the Prophet were the virtues prized in a bourgeois society, such as capacity for hard work, perseverence, frugality, seriousness of purpose. He was also depicted as full of love and compassion for his fellow human beings.[107]

The controversies fostered by the different groups of *ulama* and the debates between either of them and the Hindu revivalists or Christian missionaries also contributed in a major way to the growth of community consciousness among Muslims in north India. The main Muslim *ulama* involved in such controversies and debates were the *Deobandis* (those associated with the seminary at Deoband); the *Ahl-i-Hadis*, who rejected all the four law schools of traditional Islam as a source of religious guidance and relied only upon the Koran and *Hadis,* i.e. the teachings and practice of the Prophet, as interpreted by themselves; and the *Barelvis*, followers of Maulvi Ahmed Raza Khan of Bans Bareli in Rohilkhand Division of UP, who stood for traditional Islam, including Sufism and other religious practices which were opposed by some reforming *ulama*; and the products of *Nadvat-ul-Ulama* of Lucknow, who stood for a middle position between modernists and traditionalists and worked for the removal of sectarian differences. Some of the debates were largely attended and evoked tremendous popular enthusiasm. The printing press also played its part by making it easy for the revivalists and reformers of various schools to spread their views through pamphlets. Even the controversies among the different Muslim groups, while undoubtedly fostering discord among certain groups of Muslims, on the whole, heightened their community-consciousness and made them much more aware of their differences from Hindus and Christians than before. This was illustrated by the construction of new mosques and religious schools in UP, one of the main areas of sectarian conflict among Muslims, setting up of new printing presses and publication of more and more religious tracts in Urdu.[108]

As Rafiuddin Ahmed has shown with a profusion of details, controversies between traditionalists and reformers and between the different groups of the latter contributed, during the second half of the nineteenth century and early years of the twentieth, to the heightening of Islamic consciousness among the rural masses in Bengal and in making them feel that they were fundamentally different from the Hindus. The wide interest created by meetings held for *bahas* (debate) between the spokesmen of various groups contributed significantly to this development, for it helped to break the isolation of Muslims living in remote rural areas and made them aware of their bond with other fellow-Muslims and of the vital issues connected with their religion. The growing production of cheap books and pamphlets in Bengali containing instruction regarding religious beliefs and practices, known as *Nasihat Namas*, further contributed to this process. These books invariably called upon the Muslims to order their lives strictly according to the tenets of their religion and to give up the practices alien to it. A number of books appeared in Bengali glorifying the early history of Islam and painting an idealized picture of life in Turkey, the greatest living Muslim power. Muslims now became keenly interested in differentiating themselves from the rest of the local population and identifying themselves with Muslims in West Asian countries and those living in upper India. Indeed, it became now a vogue to describe a Muslim Bengali as just a Muslim and only a Hindu Bengali as Bengali. The Muslims began now to give up such elements of dress as *dhoti* and *chaddar* which made them indistinguishable from Hindus, to change their names from Bengali to Arabic and Persian, and to introduce more and more Arabic and Persian words into the Bengali language which they were using, calling it Mussalmani or Islamic Bengali. They began to resent any assertion of their predominantly local origin and to claim that most of them were descendants of those Muslims who had come to Bengal from abroad as rulers, teachers, administrators and soldiers, and only a small minority were converts from the local population. Some even began to assert that Bengali was not their language, but this view was ultimately given up on practical considerations. However, if Bangali was retained, a conscious effort now began to change not merely its form, but also its content, eliminating from it the descriptions and imageries of Hindu gods and practices and substituting them with Muslim themes and imageries. These developments helped to bridge the gulf between the Muslim elite and the lower middle classes and masses in Bengal, and made the latter receptive to the call of Muslim solidarity.[109]

The products of Deoband, along with those of religious seminaries inside Bengal itself, played an important part in spreading this new consciousness in Bengal. Writers and journalists helped through their publications. Among them, mention may particularly be made of Munshi Meherullah (1861-1907). Born in Jessore and a self-educated person, he began his career as a tailor, but was gradually drawn towards writing and preaching in order to meet the challenge posed by the propaganda of the Christian missionaries. His books in Bengali, meant largely to defend Islam, contained attacks not only on Christianity, but also on Hinduism and sought to remind the Muslims of their glorious heritage. He also established Islamic associations or *anjumans* and organized religious meetings called *waz mahfils*, which had a great impact on the rural Muslim community. He used such meetings to mobilize public support for spreading modern education among Muslims. Like the *bahas* meetings of the earlier days, these meetings contributed significantly towards breaking the isolation of the rural Muslims of Bengal, making them conscious of their Muslim identity and strengthening their self-confidence. At the same time, they also contributed to increasing Hindu-Muslim tension there.[110]

VIII

This growing movement for Islamization was partly the result of the propaganda carried on by the revivalists and reformers of various hues, but partly also of the growth of Pan-Islamism in India during the last quarter of the nineteenth and the first quarter of the twentieth centuries. The Muslim elite in India had always been conscious of their Pan-Islamic identity, that is, their belonging to a wider world of Islam which extended far beyond India. In one sense, Pan-Islamism, as an ideology or a sentiment, can be said to have been as old as Islam itself, for the brotherhood of all Muslims had been an essential part of the teachings of the Prophet. This feeling of brotherhood and solidarity had been buttressed over the centuries by two powerful institutions of Islam—the Hajj and the Caliphate. The former led hundreds of thousands of Muslims from different parts of the world to congregate every year at Mecca for religious pilgrimage. The holder of the Caliphate (known as Caliph or *Khalifa*), instituted immediately after the Prophet's death, was treated as the head of all Muslims wherever they might be living. Passing through numerous vicissitudes, it survived in some form or the other till the first quarter of the twentieth century. This institution had generally been treated with great reverence by Indian Muslims. Most of the Turkish Sultans of Delhi had taken pains to secure recognition and robes of honour from the Abbasid Caliphs in Baghdad. Even though his authority had become quite shadowy, the Caliph was still considered as the temporal as well as spiritual head of Muslims all over the world. The theory of the Caliph's supreme position was so widespread that his recognition was generally considered as a great source of legitimation for Muslim rulers in various parts of the world, who claimed that they were ruling on behalf of the Caliph. Sometime after the killing of the last Caliph of Baghdad, al-Musta'sim, (1258) by the Mongol ruler, Hulagu Khan, a scion of the Abbasid family was specially taken to Cairo by the Memluk ruler of Egypt and proclaimed as the Caliph (1261). In the sixteenth century, the history of the Cairo Caliphate came to an end with the conquest of Egypt by the Ottoman Sultan. The Mughal kings of Delhi declared themselves as Caliphs in addition to being Sultans, though they did not claim any authority beyond their dominions. Thus, they did not recognize any authority outside India as superior to them whose recognition had to be sought for legitimizing their rule.[111] They were, however, very much conscious of their belonging to the wider world of Islam, and administrators, preachers and scholars from the latter were always warmly welcomed at their courts and generally given precedence in the distribution of patronage and honour over the native nobles, whether Muslim or Hindu. In course of time, the Ottoman Sultans began to describe themselves as Caliphs and, beginning particularly with the eighteenth century, asserted their claim over the allegiance of all Muslims, thus emerging as symbols of Pan-Islamism. For sometime the British encouraged the growth of Pan-Islamic sentiments in India and, in 1857, even secured a proclamation from the Ottoman Sultan calling upon Indian Muslims to remain loyal to his British allies. In the beginning Syed Ahmad Khan also was quite cordial in his attitude towards the Ottoman rulers, but changed his policy later when, with a change in British foreign policy, there appeared the possibility of the pro-Turkish sentiments of the Muslims resulting in the growth of anti-British feelings among them. Nevertheless, such sentiments continued to grow and even those who followed Syed Ahmad Khan's lead in other fields, did not heed his guidance on the issue of supporting Turkey.[112] As the greatest Muslim power then in existence, it became the centre of their attention, and the fact that its ruler had also the title of Caliph further increased its attraction. Indeed many Muslims now began to consider it a religious duty to support Turkey. With the spread of the movements of Islamic revival and reform, Pan-Islamic sentiments also grew among Muslims. They felt a deep interest not only in the fate of Turkey, which was coming more and more under attack by various Western powers, but in that of every country inhabited by Muslims.

Although Pan-Islamic sentiments developed in India spontaneously and manifested themselves as early as 1877 during the Russo-Turkish War,[113] if not earlier, the teachings of the legendary Jamal al-din al-Afghani (1838-97) who visited India several times during the second half of the nineteenth century, staying on one occasion for three years (1879-82), contributed significantly to their subsequent growth. It has been remarked by a noted authority that Afghani 'stirred the soul of Islam as no one else did', and created 'a deep impression' on those whom he met during his visits to India.[114] Even those who hold that there was not much immediate impact of his visits recognize that 'a generation later, in the first decades of the twentieth century, as a symbol and a legend, his mission exercised a powerful impact on the Pan-Islamic movement'.[115] In some of his writings, he strongly attacked the thinking of Syed Ahmad Khan. However, there was not much difference in the religious views of the two thinkers, for al-Afghani also stood for modernistic reforms in the field of religion. The real difference lay in the political field. While Syed Ahmad Khan stood for adjustment between Islam and the West, al-Afghani believed in an inevitable confrontation between them. Besides, according to him, the interests of Indian Muslims could not be separated from the rest of the Muslim world; there was a basic unity tying all parts of that world and they would rise or fall together. He was not opposed to a reinterpretation of Islamic thought or a reorientation of Islamic attitudes, but these could be satisfactorily achieved only by working within the framework of Pan-Islamism under a common leadership. Such common leadership could most appropriately be provided by the Caliphate.[116]

Some impact of al-Afghani's ideas is visible in the later phase of Shibli Numani's activities when he denounced the general approach of the Aligarh School and exhorted the Indian Muslims to join hands with the Hindus in a struggle for freedom from British rule, but these ideas were really developed by the latter's disciple, Abul Kalam Azad (1888-1958) through his articles in his paper *Al-Hilal* during 1912-14, and in his speeches and writings after the First World War, especially in *Masla-i-Khilafat*, written in 1920. The writings of Mohammed Ali (1878-1930) in his paper *The Comrade* during 1911-14 and his speeches in 1919-20 also made a notable contribution to the spread of the ideology of Pan-Islamism in India. Several other Muslim journals, notably *Zamindar*, edited by Zafar Ali Khan, performed the same role. A third major force consisted of the *ulama*, particularly those associated with the Deoband School, who for the first time founded an all-India organization called Jamiyat-ul-Ulama-i-Hind in 1919. The international background was provided by such developments as the growth of a powerful reform movement in Turkey and Persia in the second decade of the twentieth century, the generally hostile attitude of most of the Western powers towards Turkey, Italy's annexation of Tripoli (1911), the rebellion of the Balkan States of the Turkish empire and the resultant Balkan wars (1912), Turkey's joining the World War on the side of Germany and against Britain (1914) and the victorious Western powers' resolve to dismember the Turkish empire, including its Asian and purely Turkish regions (1919-20). Inside India, the Aligarh policy of loyalty to the British stood discredited because of the latter's annulment of the partition of Bengal (1911), which made many Muslims realize that their interests could no longer be safeguarded by the British, who seemed to be following an anti-Muslim policy everywhere. All this, provided a very congenial environment for the spread of the Pan-Islamic ideology and it became the dominant ideology of the Indian Muslims between 1912 and 1924.

Abul Kalam Azad was the main theoretician of Pan-Islamism and his writings and speeches constituted its main intellectual prop. The working of his mind is very well revealed by what he wrote to a friend in 1912:

> Aligarh movement has paralysed the Muslims. The real aim is the promotion of Pan-Islam, which is the true foundation and link for the progress and reform of Islam, and, for this, there will never be a better opportunity than we have now. Today no local or national movement can benefit the Muslims, even if it be the tall talk of the [Aligarh] University. So long as the whole world of Islam does not come together in an international and universal alliance, how can small tracts help the forty crores of Muslims?[117]

An important concomitant of this attitude was over-emphasis on religion and its close relationship with politics. According to Azad's writings in the *Al-Hilal*, the Koran contained detailed guidance relating to all aspects of life, including politics. For a Muslim, therefore, politics could not be separated from religion. Those who sought to do so were apostates. In order to be able to fight for freedom, Muslims must first discover their own community; 'others may acquire a spirit of nationhood (*qaumiyyat*) on the basis of race, descent or the same habitat, Muslims may only acquire that spirit on the basis of their religion'.[118] Further, according to Azad, there was no need for Muslims to seek guidance in politics from any source other than the Koran. Everything would be well for them if they only followed the latter. In one of his articles in *Al-Hilal* dated 29 May 1913, he observed:

> Muslims today do not need to lay new foundations or to exercise ingenuity. They have only to revive and reaffirm what has been commended. There is no reason why we should feel distraught over the new houses to be built; we

need only to settle down in the dwellings we have forsaken. This is the difference in principle between my conviction as regards what is to be done and the methods of my contemporaries.[119]

Since Azad laid so much stress on religion guiding politics, it is important to remember that he did not interpret Islam in any narrow, sectarian sense. As he pointed out in *Al-Hilal* dated 9-16 April 1913:

Islam does not commend narrowmindedness, and racial and religious prejudice. It does not make the recognition of merit and virtue, of human benevolence, mercy and love dependent upon and subject to distinctions of religion and race. It teaches us to respect every man who is good, whatever be his religion, to let ourselves be drawn towards merits and virtues, whatever the religion or the race of the person who possesses them.[120]

Azad's reading of Islamic injunctions did not lead him to ask Muslims to keep away from Hindus in politics. On the contrary, he asked them to join hands with the latter in the struggle for India's freedom and asserted that there was no need to fear them because of their majoirty in the country. Indeed he described such fear as 'the most evil suggestion of the devil'. Who would wield power would be determined not by majority or minority, but by such factors as character, morals, fear of God and commendable deeds.[121]

According to Azad, it would not be enough for Muslims to fight for India's freedom along with Hindus; they must also support the Caliphate. He asserted that no community or nation could survive without a political centre (*siyasi markaz*) and pointed out that the Ottoman Caliphate, with all its imperfections, was the only possible centre for Muslims, for it possessed the only sword the Muslims had for the protection of their religion. Besides, it was the last important independent Muslim power and, on that ground too it deserved the support of Muslims.[122] It is, however, important to note that while elaborating this argument in *Masla-i-Khilafat,* Azad treated the Ottoman Caliph as only symbolizing the common life and religions purpose of the Muslim community and its intention to order its life according to the Holy Law of Islam and nowhere suggested that it should have the authority to enforce that law in India.[123]

Thus, the objective of Pan-Islamism was not to make India subordinate to the Caliphate. On the contrary, the struggle to maintain the Caliphate with all the honour and authority due to it,[124] together with the preservation and promotion of the Islamic way of life for Muslims in India, went hand in hand with that for achieving India's freedom. This is illustrated best by the objectives of the Jamiyat-ul-Ulama-i-Hind, in the foundation of which Azad and other leading *ulama* and leaders of the Khilafat movement in India, like Maulana Abdul Bari of Firangi Mahal, Lucknow, had played a key role. These objectives, as indicated in its constitution, were as follows:

1. To guide the followers of Islam in their political and non-political matters from a religious point of view.
2. To defend, on *Shariah* grounds, Islam, centres of Islam (the *Jazirat-ul-Arab* and the seat of the Khilafat), Islamic rituals and customs and Islamic nationalism [nationality?] against all odds injurious to them.
3. To achieve and protect the general religious and national rights of the Muslims.
4. To organize the *ulama* on a common platform.
5. To organize the Muslim community and launch a programme for its moral and social reform.
6. To establish good and friendly relations with the non-Muslims of the country to the extent permitted by the *Shriat-i-Islamiyat*.
7. To fight for the freedom of the country and religion according to the *Shariah* objectives.
8. To establish *mahakim-i-Shariyah* (religious courts) to meet the religious needs of the community.
9. To propagate Islam by way of missionary activities in India and foreign lands.
10. To maintain and strengthen the bond of unity and fraternal relations (as ordained by Islam) with the Muslims of other countries.[125]

These objectives of the Jamiyat-ul-Ulama, it has been rightly pointed out, 'reveal its dual loyalty to Islam and Islamic countries, on the one hand, and to India on the other. They also indicate the utmost emphasis on the *Shariah* and its preservation and promulgation in the Indian subcontinent.'[126] This over-emphasis on religion and the tendency to explain every political move in terms of the precepts of Islam were hallmarks of the Pan-Islamic ideology and put a severe constraint on the efforts of those Muslim leaders who were trying to build up an all-inclusive Indian nationalism. This became apparent after the collapse of the Khilafat movement.[127] In any case, the convergence of Pan-Islamism and Indian nationalism did not last long. Already weakening as a result of the impact of a number of developments, including the growing Hindu-Muslim tension as a result of the Mappila uprising (1921), the suspension of the Civil Disobedience Movement (1922) by the Congress under Gandhi's guidance, and shortly after this, the projection by the then Viceroy, Lord Reading, of himself as a champion of the Indian Muslims' concerns *vis-a-vis* Turkey it received the final blow from the abolition of the Caliphate by the rulers of the new Turkey in 1924. While some prominent leaders of the Khilafat movement, like Abul Kalam Azad and M.A. Ansari, remained associated with the Indian nationalist movement and indeed functioned as its leaders till the end of their lives, others, along with their followers became adherents of Muslim nationalism, which now began to grow by leaps and bounds.

IX

The person who provided the strongest ideological as well as emotional foundations for Muslim nationalism was Muhammad Iqbal, generally known as Allama Iqbal (1877-1938), one of the greatest poets, philosophers and political thinkers ever produced by India. He dominated Muslim religious and political thought in India in the twentieth century just as Syed Ahmad Khan had done in the nineteenth. Always responsive to the call of Islam and proud of his Islamic heritage, he began his career as a poet and an ardent Indian nationalist, then turned into even a more ardent Pan-Islamist to whom nationalism was an anathema and a menace to Islamic solidarity, and finally gave voice and vision to Indian Muslim nationalism. There is absolutely no doubt that he is the most important poet and thinker for any one seeking to understand the ideological and emotional environment of the Indian Muslim intelligentsia and youth during the first half of the twentieth century. 'Perhaps the right way to look at Iqbal', observes H.A.R. Gibb, a renowned authority on Islamic history, 'is to see in him one who reflected and put into vivid words the diverse currents of ideas that were agitating the minds of the Indian Muslims. His sensitive poetic temperament mirrored all that impinged upon it. . . .'[128] Actually, he did more so far as the main political issue before the Indian Muslims in the first half of the twentieth century was concerned, for he gave a concrete shape to 'what his fellows were vaguely beginning to feel, but were unable to formulate'.[129] He was able to do so on the basis of a synthesis of the ideology of the Aligarh movement, the Pan-Islamic ideology and the Western democratic principles, particularly the principle of self-determination.

It was at the annual functions of an institution inspired by the Aligarh movement, the Anjuman-i-Himayat-i-Islam of Lahore, founded in 1884, that Iqbal made his name as a rising Urdu poet between 1900 and 1905. On the very first occasion, in 1900, when he recited his poem, *Nala-i-Yatim* (Orphan's cry) the audiance was moved to tears. The chairman of the function, a prominent leader of the Aligarh movement, Maulvi Nazir Ahmed, remarked: 'I have heard several elegies of Anis and Debir, but never did I hear before such a heart-breaking poem.'[130] Among the poems of those days the most famous, of course, was *Tarana-i-Hind* (song of India) which became one of the most popular national songs throughout India and continued to be sung long after Iqbal himself had begun to sing a different song and indeed revoked it by writing *Tarana-i-Milli* (Muslim anthem), where he said 'We are Muslims and the whole world is our home.' The former, which many in India even today consider as the best patriotic song written by an Indian poet, opens with the following lines:

> Our India is better than the whole world
> We are her nightingales, she is our rose garden.
> Religion does not teach mutual hostility
> We are all Indians and India is our home.

In the same vein were written such poems as *Hindustani Bachon ka Qaumi Geet* (national anthem of Indian Children) and *Naya Shivala* (New Temple). The latter shows Iqbal's concern with the prevalence of dissensions between Hindus and Muslims for which he rebukes both and calls upon them to build a new temple dedicated to mutual understanding and love:

> Come, let us remove all that causes estrangement,
> Let us reconcile those that have turned away from each
> other, remove all signs of division.
> Desolation has reigned for long in the habitation of my heart—
> Come, let us build a new temple in our land.
> Let our holy place be higher than any on the earth,
> Let us raise its pinnacle till it touches the lapel of the sky;
> Let us awake every morning to sing the sweetest songs,
> And give all worshippers the wine of love to drink.[131]

It is perhaps true that the feelings expressed in these lines 'had a deep spiritual basis and did not derive from any transitory political sentiments',[132] but they did not last long. A perceptible change came in Iqbal's thinking during his sojourn in Europe for higher studies from 1905 to 1908. Being thrown into an alien culture, he looked for his roots and found them not in Indianism, but in Islam. Perhaps the rising crest of the wave of Hindu nationalism in the wake of the agitation against the partition of Bengal (1905) as well as the growth of nationalism among the Europeans (Christians) within the Turkish empire and growing sympathy in all parts of Europe for them influenced his thinking. He gradually began to look upon himself as 'Islam's messenger to the Muslims'.[133] The following lines written in 1907 illustrate this change:

> The time of unveiling has come, the beloved will be seen by all.
> The secret which was veiled by silence shall now become manifest.
> That time, cup-bearer, has gone when the lovers of wine drank in hiding;
> The whole world will now be a tavern and all will drink in the open.
> For, the silence of Mecca has proclaimed to the expectant ear at last,
> That the compact made with the desert-dwellers shall be enforced again.
> That lion which emerged out of the wilderness and upset the Empire of Rome,
> I hear from the angels, shall awaken once more.[134]

When on his return-voyage from Europe to India in 1908 his ship passed by Sicily which was once under Arab (Muslim) rule, he felt such deep nostalgia for the departed glory of the Muslims that he wrote a moving elegy, which contained these lines:

> I am the dust raised by that caravan which once broke its journey here.
> Paint me that picture of the old
> Rouse me by telling the tale of bygone days;
> I shall carry the gift to India,
> and make others weep as I weep now.[135]

That this did not indicate a mere shift in emphasis but a real change of direction soon became clear. When in 1909, he was invited to Amritsar to attend a meeting of a cultural organization called Minerva Lodge, whose membership was open to both Hindus and Muslims, he declined to go and wrote, while explaining his decision, on 28 March 1909:

I have myself been of the view that religious differences should disappear from this country, and even now, act on this principle, in my private life. But now I think that the preservation of their separate national entities is desirable for both the Hindus and the Muslims. The vision of a common nationhood for India is a beautiful ideal, and has a poetic appeal, but looking to the present conditions and the unconscious trends of the two communities, appears incapable of fulfilment.[136]

In an article on 'Islam as a Moral and Political Ideal', published in the *Hindustan Review* in July-December 1909, Iqbal emphasized that Islam was not merely a matter of private belief and conduct, guiding the individual in his relationship with God, but also connoted a social and political order. For a Muslim, therefore, the basis of nationality could only be religion and nothing else. He observed:

We know that Islam is something more than a creed, it is also a community, a nation. The membership of Islam as a community is not determined by birth, locality or naturalization; it consists in the identity of belief. The expression 'Indian Muhammedan', however convenient it may be, is a contradiction in terms, since Islam in its essence is above all conditions of time and space. Nationality with us is a pure idea; it has no geographical basis. But in as much as the average man demands a material centre of nationality the Muslim looks for it in the holy town of Mecca. . . .[137]

Iqbal's purpose in writing this article was not merely to analyse the tenets of Islam, but also to educate and inspire the Indian Muslims. Condemning all sectarian as well as social distinctions among Muslims, and making a fervent plea for unity in Muslim ranks, he wrote:

Islam is one and indivisible; it brooks no distinctions in it. There are no Wahabies, Shias or Sunnis in Islam. Fight not for the interpretations of the truth, when the truth itself is in danger. It is foolish to complain of stumbling when you walk in the darkness of night. Let all come forward and contribute their respective shares in the great toil of the nation. Let the idols of class distinctions and sectarianism be smashed for ever; let the Mussalmans of the country be once more united into a great vital whole.[138]

The most powerful expression of such views come, of course, through Iqbal's poetry in both Urdu and Persian. Among his first Urdu poems conveying his new message, mention may particularly be made of *Shikwa* (Complaint) and *Jawab-i-Shikwa* (Answer to the Complaint), composed respectively in 1909 and 1913. In the former, he reminds God of the achievements of Muslim warriors in spreading

His message in various parts of the world, and then complains about their sad plight in the contemporary world. Dwelling on the bravery and sacrifices of Muslims in spreading God's message, the poet writes:

> Of all the brave warriors, there were none but only we,
> Who fought your battles on land and often on the sea.
> Our calls to prayer rang out from the churches of European lands
> And floated across Africa's scorching desert sands.
> We ruled the world, but regal glories our eyes disdained.
> Under the shades of glittering sabres your creed we proclaimed.
> All we lived for was to battle; we bore the troubles that came,
> And laid down our lives for the glory of your name.
> We never used our strength to conquer or extend domain.
> Would we have played with our lives for nothing but worldly gain?
> If our people had run after earth's goods and gold,
> Need they have smashed idols, and not idols sold?

The poet's complaint was that in spite of such services in the cause of the Lord, He was really kind to uncultured non-believers, who were prospering in every way, but quite unkind to the believers, i.e. Muslims:

> Our complaint is not that they are rich, that their coffers overflow
> They who have no manners and of polite speech nothing know.
> What injustice! Here and now are houris and palaces to infidels given,
> While the poor Muslim is promised houris only after he goes to heaven.
> Neither favour nor kindness is shown towards us any more;
> Where is the affection you showed us in the days of yore?[139]

In the *Jawab-i-Shikwa*, we have the poet's remedy for this situation: Muslims must be animated by the feeling of belonging to one community and put an end to all their internal divisions. While answering the poet's complaint, God is made to say:

> You have one faith, one creed and to one Prophet allegiance owe.
> You have one sacred Kaaba, one God and one holy book, the Koran.
> Was it so difficult to unite in one community every single Musalman?
> It is factions at one place; divisions into castes at another.
> In these days are these the ways to progress and to prosper?

Besides, Muslims, particularly the rich, had deviated from the true path and forgotten Islam. If they wanted to revive their past greatness, they must first learn to live like Muslims:

> There is loud talk that Muslims have disappeared from the earth's face.
> We ask you: did true Muslims exist anywhere in any place?
> Your style of living is Christian, your culture that of the Hindu;
> A Jew would be ashamed if he was Muslim such as you.
> You are Saiyyads as well as Mirzas, and you are Afghans—
> You are all these, but tell us are you also Mussalmans?[140]

The core of Iqbal's message was that the Muslims, particularly the youth, must awaken, build up their strength and become active in the service of the community. This comes out again and again in his poetry, though, of course, like all great poetry, there is a lot in it which is of universal appeal. Thus, in *Asrar-i-Khudi* (Secrets of Self, 1915), he writes:

> O thou, who complainest of the cruelty of Heaven,
> Thou whose class cries out against the injustice of the store,
> How long this wailing and crying and lamentation?
> How long this perpetual beating of thy breast?
> The pith of Life is contained in action,
> To delight in the creation is the Law of Life.
> Arise and create a new world![141]

Though the book is devoted to the awakening of the individual and reminding him of his prowess, the ideal of Islamic solidarity is not ignored. Thus in its final section, which is in the form of invocation to God, Iqbal observes:

> When the people of Islam let the thread of unity go from their hands,
> They fell into a hundred mazes.
> We are dispersed like stars in the world;
> Though of the same family, we are strange to one another.
> Bind again these scattered leaves,
> Revive the law of love!
> Take us back to serve thee as of old,
> Commit thy cause to them that love thee![142]

This emphasis on Islamic solidarity without any regard for national boundaries reflected the temper of the times dominated by the Pan-Islamic movement. The abolition of the Caliphate in 1924 by the Turks under the leadership of Mustafa Kamal and their effort to build up Turkey as a nation state saddened most Indian Muslims and left them rudderless for quite sometime; but it also opened a new vista for some. Iqbal was among the latter. He realized that while the ideal of Islamic solidarity remained valid as an ultimate objective, there was no immediate prospect of realizing it in practice. Although disagreeing with some of the measures introduced in Kamalist Turkey, he ardently supported the Turks' concentration on building up their own State and felt that Muslims in other lands should also concentrate on building up their own strength and organizing themselves on sound lines. When this process was completed, the time would arrive for giving a concrete shape to the ideal of Islamic solidarity. Thus did he travel from Pan-Islamism and opposition to all manifestations of nationalism to multi-nationalism.[143] The working of Iqbal's mind is made clear from the views expressed by him towards the end of his book, *Reconstruction of Religious Thought in Islam*, consisting of lectures delivered by him at the Universities of Madras, Hyderabad and Mysore in 1928 and published in 1934:

> For the present every Muslim nation must sink into her own deeper self, temporarily focus her vision on herself alone, until all are strong and powerful to form a living family of republics. A true and living unity . . . is not so easy as to be achieved by a merely symbolical overlordship. It is truly manifested in a multiplicity of free independent units whose racial rivalries are adjusted and harmonised by the unifying bond of a common spiritual aspiration. It seems to me that God is slowly bringing home to us the truth that Islam is neither Nationalism nor Imperialism but a League of Nations which recognises artificial boundaries and racial distinctions for facility of reference only, and not for restricting the social horizon of its members.[144]

It was this reasoning which lay at the back of his mind when, giving up his earlier opposition to nationalism as something inimical to Islam, he proceeded, in course of his presidential address to the annual session of the All India Muslim League held at Allahabad in December 1930, to assert that India did not consist of only one nation and that Muslims living on its soil constituted a nation by themselves. This constituted the central theme as well as the real significance of his address and not the demand for the creation of a separate Muslim State, as has been generally imagined, particularly in Pakistan.[145] Though the latter followed the former, it need not have necessarily done so. At any rate, Iqbal at that stage did not see the necessary connection. Quoting the French philosopher Earnest Renan, he emphasized that a nation is made neither by race, nor by religion, nor by geography, but by a common moral consciousness. The main problem in India arose from the fact that the Indian people were not animated by such a common consciousness and did not constitute a single nation. This was because various caste and religious groups had not shown any inclination to sink their respective individualities in a larger whole, and each group continued to be seriously concerned with maintaining its separate identity. So far as the Muslims were concerned, Islam had been the chief factor in moulding their history and had provided 'those basic emotions and loyalties which gradually unite scattered individuals and groups and finally transform them into a well defined people'. Islam was not a religion which could be relegated to the position of a mere private belief. Its religious ideal was closely related to its social order. The one could not exist without the other. 'Therefore the construction of a polity on national lines, if it means a displacement of the Islamic principle of solidarity, is simply unthinkable to a Muslim.' In such a situation the unity of India as a nation should be sought 'not in the negation, but in the mutual harmony and cooperation of the many'. If the principle was accepted that the Indian Muslims were entitled to full and free development in accordance with their own traditions and culture, they would stake their all for the freedom of India. India was a continent consisting of groups 'belonging to different races, speaking different languages and professing different religions'. It was 'Asia in miniature'. The principles of European democracy, therefore, could not be applied to India without recognizing these different groups, 'The Muslim demand for the creation of a Muslim India within India is, therefore, perfectly justified.' Such a creation would be facilitated by the merger of the Punjab, North West Frontier Province, Sind and Baluchistan into a single Muslim state. The formation of such a consolidated state appeared to be 'the final destiny of the Muslims, at least of the north-west India'. Some areas like the Ambala Division of the Punjab, where non-Muslims predominated, might be excluded from it in order to make it more clearly Muslim in population. A redrawing of the political map of India on this pattern, involving the setting up of culturally homogeneous units, would also mean an end of the controversy regarding joint *versus* separate electorates. In any case, the setting up of a Muslim state in the north-west was essential for safeguarding the future of Islam in India. Explaining his proposal, Iqbal observed:

India is the greatest Muslim country in the world. The life of Islam as a cultural force in this country very largely depends on its centralisation in a specified territory. This centralisation of the most living portion of the Muslims of India . . . will eventually solve the problem of India as well as of Asia. It will intensify their sense of responsibility and deepen their patriotic feeling. Thus possessing full opportunity of development within the body politic of India, the North-West India Muslims will prove the best defenders of India against a foreign invasion, be the invasion one of ideas or of bayonets.

The last sentence makes it clear that at that stage Iqbal was not thinking of a completely independent Muslim State. That he was also not visualizing the establishment of a separate army, except for purely local purposes, by his projected Muslim state in the north-west becomes clear from his observations on India's defence problem in the same address. Provincial armies, he stated, might be necessary in order to maintain internal peace, but the Indian Federal Parliament could maintain on the north-west frontier 'a strong Indian Frontier Army, composed of units recruited from all provinces and officered by efficient and experienced military men taken from all communities'. He, of course, emphasized, in line with the general Muslim thinking at that time, that an unitary form of government was 'simply unthinkable in a self-governing India'. Residuary powers must belong 'entirely to self-governing states, the Central Federal State exercizing only those powers which are expressly vested in it by the free consent of federal states'. He could never advise the Muslims of India to accept a system of government which negatived the principle of 'true federation' or failed to recognize them as 'a distinct political entity'.[146]

Iqbal further clarified the main intellectual underpinning behind these ideas in the course of his presidential address to the annual session of the All India Muslim Conference at Lahore in March 1932. Politics, according to him, had its roots in the spiritual life of man. In any case, Islam was not a matter merely of private belief, but a society or a civic church. He was opposed to nationalism as understood in Europe not because, if applied to India, it was likely to bring less material gains to Muslims, but because he saw in it the germs of atheistic materialism which, according to him, constituted the greatest danger to modern humanity. Describing what, according to him, was the heart of the Indian problem, he observed:

Patriotism is a perfectly natural virtue and has a place in the moral life of man. Yet that which really matters is a man's faith, his culture, his historical tradition. These are the things which in my eyes are worth living for and dying for, and not the piece of earth with which the spirit of man happens to be temporarily associated. In view of the visible and invisible points of contact between the various communities of India I do believe in the possibility of constructing a harmonious whole whose unity cannot be disturbed by the rich diversity which it must carry within its bosom. The problem of ancient Indian thought was how the one became many without sacrificing its oneness. Today this problem has come down from its ethical heights to the grosser plane of our political life and we have to solve it in its reversed form, i.e. how the many can become one without sacrificing its plural character.[147]

In a statement issued on 6 December 1933, Iqbal again stressed that to be opposed to nationalism 'in the sense of a fusion of the communities' did not necessarily amount to being anti-national. He certainly remained opposed to such fusion, but admitted that these communities had various interests in common. An understanding among them regarding those interests was not only possible but 'bound to come'. However, for this to materialize and an united India to emerge, it was necessary to recognize 'the distinct existence of more than one people in the country'.[148]

X

In suggesting the consolidation of the Muslim majority areas of north-west India into one state, Iqbal was not saying something startlingly new, but merely reflecting one of the strands of the then prevailing opinion among the Muslim intelligentsia in the Punjab. This is borne out by the dispatch of 'A Correspondent in India' published in *The Times* (London) dated 14 March 1928. According to it, not only in Punjab but also in the valley of the Indus and its tributaries, there was to be found 'a practical vision of a constructive future, based on history'. That was the vision of 'effective Muslim rule'. He also mentioned that when the time came for the implementation of that vision, the predominantly Hindu areas of the Punjab might be separated and added to Delhi. This would result in the creation of 'a solid Muslim bloc from the Peshawar valley to the mouth of the Indus'.[149]

Some others went beyond such consolidation and began to think of more radical solutions based on the Two-nation theory. Mention may first be made of a Punjabi journalist and missionary of the Ahmediya sect, F.K. Khan Durrani, editor of *Muslim India* (Lahore), who looked forward to making the whole of India Muslim or establishing Muslim rule over India as the only solution to the communal problem. In a book entitled *The Future of Islam* in India, published in February 1929, he observed:

> The idea of unity as a solution of India's problem is an unutterable folly, against which the history of the world stands as a witness. States have never been born of pacts, and the people of India are not so extraordinarily wonderful that they should be able to achieve what the world has never been able to achieve. The idea of unity is based upon ignorance of the national characteristics of the two peoples. It is based upon ignorance of the very rudiments of political philosophy. The true solution of India's problem is elimination of one of the two elements. Either the Muslims should commit suicide and remove themselves from the stage (or grow tufts of hair on their heads and become Hindus, which means the same thing) or assert themselves like Muslims and make a bid for the empire of India. There is no other alternative.[150]

The idea of a Muslim empire, so out of tune with the then existing reality, was not picked up by any other publicist or politician. The significance of Durrani's book, therefore, lies mainly in its emphasis on the Two-nation theory and the impossibility of Muslims willingly forming part of a political set-up in which they did not constitute the dominant element. Basing themselves on this premise, some Muslims began to advocate India's partition and the setting up of an independent Muslim State. This was not an entirely novel idea. Stray individuals had off-and-on suggested this earlier as the most suitable solution of the Indian problem. Thus, for instance, the Kheiri Brothers, Abdul Jabbar and Abdus Sattar, had in a paper submitted to the Stockholm Conference of the Second International held in the autumn of 1917, suggested the partition of India into a Muslim India and a Hindu India.[151] In March-April 1920, a local Urdu paper of Badaun (UP), called *Zulqarnain*, published an open letter to Gandhi by one Muhammad Abdul Qadir Bilgrami advocating the division of India between Hindus and Muslims. The letter was subsequently published as a pamphlet running into 62 pages and containing a list of Muslim dominated districts 'fundamentally not too different from the present boundaries of Bangladesh and Pakistan'.[152] In 1921, a lawyer of Agra, Nadir Ali, published a pamphlet in which he discussed the partition of India as one of the means for settling the Hindu-Muslim problem.[153] In 1923, Sardar Gul Khan, President of the Islamic Anjuman, Dera Ismail Khan, in the course of his deposition before the North-West Frontier Enquiry Committee, suggested the division of India between

Hindus and Muslims. Asserting that Hindu-Muslim unity would never become a fact, he added: 'we would very much rather see the separation of the Hindus and the Muhammedans, 23 crores of Hindus to the South and 8 crores of Muslims to the North'.[154]

With the passage of time, the idea of partition apparently acquired more adherents. In December 1927, Malcolm Hailey, then Governor of the Punjab, recorded that he noticed 'some curious movements going on in the Muhammedan world of Northern India'. Muslims in the Punjab were realizing that they could never have the same interests as Muslims living in provinces where they were in a minority. This had set them thinking about the desirability of having a federation of their own embracing the Punjab, parts of UP, the North-West Frontier Province, Sind and Baluchistan. They openly said that that was only a preparation for a larger federation which would embrace Afghanistan and perhaps Persia. Hailey was, of course, not sure how far these ideas would grow or shape themselves into a definite policy.[155] Within two years, he reverted to this theme as Governor of UP, while reporting on his conversation with Ross Masood, then Vice-Chancellor of Aligarh Muslim University. According to that report, Masood told Hailey that the differences of Muslims from the Hindus were 'really very deep-seated', they being much more cultural than religious. Muslims felt that they would be swamped by the Hindus in a self-governing India. Their minds were turning more and more to the idea of a federation with Afghanistan, with Persia in the background and with allies in the frontier independent territories. Hailey's own comment, after recording Masood's impression, is also significant, especially in the context of the long-prevailing myth that the idea of partition first emerged in the Muslim minority provinces, particularly UP, and that Muslims of the Punjab supported it only towards the fag end of the Pakistan movement:

> Most of us, of course, have had schemes of this kind under view for some time. Circumstances have prevented their coming into the field of open discussion, and in any case, I am not sure that they will gain much support in the U.P. or Bengal. But the Punjab Muslims have long been talking among themselves of a Union of Northern Punjab (which would give them a solid position against the Sikhs and Hindu Jats), Sind, Baluchistan and Afghanistan. A generation ago a union with Afghanistan would have been regarded with horror, for the Pathan is a very unpopular person in northern India; but the memory of his raids, etc. is dying out, and at present, at all events, it seems preferable to many of them to run the risk of engaging him as an ally rather than to accept the certainty of domination by a Hinduised Central Government.[156]

Hailey's impression is corroborated by some of the Muslim writings and speeches during 1928-9, which have recently come to light. The year 1928 witnessed the publication in London of a book called *The Indian Moslems* by 'An Indian Mohammedan', whose identity was kept secret for a long time, but who has recently been identified as Nawab Sayyid Sardar Ali Khan of Hyderabad. He did not advocate partition, but did speculate on a possible 'sub-division' of India, without which Muslims were not likely to receive their due: '. . . no doubt if India ever comes again to be sub-divided, as was her usual lot before the Mogul[s] arrived, they [Muslims] will be entitled to obtain their share in a general partition. But it would not be in any India that preserved its unity.'[157] Sardar Ali Khan was also a firm believer in the Two-nation theory and emphasized that the future constitution must be based on it:

> Within the frontiers of India live two nations, the Moslem and the Hindu, which entertain for each other the same feelings as do, for instance, French and Germans, and who differ from one another more profoundly than any two nations in Europe. . . . This is the fundamental fact on which Indian society is based, and any constitution which is not founded on it will come to the ground.[158]

In December of the same year, Maulana Murtaza Ahmed Khan Maikash, a Punjabi journalist, wrote a series of four articles in the *Inquilab*, an Urdu daily of Lahore, asserting that the solution of the Indian communal problem lay in the establishment of 'a Muslim national homeland' consisting of the Punjab, Sind, Baluchistan and the North-West Frontier Province. In reply to criticism in a section of contemporary Hindu press in Lahore, he emphasized that the demand for the creation of such a State was based on 'the internationally recognised principle of the right of self-determination' and that it was 'the only goal for which Muslims could make sacrifices'.[159]

About a year later, the partition idea received powerful support from Nawab Sir Zulfiqar Ali Khan, a prominent political leader of Punjab, associated with all the three important Muslim organizations—the Muslim League, Muslim Conference and Khilafat Conference—as also a member of the Central legislature since 1921. In his address as chairman of the reception committee of the All India Khilafat Conference held at Lahore, on 31 December 1929, he strongly affirmed the Two-nation theory and suggested a partition of India on that basis, for the first time including Bengal also in the proposed Muslim homeland. In India, he argued, thanks to the Asian temperament, religion was an essential ingredient of nationality. India could, therefore, become a nation only if all its people accepted one common religion. However, this was neither practical nor necessary for ending sectarian conflicts and ensuring peace and progress. That could be easily ensured by dividing the country between Hindus and Muslims. As he put it:

> The freedom and progress of India depends on this: the Muslims should be given in northern India a territory containing two or three provinces, or one which could be made into one province, wherein their majority should not be less than 80%. Similarly, in eastern India, Bengal should be so divided as to leave the Muslims with an 80% ratio in the population. The Muslims should demand a country or a homeland, instead of asking for rights.[160]

Three years later, a Punjabi student at Cambridge, Chaudhury Rahmat Ali reiterated the partition idea in most eloquent terms, demanding the creation of a separate Muslim State out of the north-western areas of India and also giving it the name Pakistan (first spelled Pakstan). Both the demand and the name were publicized through a four-page statement entitled *Now or Never*, signed by Rahmat Ali and three others and forwarded on 28 January 1933 to important persons dealing with the Indian constitutional problem in Britain, including the members of the third session of the Round Table Conference on India then meeting in London. The signatories claimed that they were speaking 'on behalf of the thirty million Muslims of Pakstan', who then lived in the five northern units of India—Punjab, North West Frontier Province, Kashmir, Sindh and Baluchistan—and representing 'their inexorable demand for the recognition of their separate national status, as distinct from the rest of India, by the grant of a separate federal constitution on social, religious, political and historical grounds'. They strongly attacked the Muslim delegates to the Round Table Conference (who included Iqbal) for having agreed to the setting up of an All-India Federation and characterized it as 'nothing less than signing the death-warrant of Islam and its future in India'. India, according to them, was neither the name of a single country nor the home of a single nation, but 'the designation of a State created for the first time in history, by the British'. In the five northern provinces of India claimed for Pakistan, they emphasized, the Muslims constituted an overwhelming majority of the population and they had hardly anything in common with the Hindus:

> Our religion, culture, history, economic system, laws of inheritance, succession and marriage are basically and fundamentally different from those of the

people living in the rest of India. The ideals which move our thirty million brethren-in-faith living in these provinces to make the highest sacrifices are fundamentally different from those which inspire the Hindus. These differences are not confined to the broad basic principles—far from it. They extend to the minutest details of our lives. We do not inter-dine; we do not inter-marry. Our national customs and calendars, even our diet and dress are different.

They went on to clarify that what they were demanding was basically different from the suggestion made by Iqbal in 1930. While the latter had envisaged a consolidated Muslim state in the north-west to be a part of an All-India Federation, what was now being demanded was the setting up of a completely separate federation of their own for the Muslim majority areas of the north-west. 'There can be no peace and tranquillity in the land', Rahmat Ali and his comrades finally warned, 'if the Muslims are duped into a Hindu dominated federation where we cannot be the masters of our own destiny and captains of our own soul'.[161]

This was not the last statement issued by this group. Rahmat Ali set up a small organization called the Pakistan National Movement in order to carry on a continuous propaganda campaign on behalf of the demand for Pakistan. Besides he also continued to issue statements and brochures from time to time describing himself as the Founder-President, Pakistan National Movement. Thus, while the Joint Select Committee of the British Parliament was considering proposals regarding Indian constitutional reforms, a statement issued on 1 November 1933 on behalf of the Pakistan National Movement drew attention to the demand contained in the first statement entitled *Now or Never* and declared that the Pakistan National Movement was irrevocably committed to it and determined to work by all constitutional means available to it for its realization. Pakistan and Hindustan, the statement observed, had given much to the world in the past and could give more in the future, but they could give anything of value only by remaining essentially themselves. 'Political fusion could destroy their national souls and would result in hybrid nationalism from which would issue nothing but degeneration, disruption, and disintegration.' Again, when the Parliament was giving consideration to the Government of India Bill, a statement dated 8 July 1935 and issued under the signature of Rahmat Ali declared that the Bill, embodying the scheme of an All-India federation, had created 'an acute crisis in the national life of Pakistan', and had raised 'a supreme issue—an issue of life or death for its national future'. Reiterating the basic ideology of the

Pakistan movement it declared that the constitutional problem in India did not represent an inter-communal issue, but an international one and could be solved permanently only on that basis.[162]

Although not a pioneer in publicly propounding the Pakistan idea, Rahmat Ali made a most significant contribution to its spread by clothing it with such passionate arguments. These soon began to echo and re-echo in India, particularly in the Punjab and several articles appeared in the press strongly supporting them. When, after years of pondering and preparation, Jinnah at last decided to publicly demand Partition—through his presidential address to the Lahore session of the Muslim League (1940)—he used words very much reminiscent of the ones used by Rahmat Ali in 1933. The latter's name was, of course, not mentioned.

NOTES

1. Muhammad Iqbal, *Reconstruction of Religious Thought in Islam* (London, 1934), p. 162.
2. Hafeez Malik, *Moslem Nationalism in India and Pakistan* (Washington D.C., 1963).
3. Aziz Ahmad, *Studies in Islamic Culture in the Indian Environment* (Oxford, 1969), p. 201.
4. M. Mujeeb, *Indian Muslims* (London, 1967), p. 281.
5. Ibid., p. 277.
6. Ibid.
7. Aziz Ahmad, n. 3, p. 205.
8. Saiyid Athar Ali Rizvi, *Shah Wali-Allah and His Times* (Canberra, 1980), p. 249.
9. Malik, n. 2, p. 129.
10. Ibid., pp. 128-39.
11. Mujeeb, n. 4, p. 282.
12. K.A. Nizami, 'Socio-Religious Movements in Indian Islam, 1763-1898', in S.T. Lokhandwalla, ed., *India and Contemporary Islam* (Simla, 1971), pp. 102-3. Recently a serious doubt has been expressed on both these points. See Barbara Daly Metcalf, *Islamic Revival in British India: Deoband, 1860-1900* (Princeton, 1982), pp. 50-4 and Saiyid Athar Abbas Rizvi, *Shah Abd Al-Aziz: Puritanism, Sectrarian Polemics and Jihad* (Canberra, 1982), pp. 522-3.
13. Aziz Ahmad, n. 3, p. 213.
14. Refiuddin Ahmed, *The Bengal Muslims, 1871-1906: A Quest for Identity* (Delhi, 1981), p. 71.
15. On these movements, in addition to the works cited above, see also Qeyamuddin Ahmad, *The Wahabi Movement in India* (Calcutta, 1966), and Muinuddin Khan, *The Faraidi Movement: Muslim Political Thought and Activity in India during the Nineteenth Century* (Aligarh, 1969).

16. Aziz Ahmad, *Islamic Modernism in India and Pakistan, 1857-1964* (London, 1970), p. 104.
17. See Ziaul Hasan Faruqi, *The Deoband School and the Demand for Pakistan* (Bombay, 1963), pp. 20-1. It has, however, been pointed out in a recent study that there is no conclusive proof of this. See Metcalf, n. 12, pp. 82-3. See also Aziz Ahmad's Introduction in Aziz Ahmad and G.E. Von Grunebaum, eds., *Muslim Self-Statement in India and Pakistan, 1857-1968* (Wiesbaden, 1970), p. 5.
18. Metcalf, n. 12, pp. 152-3.
19. Malik, n. 2, p. 196.
20. For an account of Syed Ahmed's service to the English at Bijnor, see G.F.I. Graham, *The Life and Work of Sir Syed Ahmed Khan* (Karachi, 1974, 1st pub. 1885), pp. 15-23.
21. See Christian W. Troll, *Sayyid Ahmed Khan: A Restatement of Muslim Theology* (New Delhi, 1978), pp. xviii-xix.
22. Hafeez Malik, *Sir Sayyid Ahmed Khan and Muslim Modernization in India and Pakistan* (New York, 1980), p. 76.
23. W.C. Smith, *Modern Islam in India* (London, 1946), p. 15.
24. Graham, n. 20, p. 37.
25. Ibid., pp. 41-2.
26. Troll, n. 21, p. 99.
27. J.M.S. Baljon Jr., *The Reforms and Religious Ideas of Sir Sayyid Ahmed Khan* (Leiden, 1949), p. 17.
28. Graham, n. 20, pp. 141-56.
29. Aziz Ahmad, n. 3, p. 60.
30. Ibid., p. 64.
31. Francis Robinson, *Separatism Among Indian Muslims: The Politics of the United Provinces' Muslims, 1860-1923* (Cambridge, 1974), p. 112.
32. Ibid.
33. Graham, n. 20, pp. 125-9.
34. Malik, n. 2, pp. 98-9.
35. Mujeeb, n. 4, p. 448.
36. Baljon, n. 27, p. 25.
37. Malik, n. 22, p. 262.
38. S.M. Ikram, *Modern Muslim India and the Birth of Pakistan* (Lohore, 1970), pp. 34-5.
39. Aziz Ahmad, n. 16, pp. 40-53; Malik, n. 22, pp. 262-79.
40. Bashir Ahmad Dar, *Religious Thought of Sayyid Ahmad Khan* (Lahore, 1971), p. 268.
41. Aziz Ahmad, n. 16, p. 4.
42. Graham, n. 20, p. 48.
43. Robinson, n. 31, p. 90.
44. Ibid., p. 91.
45. Ibid., pp. 92-3.
46. Ibid., pp. 93-7; Malik, n. 22, pp. 84-93.
47. Paul R. Brass, *Language, Religion and Politics in North India* (Cambridge, 1974), p. 130.
48. Ikram, n. 38, pp. 30-1; translated from Urdu.
49. Ibid., p. 31. Emphasis added.

50. T. Morison, *History of the Muhammadan Anglo-Oriental College* (Allahabad, 1903), p. 63.
51. David Lelyveld, *Aligarh's First Generation: Muslim Solidarity in British India* (Princeton, 1978), p. 318. See also M.S. Jain, *The Aligarh Movement* (Agra, 1965), pp. 43-50.
52. Some idea of the proceedings of the various sessions of the Conference during the lifetime of Syed Ahmad Khan can be had from Shan Muhammad, ed., *The Aligarh Movement: Basic Documents: 1864-1898,* III (Meerut, 1978), pp. 767-903.
53. Malik, n. 22, pp. 219-20.
54. Ikram, n. 38, p. 38.
55. For an excellent summary of different views on this point, see Troll, n. 21, pp. 6-13; the latest contribution, of course, by an old hand, is contained in Malik, n. 22, pp. 229-53.
56. Malik, n. 22, p. 232.
57. Shan Muhammad, ed., *Writings and Speeches of Sir Syed Ahmad Khan* (Bombay, 1972), pp. 159-60.
58. Ibid., pp. 161-3, 174-6.
59. C.H. Philips and B.N. Pandey (eds.), *The Evolution of India and Pakistan, 1858-1947; Select Documents* (London, 1962), p. 185.
60. A.M. Zaidi, ed., *Evolution of Muslim Political Thought in India,* I (New Delhi, 1975), pp. 33-46.
61. Badruddin Tyabji to Syed Ahmad Khan and others, 13 January 1888, *Badruddin Tyabji Papers*, National Archives of India; also reproduced in Government of Bombay, *Source Material for a History of the Freedom Movement in India,* II, 1885-1920 (Bombay, 1958), pp. 67-8.
62. Syed Ahmad Khan to Badruddin Tyabji, 24 January 1888, ibid., pp. 70-1.
63. Badruddin Tyabji to Syed Ahmad Khan, 18 February 1888, ibid., pp. 71-3.
64. Zaidi, n. 60, pp. 47-61.
65. Ibid., pp. 65-8.
66. See, for example, Mushir U. Haq, *Muslim Politics in Modern India* (Meerut, 1970), pp. 28-33.
67. Ikram, n. 38, pp. 59-60.
68. See I.H. Qureshi, *The Muslim Community in the Indo-Pakistan Subcontinent* (S. Gravenhage, 1962), pp. 248-9.
69. See Shan Muhammad, n. 57, pp. 161-3.
70. Anil Seal, *The Emergence of Indian Nationalism* (Cambridge, 1968), p. 325.
71. C.F. Andrews, *Zaka Ullah of Delhi* (Cambridge, 1929), p. 95.
72. Ibid., pp. 110-11.
73. Ibid., pp. 112-13.
74. Ibid., p. 125.
75. A.B.M. Habibullah, 'Historical Writing in Urdu: A Survey of Tendencies', in C.H. Philips, ed., *Historians of India, Pakistan and Ceylon* (London, 1961), pp. 488-90.
76. Ibid., p. 490.
77. Muhammad Sadiq, *A History of Urdu Literature* (London, 1964), pp. 316-18.
78. Ibid.
79. Smith, n. 23, pp. 39-40.

80. Cited in N. Gerald Barrier, 'Muslim Politics in the Punjab, 1870-1890', *The Punjab Past and Present*, Vol. VI, April 1971, p. 118.
81. Andrews, n. 71, p. xiv.
82. Sadiq, n. 77, p. 267.
83. Ikram, n. 38, p. 60.
84. Ibid., p. 63.
85. Altaf Hussain Hali, *The Mussaddas: The Story of the Ebb and Tide in Islam, Syeda Saiyidain Hameed,* Trans. (to be published), stanzas 69-71.
86. Ibid., stanzas 119-20.
87. Ibid., stanza 150.
88. Ibid., stanza 212.
89. Ahmad and Grunebaum, n. 17, p. 99.
90. Ibid.
91. Ikram, n. 38, pp. 68-9.
92. Habibullah, n. 75, p. 485.
93. Ikram, n. 38, p. 67.
94. Habibullah, n. 75, p. 485.
95. Smith, n. 23, p. 49.
96. Ibid., p. 50. See also Freeland Abbott, *Islam and Pakistan* (Ithaca, New York, 1968), pp. 140-3.
97. Ahmad, n. 16, pp. 89-91.
98. Smith, n. 23, pp. 53-4. See also Ameer Ali, *The Spirit of Islam* (London, 1961); a representative selection from this book relating to Islam and Christianity is to be found in Ahmad and Grunebaum, n. 17, pp. 100-11.
99. Smith, n. 23, p. 40. See also M. Moinul Haq, *Islamic Thought and Movements in the Subcontinent* (Karachi, 1979), pp. 478-82.
100. Ahmad, n. 16, p. 77.
101. Sadiq, n. 77, pp. 274-6.
102. Ikram, n. 38, pp. 120-4.
103. Ibid., pp. 124-9.
104. Habibullah, n. 75, p. 490.
105. Quoted in Sadiq, n. 77, p. 340. See also Habibullah, n. 75, p. 491.
106. Smith, n. 23, p. 56.
107. Ibid., pp. 59-70.
108. Matcalf, n. 12, pp. 358-9.
109. See Chapters III and IV of Ahmed, n. 14, pp. 72-132.
110. Ibid., pp. 99-103.
111. Malik, n. 22, pp. 17-21.
112. Ahmed, n. 16, p. 126.
113. See Ram Chandra Shukla, *British, India and the Turkish Empire* (New Delhi, 1973), pp. 94-120.
114. Sharif Al Mujahid, 'Pan-Islamism', *A History of Freedom Movement* III (i) (Karachi, 1961), pp. 96, 104.
115. Aziz Ahmad, n. 16, p. 126.
116. Ibid., pp. 126f.
117. Ikram, n. 38, p. 137.
118. Peter Hardy, *Partners in Freedom and True Muslims: The Political Thought of Some Muslim Scholars in British India, 1912-1947* (Lund, 1971), p. 21.
119. Mujeeb, n. 4, p. 458.

120. Ibid.
121. *Al-Hilal*, 18 December 1912, cited in Hardy, n. 118, p. 22.
122. *Al-Hilal*, 6 November 1912, cited in ibid.
123. Ibid., p. 30.
124. This implied that the Caliph should have 'temporal power at all times adequate for the defence of the (Islamic) Faith'. Along with it went the demand that the Arabian peninsula, containing the holy places of Islam and known as Jazirat-ul-Arab should be kept absolutely free of all non-Muslim control. See the text of Maulana Muhammad Ali's speech in London in 1920 in Afzal Iqbal, ed., *Selected Speeches and Statements of Maulana Mohammed Ali* (Lahore, 1963), II, pp. 33-45. Also given in Ahmad and Grunebaum, n. 17, pp. 117-19.
125. Faruqi, n. 17, pp. 68-9.
126. Ibid., p. 69.
127. See Ali Ashraf, 'Khilafat Movement: A Factor in Muslim Separatism', in Mushirul Hasan, ed., *Communal and Pan-Islamic Trends in Colonial India* (New Delhi, 1981), pp. 66-84.
128. H.A.R. Gibb, *Modern Trends in Islam* (Chicago, 1947), p. 61.
129. Smith, n. 23, p. 98. See also C.M. Naim, ed., *Iqbal, Jinnah and Pakistan: The Vision and the Reality* (Syracuse, 1979), pp. 11-106.
130. Hafeez Malik, 'Life of the Poet-Philosopher', in Hafeez Malik, ed., *Iqbal: Poet-Philosopher of Pakistan* (New York, 1971), p. 16.
131. Mujeeb, n. 4, p. 485.
132. Ibid.
133. Ibid., p. 483.
134. Ikram, n. 38, p. 163.
135. Ibid., pp. 163-4.
136. Translated from Urdu, ibid., p. 164.
137. Syed Abdul Vahid, ed., *Thoughts and Reflections of Iqbal* (Lahore, 1964), pp. 50-1.
138. Ibid., pp. 54-5. See also pp. 59-60, 376-7.
139. Muhammad Iqbal, *Shikwa* and *Jawab-i-Shikwa*, translated into English by Khushwant Singh (Delhi, 1981), pp. 33-4, 43.
140. Ibid., pp. 73, 77.
141. Muhammad Iqbal, *The Secrets of the Self: Allama Iqbal's Asrar-i-Khudi*. Translated into Versified English by Reynold A. Nicholson (Lahore, 1955), p. 89.
142. Ibid., pp. 142-3.
143. See Sharif Al Mujahid, 'Muslim Nationalism: Iqbal's Synthesis of Pan-Islamism and Nationalism', *Journal of Pakistan Studies*, Vol. I, No. I, June 1979, pp. 37-49.
144. Muhammad Iqbal, *Reconstruction of Religious Thought in Islam* (Lahore, 1977), p. 159.
145. For a detailed review as well as refutation of the views of most of the Pakistani scholars who hold that because of the Allahabad Address, the credit for having first proposed a separate State for Indian Muslims from a public platform should go to Iqbal see K.K. Aziz, *A History of the Idea of Pakistan* (Lahore, 1987), I, pp. 224-327.
146. Vahid, n. 137, pp. 161-94.

147. Ibid., pp. 196-7.
148. Ibid., p. 366.
149. Aziz, n. 145, p. 154. The 'Correspondent in India' was one J.M. Ewart, ibid. p. 181, fn. 49.
150. Syed Sharifuddin Pirzada, *Evolution of Pakistan* (Lahore, 1963), pp. 119-20. For speculation on the possible impact of Durrani's thinking on Iqbal and Rahmat Ali, see Aziz, n. 145, pp. 160-7. The full text of Durrani's book has been reproduced in K.K. Aziz, ed., *Prelude to Pakistan, 1930-1940: Documents and Readings Illustrating the Growth of the Idea of Pakistan* (Lahore, 1992), I, pp. 78-106.
151. See Pirzada, n. 150, pp. 86-9. Also Majid Hayat Siddiqi, 'Bluff, Doubt and Fear: The Kheri Brothers and the Colonial State, 1904-45', *The Indian Economic and Social History Review,* XXIV, No. 3, July-September 1987, pp. 261-2.
152. Ishtiaq Husain Qureshi, *The Muslim Community of the Indo-Pakistan Subcontinent* (Karachi, 1977; 2nd edn), p. 338. Bilgrami's thesis rested primarily on the Hindu-Muslim clash over cow-killing, Aziz, n. 145, pp. 99-104.
153. Chaudhry Khaliquzzaman, *Pathway to Pakistan* (Lahore, 1961), p. 238.
154. Pirzada, n. 150, pp. 95-6. See also Aziz, n. 145, pp. 116-17.
155. Hailey to Sir Arthur Hirtzel, 15 December 1927, IOR, E220/11B, Hailey Collection.
156. Hailey to Irwin, 3 December 1929, E220/16B, ibid.
157. Aziz, n. 145, p. 152.
158. Pirzada, n. 150, pp. 118-19.
159. Aziz, n. 145, pp. 167-8.
160. Ibid., pp. 171-2. See also M. Rafiq Afzal, 'Origin of the Idea of a Separate Muslim State: Nawab Sir Zulfiqar Ali Khan's Lahore Address, 1929', *Journal of the Research Society of Pakistan,* January-April 1966.
161. IOR/P & J/8/689, Private Office Papers.
162. Ibid. All these documents are reproduced in K.K. Aziz, ed., *Complete Works of Rehmat Ali*, Vol. I (Islamabad, 1978), pp. 1-20.

CHAPTER IV

Hindu Nationalism, Ethos of Indian Nationalism and British Policy

IRONICAL THOUGH it may seem, Muslim nationalism drew considerable strength from Hindu nationalism just as the latter also drew strength from the former. Indeed, both these nationalisms helped sustain each other. Hindu nationalism also served to deepen the Muslim elite's feeling of uncertainty and insecurity, particularly in relation to the sharing of power, while visualizing their future in a free India. The limited support for such nationalism, compared to the much greater support enjoyed by Indian nationalism, failed to remove this feeling. For it was generally believed by votaries of Muslim nationalism that the forces of Hindu nationalism, regardless of their formal strength, were the true representatives of the feelings of the bulk of the Hindu population.

Movements of religious revival and reformation significantly contributed to the rise and growth of Muslim nationalism. The same process was at work amongst the Hindus. The central motivation was also similar: to spread modern education and enlightenment among Hindus on the basis of indigenous inspiration and thereby face the challenge posed by the Christian missionaries who were openly declaring that Hinduism was nothing but a bundle of superstitions, and that Hindus had no future in modern times without its abandonment and their conversion to Christianity. Most of the leaders of the Hindu revival and reformation movements—very often the two overlapped—argued that Hinduism in its original form was an ideal religion in every respect and that its objectionable features had gathered to it later. The remedy, therefore, lay in going back to the earliest time, the time of the Vedas, when the basic tenets of Hinduism had taken shape, and to get rid of the later accretions, many of them of medieval origin, due largely to contact with Islam. Thus, just as among Muslims, so among Hindus, religious revival meant going back to the remote past for inspiration and getting rid of many of the traditions and beliefs acquired as a result of contact with the followers of the other faith.This created a major schism in the intellectual or inspirational worlds of the two elites and propelled them in different directions, demolishing some of the bridges that had been built up as a result of living together on Indian soil during the medieval period.[1] Along with it, largely because of historical reasons, there also developed among some of the leading figures of the Hindu revival and reformation movements a certain feeling of antipathy towards Muslims. This was bound to endow many of their followers with an outlook which could not be conducive to the promotion of understanding between the two communities.

The process began with Raja Rammohun Roy (1772-1833), the founder of the Brahmo Samaj and generally regarded as the Father of Modern India. He tried to show that the worship of idols of innumerable gods and goddesses had not originally been a part of Hinduism, which had really been based on monotheism. He also campaigned in favour of the abolition of all caste distinctions and pernicious social customs like *sati*, and the spread of modern education and enlightenment among Hindus. A very learned man, he devoted a lot of time in studying Hindu scriptures and finding therein support for his arguments. Just as in the case of Syed Ahmed Khan, however, his interest in religious reform was motivated not so much by his interest in religion *per se* as by his desire to renovate and revitalize his community which he too treated as a nation. As he wrote in course of an important letter in 1828, he found Hindus in general more superstitious and miserable than the rest of the known 'nations on the earth'. According to him, the religion then followed by Hindus was 'not well calculated to promote their political interest'. Innumerable caste divisions and subdivisions had deprived them of patriotic feeling and preoccupation with a multitude of religious rites and ceremonies had disqualified them from undertaking any difficult enterprise. Some change was, therefore, necessary in their religion 'at least for the sake of their political advantage and social comfort'.[2]

Again, although endowed with an universalist outlook, Rammohun Roy subscribed to the widely prevalent view that Muslim rule had caused great damage to Hindu society and culture. He recognized that under Muslim rulers, 'the natives of this country' had enjoyed every political privilege in common with Muslims and had been eligible to the highest offices in the State without any disqualification or discrimination on account of their religion, but also held that their civil and religious rights had been often violated by 'the rapacity and intolerance' of Muslims, and their property 'often plundered, their religion insulted and their blood wantonly shed'. Muslims, he thought, had introduced a tyrannical government 'destroying temples, universities and all other sacred and literary establishments'.[3] This line of thought was continued by some of his prominent disciples in Bengal. Thus, Dwarkanath Tagore (1794-1846) while dilating upon some of the deficiencies of 'natives' such as 'a want of truth, a want of integrity, a want of independence', remarked that these evils had not existed in India in ancient times, but had emerged as a result of Muslim conquest and the consequent loss of liberty and national degradation. He further observed:

> The Muhammedans introduced in this country all the vices of an ignorant, intolerant and licentious soldiery. The utter destruction of learning and science was an invariable part of their system, and the conquered, no longer able to protect their lives by arms and independence, fell into opposite extremes of abject submission, deceit and fraud. Such has been the condition of the natives of Hindustan for centuries.[4]

Indeed, such thinking was so common among Hindus in Calcutta that even some non-Hindus adopted it. Thus, Henry Louis Vivian Derozio (1809-31), one of the famous names in the history of the Bengal Renaissance, wrote in one of his poems:

> The Muslim is come down to spoil the land . . .
> The Hindu hath marched forward to repel
> The lawless plunderer of his shrines,
> The savage, rude disturber of his peace.[5]

Swami Dayanand Saraswati (1824-83), founder of the Arya Samaj (1875) which developed into a powerful organization in northern India, particularly in Punjab, gave the slogan 'Back to the Vedas'. He asserted that they contained not only the highest form of monotheism, but also all conceivable wisdom and knowledge regarding various aspects of life. He wrote and preached in Hindi and spoke in a more strident, nationalistic tone than Rammohun Roy, whose utterances had been generally marked by an apologetic tone and had been aimed at showing that Hinduism was not in any way inferior to Christianity. Dayanand asserted that the Vedic religion was superior to all other religions, including Christianity and Islam. While most of his energy was devoted to combating the evils, both of belief and practice, which, according to him, had crept into Hinduism and corrupted it, he also tried to establish its superiority over other religions. His main religious treatise, *Satyartha Prakash,* first published in 1875, and revised and enlarged in 1883, contains detailed criticisms of Christianity and Islam. Although his criticism of Islam is not as bitter and sarcastic as that of Christianity,[6] it occupies a larger space in the book and is couched in extremely strong language. Its main thrust is on 'Islam's division of the world into the faithful and the infidel, plus the twin themes of brutality and sensuality.'[7] Thus commenting on the Koranic injunction, 'and fight for the cause of God against those who fight against you and kill them wherever ye shall find them . . .', Dayananda observes: 'Had not such teachings existed in the Quran, the Mohammedans would not have been so cruel to the non-Mohammedans'. According to him,

> The Quran enjoins on its believers to kill the non-Muhammedans. If they kill their co-religionists by mischance, they shall have to make amends for it by freeing a believer from slavery, but if they kill non-Muhammedans even though it be through a mistake, they shall inherit Heaven.
>
> Such teachings deserve to be utterly discarded. Such a book, such a prophet and such a religion do nothing but harm. The world would be better off without them.

At another place, Dayanand remarks: 'He would indeed be a perfect idiot who would believe the Quran to be revealed, Mohammad to be a prophet and the Mohammedan God to be an Omnipotent Lord.'[8]

Swami Vivekananda (1863-1902), the most powerful champion of Hindu revival and having the greatest impact on the thinking of the educated Hindus in modern times all over India, spoke in a different tone. Following in the footsteps of his illustrious preceptor, Ramakrishna (1834-86), he emphasized the oneness of entire mankind and the essential unity of all religions, including Christianity and Islam. Far from attacking Islam, he showed a keen appreciation for its message of social equality. Thus describing Vedantism or Advaitism, one of the main philosophical strands of Hinduism and based on the concept of oneness of mankind, as 'the last word of religion and thought' and 'the religion of the future enlightened humanity' in a letter to a Muslim admirer, he emphasized that while Hindus might get the credit for arriving at it earlier than other races because of being an older race than the Hebrews or the Arabs, practical Advaitism had never been developed among them. On the other hand, if any religion came anywhere near the concept of equality among all human beings preached by Advaitism, it was 'Islam and Islam alone'. He further added:

I am firmly persuaded that without the help of practical Islam, theories of Vedantism, however fine and wonderful they may be, are entirely valueless to the vast mass of mankind. We want to lead mankind to the place where there is neither the Vedas, nor the Bible, nor the Koran, yet this has to be done by harmonising the Vedas, the Bible and the Koran. Mankind ought to be taught that religions are but the varied expressions of THE RELIGION, which is oneness, so that each may choose the path that suits him best.

For our own motherland, a junction of the two great systems, Hinduism and Islam—Vedanta brain and Islam body—is the only hope.[9]

Though this shows remarkable broadmindedness, the type of integration based on a synthesis of Hindu philosophy and Islamic social organization, which Vivekananda seemed to have envisaged, would be based essentially on Hindu philosophical thought. Even if a syncretic approach was developed, this type of integration, particularly in religion, could not have received any appreciation from Muslims with their faith in the superiority of their own religious doctrines and deep concern with maintaining their separate identity. His appeal, therefore, was bound to remain confined only to Hindus. He was, moreover, essentially a Hindu preacher and the revitalization of Hinduism was his chief concern. In carrying out this mission, he naturally sought to remind Hindus of the greatness, almost uniqueness, of their religious heritage. Sister Nivedita, a prominent disciple of Vivekananda, observes with reference to the latter's speeches: 'The religious ideas of the Hindus were his theme at Chicago, and similarly thereafter, it was those elements which were common to, and characteristic of, orthodox Hinduism in all its parts that formed the burden of his teaching.'[10] A careful perusal of Vivekananda's speeches in different parts of India after his return from the United States in 1897, reveals that while there was much in them which would inspire a genuine Indian nationalist, there was also much which might provide a strong ideological foundation for Hindu nationalism. In almost every speech Vivekananda equated India with Hindus and India's spiritual message with the teachings of Hinduism. Mark these words:

We Hindus have now been placed, under God's providence, in a very critical and responsible position. The nations of the West are coming to us for spiritual help. A great moral obligation rests on the sons of India to fully equip themselves for the work of enlightening the world on the problems of human existence.[11]

Again, while calling upon Hindus to give the highest priority to the regeneration of their religion and spirituality which, according to him, held the key to India's regeneration as a nation, he observed on one occasion:

> Let us all work hard, my brethren; this is no time for sleep. On our work depends the coming of the India of the future. She is there ready, waiting. She is only sleeping. Arise and awake, and see her seated here, on her eternal throne, rejuvenated, more glorious than she ever was—this motherland of ours. The idea of God was nowhere else ever so fully developed as in this motherland of ours, for the same idea of God never existed anywhere else. Perhaps you are astonished at my assertion; but show me any idea of God from any other scripture equal to ours.[12]

It is not surprising that many saw in Vivekananda a Hindu Napoleon who had succeeded in taking the message of Hinduism to the whole world. The writings in the Indian press regarding him between 1893 and 1902 show a tremendous growth of community-consciousness among educated Hindus as a result of his achievement. A feeling of pride in being a Hindu and a feeling of gratefulness towards Vivekananda for having made Hinduism respectable in the West were important elements of this consciousness. Another notable feature was the increasing use of the word 'nation' for the Hindu community. Thus, the *Indian Mirror* (Calcutta) remarked on 21 February 1894 that Vivekananda's mission had immensely raised the position of Hinduism in the eyes of the civilized world and for that 'the whole Hindu community should feel grateful to the Swamy'.[13] Again commenting on the public meeting held in Calcutta on 5 September 1894, to record appreciation for Vivekananda's work in America, the same paper wrote the next day:

> The great meeting of the Hindu community last evening at the Town Hall must have furnished a striking object lesson to every one who was present at the immense gathering. The appearance of the different castes and sub-castes, into which Hindu society is split up at the present time, on a common platform, the oneness of feeling that animated all, the common enthusiasm, the united applause, as speaker after speaker rose and resumed his seat, and the absolute sincerity of the entire proceedings, all went to show that life has begun to beat with strong pulsation once more into the veins of the Hindu nation.[14]

According to the detailed report of the proceedings of that meeting, published on 6 September 1894, the mover of the first resolution adopted there, Narendra Nath Sen, underlined the significance of such meetings being held at that time in different parts of India. 'It is evident', he remarked, 'national life is springing up everywhere; and nobody can say now that the Hindus are a dead or inert nation.'[15] The

Amrit Bazar Patrika (Calcutta) observed on 1 September 1894 that Vivekananda richly deserved recognition by his countrymen for his 'services to the Hindu nation'. It further added: 'He has done much more to elevate our nation in the estimation of the people of the West than what has hitherto been done by all our political leaders put together.'[16]

Mahadeo Govind Ranade (1842-1901), a prominent leader of the social reform movement amongst the Hindus in the second half of the nineteenth century, seldom spoke in revivalist terms and tried to foster the growth of a rational, secular approach among his countrymen. He did not believe in the theory that Muslim rule did not bring any advantage to India and emphasized that no progress was possible in India unless Hindus and Muslims joined hands again as they had done during Akbar's rule.[17] Even while propounding such ideas, however, in his inaugural address to the thirteenth Indian Social Conference held at Lucknow in 1899, he spoke in terms which show that he equated India with Hindus and looked upon Muslims as foreigners. Referring to Hindus and Muslims as 'two races', he observed:

> Of one thing we are certain, that after lasting over five hundred years, the Muhammedan Empire gave way, and made room for the re-establishment of the old native races in Punjab, and throughout central Hindustan and South India, on foundations of a much more solid character than those which yielded so easily before the assaults of the early Muhammedan conquerors.[18]

By the 'old native races', Ranade, of course, meant the Sikhs, Rajputs and Marathas, who had established their rule in Punjab, Central India and Deccan, respectively, in the eighteenth century. He referred to this point more clearly, and with evident pride as a Hindu, in course of his study of the rise of Marathas in the seventeenth and eighteenth centuries. 'The immediate predecessors of the British rulers of India', he observed, 'were not the Muhammedans, as is too often taken for granted, but they were the native rulers of the country, who had successfully thrown off the Muhammedan yoke.'[19] Indeed, some of Ranade's utterances make it clear that he looked upon Hindus and Muslims as two nations, though, of course, he never faltered in his belief that they should cooperate among themselves and live together in harmony. Thus, while delivering the inaugural address at the second Social Conference held at Allahabad in 1888, he referred to the manifold differences based on creed, race and custom among the members of the Hindu community, and remarked: 'We are in a sense as strictly national socially, as we are politically.' Though recognizing that some of the differences among the Hindus were quite evident, particularly relating to matters of practical reform, he drew attention to the fact that there was 'a background of common traditions, common religion, common laws and institutions and customs and perversions of such customs'.[20] Again, in course of the inaugural address to the Seventh Social Conference held in Lahore in 1893, he proudly declared that he was speaking there 'as a member of the great Hindu community which peoples this land and forms one-sixth of the human race'. He added: 'The Hindu community is not a festering mess of decay and corruption. It is no doubt conservative to a degree, but that conservatism is its strength. No nation has any destined place in history which changes its creed and its morals, its customs and its social polity, with the facility of fashions.'[21] Ranade's pride in belonging to the Hindu 'nation' comes out more clearly in course of his tribute to the memory of Rammohun Roy:

> What Raja Ram Mohan felt was that we had in India a nation, gifted with a religious history transcending all the records of every other race. Here was a nation, which was gifted, was well endowed, was spiritual in all its real aspirations. This nation had gradually ascended to the conception of the purest form of monotheism that the world has yet seen.[22]

In a veiled reference to Christianity and Islam, Ranade added that in the Upanishads and the *Gita*, the 'Hindu nation' had developed such monotheism 'not by a mere impulse, not by the command of any single prophet, but by the slow process of growth and evolution'.[23] Needless to add, Ranade considered such process the ideal method for achieving progress and reform.

Pride in ancient Indian polity went hand in hand with that in ancient Indian monotheism. And while giving expression to such pride, Ranade did not limit himself to a veiled reference, but openly contrasted it with the system of despotism he thought had prevailed in India under the Muslim rulers. While pleading for a reconsideration of British policy on land assessments, he wrote in 1884:

> The Government must retrace its steps, forget its Muhammedan antecedents of absolutism, and return to the old Hindu traditions, where the King's power was restrained in all directions by the rights of the people among whom the king was more of a father and a manager than a conqueror or a sovereign lord, and cultivated land belonged in absolute right to private owners who paid as tax a fixed share of the produce to the king like any of his other subjects for the expenses of protection.[24]

II

The rising tide of Hindu revivalism in late nineteenth century was widely reflected in contemporary Indian literature. Here it may not be inappropriate to begin with the writings of Bankim Chandra Chatterjee (1838-94), one of the greatest names in Bengali literature and regarded by some as 'the creator of Hindu nationalism'.[25] According to Bankim, religion encompassed all aspects of life and there was no religion equal to Hinduism. The following is a good illustration of his general approach:

> If religion is the source of true happiness, the whole human life should be governed by religion. This is the essence of Hindu *dharma*. Other religions do not say so; that is why they are incomplete; only Hindu religion is the most complete religion. Other people believe that religion is concerned with only God and the life beyond. To the Hindu religion encompasses this life, the life beyond, God, man, all living beings, the whole of creation. Is there any other religion so all encompassing, so full of bliss and so pure?[26]

Although he talked of the need to discard all impurities which had entered the Hindu religion through the centuries, he did not really see any need for reform in the essentials of Hindu religion and offered rationalizations for all kinds of faiths and practices, including idol-worship. As has been pointed out by M.K. Haldar, 'Bankim, through a remarkable sophistry, could extol idolatry, monotheism, polytheism, Vedantic transcendentalism and such other divergent ideas in the same breath'.[27] He made his most powerful contribution to nationalist lore through his poem *Bande Mataram*, depicting the motherland virtually as a Hindu goddess, composed sometime in 1875 and published as part of his novel *Anandmath*, in 1882. The first three stanzas, translated from Bengali into English by Aurobindo, are as follows:

> Mother, I bow to thee!
> Rich with thy hurrying streams,
> Bright with thy orchard gleams,
> Cool with the winds of delight,
> Dark fields waving, Mother of might,
> Mother free.
>
> Glory of moonlight dreams
> Over thy branches and lordly streams,
> Clad in thy blossoming trees

Mother, giver of ease,
Laughing low and sweet,
Mother, I kiss thy feet,
Speaker sweet and low
Mother, to thee I bow.

Who hath said thou are weak in thy lands,
When the swords flash out in seventy million hands,
And seventy million voices roar
Thy dreadful name from shore to shore?
With many strengths who art mighty and stored,
To thee I call, Mother and Lord.[28]

Anandmath is the story of a Hindu rebellion against Muslim rule in Bengal. It ends with an injunction by a divine voice to the commander of the rebels to stop fighting, as power in Bengal had passed from Muslim to English hands. The opportunity provided by it, the divine injunction continues, should be utilized by the Hindus to acquire knowledge of the physical world from the English, who are masters of such knowledge and also good teachers:

> Once the people of India have acquired knowledge of the physical world from the English, they will be able to comprehend the nature of the spiritual. There will then be no obstacle to the true faith. True religion will then shine forth again of itself. Until that happens, and until Hindus are wise and virtuous and strong, the English power will remain unbroken. Under the English our people will be happy; and there will be no impediment to our teaching our faith. So, wise one, stop fighting against the English and follow me.[29]

It has been often argued that this was a cover for the real intention of the author which was to preach rebellion against British rule. There is even a view that the first edition mentioned the rebellion to have occurred against British rule and, in order to avoid persecution, this was changed to Muslim rule in the second edition.[30] This does not, however, seem convincing, not only because, it would amount to attributing 'the worst cowardice, deception and chicanery' to a writer of Bankim's stature,[31] but also because there is a strong anti-Muslim sentiment running through many of his novels and the sentiments expressed in *Anandmath* fit in with them. Bankim's references to Muslims in his novels are 'generally unfriendly, and in many places unmistakenly hostile'. In his essays as well as novels, he uses 'Hindu' and 'Indian' as synonymous terms. Nowhere does he write in such a way as to indicate, even by implication, that he includes Muslims among Indians. This can only mean that he treated Muslims as aliens. In a few cases in his novels, Muslim characters are, of course, treated sympathetically, but generally they are presented as tyrants and oppressors.[32] Amalas Tripathi differs from this view and argues that 'Bankim's target was not the upright Muslim but the decadent tyrant'.[33] This, however, does not seem convincing.[34]

Though Bankim gave the most powerful expression to anti-Muslim as well as Hindu nationalist sentiments in late nineteenth century, he was by no means unique so far as the expression of such sentiments was concerned. The most important writers in some other Indian languages in that period wrote in a similar vein, often using Indians and Hindus as synonymous terms, treating Muslims as foreigners and praising British rule over India in comparison with the so-called Muslim rule in the past. This is very well illustrated by the writings of Bhartendu Harishchandra (1850-85), Pratap Narain Misra (1856-94), and Radha Charan Goswami (1859-1923), the pioneers of modern Hindi literature. The irony is that they freely gave expression to anti-Muslim sentiments while at the same time emphasizing the virtues of patriotism and the need for Hindu-Muslim unity. Thus, in his poem welcoming the Prince of Wales in 1875, Bhartendu expressed his happiness at the end of centuries of oppression by the Muslims through the establishment of British rule in India and referred to the 'wounds in the heart' that were preserved through the presence of the mosque built by Aurangzeb just by the side of the sacred Vishwanath Temple in Varanasi. In another poem written two years later, he wrote that the happiness of Hindus had departed with the establishment of Muslim rule. Next year, he wrote a poem in which he accused the Muslims of having deprived Hindus of their religion, wealth and women. Misra shared this characterization of Muslim rule in India and described the Muslims as 'abominally impure *mlechchas*'. He charged the Hindus with cowardice on the ground that although they were much superior to Muslims not only in number, but also in education and wealth, the latter went on killing cows, abusing Hindu gods and interfering with the taking out of Hindu religious processions. A character in a play entitled *Bharat Mein Yavan Raj* (Foreign Rule in India) and written by Goswami thanks the British for freeing the 'Hindustanis' from rule by Muslims who had been killing cows, desecrating temples and robbing the people. Balkrishna Bhatt (1844-1914) and Balmukund Gupta (1864-1907) show similar tendencies.[35] The ancient past which they eulogized was the one which was supposed to be the golden age of the Hindus. And when they selected the Rajput heroes of medieval India for special treatment, the purpose generally was to darken the image of their Muslim contemporaries.[36]

The works of Maithili Sharan Gupta (1886-1964) who is generally acclaimed as the greatest among nationalist Hindi poets, echo somewhat similar sentiments, though in a more refined form. *Bharat Bharati*, first published in 1912 and reprinted several times, is the most important among his poems eulogizing patriotism. Seeking to do for the Hindus what Hali had done for the Muslims, he depicts the ancient past of the Hindus when they were supposed to have reached the heights of civilization in the most idealistic terms. He proceeds to depict the generally miserable condition of the Hindus during the medieval period under Muslim rule, when they often had to choose between their religion and life, thus many of them being converted to Islam by force. He, of course, praises liberal Muslim rulers like Akbar and emphasizes that no community is totally devoid of good men, but treats the period of supposed Muslim rule as a whole as a kind of dark age for Indians or Hindus, both of which are generally used as synonymous terms. While looking to the future, his major concern is that the Hindu community should recapture its old glory.[37]

The same can be said of the pioneers of modern Gujarati literature like Dalpatram (1820-98) and Narmadashankar (1838-86).[38] About the latter in particular, it has been authoritatively stated that his 'India is exclusively a Hindu India. He extols the glory of the Hindus as the glory of India, and holds the flaws in the character of the Hindus and their socio-economic inequities responsible for the decline and degeneration of India.'[39]

The pioneers of modern Marathi literature, whether belonging to the reformist or the revivalist camp, expressed pronounced anti-Muslim sentiments. Gopal Hari Deshmukh (1823-92), popularly known as Lokahitwadi, who championed the cause of reform, writes that five centuries of Muslim rule had turned the Hindus into a degenerate lot as they had adopted many Muslim customs and manners, particularly those relating to women. He also asserts that the British rule was much better for Hindus than Muslim rule. Another important writer of the reformist camp, Gopal Ganesh Agarkar (1856-95), also ascribes the subordinate status of women in the Hindu society to the impact of Muslim rule. Describing the nature of that rule, he observes: 'Muslims terrorised the Hindu population from one end of India to the other, persecuted them, carried out forced conversions, destroyed temples and abducted Hindu women.' According to him Muslims were 'bullies and fanatics'.[40]

Prominent Marathi writers of the revivalist camp exhibit a similar attitude towards Muslims. Thus Vishnushastri Chiplunkar (1850-82), while writing long essays in opposition to Lokahitawadi on several points, agrees with the latter that the Hindus had degenerated because of their tendency to adopt evil Muslim habits such as indolence. He also refers to the existence of deep dislike and distrust for each other among Hindus and Muslims. 'The Muslim', he says, 'attempts to counteract the sin of the sight of a non-Muslim by reciting the name of Allah, while the Hindu goes to the extent of physically washing off the sin; Bajirao II avoided the sight of a Muslim until late in the day.' Bal Gangadhar Tilak (1856-1920) refers to the destruction of temples undertaken by Muslim invaders and rulers, and ascribes their success to the prevalence of certain weaknesses among the Hindus. The rise of the Marathas in the second half of the seventeenth century is interpreted by him as a striking example of Hindu resurgence. He also refers to the evil influence of certain pernicious Muslim customs such as the *purdah* and emphasizes that while Hindus had changed their social outlook for the better in modern times the Muslims had remained 'as fanatical as ever'. Shivarama Mahadeva Paranjape (1864-1929), a veteran journalist and editor of the popular weekly *Kal*, writes in the same vein. He characterizes Muslim rule as despotism and underlines 'the provocative boastfulness of Muslim rulers' who publicly killed a cow and thereby raised a furore among the Hindus when they could have privately killed hundreds of cows without creating any problem. He uses considerable poetical imagination to describe the pitiable condition of Hindus before the rise of Shivaji and rises to poetical heights while describing the latter's exploits. A large number of poems and novels were written with these exploits as their major theme. The most noteworthy among them are the historical novels of Hari Narayana Apte (1864-1919), particularly *Gada Ala Pana Simha* (The Fort was conquered though the Hero Was Killed) and *Ushahkala* (Dawn).[41]

III

The growing community-consciousness among certain sections of the Hindu elite was also reflected in historical writings. Many Hindu scholars wrote books dealing with the struggles of the Rajputs, Sikhs and Marathas against the Mughals, underlining their 'heroic fights against Muslims'.[42] Unlike poets and novelists, who gradually changed their tone in the twentieth century as the Indian nationalist movement gathered momentum, historians continued to lay stress on the struggles of Hindus against Muslim domination during the pre-British period.

The rise of the Marathas, particularly the personality and achievements of Shivaji, provided the most attractive theme for such historians and their writings on it may appropriately be utilized for illustrating the role of historians in fostering a Hindu national consciousness. Almost without any exception, they interpreted that rise as principally representing the struggle of Hindus against Muslim tyranny. The tone was set by Mahadev Govind Ranade in *Rise of the Maratha Power* published in 1900. According to him, 'the rise of the Maratha power was not a mere accident due to any chance combination, but was a genuine effort on the part of a Hindu nationality, not merely to assert its independence, but to achieve what had not been attempted before—the formation of a Confederacy of States animated by a common patriotism'.[43] Dilating on the greatness of Shivaji, he lays the main stress on the former's contribution to the reestablishment of Hindu political power. As he puts it:

> He did not create the Maratha power; that power had been already created, though scattered in small centres all over the country. He sought to unite it for a higher purpose by directing it against a common danger. This was his chief merit and his chief service to the country, and in this consists his chief claim upon the grateful remembrance of his people. It was not for nothing that the people looked up to him as their inspired leader. He felt the inspiration himself, and communicated it to those about him, not only in one generation, but for generations more to come after him, till the idea of reestablishing Hindu power throughout the country was realised at once in the great centres or camps which the Marathas established in all parts of the Indian continent.[44]

Several authors in Maharashtra wrote in the 1920s and 1930s on Shivaji and the rise and expansion of Maratha power. They generally propounded the view that Shivaji was primarily motivated by a religious inspiration to fight against the injustices and oppressions inflicted by Muslim rulers on their Hindu subjects.[45] The work of V.D. Savarkar, who became the chief spokesman of Hindu nationalism in the 1930s and 1940s falls into this genre. In his book on Shivaji, published in 1925, he emphasized that not only the generation of Shivaji, but also the generations after him were animated by 'the same noble spirit of patriotism, the consciousness of continuing the same sacred mission of winning back the political independence of the Hindu race and defending the Hindu Dharma from the attacks of an alien and barbarous foe'.[46]

It was not merely the scholars in Maharashtra who were engaged in eulogizing the achievements of Shivaji as a great leader of Hindu resistance against Muslim tyranny. Savarkar's book contains a brief introduction by R.C. Majumdar, hailing from Bengal and occupying a distinguished position among India's historians in the 1920s when Savarkar's book was first published. Majumdar is most enthusiastic in his praise for Savarkar's achievement and particularly draws attention to the fact that he had succeeded in bringing out that behind the rise of Marathas there was 'a noble and inspiring ideal', the ideal of 'Hindu-Padshahi, the establishment of an independent Hindu Empire'. He also shares Savarkar's hopes for the future: 'Standing on the grave of the last and one of the most glorious of our Hindu empires the author has asked us to watch and hope. Let us say "amen".'[47]

The most important scholarly work on Shivaji was, of course, produced by Jadunath Sarkar (1870-1958), generally acknowledged as the greatest Indian historian of modern times. He first wrote at length on Shivaji in the fourth volume (1919) of his work on Aurangzeb. His summing up of the achievements of Shivaji brings out his most enthusiastic admiration for Shivaji as a great Hindu as also his assumption of Hindus being Indians and Muslims foreigners:

> Shivaji was the first to challenge Bijapur and Delhi and thus teach his countrymen that it was possible for them to be independent leaders in war. Then, he founded a state and taught his people that they were capable of administering a kingdom in all its departments. He has proved by his example that the Hindu race can build a nation, found a state, defeat enemies. He taught the modern Hindus to rise to the full stature of their growth.[48]

Sarkar published a full-length study on Shivaji during the same year that the fourth volume of his work on Aurangzeb was published (1919). Here he repeated the same estimate of the achievements of his hero word by word which has been cited above from the other work. Not content with it, however, he added the following, again emphasizing the significance of Shivaji as a Hindu leader fighting against Muslim tyranny:

> He has proved that the Hindu race can still produce not only *jamadars* (non-commissioned officers) and *chitnises* (clerks), but also rulers of men, and even a king of kings (*chhatrapti*).

Shivaji has shown that the tree of Hinduism is not really dead, that it can rise from beneath the seemingly crushing load of centuries of political bondage, exclusion from the administration, and legal repression; it can put forth new leaves and branches; it can again lift its head upto the skies.[49]

Needless to add, the picture of Shivaji and the Peshawas symbolizing a struggle for freedom from the Muslim rulers, who were supposed to be foreigners, remained the dominant theme among most Hindu historians who wrote on the Marathas right up to independence. An apt illustration is provided by G.S. Sardesai, one of the prominent Indian historians of the Marathas. In the preface to the first volume (of his three volume study) which was published in 1946, he observes with reference to the character and achievements of Shivaji and the Peshawas:

They form the most recent example of our genius for nation-making of which we today may well be proud. Of all the diverse races inhabiting the Indian Continent, each gifted with a peculiar trait of its own, the Marathas alone can claim to have made a distinct contribution to the political fortunes of this land by daring to establish Indian self-rule throughout the country, although measured by the length of time their construction proved too short-lived.[50]

How all this influenced the minds of the educated Hindu youth belonging to middle-class families during the early years of the twentieth century comes out clearly in the recollections of Nirad C. Chaudhury. According to him, the general Hindu attitude towards Muslims in eastern Bengal before the Swadeshi movement (1905-8) was marked by 'a retrospective hostility' towards them. This was quite 'well-organized intellectually' and possessed 'very deep roots'. Elucidating this point he observes:

Nothing was more natural for us than to feel about the Muslims in the way we did. Even before we could read we had been told that the Muslims had once ruled and oppressed us, that they had spread their religion in India with the Koran in one hand and sword in the other, that the Muslim rulers had abducted our women, destroyed our temples, polluted our sacred places. As we grew older we read about the wars of the Rajputs, the Marathas and the Sikhs against the Muslims, and of the intolerance and oppression of Aurangzeb.[51]

IV

The growing community consciousness among the Hindus found a powerful expression in the demand for the replacement of Urdu by Hindi both as the language of courts and as the medium of instruction in primary schools in UP, then known as the North-Western Provinces and Oudh. When the Government decided in 1837 to replace Persian by English and the vernacular of a province, it had decided in favour of Urdu in the North-Western Provinces and Oudh under the impression that it was the dominant vernacular there. This was, however, not acceptable to large sections of the Hindu elite, who started a strong agitation in favour of Hindi, though a small section, consisting largely of Kayastha and Kashmiri Pandit families, felt quite at home with Urdu and supported its continuance. There was not much difference in the content of the two languages, the difference really related to the script, for Urdu was written in the Persian script and Hindi in Devanagari.

This agitation began in the 1860s. In the previous chapter, we have noticed how it contributed to the belief of Syed Ahmad Khan that Hindu and Muslim elites were not likely to work together for the country's advancement. That shows how strongly the Muslim elite reacted to this agitation. Here it may be pertinent to notice the intensity of feelings of the dominant Hindu elite on this issue. This comes out first of all in a memorandum submitted to the authorities in 1868 by Sivaprasad of Banaras, who later on became known as Raja Sivaprasad. Asking the Government to drive 'Persian letters' out of the courts just as the language had been, he described them as the relic of the authoritarian ways of the Muslim rulers and asserted that Hindi had always been the language of the vast majority of the people. As he put it:

> When the Muhammedans took possession of India, they found Hindi the language of the country. . . . The Muhammedans did not force their countrymen, Persian, Afghan and Turkish officers, as the British Government does, to pass in the Vernaculars; they forced the Hindus to learn their language, and in it the whole business of the state was carried on. . . . High rewards were given to Persian poets, and a knowledge of Persian was the only passport to the portals of power and affluence. Yet this Persian did not become the language of the millions; beyond towns and towns people or the upper 'ten thousand', Persian was seldom studied. The Patwaree still kept his village papers in Hindi; the bankers, merchants, and shopkeepers still carried on all their transactions in Hindi. Those who did not aspire or seek to gain the favour of the Muhammedans by becoming, if not altogether, half Muhammedanised, still valued Hindi works left by Tulsidas, Surdas, Bihari, etc. . . . [52]

Another document which has come down to us from those days is a memorial submitted in 1873 to the then Lieutenant-Governor of the

North-Western Provinces, William Muir. Echoing Sivaprasad's memorandum on the language issue submitted five years earlier, this memorial declared that the Persian characters were 'foreign to this country'. It further added that in spite of their long use in courts and public offices, their 'inherent defects' made them 'incapable of being adopted in the daily transactions of life by the generality of the people'. Pointing out that it was only a portion of the higher classes, forming a small section of the population, that was habituated to the use of Persian characters, it asserted that 'where the interests of the majority are concerned, those of the few should yield'. It did not deny that the change from Persian to Nagari characters would not be liked by the Muslims, but pointed out that their proportion in the population to those who would be benefited by it was only one-eighth. Even among these one-eighth, the majority lived in the villages and they used Hindi in day-to-day life. It finally affirmed that the fact that Hindi maintained its position in the day-to-day life of the generality of the people in spite of its neglect by the State over a long period of time showed 'the deep-rooted and permanent hold' it had upon the popular mind, and clearly indicated 'its being national in the country'.[53]

The protagonists of the Hindi Movement in the North-Western Provinces and Oudh intensified their agitation after 1881 when Hindi in Devanagari script replaced Urdu in Persian script as the language of the courts in Bihar and Central Provinces. This is borne out by the fact that they were responsible for not less than 118 out of a total of 145 petitions submitted to the Indian Education Commission of 1882. The objective of these petitions was the replacement of Urdu by Hindi as the medium of instruction in the primary schools.[54]

For an idea of the general tone of these petitions, reference may here be made to the one presented on behalf of the residents of the city and district of Allahabad. Drawing attention to the fact that Muslims constituted only about 13 per cent of the population of the province, it observed: 'The bulk of the people being Hindus, they speak, with few exceptions, Hindi, which is in some form or other their mother-tongue.' It further argued that even the rural Muslims used Hindi and not Urdu in conversation. It also contended that the 'inherent difficulties' of Urdu made it quite unsuitable for mass education in northern India. For, although its verbs were generally conjugated according to the rules followed in Hindi, 'the facts of its being written in uncouth and outlandish characters, and its being surcharged with Arabic, Persian and Turki terms, make it an altogether foreign tongue to the Hindu population of villages and hamlets'.[55]

It is significant that ardent pleas in favour of Hindi as the medium of instruction in schools were made not merely in UP, but also in the Punjab. Of the total 96 petitions submitted to the Commission, 46 dealt with this theme.[56] The language used in these petitions as also in answers to the questions put by the Commission show the strong feelings of the Hindu elite on the language issue as also the extent of the growth of community consciousness, based on religious affiliation, among them. Thus, referring to Urdu, the Arya Samaj of Lahore contended that the vernacular recognized and taught in the schools of the Punjab did not represent the dialect of the people. It was a foreign language spoken neither by the Muslims nor by the Hindus. 'Urdu', it further added, 'besides, being a foreign language, is written in perfectly redundant, imperfect and unphonetic characters, and thus taxes the energies and the time of the students to an unnecessary extent.'[57] The Punjab Brahmo Samaj observed that the use of Urdu as the medium of instruction in the primary schools adversely affected the soundness of the system of primary education in the Punjab, for Urdu was neither the national language of the people nor capable of raising the nation intellectually and morally to the level of other civilized nations.[58]

The memorial from the Gujarat Bhasha Pracharini Sabha in the Punjab, signed by its president, Narayan Das and 5,506 others, observed that it was wrong to hold that the Nagari character and Hindi language, if adopted as medium of primary education, would not suit the Muslims. They accepted the fact that a large number of Indians had adopted Islam, but argued that this did not mean that they had also changed their language. 'The language spoken by the Hindus and Muhammedans of a locality', their statement continued, 'is the same, and as a general rule, very few Arabic and Persian words are met with in the spoken language of our Muhammedan brethren as compared with words of the Sanskrit stock in their speech.' The songs current among Muslim women, particularly those sung on certain special occasions such as marriage, were 'conspicuous by the rarity, if not absence, of Arabic and Persian words. This proved that the mother-tongue of no class of the people in the Punjab was Urdu which abounded in foreign words.' The members of the Sabha were content to leave the question of extending primary education among Muslims to the Government through any language it wished, but prayed that 'at least, for Hindus, the Government might be pleased to impart primary education through Nagari characters and the Hindi language'.[59]

Some of the associations in the Punjab which had a membership of both Hindus and Muslims could not come to any unanimous conclusion on the issue of the medium of instruction in primary schools. This is illustrated by comments on the language issue offered by the Select Committee of the Anjuman-i-Punjab, appointed for the purpose, and confirmed by the general meeting of the society held in July 1882. Thus, the three Hindu members of the Committee (Baboo Navina Chandra Rai, Pandit Guru Purshad and Pundit Bhagwan Dass) took the position that the vernacular (Urdu) recognized and taught in the schools of Punjab was not the dialect of the people, and hence the schools were neither popular nor useful. On the other hand, the sole Muslim member (Dr Rahim Khan) held that although Urdu was not the dialect of the country, still on that account it did not affect the number of pupils in schools. Besides, no complaints had ever been heard against Urdu from the public at large, but only from a few who were 'prejudiced against Urdu from a religious point of view' and were desirous of introducing Hindi which was 'just as much foreign to the country as Urdu'. It was further contended that no one understood Hindi except a few Brahmins.[60]

Another society with mixed membership, the Delhi Literary Society, also could not come to any unanimous recommendations on Urdu *versus* Hindi though the division was perhaps not strictly on the basis of religious or communal affiliation. According to the statement issued by the society, its 'more conservative members' were of the opinion that Urdu, which was recognized and taught in schools in the Punjab, was spoken and understood by the educated classes in almost all towns of the Punjab, including Delhi. They also expressed the view that being the language of the courts, and the only dialect in northern India which had been greatly enriched by translations and compilations, it had acquired at least some capability of expressing scientific ideas. They also felt that its study was 'very ardently sought for by all classes of the community'. At the same time, however, they recommended that in some agricultural districts where the population was chiefly Hindu and a desire was expressed by the latter for Hindi schools, it might be desirable to establish more such schools than was the case at that time. On the other hand, the advocates of Hindi, the statement of the Delhi Literary Society continued, asserted that the schools would become more popular if Hindi were adopted instead of Urdu. According to them, Urdu was a language 'perfectly foreign to this part of the country'. It was 'the growth of Muhammedan times', and was indeed not even a hundred years old. In any case, it was 'not the mother tongue of the people'. Particularly was this true of people living in rural areas, whether they were Hindus or Muslims. Even in towns Urdu was not spoken at home, but only in public societies, courts and offices. Women everywhere used only Hindi and the language they spoke was the mother tongue of the people. In the end, a hope was expressed that the Government would not force 'a foreign language' on the people who are entirely averse to it.[61]

There was one memorial claiming to speak on behalf of the residents of Lahore and signed by nearly four thousand persons, including Hindus, Muslims and Christians, which expressed itself in favour of the retention of Urdu and declared that some Bengalis had been the real movers of the agitation in favour of Hindi. Further, it expressed regret at the fact that a number of memorials supporting the cause of Hindi had been sent to the Education Commission by 'some young inexperienced Hindus . . . , actuated by religious prejudices and sectarian views'.[62] Another memorial in support of Urdu emanated from the Anjuman-us-Sabha of Gujarat and claimed to speak for nearly three thousand persons including Hindus and Christians as well as Muslims. However, the Chairman of the Education Commission, W.W. Hunter, after a scrutiny of its signatories, came to the conclusion that they were almost entirely Muslims. Of the exceptions, several were Hindus or Europeans employed in government offices, schools or courts. The proportion of non-official signatories, not Muslim, was very small. This memorial spoke in a quite strident tone in support of Urdu. It pointed out that unlike Hindi, Urdu was not the language of one race and hence to make Hindi the language of India and 'to obliterate the footprints of the races that from time to time overran India and still reside within her borders, would savour of violence and even of injustice to them'. It further added that being the end-product of the interaction of the languages of the successive conquering races that entered India with the language originally spoken in various parts of India, Urdu was 'a language found without respect of race or religion' and extensively used throughout Hindustan, and that was the main reason behind its adoption by the government as the language of courts and business offices. Hindi, on the other hand, was a dead language and the movement in its favour was being championed by educated Hindus as a result of religious prejudice, because of the presence of Arabic and Persian words in Urdu. Finally, they warned that the movement in favour of Hindi with Devanagari characters was prompted by 'religious and party prejudices, injuriously calculated to encourage unnecessary antagonism between Hindus and Mussalmans'. They also added that it should not be ignored that Muhammedans would never accept Hindi characters or agree to the removal of Persian ones which would be tantamount to the 'the destruction of all the traditions of their race and religion'.[63]

The position taken by the protagonists of Hindi and Urdu in the Punjab should help us to realize that, just like UP, the Punjab was also an important cradle of both Hindu political consciousness and Muslim political consciousness. One of the signatories of a memorial in support of Hindi was Lala Lajpat Rai (1864-1928) who became in due course one of the most prominent leaders of the Indian nationalist movement. According to him, the language controversy provided him his 'first lesson in Hindu nationalism'.[64] The Arya Samaj played a major role in the development of the latter.[65] As Lajpat Rai recalled later, 'The tiny barge of the Arya Samaj was at that time to me the barge of Hindu nationality.'[66] Recent research has established that within fifteen years of its formation in 1877, the Punjab Arya Samaj included among its members quite a large proportion of the Hindu commercial castes (Khatri, Arora and Bania) which virtually monopolized the modern educational institutions and professions and also became the strongest supporters of national as well as provincial political activities in the Punjab.[67] According to N. Gerald Barrier, the systematic attack on Islam carried on by the preachers of the Arya Samaj 'contributed to a more intense level of Hindu-Muslim antagonism and produced a regularized pattern of conflict'. The Arya Samajists, following the methods of religious propaganda adopted by the Christian missionaries, sent a number of preachers to various parts of the province and published several pamphlets and posters attacking Islam. The followers of Islam returned the compliment.[68] On the other hand, according to the protagonists of the Arya Samaj, it is the Muslims, particularly the Ahmadiyas,[69] who had taken the initiative by launching a propaganda-offensive against the Arya Samaj in the Punjab.[70] Whatever that might have been, it is important to note that such religious polemics sometimes resulted in violence and this further heightened the atmosphere of communal antagonism. Mention may, in this connection, be made of the publication in 1892 of a strong attack on Islam and its Prophet by a well-known Arya Samaj leader of the Punjab, Pandit Lekh Ram, followed by his assassination by a Muslim five years later.[71] Communal tension in the Punjab had increased to such an extent that henceforward the religious or communal identity became the most dominant form of identity in that province. This did not, of course, mean that each community was solidly organized under an unified leadership, but there is no doubt that from now onward 'in one form or another religious identification tended to receive much greater loyalty than any type of secular identity'.[72] The organization of cow-protection societies in the early 1880s, in which the Arya Samajists played a leading role, further aggravated the situation. Between 1883 and 1891, there took place fifteen major riots in the Punjab over cow-killing and other related matters.[73]

V

Originating from the Punjab, the movement for cow-protection soon engulfed large parts of northern India and became particularly strong in the Bhojpuri speaking areas of UP and Bihar. Along with the movement for the replacement of Urdu by Hindi, the cow-protection movement must be considered as one of the most powerful manifestations of Hindu resurgence in late nineteenth-century India. That movement had behind it a complex of motivations, including economic, and had been supported not only by Hindus and Sikhs, but, at least in Bombay, also by some rich Parsis and Khoja Muslims. There can be no doubt, however, that the central core of the movement as well as the bulk of its vast expanse consisted of Hindus who were determined to assert their position and to enforce their demand that what was one of the objects of their deepest veneration could not be slaughtered in a land where they constituted an overwhelming majority. Beginning with the *kuka* Sikhs in the Punjab in the 1870s, the cow-protection movement was later championed by Dayanand, continued by his followers belonging to the Arya Samaj and swamped by a large number of other Hindus who had absolutely no sympathy with the reformist aims of the Arya Samaj, but were quite keen to assert their Hinduness by working for cow-protection. As the movement progressed and assumed an aggressive character, many Muslims, equally determined to assert their Muslimness, decided to protect what appeared to them their inherent right to kill cows according to their religious and other needs, and even do so in a demonstrative manner. This juxtaposition of a growing Hindu consciousness with an equally powerful Muslim consciousness resulted in widespread riots in 1893. Starting with an attack by Hindus on Muslims on the occasion of a reported move for cow-killing in Azamgarh district in eastern UP, Hindu-Muslim riots spread like wildfire in several districts of eastern UP and Bihar. Hindu aggression in these riots was sought to be answered by Muslim aggression in western India, first in Prabhas Patan in Junagadh, then in Bombay city. The final tally came to 45 riots and 107 deaths, the bulk of them in Bombay city where 80 persons (a majority of them Muslims) lost their lives in three days and 300 temples, mosques and shops were damaged or destroyed. The number of Muslims killed was much larger than Hindus because, as the Government of Bombay pointed out, the Hindu labourers working in the Bombay mills 'not only retaliated upon their Muhammedan aggressors, but did so in large and apparently organized gangs'. Hindu-Muslim riots spread even to Rangoon.[74]

John R. McLane, who has provided the most detailed account of these riots, misses their deeper significance. According to him, the timing of the cow-protection movement and the contemporary newspaper comments on it show its connection with the Hindu-Muslim disagreements over the Legislative Council reforms of 1892. As Gyan Pandey has pointed out, if apart from the timing, McLane had paid equal attention also to the scale of the riots, the identity of the participants and the slogans and symbols used by them, it would have been clear to him that the Indian Councils Act of 1892 and the aspirations of a few Hindu politicians constituted 'too narrow a reason for the outbreak of agitation on this scale'.[75] It is particularly noteworthy that along with the people belonging to the chief zamindar (upper) castes of Rajputs, Brahmins and Bhumihars, a large number of Ahirs or Yadavas, one of the important middle castes, actively participated in these riots in the Bhojpuri region of UP and Bihar. This pattern was repeated on an even larger scale in similar riots in that region in 1917.[76]

The riots of 1893, which had innumerable successors, showed that by that year the spirit of Hindu resurgence was no longer confined to the people of the upper castes or the elite groups, but had also travelled to various middle and lower castes. For though the former continued to play the leading role, the latter too were represented by substantial members of their class. This was particularly true of the Ahirs, though the Chamars, a major caste-group among the so-called untouchables or the depressed castes, had stayed out. Again, if the anti-Urdu and pro-Hindi agitation was led by the elites in the provincial capitals and other big towns, the violent outbursts for cow-protection were led by the elites in the districts and the localities. For although members of the Hindu elite at the national level had fathered and patronized the cow-protection movement, they had no hand in the violent attacks on Muslims in Azamgarh, which marked the beginning of the riots in 1893. This was another pointer to the spread of Hindu consciousness among the lower middle classes and the masses towards the end of the nineteenth century. Indeed, the latter now emerged as a fairly autonomous element in this regard and quite often functioned without any coordination with or guidance from the elites at higher levels. This is particularly borne by the fierce attacks on Muslims in Shahabad, Bihar in 1917, in the name of cow-protection, at a time when the leaders of the Congress and the Muslim League were warmly cooperating among themselves at the national level after adopting the joint scheme of constitutional reforms in 1916.

The very size of the crowds taking part in some of these incidents is illustrative of the emergence of an aggressive communal consciousness among the Hindu lower middle classes and masses. At Mau, in Azamgarh district, which saw the beginning of these riots, the local Hindus were joined by 2,000 men from the adjoining Ballia district in the south and 4,000 men from the Ghazipur district in the east. A Muslim is reported to have remarked that 'for three days it looked as if British rule had ceased in the district'.[77] According to the divisional commissioner, the incidents at Mau were 'not so much riots . . . as an actual invasion of enemies bound on intimidating and robbing and killing'.[78]

Indeed the size of the attacking crowds was so large that several British officials, right up to the Viceroy and the Secretary of State for India, believed that the attacks on Muslims for cow-protection in 1893 had been pre-planned and really engineered by the Congress. Thus reporting the incidents in the districts of Azamgarh, Ballia and Ghazipur, the Lieutenant-Governor of the North-Western Provinces and Oudh reported to the Viceroy that they represented 'a serious rising, not only on account of the numbers engaged, but because it was not the result of local squabbles, but of the widespread cow-protection movement, and it was organized and concerted'.[79] A few weeks later, he recorded his agreement with the prevailing Muslim view that 'these acts were the result of an organized and well-planned conspiracy of which the Gaurakshini Sabhas were the agents . . . behind the Sabhas is the Congress agitation'.[80] The Viceroy apparently accepted this version and wrote to the Secretary of State for India:

The more I see of this [anti cow-killing] agitation the more serious does it seem to me. The advanced wing of the Congress party, which is profoundly disloyal to us, has found in this fanatical and powerful movement a means of establishing a connection between itself and the great mass of the Hindu population. The subterranean connection which has now been established between Congress and the cow will, unless I am mistaken, convert the former from a foolish debating society into a real political power, backed by the most dangerous elements in Native society.[81]

Actually, this assumption had no basis in fact and this was shortly realized by none other than the Lieutenant-Governor of North-Western Provinces and Oudh himself, who had first transmitted it to the Viceroy. Although he noted that the local Congress leaders supported the cow-protection societies, the chief instruments of the anti-cow-killing movement, he agreed with the Viceroy that it would be 'impossible to prove that the Congress is one with these Societies, and that it should not be said publicly'. He further added:

That the Congress, as a body, or through its officers, desires a disturbance, or had anything whatever directly to do with it, I do not believe. It is contrary to their interests, especially at the present time. Their object is to make use of the Societies in order to get, what they could not obtain otherwise, a popular following.[82]

The really significant thing about the cow-protection movement was the wide support it was able to muster among the Hindus in the north, showing the strength of their emerging communal consciousness and their growing antipathy towards Muslims, who were generally hostile to that movement and its main victims. The Lieutenant-Governor of North-Western Provinces and Oudh had noted in one of his letters several weeks before the outbreak of the riots of 1893 that there were few Hindus who did not sympathize with the cow-protection movement. 'Even men who had, I thought', he added, 'emancipated themselves, seem to be unable to throw off the veneration for the cow, although they take care to put forward purely utilitarian and agricultural reasons.'[83]

As for the landlords, most of them in the North-Western Provinces and Oudh were thought to be supporters of the cow-protection societies 'partly from religious motives, but greatly from fear'. The situation was made particularly difficult for the landlords by the strong support extended to the societies by the Brahmins. Even those among the landlords who in private professed not to have much veneration for the cow and made critical remarks regarding the cow-protection movement were not prepared to take a public stand against it. In this connection it is interesting to refer to the case of Raja Rampal Singh of Kalakankar, who was associated with the Congress and was recommended by the District Boards in the North-Western Provinces for nomination to the Provincial Council. He was considered in official circles as a renegade Hindu who ate beef openly, at any rate, in the company of British officials. When in a conversation with the Lieutenant-Governor, he mentioned that the cow-protection societies were causing harm, the former suggested that he might ask in the Council whether the Government knew that these societies were mischievous and whether steps would be taken to suppress them. 'He replied seriously', noted the Lieutenant-Governor, 'that if he asked such questions, it might cost him his life, and, in any case, he would never be recommended for Council again.'[84]

On the other hand, in Bihar feelings ran so high among the common people that the officiating Lieutenant-Governor of Bengal (of which Bihar was then a part) suggested to the Viceroy that it might be better to deal with the cow-protection movement through the zamindars, keeping the police in the background as far as possible. 'The feelings of intense animosity which the subject excites', he observed, 'affect the individual members of the Police as well as the strata of society from which they are drawn, and they cannot be trusted to act impartially'.[85]

The cow-protection riots should not, of course, lead us to conclude that they united all Hindus in action or that the distinctions and tensions between upper castes and lower castes vanished. A wholly united Hindu community free from deep inner contradictions never emerged. But these riots do indicate a tendency on the part of large sections of Hindus to unite temporarily in fights against Muslims. These fights too were not a constant feature of Indian life. It happened again and again that, after the most fierce and bitter rioting, Hindus and Muslims reverted to their normal, peaceful lives as neighbours. There existed, however, a latent feeling of hostility between sections of the two communities which had a tendency to burst forth in attacks on one or the other in certain situations.

Hindus were not always the aggressors; sometime the provocation came from Muslims.[86] There is, however, no boubt that most of these riots were caused by the deep resentment nurtured by Hindus at the continuance of cow-slaughter. Indeed, the depth of their resentment indicates that this had not emerged all of a sudden, but had been festering like a sore in the Hindu psyche for a long time. Just as the use of Persian character in courts, cow-slaughter was associated in that psyche with the so-called Muslim rule, and now that that rule had ended, Hindus saw no reason for tolerating its continuance, little realizing that their new rulers too were beef-eaters. The District Magistrate of Azamgarh seems to have correctly assessed the feelings of the majority of Hindus when he remarked: 'Underlying their zeal for the protection of cattle is the old grudge against the Muhammedans. The Hindus appear to have suddenly woken up to the fact that the Muhammedans are no longer their masters, and the insolent aggressiveness of their attitude towards them is a natural reaction from their former enforced submissiveness.' Such feelings were not confined to the Hindu gentry and masses, but also extended to Hindus working in government offices. 'A striking feature of the movement', added the District Magistrate of Azamgarh, 'is the favour it finds among the lower subordinate Hindu officials. They either wilfully ignore what is going on around them, or else they deliberately set themselves to misrepresent the true state of affairs.'[87]

VI

Along with the movements in support of Hindi and cow-protection, there also emerged in the late nineteenth century a clearly formulated ideology of Hindu nationalism and attempts to set up political organizations in the light of that ideology. This was a natural development in view of the consistent fostering of a Hindu consciousness by the leaders of the various religions reformation and revitalization movements and distinguished men of letters. Rajnarain Bose (1826-99), a member of the Adi Brahmo Samaj and described by many as the Grandfather of Indian nationalism,[88] can legitimately be regarded as the first prophet of Hindu nationalism. In 1866, he founded in Midnapore a Society for the Promotion of National Feeling among the Educated Natives of Bengal. By 'natives', of course, he meant Hindus, as was the vogue in those days in Bengal, as indeed in other parts of the country.[89] This becomes clear from the very first paragraph of his pamphlet which set out the objectives of his society. Expressing concern with the indiscriminate copying of Western modes by educated Hindus, he stressed the need for an effort to see that the entire Hindu heritage was not lost. As he put it:

> Already a band of youngmen have expressed a desire to sever themselves at once from Hindu society and to renounce even the Hindu name. It is to be feared that the tide of revolution may sweep away whatever good we have

inherited from our ancestors. To prevent this catastrophe and to give a national shape to reforms, it is proposed that a Society be established by the influential members of native society for the promotion of national feeling among the educated natives of Bengal. Without due cultivation of national feeling, no nation can be eventually great.

With this end, the Nationality Promotion Society, as Bose called the proposed organization, was to seek to revive the national gymnastic exercises, establish schools for instruction in 'Hindu music' and 'Hindu medicine', encourage the cultivation of Sanskrit and instruction of the mother-tongue (Bengali) before the start of instruction of English, oppose the trend to mix English words with those in Bengali in common conversation, make it obligatory for its members to correspond among themselves in Bengali, and encourage the use of Bengali in meetings and associations and the use of Indian forms of etiquette. The main object of the society would be 'to promote and foster national feelings which would lead to the formation of a national character and thereby to the eventual promotion of the prosperity of the nation'.[90]

The text of this pamphlet was published in the *National Paper*, which had been started by Nabagopal Mitra, a member of the Brahmo Samaj like Rajnarain Bose, and holding similar views. In 1867, Mitra started an annual gathering, called Jatiya Mela, which became famous later as the Hindu Mela, with a view to promoting 'national feeling, sense of patriotism and a spirit of self-help among the Hindus'.[91] The main items in the programme of these gatherings were the singing of patriotic songs, addresses by distinguished persons, gymnastic displays and exhibition of Indian arts and crafts. As Susobhan Sarkar has remarked, 'these annual meetings stirred up all Calcutta'.[92] After the fourth session of the Hindu Mela (1870), an organization called National Society or Jatiya Sabha began functioning and took charge of its organization. The main objective of this Sabha was declared to be the 'advancement of nationalist feeling (*jatiya bhaaw*) among all sections of the Hindu *jati* and their development through self-reliance'.[93] When some critics questioned the use of the word 'national' for the society when its membership was confined to Hindus only, the *National Paper* in its issue of 4 December 1872 replied that the Hindus 'certainly form a nation by themselves, and as such a society established by them can very properly be called a National Society'.[94]

As other, more important organizations emerged in Calcutta in due course, the Hindu Mela ceased to meet after 1880. Not much was heard of the National Association either. But some important persons in Bengal continued to hold the view even after the foundation of the Indian National Congress that while the latter should be supported, Hindus, since they formed a nation by themselves, must also have their own political organization. This view was quite forcefully expressed in a pamphlet, titled *Old Hindu's Hope*, running into more than 50 pages, published in 1887 in Bengali and 1888 in English.[95] Although the author's name was not mentioned, it is generally believed to have been the work of Rajnarain Bose.[96] Here the 'Old Hindu', as Bose was content to describe himself, expressed the hope that all Hindus would unite under the banner of 'God and Motherland' and do their best 'to promote the improvement of their nation in every respect'. While doing so, they must act under the dictates of their religion 'which admits no such distinction as sacred and profane duties or sacred and profane knowledge, and which ordains that every action of life should be considered as a part of religion and be performed with devoutness of mind and an eye to the supreme'.[97]

The proposed organization was to be called Maha Hindu Samiti or the Great Hindu Union, with branches in all parts of the country and having Hindus of all classes and denominations as its members. Its objects would be 'to advocate and uphold the religious rights and privileges of the Hindus, rouse Hindu national feeling, create Hindu national unity and promote Hindu improvement in general'. Bose regretted that such an union could not embrace the Muslim Indians, as according to him, their religion, manners and customs and past traditions were different from those of the Hindus. However, he had no ill-will towards them and observed that as they were living in the same country and under the same sovereign, 'political union can be effected with them'. Muslims could have their own national organization and the two national organizations could cooperate with each other in political agitation. However, the desire for cooperation with the Muslims should not be allowed to come in the way of the organization of the Hindus, just as the latter should not be made the ground for promoting ill-will towards the Muslims. As Bose put it: 'We should not allow nationality to stand in the way of cultivating love and good feeling towards our Muhammedan brethren, nor the said love and good feeling in that of performing our most important duties to our own nation.'[98] In one of his letters to the *Indian Mirror*, appearing in the pamphlet as an appendix, Bose, though not opposed to the Indian National Congress, warned against the growth of too much of Indian consciousness among the Hindus at the cost of Hindu consciousness and emphasized that both were necessary. Declaring the Hindu society to be 'dead-dead-totally dead', he observed:

> If it be alive, it is only alive to the calls of an all engrossing Indianism. I mean by the word 'Indianism' undue Indian national feeling as contradistinguished from Hindu national feeling. We are Indians and Hindus at the same time. We should possess both Indian national feeling as well as Hindu national feeling without sacrificing one to the other. Indian patriotism is common in these days. Hindu patriotism is rare, but Hindu patriotism is true patriotism.[99]

This shows that Hindu nationalism pure and simple was already in retreat in Bengal by the eighties of the nineteenth century. Bose, however, realized that it could still have a future if allied to Indian nationalism. Referring to the second session of the Congress held in Calcutta in December 1886, he remarked that it was a 'dry business meeting' and naturally so because the Congress 'could not be called a society, being only a meeting taking place once a year'. Human beings, however, were not merely intellectuals and a patriotic society must appeal to the feelings of the people. Here came the utility of an organization like the proposed Hindu Union:

> The Great Hindu Union . . . has plenty of material for appealing to the feelings of the people. If established, it would afford much scope for the cultivation of the patriotic feeling by young people, and gradually training them for becoming fit members of the Indian National Congress. This would be an advantage to that Congress and the Great Hindu Union would prove a valuable ally to the same in this and other respects also.[100]

While the plea for setting up the Great Hindu Union did not evoke much positive response from the majority of the politically conscious Hindu elite, who continued to work through the Congress, the need for appealing to the feelings of the people by the use of symbols associated with Hindu religious traditions was realized in due course by a section of the leadership of that elite.

In the meanwhile, it may be useful to refer to some of the songs that became popular in Bengal during the sixties and seventies of the nineteenth century. They bring out, as nothing else does, the ethos of Hindu nationalism. Bose had included a number of such songs in his pamphlet, giving both the original Bengali version and the English translation. The first among them is *Bande Mataram* by Bankim Chandra Chatterjee, followed by what perhaps was its first English translation. Almost all the songs are full of references to India's ancient past and to its heroes and heroines and do not recall a single event or person of medieval times. The *Bharat Sangeet* or Song of India by

Hemchandra Bannerjee, which was perhaps the most popular among these songs during the days of the Hindu Mela, warmly invoked the past Hindu greatness in order to inspire the Hindus of that generation:

> But where is that bright like flaming fire
> Hindu heroic pride, intelligence and might,
> At which animate and inanimate nature used to quake,
> From Gandhara to the ocean?
> Everything still the same but
> Where that courage of yore?
> Where is that deep wisdom, that skill?
> Where is that strong torrent of improvement?
> All that glory has departed.[101]

'Hemchandra', recalls Bipin Chandra Pal, a young college student then who later became one of the most prominent leaders of Bengal, nay of the whole of India, during the Anti-Partition movement in Bengal (1905-10), 'was our special favourite. The intense patriotic passion that breathed through his poems captured our youthful minds in a way which no other Bengalee poems had done.'[102]

Efforts at Hindu political organization were not confined to Bengal. A Hindu Sabha, for instance, was founded in Madras in 1881.[103] Punjab in particular witnessed a series of such efforts. Thus, some Hindus in Lahore founded the Lahore Hindu Sabha in 1882 for protecting the so-called Hindu interests. This was to be attempted by fostering brotherly feelings among the members of the different sections of the Hindu community, advocating the political rights and privileges of the Hindu community, establishing schools for the education of Hindu children and encouraging the use of Hindi, 'the vernacular of the country'. The way this move was defended by one Sangam Lal in the course of an article in the *Arya* shows that it was spurred by the activities of the National Muhammedan Association, founded by Syed Ameer Ali in 1877, particularly the submission of a memorial to the government in 1882 listing various Muslim grievances and demands.[104] The British acceptance of the principle of separate electorates in 1906 and the organization of the All India Muslim League during the same year further spurred such efforts. By the summer of 1908, there were Hindu Sabhas in each of the districts of Punjab and at their head stood the Punjab Hindu Sabha.[105] It was the latter's initiative which led to the foundation of the All India Hindu Mahasabha at Hardwar in 1915.[106]

Although not a large organization, the Mahasabha's role in expressing or moulding general Hindu opinion on communal issues could not be completely ignored. For over two decades several Hindu leaders of the Congress attended its annual sessions, without necessarily subscribing to its ideology or programme. Such association continued till 1937 when it was formally banned by the Congress. (This was, of course, in line with the similar association of several Muslim leaders of the Congress with the Muslim League.) Some Congress leaders like Lala Lajpat Rai and Madan Mohan Malaviya even presided over the sessions of the Mahasabha. Even those Congress leaders who kept themselves generally aloof from the Mahasabha occasionally tried to influence its decisions and extend the hold of their supporters over it.[107] This to some extent blurred the difference between the Congress and the Mahasabha in the eyes of many politically conscious Muslims. The latter generally believed that, by and large, the Congress leadership felt the same way as its counterpart in the Hindu Mahasabha; only it might not express itself as frankly. This was particularly unfortunate in view of the fact that the Mahasabha adopted an openly partisan attitude on the issue of Hindu-Muslim riots and strongly supported the *shuddhi* and *sangathan* movements in the twenties,[108] which caused considerable resentment among Muslims. Besides, its rigid stand, from the supposedly Hindu point of view, on such issues as the quantum of representation of the different communities in the legislatures, which became a major bone of contention between the leaders of Hindu and Muslim sectional organizations in the late twenties and early thirties, made it extremely difficult for the Congress to hammer out a generally acceptable settlement.[109] For the Congress could not completely ignore the Mahasabha's views, particularly in view of its growing influence among the Hindus in the years immediately following the Khilafat movement and involvement with electoral politics. The Mahasabha, of course, never became a really powerful organization, but its views on matters connected with the supposed Hindu interests were often assumed to be widely shared by the politically conscious Hindus.

The elections of 1937 marked the emergence of the Congress as a powerful parliamentary as well as mass-based party, completely eclipsing the Hindu sectional organizations like the Mahasabha, but instead of being discouraged, the latter, under the leadership of the ex-revolutionary, V.D. Savarkar, now acquired a much more strident tone, basing itself openly on Hindu nationalism and strongly opposing any concession to Muslims at the cost of supposed Hindu interests. Thus, at the annual session of the Mahasabha at Ahmedabad in 1937, Savarkar declared in course of his presidential address that Hindus were 'bound and marked out as a nation by themselves', and that all the various tests of nationhood such as country, race, religion and language entitled the Hindus to claim nationhood by themselves much more than many other nations. The Mahasabha, he further claimed, was 'preeminently a national body representing the Hindu Nation as a whole'.[110] Obviously referring to Hindus and Muslims, he observed that these were 'two antagonistic nations living side by side in India' and their antagonism was not likely to end soon. In any case, hankering after Hindu-Muslim unity by Hindus would not serve any purpose, except to further worsen the situation. The only wise thing to do was to make it clear that Muslims would have the same rights as other Indians, but no special privileges. If on this basis they were prepared to join the Hindus in the struggle for freedom, they would be welcome. Savarkar, however, felt that because of their religious fanaticism and Pan-Islamic tendencies, Muslims were not likely to work with Hindus. Hindus must, therefore, he asserted, 'look to themselves and stand on their own legs, and fight single-handed as best as they can for the liberation of India from any non-Hindu yoke, be it English or Moslem or otherwise'.[111] Thus was the two-nation theory elucidated from the rostrum of the Hindu Mahasabha, seven years after Iqbal had expouned it from the rostrum of the Muslim League, but about three years before Jinnah publicly adopted it and made it the basis for the Muslim League's demand for India's partition.

Savarkar expounded the ideology of Hindu nationalism with much greater force and at much greater length in course of his presidential address at the next annual conference of the Hindu Mahasabha at Nagpur (1938). Tracing the history of India since times immemorial, he asserted that 'ever since the Vedic ages for some five thousand years at least in the past, our forefathers had been shaping the formation of our people into a religious, racial and cultural and political unit'. According to him,

> No other nation in the world, excepting perhaps the Chinese, can claim a continuity of life and growth so unbroken as our Hindu Nation does. The Hindu Nation is not a mushroom growth. It is not a treaty nation. It is not a paper-made toy. It was not made to order. It is not an outlandish makeshift. It has grown out of this soil and has its roots struck deep and wide in it. It is not a fiction invented to spite the Moslems or any body [else] in the world.

But it is a fact so stupendous and solid as the Himalayas . . . that border our North.[112]

Turning to the concept of Indian nationalism, propounded by the Congress, Savarkar emphasized that its failure, after continuous effort over a long period of time, to win over the Muslims and persuade them to merge themselves into an united Indian nation was not at all surprising. For the Congress had since its very inception overlooked 'the fundamental social and political principle that in the formation of Nations, religious, racial, cultural and historical affinities counted immensely more than their territorial unity, the fact of having a common habitat'.[113] Citing examples from modern European history, Savarkar pointed out that 'a common territorial unit, a common habitat cannot by itself weld peoples differing in religions, racial, cultural and such other affinities into a national unit'. This was rooted in human nature. 'It is not only a political fact', emphasized Savarkar, 'but a human one that religious, racial, cultural, linguistic or historical affinities make men feel more akin to each other than the only fact of their residing in a common habitat unless that is an addition to those common ties.'[114] Because of the working of this principle and the legacy of history, Muslims would be 'about the last people to join the Hindus in forming any common political Nation on equal footing in India based on the only common bond of our territorial unity, out of a merely territorial Indian patriotism'. The Hindus should, therefore, cease running after 'the mirage of a territorial Indian Nation' and seeking in that process to kill 'an organic Hindu Nation'. Instead, they should resume the thread of their national life where their forefathers had left them at the fall of the Maratha and Sikh empires. 'The life and organic growth of the self-conscious Hindu Nation that was suddenly struck with an atrophy of self-forgetfulness must again be revived, resurrected.' Hindustan was the land of the Hindus and it was the Hindu Nation which owned it. 'If you call it an Indian Nation it is merely an English synonym for the Hindu Nation. To us Hindus, Hindusthan and India mean one and the same thing. We are Indians because we are Hindus and vice-versa.' Savarkar added:

> Yes, we Hindus are a Nation by ourselves. Because, religious, racial, cultural, historical affinities bind us intimately into an homogeneous nation and added to it we are most pre-eminently gifted too with a territorial unity as well. Our racial being is identified with India—our beloved Fatherland, our Holy land. . . .
>
> It is absurd to call us a community in India. The Germans are the Nation

in Germany and the Jews a community. The Turks are the Nation in Turkey and the Arab or the Armenian minority community. Even so the Hindus are the Nation in India, in Hindusthan, and the Muslim minorities a community.[115]

The Hindu Nation, in its own interests, Savarkar clarified, would not like to rule out the possibility of an united Indian Nation, provided it was 'based on an equitable and equal footing'. The Hindus would be ever ready to grant equal rights and representation to all minorities in India in various walks of life, but no special privileges, over and above that enjoyed by the majority. The minorities would also be free to pursue their own religion and culture. If the Muslims agreed to join the Hindus on the basis of these conditions and to bear 'undivided loyalty to the Indian State and the Indian State alone', the Hindus would welcome that; otherwise, their stand would be: 'If you come, with you, if you don't without you; but if you oppose, in spite of you, we Hindus will fight out the good battle of achieving the independence of India and herald the rebirth of a free and mighty Hindu Nation in near future.'[116]

In his presidential address to the next annual session of the Hindu Mahasabha (Calcutta, 1939) Savarkar reiterated that, in India, the Hindus constituted a nation by themselves, their numerous internal differences notwithstanding:

> We Hindus, in spite of thousand and one differences within our fold, are bound by such religious, cultural, historical, racial, linguistic and other affinities in common as to stand out as a definitely homogeneous people as soon as we are placed in contact with any other non-Hindu people—say the English or Japanese or even the Indian Moslems. That is the reason why today we the Hindus from Kashmere to Madras and Sindh to Assam will be a Nation by ourselves—while the Indian Moslems are on the whole more inclined to identify themselves and their interests with Moslems outside India than [with the] Hindus who live next door, like the Jews in Germany.[117]

The same ideology of Hindu nationalism was also being propagated by another organization, the Rashtriya Swayamasevak Sangh (RSS) founded in 1925 by Keshav Baliram Hedgewar (1889-1940), who remained its supreme leader till his passing away in 1940. By that time, the RSS could claim about one hundred thousand persons in the whole country as its adherents.[118] It considerably expanded the circle of its adherents under its new leader, Madhavrao Sadashiv Golwalkar (1906-73) though, of course, it cannot be said to have become a really far-flung organization by 1947. What distinguished it from the Hindu Mahasabha was the regular training of its volunteers in physical culture and their intensive indoctrination in the ideology of Hindu nationalism. The ideology can be found in a nutshell in a small book, published a year before Golwalkar assumed the leadership of the RSS. Having proved therein, to his satisfaction, that 'Hindusthan is the land of the Hindus and the *terra firma* for the Hindu nation alone to flourish upon', he proceeds to ask 'what is to be the fate of all those, who, today, happen to live upon the land, though not belonging to the Hindu Race, Religion and Culture?' and answers:

> There are only two courses open to the foreign elements, either to merge themselves in the national race and adopt its culture, or to live at its mercy so long as the national race may allow them to do so and to quit the country at the sweet will of the national race. That is the only sound view on the minorities problem. That is the only logical and correct solution. That alone keeps the national life healthy and undisturbed. That alone keeps the Nation safe from the danger of a cancer developing into its body politic of the creation of a state within the state. From this standpoint, sanctioned by the experience of shrewd old nations, the foreign races in Hindusthan must either adopt the Hindu culture and language, must learn to respect and hold in reverence Hindu religion, must entertain no idea but those of the glorification of the Hindu race and culture, i.e. of the Hindu nation, and must lose their separate existence to merge in the Hindu race, or may stay in the country, wholly subordinated to the Hindu Nation, claiming nothing, deserving no privileges, far less any preferential treatment—not even citizen's rights.[119]

It is remarkable that this book contains a lengthy foreword by M.S. Aney, who was until 1934 one of the prominent leaders of the Congress, having served on its Working Committee during 1924-5 and 1931-4 and acted as its president in 1933.[120] Although he had resigned from all positions of leadership in the Congress in 1934 on account of difference with its dominant section over policy towards the Communal Award (1932) and founded the Congress Nationalist Party, in collaboration with Madan Mohan Malaviya, to contest elections separately from the Congress,[121] he figured among the special invitees to the historic meeting of the Congress Working Committee held in September 1939 to deliberate upon the policy to be adopted on the war issue.[122] As mentioned earlier, this was by no means a solitary example of persons with marked Hindu nationalist leanings walking into and out of Congress leadership according to their convenience. Lajpat Rai and Madan Mohan Malaviya were other illustrious examples. There must have been several other such persons among less prominent leaders. It is not, therefore, surprising that many Muslims believed that the appeal of Hindu nationalism went much beyond the narrow circle represented by the memberships of the Mahasabha and the RSS. And such belief could not but strengthen the foundations of Muslim nationalism.

VII

Indian nationalism, as represented by the Indian National Congress, was based on an ideology quite different from that of Hindu nationalism. In a land whose overwhelming majority belonged to the Hindu faith the majority of its ordinary members as well as leaders were bound to be, and were Hindus, but it always had people belonging to other faiths like Sikhism, Islam, Christianity and Zoroastrianism within its ranks, both as ordinary members and as leaders. It also always sought to speak in the name of all the inhabitants of India and to appeal to their sentiments on the basis of their attachment to their country and its interests. For its leaders, the country and the nation were synonymous terms. They were, of course, aware from the very beginning that there were religious and cultural differences of various kinds between the different sections of the Indian population, but they tried to steer clear of them as far as possible. In order to be better able to do so, they avoided any consideration of issues relating to social reform or to any other matter which would be of interest only to one particular community. This was made clear by one of the founder leaders of the Congress, Dadabhai Naoroji, in the course of his presidential address to the second Congress Session in Calcutta in 1886. Using the word class for community, he observed:

> How can this gathering of all classes discuss the Social Reforms in each individual class? What do any of us know of the internal home-life, of the traditions, customs, feelings, prejudices of any class but his own? Only the members of that class can effectively deal with the reform therein needed. A National Congress must confine itself to questions in which the entire nation has a direct participation, and it must leave the adjustment of Social Reforms, and other class questions, to class Congresses.[123]

On the other hand, the Congress took early steps to assure the members of the minority communities, particularly the Muslims, that the Hindu majority in it would not be allowed to ride roughshod over their interests and/or sentiments. For this purpose it adopted a resolution at its fourth session (1888) providing that no subject would be allowed to be discussed at a Congress session the introduction of which was objected to by either the Hindu or the Muslim delegates as a body, unanimously or near unanimously.[124] The adoption of such a resolution was considered especially necessary in order to provide an answer to the campaign launched against the Congress by the most towering Muslim leader of the times, Syed Ahmad Khan, who contended that Muslim interests would not be served by joining the Congress. With the same end in view, the next Congress session (1889), while asking for an expansion of the legislative councils with enlarged Indian representation, suggested reservation of seats for members of the minority communities according to their proportion in the population of the province in which they resided.[125] The Congress thus recognized, quite early in its career, the Indian reality based on the diversity of its population.

An important element of the same reality, however, was the preponderance of the Hindus in that population and this was bound to be reflected in the Congress. One result of this was that even while its leadership adhered to a secular ideology, based on territorial nationalism, some sections of its rank and file were swayed by the powerful current of Hindu nationalism flowing in the country at that time. The problem was made more difficult by the fact that many of the people so swayed were not conscious of the contradictions between the two streams of thought. Belonging to the majority community, they often tended to consider their own sentiments as those of the country as a whole. The Congress leadership also could not ignore such sentiments beyond a point. This often landed the Congress in ironical situations and some of its postures and actions, adopted with a view to strengthening Indian nationalism by providing it a mass base and actually serving that purpose, also indirectly strengthened the foundations of Muslim nationalism by underlining the Hindu ethos of Indian nationalism.

Thus, while there is no evidence to support the assumption of the then Viceroy of India, Lord Lansdowne, that the Congress was behind the cow-protection agitation of the 1890s,[126] it cannot be denied that a number of Congressmen, not, of course belonging to the leadership, participated in that agitation, and also that both the Congress and the cow-protection agitation had some common patrons or financiers, particularly in the Punjab, UP, Bihar, Central Provinces and Maharashtra.[127]

During the years following the riots of 1893, Hindu nationalism cast a growing shadow over Indian nationalism. Although some Arya

Samajists had always belonged to the Congress in the Punjab, between 1894 and 1900 they became particularly interested in provincial politics, joined the Congress in bulk and assumed its leadership.[128] The nature of their debt to the Arya Samaj has been vividly expressed by their most prominent figure, Lala Lajpat Rai (1865-1928), who soon acquired an all-India stature and eminence:

> It was the Arya Samaj that taught me to love the Vedic religion and to be proud of Aryan greatness. It was the Arya Samaj that linked me with the ancient Aryas and made me their admirer and devotee. It was the Arya Samaj that instilled into me the spirit of truth, of Dharma and of liberty. My organizing capacity too I owe to the Arya Samaj. It was the Samaj again that taught me that Society, Dharma and country command our worship and that those shall inherit the kingdom of Heaven who make sacrifices to serve these.[129]

In Maharashtra, the spokesman of Hindu resurgence was Bal Gangadhar Tilak (1856-1920), who also rose to be one of the greatest leaders of Indian nationalism during the first two decades of the twentieth century. Writing in his Marathi paper, *Kesari,* dated 15 August 1893, he openly defended those Hindus of Maharashtra who had participated in Hindu-Muslim riots that year and asserted that they had acted not as a result of religious fanaticism or thoughtlessness, but purely in self-defence. If the police had acted promptly against the Muslims who had attacked first, the Hindus might not have taken to violence. Writing in a subsequent issue of *Kesari*, he observed: 'The Hindus did not of their own accord attack others; but it is a piece of good fortune that the Hindus, in any case the Marathas, have not developed that type of cowardice which would ask them to suffer meekly the miseries inflicted by others without retaliation.'[130] Still later, Tilak wrote that the Hindu mill-hands of Bombay had not done anything improper by going out 'with lathis in hand as a body'. On the contrary, since the police had failed to establish order, they had in a way helped the Government 'in quelling the disturbances'. He took the stand that the religious rights of both Hindus and Muslims should be protected and the Government should impartially punish those who violated those rights.[131] It was as a result of Tilak's initiative that after the riots of 1893, Hindus of Poona stopped joining the Muharram celebrations and started their own public celebrations of the Ganapati festival, dedicated to the god Ganesh.[132] Tilak was overjoyed at their success and sought to use it to foster unity among various sections of the Hindu community. He wrote in the *Kesari*:

During the last fortnight, all the roads in Poona were crowded with people in the night. Every lane had its own public Ganapati and all possible decorations were made. The Brahmins of course gave their help to the best of their ability; but the particular point to be noted in that it was the Marathas [as people belonging to the non-Brahmin Hindu middle castes in Maharashtra are generally called] who largely helped to make the festival a success. . . . We are happy to note that in spite of the ravings of the Christian Missionaries and the atheist reformers, the core of our society, viz. the Marathas, is sound so far as our religion is concerned. Our minds derived the same satisfaction as when one finds that the foundations of the supporting pillars are sound in a building which was showing cracks.[133]

While the Ganapati festival represented the public celebration of a religious festival which had long been in vogue in Maharashtrian Hindu homes, beginning with 1896 there developed a new celebration, called the Shivaji festival and held every year on the birth anniversary of Shivaji who had fought against Aurangzeb and established an independent kingdom in Maharashtra in the seventeenth century. Tilak played a crucial role in inspiring this celebration, describing it as a national festival which could play an important part in the 'all-round development of the nation'. Explaining the dynamics of such festivals, he wrote in the *Kesari* in 1896 that they were not as strenuous or expensive as the work of the Congress, but the educated people could achieve results through them which it would be impossible for the Congress to achieve and make the mass of the people living in the village interested in political issues.[134]

While the words 'nation' and 'national' were freely used, Tilak was really appealing to the Hindus of Maharashtra and he was fully aware of it. Thus, on the eve of the first Shivaji festival in 1896, he observed in course of his article in the *Kesari*:

Should we not have to hang down our heads if we are asked by a foreigner how we have till this day forgotten the event about which we should always be thinking, which we should never forget even in dreams?. . . The people of no other country in the world have forgotten the great man who laid the foundation of our empire, *who upheld our self-respect as Hindus, and who gave particular direction to our religion*.[135]

That Tilak was consciously working with a view to drawing the Hindu masses into the national movement and found an appeal to their religious sentiments most efficacious from this point of view is also indicated by his comment on the celebration of the Ganapati festival in 1896. Thus, he wrote in the *Mahratta*:

> No man can deny that our country is badly in want of a religious revival. Well, such a revival is taking place; only it is observable in different phases. Swami Vivekananda and the high philosophy of the Upanishads have appealed to the B.A.s and M.A.s of our universities. The God Ganapati and the vigorous preachings of Ramdas have appealed to the common people. Religion is the mainstay, the only prop for a falling nation and some of our friends are committing a national suicide in withholding themselves from a movement which is making us hopeful for the future.[136]

In the wake of the Anti-Partition agitation in Bengal (1905-8), such ideas acquired a wider appeal. Although some Muslims initially joined that agitation and its leaders showed consciousness of the need to attract larger Muslim support, as it gathered momentum it more and more acquired a wholly Hindu character. Bankim's song 'Bande Mataram' now began to be sung as a national anthem, vows to work for Swadeshi began to be taken in temples before the image of the goddess Durga and even the Shivaji festival was imported from Maharashtra and began to be celebrated with great enthusiasm. Indeed, orthodox Hinduism, emerged as 'the primary communication medium through which the leaders sought contact with the masses, and it was used also to raise the morale of the activists of the movement'.[137] Nor did its leaders see any cause for being apologetic about it. Thus brushing aside criticism of the celebration of the Shivaji festival in Calcutta in 1906, with the picture of the goddess Bhawani in the background, Tilak observed: 'We are all Hindus and idolators and I am not ashamed of the fact. . . . We cannot conceive of Shivaji without Bhawani.'[138] Already, in a speech at Varanasi, he had declared:

> Religion is an element of nationality. . . . Hindu religion . . . provides for a moral as well as social tie. . . . During Vedic times India was a self-contained country. It was united as a great nation. That unity has disappeared bringing on us degradation and it becomes the duty of the leaders to revive that union. A Hindu of this place is as much a Hindu as the one from Madras or Bombay . . . the inner sentiments which move you all are the same. . . . If we lay stress on it forgetting all the minor differences that exist between different sects, then by the grace of providence we shall ***ere long be able to consolidate all the different sects into a mighty Hindu nation***. This ought to be the ambition of every Hindu.[139]

Tilak had by now become a popular figure not merely in Maharashtra, but all over India. He was the acknowledged leader of the group of Congressmen, generally known as Extremists as distinguished from the Moderates, led by Gopal Krishna Gokhale (1866-1915), who still controlled the Congress, and were attacked by the former for following a policy of mendicancy. The Extremists were eager to step up the tempo of the Indian nationalist movement and broaden its base by bringing in the masses. For achieving these objectives in the then existing social context, they perhaps felt that they had no other option but to appeal to the religious sentiments of the Hindus. This led to increasing use of Hindu religious symbols, not merely by Tilak, but also by other extremist leaders.[140] Aurobindo (1872-1950), one of the greatest thinkers of modern India and the chief ideologue of the Extremists, explained their approach while paying tribute to Bankim for composing the song 'Bande Mataram':

> It is not till the Motherland reveals herself to the eye of the mind as something more than a stretch of earth or a mass of individuals, it is not till she takes shape as a great Divine and Maternal power in a form of beauty that can dominate the mind and seize the heart that . . . petty fears and hopes vanish in the all-absorbing passion for the Mother and her service, and the patriotism that works miracles and saves a doomed nation is born.[141]

In *Bhawani Mandir*, a tract meant to serve as the blue-print of an organization of whole-time, selfless workers solely devoted to the cause of national liberation, Aurobindo drew attention to the fact that in India all great awakenings had 'drawn their vitality from the fountain-heads of some deep religious awakening'. This phenomenon had been so persistent as to suggest that it was 'ingrained in the temperament of the race'. If any other method was followed, the objective might be gained after a long, tedious process, or might not be gained at all. In view of this Aurobindo asked: 'Why abandon the plain way which God and the Mother have marked out for you, to choose faint and tenuous paths of your own treading?' Finally, he appealed to the youth: 'Come then, hearken to the call of the Mother. She is already in your hearts waiting to manifest herself, waiting to be worshipped.'[142] In speeches and writings addressed to a wider audience, he tried to present nationalism itself as a new religion. In course of a speech in Bombay in January 1908, he declared:

> Nationalism is not a mere political programme; Nationalism is a religion that has come from God; Nationalism is a creed which you shall have to live . . . Nationalism is immortal; Nationalism cannot die; because it is no human thing. . . God cannot be killed, God cannot be sent to jail.[143]

Aurobindo made no mention of the Hindu religion here, but after his release from prison in 1909, in his famous speech at Uttarapara in Calcutta, in course of which he sought to communicate to the people what he claimed had been communicated to him by God while he was in prison, he modified the emphasis and brought the Hindu religion more clearly into the picture:

> I say no longer that nationalism is a creed, a religion, a faith; I say that *it is the Sanatan Dharma which for us is nationalism. This Hindu nation was born with the Sanatan Dharma, with it, it moves and with it, it grows*. When the Sanatan Dharma declines, then the nation declines and if the Sanatan Dharma were capable of perishing, with the Sanatan Dharma it would perish. The Sanatan Dharma, that is nationalism.[144]

Such ideas and such expressions could only provide a foundation for Hindu nationalism and not for an all-encompassing Indian nationalism. Even if this formulation is not fully accepted, there can be no doubt that they could not have any appeal for non-Hindus and would indeed tend to keep them away from Indian nationalism.

During the period covered by Gandhi's leadership (1919-47), Indian nationalism recaptured its distinct identity and ceased to be identical with Hindu nationalism, as it had become during the Anti-Partition movement in Bengal (1905-9). There was no end, however, of the Hindu ethos or, to use a phrase coined by Nehru, of the 'Hinduised look', of Indian nationalism.[145] To a certain extent, this was, of course, natural in view of the fact that Indian nationalism, as indeed India itself, was dominated by the Hindus. But because of the style of Gandhi's leadership, this 'Hinduised look' perhaps remained much more pronounced than it might have otherwise been.

There was hardly any other leader who was more concerned than Gandhi with the need to foster Hindu-Muslim unity. He was, however, a deeply religious person and made it clear more than once that for him politics flowed from religion, which always remained for him the highest source of inspiration. His effort to provide an ethical base to politics also led him to refer frequently to religion. Although while doing so he did not refer to any particular religion and took special care to profess equal respect for all religious faiths, he also very often proclaimed his allegiance to Sanatan Dharma, the traditional faith of the overwhelming majority of Hindus and even took pains to defend some of its outdated practices and traditions, including the caste system.[146] His constant emphasis on such items of his programme as cow-protection and removal of untouchability together with strong resistance, even at the risk to his life, to Harijans being treated as separate from Hindus were bound to give him the image of a primarily

Hindu leader, at any rate to many non-Hindus. His frequent references to *Ram Rajya* as the ideal society of the future, though popular among the Hindu masses, was too much identified with Hindu religious tradition to evoke a response from non-Hindus, especially because of hostile propaganda by the protagonists of the Muslim League.[147]

The predominance of the Hindu ethos in Indian nationalism, sketched above, was perhaps inevitable, keeping in view the overwhelming predominance of the Hindus (about 75 per cent) in the total population of the country and the need to widen the social base of that nationalism in a land where the bulk of the people were illiterate and the religious idiom provided the most, if not the only, effective means of mass communication. Moreover, while this must have limited the primary support-base of the Congress and inhibited some members of the Muslim elite in joining it,[148] the bulk of them were in any case out of it, on other grounds. Note must also be taken of the fact that, although always keen on maintaining their separate political as well as cultural identity, the latter were prepared to join hands with Indian nationalism, in spite of its Hindu ethos, when in their perception the interests of Muslim nationalism converged with those of Indian nationalism. This is borne out by the fact that leaders like Tilak and Gandhi, in spite of their close identification with the Hindu ethos, succeeded on certain occasions (in 1916 and 1920-2) in building bridges with Muslim nationalism in its early phase. On the other hand, when, with the passage of years, Muslim nationalism, just as Indian nationalism, gathered greater momentum, leaders like Motilal Nehru and Jawaharlal Nehru, not associated with the Hindu ethos in any marked way, utterly failed in their efforts to build such bridges. This should make us wary of attaching too much significance to the Hindu ethos of Indian nationalism as a factor in the emergence and growth of Muslim nationalism.

VIII

Another factor which played a key role in strengthening the foundations of Muslim nationalism was British policy. Although not perhaps to the same extent as Hindus, Muslims, too were divided on the basis of sects, origin, region and class, but the British always lumped them together while considering the political situation in India and referred to them as one community and also as totally hostile to the Hindus. In the beginning, this was not based on any deliberate policy, but reflected their understanding of the Indian social reality. Almost all the early British travellers in India had underlined the contrast between the Hindus and Muslims, not merely in religious belief and social organization but also in personal mannerisms. Thus the mild Hindu was often contrasted to the insolent Muslim. Islam, with its monotheism, seemed somewhat similar to Christianity and, therefore, easier to understand than Hinduism with its innumerable gods and goddesses. Even when, at the popular level, Hindus and Muslims were found celebrating each other's festivals, possibilities of tension and quarrel always seemed present, particularly when Hindu and Muslim festivals fell on the same dates. Besides, many travellers noted a general feeling of mutual dislike among the members of the two communities.[149]

What Sir William Henry Sleeman, an official of wide experience and understanding, wrote in his recollections, first published in 1844, may safely be taken as indicative of the general British impression around that time of the nature of Hindu-Muslim relations:

> Though every mosque and mausoleum was a seat of learning, that learning, instead of being a source of attraction and conciliation between the Muhammedans and Hindoos, was, on the contrary, a source of perpetual repulsion and enmity between them. It tended to keep alive in the breasts of the Mussalmans a strong feeling of religious indignation against the worshippers of idols; and of dread and hatred in those of the Hindoos. . . .[150]

This impression was confirmed by the publication in 1847 of the first major work (in six volumes) on Indian history by James Mill. It set the pattern for such works in the future by treating Hindus and Muslims as representing two distinct civilizations and ways of life, and dividing Indian history into the Hindu period, Muslim period and British period.[151] All British historians of India followed Mill's lead in this respect, however much they might differ from him on other matters.[152] While Muslims were generally considered by these historians as having been more advanced in culture and civilization than the Hindus, they were at the same time portrayed as religious bigots who had inflicted untold miseries on the Hindus. Sir Henry Elliot's original preface, written in 1849, for his monumental collection of histories of medieval India written by contemporary scholars, illustrates the general British interpretation of the state of Hindu-Muslim relations in the period.[153] The common assumption of all the leading British historians of India before 1857 was that 'Hindus and Muslim had, and indeed could have, no political feelings in common'.[154]

These travellers, scholars and officials were also aware of the advantage provided to the British by the supposed division in the Indian society. Thus Sleeman, after describing the tension and conflict generated by the juxtaposition of Hindu and Muslim festivals on the same date, remarked: 'These processions and occasional outrages are really sources of great strength to us; they show at once the necessity for the interposition of an impartial tribunal, and a disposition on the part of the rulers to interpose impartially.[155] Some even stressed the advisability of deepening this division further by painting the picture of the so-called Muslim rule in India in dark colours. Thus writing much earlier than Sleeman, Bishop Heber, whose account of his travels in northern India during 1824-5, was first published in 1828, after recounting a conversation with a Bengali Babu (as an educated Bengali Hindu was generally called by the British) in which the latter contrasted the lenient and liberal treatment meted out by the British with the harsh treatment meted out by Muslims to the Hindus in the past, observed: 'It is desirable that the Hindoos should always be reminded that we did not conquer them, but found them conquered, that their previous rulers were as much strangers to their blood and to their religion as we are, and that they were notoriously far more oppressive masters than we have ever shown ourselves.'[156] Elliot emphasized the same point. Pointing out the advantages of bringing to light the histories of medieval India which he had collected together for publication, he wrote in his preface:

> They will make our native subjects more sensible of the immense advantage accruing to them under the mildness and equity of our rule. . . . We should no longer hear bombastic Babus, enjoying under our Government the highest degree of personal liberty, and many more political privileges than were ever conceded to a conquered nation, rant about patriotism, and the degradation of their present position. If they would dive into any of the volumes mentioned herein, it would take these young Brutuses and Phocions a very short time to learn that in the days of that dark period for whose return they sigh, even the bare utterance of their ridiculous fantasies would have been attended, not with silence and contempt, but with the severer discipline of molten lead and impalement.[157]

Apart from an awareness of the division between Hindus and Muslims, these writings also indicate deep British dislike for the Muslims whom they encountered in various parts of India while expanding their dominion and suspected of harbouring rebellious intentions in contrast to the mild and subservient Hindus who apparently seemed to be quite happy at being relieved of the oppression of their former rulers. This dislike comes out vividly in the following comment on Muslims by *The Friend of India*, a British paper published from Calcutta on 25 June 1857:

> Cruel, sensual and intolerant, they are unfit to rule and unwilling to serve. Claiming to exercise sway as of Divine right and yet, destitute of every gift with which nature has endowed the races meant by destiny to dominate over the world, they fell by necessity under the power of a nation replete with energy and resolution, and loathe with all the bitterness of hate the infidels who have subdued them. They will never tolerate our gifts or forgive our supremacy. We may load them with blessings but the reward will be curses.[158]

The uprising of 1857 further deepened the British dislike of Muslims. Although Muslims and Hindus had both participated in that rebellion, it was generally felt in British circles that 'it was Muslim intrigue and Muslim leadership that converted a sepoy mutiny into a political conspiracy, aimed at the extinction of the British Raj'.[159] Although, as has been pointed out in the second chapter, the impact of this feeling on the fortunes of Muslims has generally been exaggerated, there is no doubt that it did result in loss of government patronage and favour by many Muslims. That the damage was not much more was due principally to the fact that all British officials in India did not share the general view about Muslim responsibility for the outbreak of 1857 and among them was the then Governor-General and Viceroy of India, Lord Canning. As he stood firm and refused to follow a policy of vengeance against Indians in general,[160] he refused also either to accept the general British view regarding Muslim responsibility for the rebellion or to sanction a policy of repression against them. Writing on 5 June 1857 to Vernon Smith, President of the Board of Control, he remarked that the rebellion was 'not more Mussalman than Hindu'.[161] When a suggestion was made by no less a person than the then Prime Minister of Britain, Lord Palmerston, that all civil buildings associated with Muslim tradition should be razed to the ground, Canning wrote to Smith on 21 November 1857, conveying his disagreement with such a policy and his refusal to carry it out. Religion, he said, had played a part in swaying the emotions not only of Muslims, but also of Hindus. If, therefore, the British razed Muslim religious buildings to the ground, they would also have to do the same regarding Hindu religious buildings. If they did so, that would amount to doing 'exactly what is wanting to band the two antagonistic races against ourselves'. Proceeding further, he showed a keen awareness of the great value of the division between the Hindus and the Muslims for the British and the advisability of doing nothing to end it. 'As we must rule 150 million of people by a handful (more or less small) of Englishmen', he wrote, 'let us do it in the manner best calculated to leave them divided (as in religion and national feeling they already are). . . .'[162] This prescription was faithfully followed right up to the end of British rule in India. Indeed Canning's successors went beyond it and, whenever opportunities presented themselves, did their best to ensure that the Hindu-Muslim divide grew deeper and deeper with the passage of time.

Within a decade or so of 1857, the Government began to be increasingly concerned with the attitude of the Muslims towards it. It was felt that the continued hostility of a community like the Muslims might not be in the best interests of the British. The so-called Wahhabi rebellion seemed never to come to an end and its followers continued to be active both on the north-west frontier of India and in Bengal and Bihar. There was also the feeling that if the British became involved in any action against a Muslim country or power, the sympathy of Indian Muslims would be on the opposite side. At the same time, there gradually developed a certain amount of respect for and interest in Muslims as a martial and conquering race, full of manly qualities even though hostile. This was reflected in several novels written by Englishmen and women in the second half of the nineteenth century in which most of the Indian characters, particularly those admired, were Muslim. This admiration for the Muslims contrasted with the growing contempt for the Hindus who seemed to the British to lack in manly qualities. Besides, in British eyes, the Hindu was generally identified with the commercial and educated middle class whom they disliked most, and the Muslim with the hardworking, simple peasantry, whom they liked best. Besides, as Christians, the English writers also felt a certain affinity with Islam. Hinduism, on the other hand, appeared as a strange religion, full of negativism and cruelty.[163] The fact that some Hindu members of the educated middle class had begun to criticize the various acts of omission and commission on the part of British bureaucracy in India and to demand political rights of various kinds contributed significantly to the emergence of such an attitude.

Whatever that may have been, there definitely began a move to conciliate or woo the Muslims towards the end of Lord Mayo's Viceroyalty (1869-72). The latter became quite seriously concerned with the comparative lack of interest on the part of Muslims in sending their children to modern schools. On 30 May 1871, he called upon

W.W. Hunter to write a book presenting his assessment whether the Indian Muslims were bound by their religion to rebel against the English. On 26 June 1871, he followed this up with a note on means to secure increased Muslim participation in modern educational institutions. On 7 August 1871, the Government of India issued a resolution calling attention to the need for special encouragement to Muslim education. Hunter's book *The Indian Mussalmans: Are They Bound in Conscience to Rebel against the Queen?* was published during the same year. It took great pains to emphasize the dangers likely to arise from Muslim backwardness in education and called for special measures to encourage Muslims to send their wards to modern educational institutions. In doing so, it was actually reflecting the new policy of the Government which had already taken shape in the form of Lord Mayo's note of 26 June 1871, on the need to encourage Muslim education while the book was still under preparation.[164] The assassination of Chief Justice Norman of the Calcutta High Court on 20 September 1871, within five weeks of the publication of Hunter's book, by a Muslim suspected to be a Wahhabi, followed by that of Lord Mayo himself five months later, further underlined the urgency of measures to conciliate the Muslims.[165]

At least one section of the Muslims, the remnants of the traditional Muslim aristocracy now in course of transition to a bourgeoisie and seriously concerned with the lead in this respect already established by the Hindus, were more than willing to be so conciliated. Their leader was Syed Ahmad Khan, the herald of the modern age among Muslims, whose ideas have been discussed at some length in the previous chapter. Thus were laid the foundations of a virtual Anglo-Muslim alliance which lasted, but for one interruption between 1912-22, till the end of British rule. In the beginning, this was represented by the deep British interest in the development of the M.A.O. College at Aligarh, whose foundation-stone was laid in 1877 by the then Viceroy, Lord Lytton, and which was visited by every Lieutenant-Governor of the North-Western Provinces and most of the Viceroys in the nineteenth century. Government's patronage of the Aligarh College and its organizers became a crucial factor in the role of leadership which the latter acquired in Muslim politics during its formative phase. As has been acknowledged by Francis Robinson in his authoritative work on Muslim politics:

> Syed Ahmed was the genius behind Aligarh but it was Government's patronage that made the College and its managers a major political force. Without

Government's aid it is unlikely that the College would have been founded; it is even less likely that it would have been so successful. Without the favour of the Government of India, Syed Ahmed would never have acquired the position and reputation that enabled him to found and lead all-India political organizations. . . .[166]

While Robinson considers it 'undeniable that British policy in the second half of the nineteenth century made a great contribution to the development of Muslim separatism', he takes care to add that 'this is not to say that division was intended'.[167] For this, he relies on some observations made by John Strachey and Lord Dufferin. Both, of course, disclaimed any intention to foster division in Indian ranks, but the former gave away his real intentions almost simultaneously with his disclaimer and the latter's actions speak for themselves. 'Nothing', said Strachey, 'could be more opposed to the policy and universal practice of our Government in India than the old maxim of divide and rule. . . .'[168] He, however, also observed:

> The truth plainly is that the existence side by side of these hostile creeds [Hinduism and Islam] is one of the strong points in our political position in India. The better classes of Muhammedans are already a source to us of strength and not of weakness and a continuously wise policy might, I believe, make them strong and important supporters of our power. They constitute a small but energetic minority of the population, whose political interests are identical with ours and who, under no conceivable circumstances, would prefer Hindu dominion to our own.[169]

If this does not smack of divide and rule, what else will? It is significant that K.K. Aziz, a Pakistani scholar, who has written a whole book to prove that 'Muslim nationalism was never supported in England while Indian nationalism was',[170] refers to Strachey's observation, as one of the 'confessions of the divide and rule policy'.[171] Robinson may be right in saying that the main motivation behind the British policy towards the end of the nineteenth century was to reconcile the Muslims, still sulking in hostility to their rule, but there can be no doubt that the attraction for such a policy was very much increased by the prospect of keeping the Muslims separated from the Hindus.

Dufferin, in his letter to George Allen, editor of *The Pioneer*, on 1 January 1887, did strongly disavow any intention to follow a divide and rule policy. He, of course, openly acknowledged that the racial diversity in India and the presence of a powerful Muslim community were favourable to the maintenance of British rule, but asserted that the British found these circumstances and did not create them. If these circumstances did not exist, the British would not have been justified in artificially creating them. 'It would have been a diabolical policy on the part of any Government', he added, 'to endeavour to emphasize or exacerbate race hatred among the Queen's Indian subjects for a political object.'[172] He certainly did not do so. It is also a fact that the British did not create the Hindu-Muslim divide in India; it was already there. But they did accentuate this divide by encouraging Muslim separatism. And Dufferin did not lag behind anyone in pursuing this policy. He did so by encouraging the Muslims to look upon themselves as a distinct political entity and by repeatedly assuring them that he was anxious to promote both the spread of modern education among them and their increased employment in government service. As his right hand man, Mackenzie Wallace, put it, 'Without being in the least hostile or unjust to the Hindoos, Lord Dufferin is rapidly acquiring the reputation of the benevolent protector of the Muslims.'[173]

Successive Viceroys emulated Dufferin and jealously guarded the position of the British Government as the protector and promoter of 'the special interests' of Muslims. Thus, by the end of the nineteenth century, there emerged a virtual Anglo-Muslim alliance. In the beginning symbolized by Aligarh, it was later strengthened by Lord Curzon's partition of Bengal (1905), which was openly justified by him on the ground that it would result in the creation of a new province with a clear Muslim majority, and by Lord Minto's enthusiastic support for separate electorates for Muslims (1906-9). Due to the annulment of the partition of Bengal and the growth of the Pan-Islamic movement among Indian Muslims, which threw them into a close embrace with Indian nationalism, this alliance suffered an interruption for about a decade between 1912 and 1922. As soon as the non-cooperation movement slackened and the Hindu-Muslim alliance began to show cracks, however, the British saw their opportunity again and soon reestablished the old position. The main objective behind the pursuit of such a policy was to keep the Muslims away from the Indian nationalist movement which was seen as a great danger to the future of British rule in India. Thus wrote the then Viceroy, Lord Reading to Viscount Peel, Secretary of State for India on 21 September 1922:

> I have just sent you a telegram which will show you how near we have been to a complete break between the Moslem and the Hindu. I have been giving the greatest attention for some time to this possibility. . . . If this should happen, it would be a grave blow to non-cooperation. I am most anxious to

get the Moslems into line with us, even though we cannot give them all that they want. But we must get back to the position of Britain, the friend and protector of the Moslems. We must be able to rely upon the Moslem; we must not have him arrayed against us, and if only you and I can restore the former position in this respect, we shall have taken a great step for the pacification of India and for the restoration of our authority and prestige. . . . Whatever other considerations may be thrown into the scale against us, they are all outweighed by the supreme consideration of maintaining our position in India.[174]

This was by no means an exception, but the rule. When in 1927, the Secretary of State for India, Lord Birkenhead, said a few vague words expressing his willingness to consider joint electorates if all parties in India were agreed upon them, the Viceroy Lord Irwin, wrote to him on 3 April 1927, telling him that it would be dangerous for the British to go further than the Secretary of State had done in that respect unless Muslim opinion was disposed to agree. 'They are, after all', Irwin added, 'our best friends, and however impartial it may be our duty to be, we are not called upon as I see it to throw over our friends for new allies whose friendship has been a very uncertain quantity.'[175] In 1931, when the Round Table Conference was meeting in London, Irwin became worried after receiving news conveying Muslim apprehensions regarding their inability to secure adequate safeguards for their interests; they feared that the Prime Minister might make some pronouncement favouring the establishment of responsible government at the centre 'without such qualifying conditions as would leave the Muslim position unimpaired in the absence of a communal settlement'. Irwin immediately sent a telegram to the Secretary of State, Lord Birkenhead, telling him of the danger of doing anything which might alienate the Muslims or throw them into an embrace with the Congress. That he warned, would result in 'a situation of utmost gravity'.[176]

The next Viceroy, Lord Willingdon, was both more insistent and more explicit about the need of keeping Muslims with the British and away from the Congress. In 1932, he wrote to the Secretary of State for India, Sir Samuel Hoare, emphasizing the urgency of meeting the Muslim demands regarding the quantum of representation in the legislatures of Bengal and the Punjab under the new constitution then under discussion. Thus on 25 January 1932, with the resumption of the civil disobedience campaign by the Congress in the background, he wrote that he was getting very disturbed about the general political situation and added: 'The Muhammedans are the people who have mainly supported us through these troubles, and I do not want to lose them if I can possibly avoid it.'[177] Pressing his suggestions regarding meeting the Muslim demands relating to Bengal and Punjab in the Communal Award which the Prime Minister was soon going to announce, Willingdon wrote to Hoare on 10 July 1932:

> Do please visualise the political situation out here. The Congress are against us, the Moderates are not cooperating and remember these two bodies are nearly all Hindu, who, while there are many really good men amongst them, have as a community been the leaders of every subversive movement during the past 20 years. The Moslems who, on the whole, have generally supported Government are, with the princes, at present on our side. . . . I can only add that if owing to your decision I lost their support as well, I should probably have to ask you to send someone else here to take up the role of Akbar which I have hitherto so inefficiently filled.[178]

This concern with keeping Muslims away from Indian nationalism sometimes even led some of the top British functionaries to secretly welcome a deterioration in the communal situation and the growth of communal tension between Hindus and Muslims, for it advertised to all concerned the value of British presence as a third, neutral party. When in 1925, for instance, Reading deplored the recrudescence of Hindu-Muslim riots in course of a speech before the central legislature, he received this comment from the Secretary of State, Lord Birkenhead:

> Both you and I must of course speak of these outbreaks in the tone you used; and obviously their occurrence must involve you and your local representatives, as trustees for the maintenance of order, in the greatest anxiety. But surely the complete breakdown of a Hindu-Muhammedan anti-reform unity, looked at very broadly, spells a death-blow to [C.R.] Das and the whole of the Hindu campaign. . . . In ultimate, analysis, the strength of the British position is that we are in India for the good of India. The most striking illustration of the truth of the position is of course supplied by the infinite variation of nationality, sect and religion in the subcontinent. The more it is made obvious that these antagonisms are profound, and affect immense and irreconcilable sections of the population, the more conspicuously is the fact illustrated that we, and we alone, can play the part of composers.[179]

The deep British interest in fostering separatism among Muslims also manifested itself in their high regard for those Muslim leaders who championed separatism and utter dislike, verging on detestation, of those among them who supported Indian nationalism. This is best illustrated by their attitude towards M.A. Jinnah. In a subsequent volume, we shall notice the close relationship between him and Viceroy Lord Linlithgow, as well as the prominence given to him after the outbreak of the Second World War when he emerged as the most powerful leader of Muslim separatism. He was, however, deeply disliked by the heads of the British administration during the 1920s and early 1930s when, even though leading the Muslim League, he was exploring avenues of cooperation with the Congress. The British particularly disliked him for supporting the boycott of the Simon Commission and showing his preparedness to agree to joint electorates if other important demands of the Muslims were met. During those days, the British treated Jinnah as an ambitious and scheming politician without much interest or influence in his community. Thus, when the unity conference, sponsored by Jinnah and some other leaders and held in Simla in 1927, failed to come to a satisfactory conclusion, Irwin wrote to Birkenhead:

> Jinnah's motives in promoting the Conference were perhaps not uninfluenced by a desire to pose as the man who brought national unity to India, and he is probably flattered by a few Hindus who want to use him as a tool to help them to get the Joint Electorate. His ambition is to play an important political part, occupying a kind of centre position, and for this reason he has little influence with ordinary Muhammedans.[180]

Equally revealing of the working of the British mind is Irwin's reference to Firoz Khan Noon, one of the Muslim ministers in the Punjab, then opposed to Jinnah and supporting leaders like Muhammed Shafi and Fazli Husain, who were for cooperating with the Simon Commission and sticking on to separate electorates. Obviously pleased by a conversation with Noon, Irwin wrote: 'He is a young Mussalman of good position and considerable intellectual ability. He has been active in organizing Muslim opinion against what he regards as the insiduous intrigues of Jinnah, and, so far as I can judge, his activity has been productive of considerable result.'[181]

The dislike for Jinnah was equally strong in London. And so was the determination to patronize those Muslim leaders who were cooperating with the Simon Commission and to project them as the real leaders of the Muslim community. Along with it went the design to play off Muslims against Hindus. The following from Birkenhead to Irwin in 1928 illustrates this attitude:

> I should advise Simon to see at all stages important people who are not boycotting the Commission particularly Moslems and the depressed classes. I

should widely advertise all his interviews with representative Moslems. The whole policy is now obvious. It is to terrify the immense Hindu population by the apprehension that the Commission is being got hold of by the Moslems and may present a report altogether destructive of the Hindu position thereby securing a solid Moslem support, and leaving Jinnah high and dry.[182]

Such an attitude continued even after the Simon Commission ended its endeavours. This is borne out by Samuel Hoare's correspondence with Willingdon during 1934-5 containing the most uncomplimentary references to Jinnah. Thus, peeved by Jinnah's opposition to the White Paper on Indian Constitutional Reforms, Hoare wrote to Willingdon in 1934: 'Of all the Indians I have met I think I have disliked Jinnah the most. Throughout the Round Table discussions he invariably behaved like a snake, and no one seemed to trust him. I greatly hope that he is not getting a following among the Muslims.'[183] Willingdon, on his part, used the choicest adjectives for Jinnah, referring to him in one letter as 'a thoroughly spiteful person whose chief desire in life is to make it difficult for everybody all round',[184] and in another as 'that very unpleasant fellow'.[185] Linlithgow's references to Jinnah were also not very different in the beginning. Thus when, after the refusal of the Congress to form a ministry in Bombay in March 1937, a minority ministry under the leadership of the Muslim League leader, Dehlavi, also could not be formed, Linlithgow saw no adequate reason for it 'other than the rather maleficent presence of Jinnah'.[186] Linlithgow's attitude towards Jinnah, however, became quite different in the changed political context after the outbreak of the Second World War in 1939. Jinnah then became a most valuable ally in keeping the Congress at bay and was treated with all deference and attention, at par with Gandhi.

Still another manifestation of British policy took the shape of an excessive emphasis on Hindu-Muslim differences in the reports on the Indian constitutional problem published from time to time. As the demand for Indian independence gathered momentum, the existence of these differences was used as the most important argument for justifying the continuance of power in British hands. Thus, for example, the Indian Statutory Commission, popularly known as the Simon Commission, referred to these differences in its report of 1930 in the following terms:

It would be an utter misapprehension to suppose that Hindu-Muslim antagonism is analogous to the separation between religions denominations in contemporary Europe. Differences of race, a different system of law, and the absence of inter-marriage constitute a far more effective barrier. It is a basic opposition manifesting itself at every turn in social custom and economic competition, as well as in mutual religious antipathy. Today in spite of much neighbourly kindliness in ordinary affairs, and notwithstanding all the efforts made by men of goodwill in both communities to promote Hindu-Muslim concord, the rivalry and dissension between these two forces are one of the chief stumbling blocks in the way of smoother and more rapid progress.[187]

The Joint Select Committee on Indian Constitutional Reform (1934) further improved upon this description and made the Hindu-Muslim differences look much more fundamental than ever before:

India is inhabited by many races . . . often as distinct from one another in origin, tradition and manner of life as are the nations of Europe. Two-thirds of its inhabitants profess Hinduism in one form or another as their religion; over seventy-seven millions are followers of Islam; and the difference between the two is not only one of religion in the stricter sense, but also of law and of culture. They may be said indeed to represent two distinct and separate civilizations.[188]

It is not surprising that both Rahmat Ali[189] and Jinnah[190] cited this section of the report to buttress their arguments in support of the two-nation theory.

These illustrations of British policy should give us some idea of the nature of that policy—emanating not from any innate malevolence of the British people, but from their position as rulers in a vast and distant land and from their natural desire to prolong their rule as long as possible in spite of the rising tide of Indian nationalism. A full picture of the working of that policy and its role in fostering Muslim nationalism and keeping it on a collision course with Indian nationalism can be had only through a study of the evolution of Muslim politics between 1877 and 1947.

NOTES

1. See Beni Prasad, *The Hindu-Muslim Questions* (Allahabad, 1941), pp. 25-6; also Barun De, 'A Historiographical Critique of Renaissance Analogues for Nineteenth Century India', in Barun De, ed., *Perspectives in Social Sciences*, I (Calcutta, 1977), pp. 205-9.
2. *Selected Works of Raja Rammohan Roy* (Delhi, 1977), p. 126.
3. M.K. Haldar, *Renaissance and Reaction in Nineteenth Century Bengal* (Calcutta, 1977), pp. 121-2. See also Sumit Sarkar, 'Rammohun Roy and the Break with the Past', in V.C. Joshi, ed., *Rammohun Roy and the Process of Modernisation*

in India (Delhi, 1975), p. 58; and S. Crawford Cromwell, *Rammohun Roy: His Era and Ethics* (New Delhi, 1984), p. 126.

4. R.C. Majumdar, *The Glimpses of Bengal in the Nineteenth Century* (Calcutta, 1960), p. 20.
5. Henry Louis Vivian Derozio, *Poems* (Calcutta, 1972), p. 15. Cited in Haldar, n. 3, p. 129.
6. J.T.F. Jordens, *Dayananda Sarasvati: His Life and Ideas* (Delhi, 1976), p. 269.
7. Kenneth W. Jones, *Arya Dharm: Hindu Consciousness in 19th Century Punjab* (Berkeley, 1976), p. 145.
8. *Light of Truth or An English Translation of the Satyartha Prakash* (New Delhi, 1927), Chiranjiva Bharadwaja, ed., pp. 626, 633. For the full text of Dayananda's criticism of Islam, see Chapter XIV, pp. 613-76.
9. Vivekananda to Mohammad Sarfraz Husain of Nainital, 10 June 1898, *Complete Works of Swami Vivekananda,* (Calcutta, 1956), VI, pp. 415-16. For an understanding of Vivekananda's attitude to Islam, see editor's Introduction in *Swami Vivekananda: An Anthology*, Bimal Prasad, ed. (New Delhi, 1994), pp. XV-XVII.
10. Sister Nivedita, *The Master as I Saw Him* (Calcutta, 1977), pp. 1-2.
11. *Complete Works of Swami Vivekananda,* n. 9, III, p. 139.
12. Ibid., p. 154. See also Prabha Dixit, 'The Political and Social Dimensions of Vivekananda's Ideology', in *The Indian Economic and Social History Review*, Vol. XXI, No. 3, July-September 1975, pp. 294-314.
13. *Vivekananda in Indian Newspapers, 1893-1902*, Sankari Prasad Basu and Sunil Bihari Ghosh, eds. (Calcutta, 1969), p. 12.
14. Ibid., p. 48-9.
15. Ibid., p. 57.
16. Ibid., p. 304.
17. *The Miscellaneous Writings of the late Hon'ble Mr. Justice M.G. Ranade,* Ramabai Ranade, ed. (Bombay, 1915), pp. 219, 226.
18. Ibid., pp. 219-20.
19. Mahadev Govind Ranade, *Rise of the Maratha Power* (Delhi, 1961), p. 2.
20. Ranade, n. 17, pp. 88-9.
21. Ibid., n. 17.
22. *Religious and Social Reform: A Collection of Essays and Speeches by M.G. Ranade,* M.B. Kolaskar, ed. (Bombay, 1902), p. 129.
23. Ibid.
24. Cited in Richard P. Tucker, *Ranade and the Roots of Indian Nationalism* (Bombay, 1977), pp. 155-6.
25. See Nirad C. Chaudhury, *The Autobiography of an Unknown Indian* (London, 1951), p. 188.
26. Haldar, n. 3, p. 97.
27. Ibid., p. 98.
28. Sri Aurobindo, *Birth Centenary Library* (Pondicherry, 1972), VIII, pp. 309-10.
29. C.H. Philips, ed., *The Evolution of India and Pakistan 1858 to 1947: Select Documents* (London, 1962), p. 119. See also Dusan Zbarite, *Bengali Literature* (Wiesbaden, 1976), pp. 241-2.
30. Bimanbehari Majumdar, 'The Anandmath and Phadke', *Journal of Indian History*, Vol. XLIV, pt. I (April 1966), pp. 97ff.

31. Chaudhury, n. 25, p. 429.
32. T.W. Clark, 'The Role of Bankim Chandra in the Development of Nationalism', in C.H. Philips, ed., *Historians of India, Pakistan and Ceylon* (London, 1961), p. 439. For a similar strand in some novels of R.C. Dutt, the economic historian of early Indian nationalism, see Sudhir Chandra, 'The Cultural Complement of Economic Nationalism: R.C. Dutt's "The Lake of Palms"', *Indian Historical Review*, XII, 1-2, pp. 106-20; and Gyanendra Pandey, *The Construction of Communalism in Colonial North India* (Delhi, 1990), pp. 224-7. See also Joya Chatterjee, *Bengal Divided: Hindu Communalism and Partition, 1932-1947* (Cambridge, 1995), p. 160.
33. Amalas Tripathi, *The Extremist Challenge* (Calcutta, 1967), p. 17.
34. See Kamal Kumar Ghatak, 'Bankim Chandra Chattopadhyaya (1836-1894) and the Revival of Hinduism in Bengal', *The Calcutta Historical Journal*, Vol. VII, No. 2, January-June 1983, pp. 43-57. Also, Amit Sen, *Notes on the Bengal Renaissance* (Bombay, 1946), p. 35.
35. Sudhir Chandra, 'Communal Consciousness in Late 19th Century Hindi Literature', in Mushirul Hasan, ed., *Communal and Pan-Islamic Trends in Colonial India* (New Delhi, 1981), pp. 170-86. See also Pandey, n. 32, pp. 214-18; Jitram Pathak, *Aadhunik Hindi Kavya Me Rashtriya Chetna Ka Vikas* (Allahabad, 1976), pp. 75-93; and Devaraj Sharma Pathik, *Hindi Ki Rashtriya Kavya Dhara* (Delhi, 1979), pp. 142-61.
36. Sushma Narain, *Bhartiya Rashtravad Ke Vikas Ki Hindi Sahitya Me Abhivyakti* (Delhi, 1966), p. 46.
37. Maithili Sharan Gupta, *Bharat Bharati* (Jhansi, 1960). For selected excerpts and commentary in Hindi, see Pathik, n. 35, pp. 133-4; Kranti Kumar Sharma, *Hindi Sahitya Me Rashtriya Kavya Ka Vikas* (Bhopal, 1970), p. 256; and Sudhesh, *Aadhunik Hindi aur Urdu Kavya ki Pravritiyan* (Delhi, 1974), pp. 85-6. For an English rendering of a few stanzas depicting India's ancient glory, see Dharam Paul Sarin, *Influence of Political Movements on Hindi Literature* (Chandigarh, 1967), pp. 58-9.
38. J.E. Sanjana, *Studies in Gujarati Literature* (Bombay, 1950), pp. 75ff.
39. Mansukhlal Jhaveri, *History of Gujarati Literature* (New Delhi, 1978), p. 80.
40. Balkrishna Govind Gokhale, 'Hindu Responses to the Muslim Presence in Maharashtra', in Yohanan Friedmann, ed., *Islam in Asia*, Vol. I, South Asia (Jerusalem, 1984), pp. 162-5.
41. Ibid., pp. 164-8.
42. R.C. Majumdar, 'Nationalist Historians', in *Philips*, n. 2, p. 423.
43. Ranade, n. 19, p. viii.
44. Ibid., p. 17.
45. Gokhale, n. 40, p. 169.
46. V.D. Savarkar, *Hindu-Pad-Padshahi or A Critical Review of the Hindu Empire of Maharashtra* (Madras, 1925), p. 20.
47. Ibid., pp. vi-vid.
48. Jadunath Sarkar, *Histoy of Aurangzeb*, IV (Calcutta, 1919), p. 238.
49. Jadunath Sarkar, *Shivaji and His Times* (Calcutta, 1961, 6th edn), pp. 389-90.
50. Govind Sakharam Sardesai, *New History of the Marathas*, I (Bombay, 1957; 2nd edn), p. 5.
51. Chaudhury, n. 25, pp. 229-30.

52. Madan Mohan Malaviya, *Court Character and Primary Education in the North Western Provinces and Oudh* (Allahabad, 1897). No author is mentioned in this publication, running into 65 pages of text and 100 pages of appendices, but the British Museum, which possesses a copy, lists it under the name of Malaviya. See also Paul R. Brass, 'Muslim Separatism in the United Provinces', in his *Language, Religion and Politics in North India* (Delhi, 1975), pp. 127-34; and Christopher R. King, *One Language, Two Scripts: The Hindi Movement in Nineteenth Century North India* (Bombay, 1994), pp. 126-48.
53. Malaviya, n. 52, pp. 74-5.
54. *Report of the Indian Education Commission*: (Calcutta, 1883), Appendix C, pp. 635-7.
55. *Report of the Indian Education Commission*: *North-Western Provinces and Oudh* (Calcutta, 1884), pp. 422-8.
56. *Report of the Indian Education Commission*, n. 54, pp. 637-9.
57. *Indian Education Commission*: *Report of the Punjab Provincial Committee* (Calcutta, 1984), p. 471.
58. Ibid., p. 490.
59. Ibid., p. 548.
60. Ibid., p. 507.
61. Ibid., pp. 523-4.
62. Ibid., p. 576.
63. Ibid., p. 578.
64. Lala Lajpat Rai, *Autobiographical Writings*, V.C. Joshi, ed. (New Delhi, 1965), p. 29.
65. Kenneth W. Jones, 'Communalism in the Punjab: The Arya Samaj Contribution', *The Journal of Asian Studies,* Vol. XXVIII, No. 1, November 1968, pp. 39-54.
66. Lajpat Rai, n. 64, p. 29.
67. Norman G. Barrier, 'The Arya Samaj and Congress Politics in the Punjab, 1894-1908', *The Journal of Asian Studies,* Vol. XXVI, No. 3, May 1967, pp. 363-79.
68. N. Gerald Barrier, 'The Punjab Government and Communal Politics, 1870-1908', ibid., Vol. XXVII, No. 3, May 1968, p. 528.
69. The Ahmadiyas were the followers of Mirza Ghulam Ahmad (1838-1908) of Qadian in the Punjab, who sought to revitalize and popularize Islam by following a somewhat heretical path and proclaimed himself to be a minor prophet. They pray in separate mosques and are not considered as followers of Islam by orthodox Muslims. See Aziz Ahmad's Introduction in Aziz Ahmad and G.E. Von Grunebaum, eds., *Muslims Self-Statement in India and Pakistan, 1857-1968* (Wiesbaden, 1970), pp. 7-8. For selections from important Ahmadiya texts see ibid., pp. 77-84.
70. See Satyaketu Vidyalankar, ed., *Arya Samaj ka Itihas*, IV (New Delhi, 1985), p. 181.
71. Jones, n. 7, pp. 146-53, 193-5.
72. Jones, n. 65, p. 54.
73. Barrier, n. 67. See also Ikram Ali Malik, *Hindu-Muslim Riots in the British Punjab, 1849-1900* (Lahore, 1984).
74. John R. McLane, *Indian Nationalism and the Early Congress* (Princeton, 1977), pp. 271-321. See also Peter Robb, 'The Challenge of Gau Mata:

British Policy and Religious Change in India 1880-1916', *Modern Asain Studies*, Vol. XX, No. 2.

75. Gyanendra Pandey, 'Rallying Round the Cow: Sectarian Strife in the Bhojpuri Region, *c.* 1888-1917', in Ranajit Guha, ed., *Sabaltern Studies,* II (Delhi, 1983), p. 62.
76. Ibid., p. 104.
77. McLane, n. 74, p. 315.
78. Ibid.
79. Sir C.H.T. Crosthwaite to Lord Lansdowne, 1 July 1893, Mss. Eur. D. 558/25, Lansdowne Collection, India Office Library & Records.
80. Enclosure to Crosthwaite to Lansdowne, 18 August 1893, ibid.
81. Lansdowne to Earl of Kimberbey, 22 August 1893, D. 558/25, ibid.
82. Crosthwaite to Lansdowne, 26 September 1893, D 558.25 ibid.
83. Crosthwaite to Lansdowne, 21 June 1893, ibid.
84. Enclosure to Crosthwaite to Lansdowne, 18 August 1893, ibid.
85. Sir A.P. MacDonnell to Lansdowne, 4 August 1893, ibid.
86. Pandey, n. 75, pp. 106-7.
87. McLane, n. 74, p. 315.
88. See Nemai Sadhan Bose, *The Indian Awakening and Bengal* (Calcutta, 1960), p. 170.
89. Ibid., p. 172.
90. Text in Jogesh C. Bagal, 'Rajnarain Bose and Indian Nationalism', *Modern Review*, Vol. IXXV, No. 6, June 1944, pp. 444-7; also the same author's *Hindu Melar Itivritta* (Calcutta, 1968), pp. 91-101.
91. R.C. Majumdar, *History of the Freedom Movement in India,* I (Calcutta, 1962), p. 330.
92. Susobhan Sarkar, *On the Bengal Renaissance* (Calcutta, 1979), p. 49. For examples of contemporaneous manifestations of Hindu socio-political consciousness in UP, see C.A. Bayly, *The Local Roots of Indian Politics: Allahabad, 1880-1920* (Oxford, 1975), pp. 104-17.
93. Bagal, *Hindu Melar Itivritta*, n. 90, p. 61.
94. Ibid., p. 64.
95. See *Old Hindu's Hope or a Proposal for the Establishment of a Hindu National Congress* (Calcutta, 1888). A copy is available in the National Library, Calcutta. I owe this information to Professor Somnath Roy of Bardwan University who kindly secured for me a typed copy.
96. See Shrimati Ashru Kole, *Rajnarain Basu: Jivan o Sahitya* (in Bengali), (Calcutta, 1975), p. 406, fn. 1.
97. *Old Hindu's Hope*, n. 95, p. ii.
98. Ibid., pp. 1-3
99. Ibid., p. 29.
100. Ibid., pp. 31-2.
101. Ibid.
102. Bipin Chandra Pal, *Memories of My Life and Times*, I (Calcutta, 1932), p. 228.
103. Indra Prakash, *Hindu Mahasabha: Its Contribution to Indian Politics* (New Delhi, 1966), p. 13.
104. See Jones, n. 7, pp. 65-6.
105. Barrier, n. 67, pp. 378-9.
106. Indra Prakash, *A Review of the History and Work of the Hindu Mahasabha and*

the Hindu Sangathan Movement (New Delhi, 1952), p. 18. See also B.B. Misra, *The Indian Political Parties* (Delhi, 1976), p. 164.

107. Richard Gordon, 'The Hindu Mahasabha and the Indian National Congress, 1915 to 1926', *Modern Asian Studies*, 9, 2 (1975), pp. 145-203.
108. S.L. Gupta, *Pandit Madan Mohan Malaviya* (Allahabad, 1978), pp. 291-307. For further details, see the summary of the proceedings of the annual sessions of the All India Hindu Mahasabha in the twenties and thirties in the volumes of the *Indian Annual Register* concerning that period.
109. Uma Kaura, *Muslims and Indian Nationalism, 1928-40* (New Delhi, 1977), pp. 46-7, 74.
110. V.D. Savarkar, *Hindu Rashtra Darshan* (Bombay, 1945), pp. 5, 11.
111. Ibid., pp. 23-7.
112. *Indian Annual Register*, 1938, II, p. 320.
113. Ibid., p. 320
114. Ibid., p. 326.
115. Ibid., p. 328.
116. Ibid., pp. 329-30.
117. Ibid., 1939, II, pp. 317-18.
118. Jean A. Curran Jr., *Militant Hinduism in Indian Politics: A Study of the R.S.S.* (New York, 1951), p. 14.
119. M.S. Golwalkar, *We or Our Nationhood Defined* (Nagpur, 1939), pp. 45, 47-8.
120. S.P. Sen, ed., *Dictionary of National Biography*, I (Calcutta, 1972), p. 61.
121. *Indian Annual Register*, 1934, II, p. 202.
122. Ibid., 1939, II, p. 223.
123. A. Moin Zaidi and Shabeda Zaidi, eds., *The Encyclopaedia of Indian National Congress* (hereinafter referred to as Congress Encyclopaedia), I (New Delhi, 1976).
124. Ibid., p. 311.
125. Ibid., p. 439.
126. S. Gopal, *British Policy in India, 1858-1905* (Cambridge, 1965), pp. 194-5.
127. MacLane, n. 74, pp. 286-308. Also C.A. Bayly, 'Patrons and Politics in Northern India', *Modern Asian Studies,* Vol. VII, July 1973; and Mushirul Hasan, ed., *Communal and Pan-Islamic Trends in Colonial India* (New Delhi, 1981), pp. 199-223.
128. Barrier, n. 67, pp. 367-79.
129. Lala Lajpat Rai, n. 64, p. 30.
130. D.P. Karmarkar, *Bal Gangadhar Tilak: A Study* (Bombay, 1956), pp. 60-1.
131. Ibid., pp. 64-9.
132. Vishwanath Prasad Varma, *The Life and Philosophy of Lokamanya Tilak* (Agra, 1978), p. 65.
133. Karmarkar, n. 130, p. 73.
134. Ibid., pp. 77-9.
135. Stanley A. Wolpert, *Tilak and Gokhale: Revolution and Reform in the Making of Modern India* (Berkeley, 1961), p. 80. Emphasis added.
136. Gordon Johnson, *Provincial Politics and Indian Nationalism: Bombay and the Indian National Congress, 1880 to 1915* (Cambridge, 1973), p. 89.
137. Sumit Sarkar, *The Swadeshi Movement in Bengal, 1903-1908* (New Delhi, 1973), pp. 303-16, 418-64, the lines cited are on p. 308.

138. Ibid., p. 422.
139. Wolpert, n. 135, pp. 178-9. Emphasis added.
140. Tripathi, n. 33, pp. 46-84.
141. Cited in Charles H. Heimsath, *Indian Nationalism and Hindu Social Reform* (Princeton, 1964), p. 138.
142. Sri Aurobindo, n. 28, I, pp. 62-71. The lines cited are on pp. 68, 71.
143. Ibid., pp. 652-3.
144. Ibid., II, pp. 9-10. Emphasis added.
145. Jawaharlal Nehru, *The Discovery of India* (Bombay, 1977), p. 351.
146. For Gandhi's references to religion, see M.K. Gandhi, *In Search of the Supreme*, V.K. Kher (ed.), 3 Vols, (Ahmedabad, 1961-2). For an interpretative study, see Margaret Chatterjee, *Gandhi's Religious Thought* (London, 1983).
147. Razi Ahmed, *Gandhiji our Musalman* (in Urdu) (New Delhi, 1985), p. 167. See also Sadiq Ali's Foreword to this book.
148. For a recent exposition of this view see Bipan Chandra, *Communalism in Modern India* (New Delhi, 1984), pp. 298-9.
149. Ketaki Kushari Dyson, *A Various Universe: A Study of the Journals and Memoirs of British Men and Women in the Indian Subcontinent, 1765-1856* (Delhi, 1978), pp. 46-7, 51-5, 148-9, 165-7, and 230-2. See also Ronald Inden, 'Orientalist Constructions of India', *Modern Asian Studies*, Vol. XX (1986) and Thomas R. Metcalf, *Ideologies of the Raj* (Cambridge, New Delhi, 1995), pp. 132-4.
150. Sleeman, *Rambles and Recollections of an Indian Official* cited in Dyson, n. 149, p. 53.
151. James Mill, *The History of British India* (London, 1826, 3rd edn) II, Chapter V entitled 'A Comparison of the State of Civilization among the Muhammedan Conquerors of India with the State of Civilization among the Hindus', pp. 424-60.
152. J.S. Grewal, *Muslim Rule in India: The Assessments of British Historians* (Oxford, 1970), p. 168.
153. Henry M. Elliot and John Dowson, *The History of India As Told by Its Own Historians* (London, 1867), I, pp. xxii-xxiii.
154. P. Hardy, *The Muslims of British India* (Cambridge, 1972), p. 89.
155. Sleeman, n. 150 cited in Dyson, n. 149.
156. M.A. Laird, ed., *Bishop Heber in Northern India: Selections from Heber's Journal* (Combridge, 1971), pp. 63-4.
157. Elliot and Dowson, n. 153.
158. Cited in Rafiq Zakaria, *Rise of Muslims in Indian Politics* (Bombay, 1971, 2nd edn), p. 5.
159. Thomas R. Metcalf, *The Aftermath of Revolt: India, 1857-1870* (Princeton, 1965), p. 298.
160. Gopal, n. 126, p. 2.
161. Hardy, n. 154, pp. 68-9.
162. Ibid., pp. 71-2.
163. See Allen J. Greenberger, *The British Image of India: A Study in the Literature of Imperialism, 1880-1960* (London, 1969), pp. 45-52.
164. See Hardy, n. 154, pp. 85-8.
165. Francis Robinson, *Separatism among Indian Muslims* (New Delhi, 1975), pp. 102-4.

166. Ibid., p. 131.
167. Ibid.
168. Ibid.
169. Sir John Strachey, *India* (London, 1888), p. 225.
170. K.K. Aziz, *Britain and Muslim India* (London, 1963), p. 22.
171. Ibid., p. 34.
172. Cited in Gopal, n. 126, p. 160.
173. Ibid., pp. 158-60.
174. IOR, Mss. Eur. E. 238/5, Reading Collection.
175. IOR, Mss. Eur. C. 152/4, Halifax Collection.
176. IOR, Mss. Eur. C. 152/11, ibid.
177. IOR, Mss. Eur. E. 240/5, Templewood Collection.
178. Ibid.
179. Birkenhead to Reading, 22 January 1925, IOR, Mss. Eur. E. 238/8, Reading Collection.
180. Irwin to Birkenhead, 29 September 1927, IOR, Mss. Eur. C. 152/4, Halifax Collection.
181. Ibid.
182. Ibid.
183. Samuel Hoare to Willingdon, 5 April 1934, IOR, Mss. Eur. E. 240/4, Templewood Collection.
184. Willingdon to Samuel Hoare, 13 January 1935, E. 240/8, ibid.
185. Ibid., 28 January 1935.
186. Linlithgow to Zetland, 30 March 1937, IOR, Mss. Eur. F. 125/4, Linlithgow Collection.
187. *Report of the Indian Statutory Commission* (London, 1930), I, p. 25.
188. *Report of the Joint Select Committee on Indian Constitutional Reform* (London, 1934), I, p. 1.
189. See the printed letter dated 8 July 1935, issued by Rahmat Ali from Cambridge, IOR I/P&J/8/689, p. 2.
190. See the text of M.A. Jinnah's article on 'The Constitutional Maladies of India' written for *Time and Tide* (London) in January 1940, and reproduced in Jamil-ud-Din Ahmad, ed., *Speeches and Writings of Mr. Jinnah* (Lahore, 1968), I, p. 123.

APPENDIX I

SYED AHMED KHAN'S SPEECH AT LUCKNOW, 28 SEPTEMBER 1887*

Gentlemen,—I am not given to speaking on politics, and I do not recollect having ever previously given a political lecture. My attention has always been directed towards the education of my brother Mohammedans, for from education I anticipate much benefit for my people, for Hindustan, and for the Government. But at the present time circumstances have arisen which make it necessary for me, I think, to tell my brother Mussalmans clearly what my opinions are. The object, gentlemen, of this lecture is to explain the attitude which the Mohammedan community ought to adopt with regard to the political movements of the time. I am not going to give a philosophical discourse, nor to speak of those abstract questions on political economy which would require many lectures fully to deal with; but I am simply going to express my opinions in a plain and straightforward manner, leaving it to everyone who hears me to agree with me or differ from me. The reason why I stand here to address you to-day is because there has grown up in India a political agitation, and it is necessary to determine what action should be taken by the Mohammedan community with regard to it. Although my own thoughts and desires are towards my own community, yet I shall discuss whether or not this agitation is useful for the country and for the other nations who live in it. If it be useful, we must follow it, but if dangerous for the country or our nation, we must hold aloof.

Before I enter on this subject, let me briefly describe the methods of rule adopted by our Government, which has now been here for nearly a hundred years. Its method is this: to keep in its own hands all questions of foreign policy and all matters affecting its army. I hope that we, who are subjects of the Empire, will not seek to interfere in those matters which Government has set apart as its own. If the Government fights Afghanistan or conquers Burma, it is no business of ours to criticise its policy. Our interests will not suffer from these matters being left in the hands of Government. But we are concerned with matters affecting internal policy, and we have to observe what method Government has adopted for dealing with them. Government has made a Council for making laws affecting the lives, property, and comfort of the

*Source: Sayyid Ahmad Khan, *The Present State of Indian Politics: Speeches and Letters* (Allahabad, 1888).

people. For this Council, she selects from all Provinces those officials who are best acquainted with the administration and the condition of the people, and also some *Raises*, who, on account of their high social position, are worthy of a seat in that assembly. Some people may ask—Why should they be chosen on account of social position instead of ability? On this, gentlemen, I will say a few words. It is a great misfortune—and I ask your pardon for saying it—that the landed gentry of India have not the trained ability which makes them worthy of occupying those seats. But you must not neglect those circumstances which compel Government to adopt this policy. It is very necessary that for the Viceroy's Council the members should be of high social position. I ask you—Would our aristocracy like that a man of low caste or insignificant origin, though he be a B.A. or M.A., and have the requisite ability, should be in a position of authority above them and have power in making laws that affect their lives and property? Never! Nobody would like it (Cheers). A seat in Council of the Viceroy is a position of great honour and prestige. None but a man of good breeding can the Viceroy take as his colleague, treat as his brother, and invite to entertainments at which he may have to dine with Dukes and Earls. Hence no blame can be attached to Government for making those great *Raises* members of the Council. It is our great misfortune that our *Raises* are such that they are unable to devise laws useful for the country. The method of procedure in the Council is this. If any member introduces a subject of importance and difficulty, a commission is appointed which collects evidence and digests it. The matter is discussed in every newspaper, and memorials are invited from Associations. The Council then discusses the matter, every member speaking his views with great vigour and earnestness, more even than was displayed in the discussion on the third resolution of the Mohammedan Educational Congress, advocating what he thinks necessary for the welfare of the country, and as regardless of the Viceroy's presence as if he were a figure of white stone. I have had the honour of being in this Council. I do not recollect any matter of importance concerning which ten or twenty memorials were not sent in. A Select Committee was then appointed, which read through these memorials and discussed them at length, many of which on consideration turned out to be thorough nonsense. Extracts from Urdu papers were also considered. Although not in my presence, yet often amendments suggested by these memorials have been adopted. This is the method of our Government. After this the law is passed and sent to the Secretary of State, who is assisted by the Council of State, which consists of men of the highest ability, who have lived for a long time in India and have often held all offices, from that of Assistant Collector to Lieutenant-Governor. If they think it expedient it is passed, otherwise a short note of four lines cancels it. Often people make objections to the laws so passed, and in some cases they are perhaps right; but in the majority of cases, as far as my experience goes, those very people who sit in their houses and make objections would, if they had been on Viceroy's Council, have supported them. Many details appear wrong on superficial consideration, but when all the circumstances and difficulties are taken into account, they are seen to be right. In conclusion, whether the laws be good or bad, no one can say that Government acts independently of the wishes and opinions of its subjects. Often it adopts some of the views expressed in newspapers and memorials. Can we say that Government, in the method it has adopted for legislation, acts without regard to the opinions of the people? Can we say that we have no share in the making of the laws? Most certainly not (Cheers).

There is now another great duty of Government. That is, that in whatever country Government establishes its dominion, that dominion should be made strong, firm, and secure. I believe that if any of my friends were made Viceroy, he would be as loyal to Her Majesty the Queen-Empress of India as is our present Viceroy, Lord Dufferin. And his first duty would be to see that the Empire of Her Majesty were made so firm that no enemy, external, or internal, could shake it (Cheers). If it were my fortune to be Viceroy, I speak from my heart when I say I would not be equally but more anxious to see the rule of the Queen placed on a firm basis (Cheers). It is a first principle of Empire that it is the supreme duty of every one, whether Hindustani or Englishman, in whose power it rests, to do what he can to strengthen the Government of Her Majesty the Queen. The second duty of Government is to preserve peace, to give personal freedom, to protect life and property, to punish criminals and to decide civil disputes. Now, every one will admit that Government completely fulfils its duty in this respect. Many people think that the laws have become too numerous and consequently that law-suits have become more complicated, and thus, lead to disputes between the *zamindar* and *kashtkar*.* But this is the opinion of the critics who sit in their houses, who if they sat on the Viceroy's Council, would change their views. The multiplicity of laws depends upon the condition of the country and of its people. New companies and new industries are springing into existence. New and unforeseen legal rights have arisen which are not provided for in the Mohammedan law. Hence, when the country is changing at such a rate, it is absolutely necessary that new laws should be brought forward to deal with the new circumstances. Government does not want to increase the number of laws, but when the conditions of the country change, it becomes unavoidable. Taking all these things into account I cannot but think that there is no requirement of the country that cannot be brought to the notice of Government. And nothing can prevent our expressing our views on the subject and being heard by Government. So that whatever comfort we can experience under any Government, we have under the British Government (Cheers).

I come now to the main subject on which I wish to address you. That is the National Congress and the demands which that body makes of Government. I cannot allude to its proposals in detail because, as far as I am

*Cultivator.

aware, there are forty-nine of them, and the time at my disposal is short. I must therefore select the most important. That about which the greatest agitation has taken place is the following. When the Government of India passed out of the hands of the East India Company into those of the Queen, a law was passed, saying that all subjects of Her Majesty, whether white or black, European or Indian, should be equally eligible for appointments. This was confirmed by the Queen's Proclamation. We have to see whether, in the rules made for admission to civil appointments, any exception has been made to this or not; whether we have been excluded from any appointments for which we are fitted. Nobody can point out a case in which for any appointment a distinction of race has been made. It is true that for the Covenanted Civil Service a special set of rules has been made, namely, that candidates have to pass a competitive examination in England. Perhaps it will occur to every one that this examination ought not to be held in England, and the proposal about which the greatest agitation has taken place is that it should be held in India. And to this is added another proposal that all posts in the subordinate service, from that of Tahsildar to Subordinate Judge, should also be given by competitive examination.

I do not think it necessary for me on this occasion to discuss the question why the competitive examination is held in England, and what would be the evils arising from its transference to India. But I am going to speak of the evils likely to follow the introduction into India of the competitive principle. I do not wish to speak in the interest of my own co-religionists, but to express faithfully whether I think the country is prepared for competitive examination or not. What is the result of competitive examination in England? You know that men of all social positions, sons of Dukes or Earls, of *darzies* and people of low rank, are equally allowed to pass this examination. Men of both high and low family come to India in the Civil Service. And it is the universal belief that it is not expedient for Government to bring the men of low rank; and that the men of good social position treat Indian gentlemen with becoming politeness, maintain the prestige of the British race, and impress on the hearts of the people a sense of British justice; and are useful both to Government and to the country. But those who come from England, come from a country so far removed from our eyes that we do not know whether they are the sons of Lords or Dukes or of *darzies*, and therefore, if those who govern us are of humble rank, we cannot perceive the fact. But as regards Indians, the case is different. Men of good family would never like to trust their lives and property to people of low rank with whose humble origin they are well acquainted (Cheers). Leave this a moment, and consider what are the conditions which make introduction into a country of competitive examinations expedient, and then see whether our own country is ready for it or not. This is no difficult question of political economy. Every one can understand that the first condition for the introduction of competitive examination into a country is that all people in that country, from the highest to the lowest should belong to one nation. In such a country no particular difficulties are likely to arise. The second case is that of a country in which there are two nationalities which have become so united as to be practically one nation. England and Scotland are a case in point. In the past many wars were waged between those countries and many acts of bravery were done on both sides, but those times have gone, and they are now like one nation. But this is not the case with our country, which is peopled with different nations. Consider the Hindus alone. The Hindus of our Province, the Bengalis of the East, and the Mahrattas of the Deccan, do not form one nation. If, in your opinion, the peoples of India do form one nation, then no doubt competitive examination may be introduced; but if this be not so, then competitive examination is not suited to the country. The third case is that of a country in which there are different nationalities which are on an equal footing as regards the competition, whether they take advantage of it or not. Now, I ask you, have Mohammedans attained to such a position as regards higher English education, which is necessary for higher appointments, as to put them on a level with Hindus or not? Most certainly not. Now, I take Mohammedans and the Hindus of our Province together, and ask whether they are able to compete with the Bengalis or not? Most certainly not. When this is the case, how can competitive examination be introduced into our country (Cheers). Think for a moment what would be the result if all appointments were given by competitive examination. Over all races, not only over Mohammedans but over Rajas of high position and the brave Rajputs who have not forgotten the swords of their ancestors, would be placed as ruler a Bengali who at sight of a table knife would crawl under his chair (Uproarious cheers and laughter). There would remain no part of the country in which we should see at the tables of justice and authority any face except those of Bengalis. I am delighted to see the Bengalis making progress, but the question is—What would be the result on the administration of the country? Do you think that the Rajput and the fiery Pathan, who are not afraid of being hanged or of encountering the swords of the police or the bayonets of the army, could remain in peace under the Bengalis? (Cheers). This would be the outcome of the proposal if accepted. Therefore if any of you—men of good position, *Raises*, men of the middle classes, men of noble family to whom God has given sentiments of honour—if you accept that the country should groan under the yoke of Bengali rule and its people lick the Bengali shoes, then, in the name of God jump into the train, sit down, and be off to Madras, be off to Madras! (Loud cheers and laughter). But if you think that the prosperity and honour of the country would be ruined, then, brothers, sit in your houses, inform Government of your circumstances, and bring your wants to its notice in a calm and courteous manner.

The second demand of the National Congress is that the people should elect a section of the Viceroy's council. They want to copy the English House of Lords and the House of Commons. The elected members are to be like members of the House of Commons; the appointed members like the House of Lords. Now, let us suppose the Viceroy's Council is made in this manner.

And let us suppose first of all that we have universal sufferage, as in America, and that everybody, *chamars** and all, have votes. And first suppose that all the Mohammedan electors vote for a Mohammedan member and all Hindu electors for a Hindu member, and now count how many votes the Mohammedan members have and how many the Hindu. It is certain the Hindu members will have four times as many because their population is four times as numerous. Therefore we can prove by mathematics that there will be four votes for the Hindu to every one vote for the Mohammedan. And now how can the Mohammedan guard his interests? It would be like a game of dice, in which one man had four dice and the other only one. In the second place, suppose that the electorate be limited. Some method of qualification must be made; for example, that people with a certain income shall be electors. Now, I ask you, O Mohammedans! Weep at your condition! Have you such wealth that you can compete with the Hindus? Most certainly not. Suppose, for example, that an income of Rs. 5,000 a year be fixed on, how many Mohammedans will there be? Which party will have the larger number of votes. I put aside the case that by a rare stroke of luck a blessing comes through the roof and some Mohammedan is elected. In the normal case no single Mohammedan will secure a seat in the Viceroy's Council. The whole Council will consist of Babu so-and-so Chuckerbutty (Laughter). Again, what will be the result for the Hindus of our Province, though their condition be better than that of the Mohammedans? What will be the result for those Rajputs the swords of whose ancestors are still wet with blood? And what will be the result for the peace of the country? Is there any hope that we and our brave brothers the Rajputs can endure it in silence? Now, we will suppose a third kind of election. Suppose a rule is to be made that a suitable number of Mohammedans and a suitable number of Hindus are to be chosen. I am aghast when I think on what grounds this number is likely to be determined. Of necessity proportion to total population will be taken. So there will be one number for us to every four for the Hindus. No other condition can be laid down. Then they will have four votes and we shall have one. Now, I will make a fourth supposition. Leaving aside the question as to the suitability of members with regard to population, let us suppose that a rule is laid down that half the members are to be Mohammedan and half Hindus, and that the Mohammedans and Hindus are each to elect their own men. Now, I ask you to pardon me for saying something which I say with a sore heart. In the whole nation there is no person who is equal to the Hindus in fitness for the work. I have worked in the Council for four years, and I have always known well that there can be no man more incompetent or worse fitted for the post than myself (No, No!). And show me the man who, when elected, will leave his business and undertake the expense of living in Calcutta and Simla, leaving alone the trouble of the journeys. Tell me who there is of our nation in the Punjab, Oudh, and North-

*Cobblers.

Western Provinces, who will leave his business, incur these expenses, and attend the Viceroy's Council for the sake of his countrymen. When this is the condition of your nation, is it expedient for you to take part in this business on the absurd supposition that the demands of the Congress would, if granted, be beneficial for the country? Spurn such foolish notions. It is certainly not expedient to adopt this cry—Chalo Madras! Chalo Madras!—without thinking of the consequences.

Besides this there is another important consideration, which is this. Suppose that a man of our own nationality were made Viceroy of India, that is, the deputy of Her Most Gracious Majesty the Queen-Empress. Could such a person grant demands like these, keeping in view the duty of preserving the Empire on a firm and secure basis? Never! Then how absurd to suppose that the British Government can grant these requests? The result of these unrealizable and impossible proposals can be only this, that for a piece of sheer nonsense the hearts of everybody will be discontented with Government, and everybody will believe that Government exerts over us a tyrannical rule, and turns a deaf ear to our requests. And thus anger and excitement will spread throughout the people, and the peace of the country will be destroyed.

Everybody knows well that the agitation of the Bengalis is not the agitation of the whole of India. But suppose it were the agitation of the whole of India, and that every nation had taken part in it, do you suppose the Government is so weak that it would not suppress it, but must needs be itself overwhelmed? Have you not seen what took place in the Mutiny? It was a time of great difficulty. The army had revolted; some *badmashes* had joined it; and Government wrongly believed that the people at large were taking part in the rebellion. I am the man who attacked this wrong notion, and while the Government was hanging its officials, I printed a pamphlet,* and told Government that it was entirely false to suppose that the people at large were rebellious. But in spite of all these difficulties, what harm could this rebellion do to the Government? Before the English troops had landed she had regained her authority from shore to shore. Hence, what benefit is expected from all this for the country, and what revolution in the Government can we produce? The only results can be to produce a useless uproar, to raise suspicions in Government and to bring back again that time which we experienced thirty or thirty-one years ago. This is on the supposition that by all of us coming together we could do something: but if you take the agitation as it is, what could it accomplish? The case of Ireland is held up as an example. I will not discuss the question whether that agitation is right or wrong. I will only point out that there are at this moment in Ireland thousands of men ready to give up their lives at the point of the sword. Men of high position who sympathise with that movement fear neither the prison nor the bayonets of the police. Will you kindly point out to me

**Asbab-e-Baghawat-e-Hind*, later translated into English—*Causes of the India Revolt.*

ten men among our agitators who will consent to stand face to face with the bayonets? When this is the case, then what sort of an uproar is this, and is it of such a nature that we ought to join it? We ought to consider carefully our own circumstances and the circumstances of Government. If Government entertains unfavourable sentiments towards our community, then I say with the utmost force that these sentiments are entirely wrong. At the same time if we are just, we must admit that such sentiments would be by no means unnatural. I repeat it. If Government entertains these bad sentiments it is a sign of incompetence and folly. But I say this, we ought to consider whether Government can entertain such thoughts or not. Has she any excuse for such suspicions or not? I reply that she certainly has. Think for a moment who you are. What is this nation of ours? We are those who ruled India for six or seven hundred years (Cheers). From our hands the country was taken by Government into its own. Is it not natural then for Government to entertain such thoughts? Is Government so foolish as to suppose that in seventy years we have forgotten all our grandeur and our empire? Although, should Government entertain such notions, she is certainly wrong, yet we must remember she has ample excuse. We do not live on fish; nor are we afraid of using a knife and fork lest we should cut our fingers (Cheers). Our nation is of the blood of those who made not only Arabia, but Asia and Europe to tremble. It is our nation which conquered with its sword the whole of India, although its peoples were all of one religion (Cheers). I say again that if Government entertains suspicions of us it is wrong. But do her the justice and admit that there is a reasonable ground for such suspicions. Can a wise ruler forget what the state of things was so short a time ago? He can never forget it. If then the Mohammedans also join these monstrous and unreasonable schemes, which are impossible of fulfilment, and which are disastrous for the country and for our nation, what will be the result? If Government be wise and Lord Dufferin be a capable Viceroy, then he will realise that a Mohammedan agitation is not the same as a Bengali agitation, and he will be bound to apply an adequate remedy. If I were Viceroy, and my nation took part in this affair, I would first of all drop down on them, and make them feel their mistake. Our course of action should be such as to convince Government of the wrongness of her suspicions regarding us, if she entertains any. We should cultivate mutual affection. What we want we should ask for as friends. And if any ill-will exists it should be cleansed away. I am glad that some Pathans of the N.W.P. and Oudh are here to-day, and I hope some Hindu Rajputs are also present. My friend Yusuf Shah of the Punjab sits here, and he knows well the mood of mind of the people of the Punjab, of the Sikhs and Mussalmans. Suppose that this agitation that has arisen in Bengal—and I imagine that no danger can spring from it there—suppose that this agitation extends to these Provinces, to the Rajputs and Pathans of Peshawar, do you think it will confine itself to writing with the pen—giz, giz, giz, giz, giz,—and to mere talking—buk, buk, buk, buk? It will then be necessary for Government to send its army and show by bayonets what the proper remedy for this agitation is. I believe that when Government sees the Mohammedans and other brave races taking part in this stupid agitation, it will be necessary for Government to pass a new law and to fill the jails. O my brothers! children of my heart! This is your relationship to Government. You should conduct yourself in a straightforward and calm manner; not come together to make a noise and a hubbub like a flock of crows (Cheers and laughter).

I come now to some other proposals of the Congress. We have now a very charming suggestion. These people wish to have the Budget of India submitted to them for sanction. Leave aside political expenses; but ask our opinion about the expenses of the army. Why on earth has Government made so big an army? Why have you put Governors in Bombay and Madras? Pack them off at once. I am also of the opinion that their ideas should certainly be carried out. I only ask them to say who, not only of them but of the whole people of India, can tell me about the new kinds of cannon which have been invented—which is the mouth and which the butt end. Can any one tell me the expense of firing a shot? Does any one understand the condition of the army? One who has seen the battlefield, the hail-shower of shots, the falling of the brave soldiers one over another, may know what equipments are needed for an army. If then, under these circumstances, a Mohammedan were on this Council, or a Bengali—one of that nation which in learning is the crown of all Indian nations, which has raised itself by the might of learning from a low to a high position—how could he give any advice? How ridiculous then for those who have never seen a battlefield, or even the mouth of a cannon, to want to prepare the Budget for the army?

A still more charming proposal is the following: When some people wrote articles in newspapers, showing that it was impossible to establish representative government in India, and bringing forward cogent reasons, then they came down a little from their high flight and said: 'Let us sit in the Council, let us chatter; but take votes or not, as you please'; can you tell me the meaning of this, or the use of this folly?

Another very laughable idea is this. Stress is laid on these suggestions: that the Arms Act be repealed, that Indian Volunteers be enlisted, and that army schools be established in India. But do you know what nation is proposing them? If such proposals had come from Mohammedans or from Rajput brothers, whose ancestors always wore the sword, which although it is taken from their belts, yet still remains in their hearts, if they had made such proposals there would have been some sense in it. But what nation makes these demands? I agree with them in this and consider that Government has committed two very great mistakes. One is not to trust the Hindustanis and to allow them to become volunteers. A second error of Government of the greatest magnitude is this, that it does not give appointments in the army to those brave people whose ancestors did not use the pen to write with; no, but a different kind of pen—(Cheers)—nor did they use black ink, but the ink they dipped their pens in was red, red ink which flows from the bodies of men (Cheers). O brothers! I have fought the Government in the harshest language about these points. The time is, however, coming when my brothers, Pathans, Syeds, Hashmi and Koreishi, whose blood smells of the blood of Abraham, will appear in glittering uniform as Colonels and Majors in the army. But we must wait for that time. Government will most certainly attend to it; provided you do not give rise to suspicions of disloyalty. O brothers! Government, too, is under some difficulties as regards this last charge I have brought against her. Until she can trust us as she can her white soldiers she cannot do it. But we ought to give proof that, whatever we were in former days, that time has gone, and that now we are as well-disposed to her as the Highlanders of Scotland. And then we should claim this from Government. I will suppose for a moment that you have conquered a part of Europe and have become its rulers. I ask whether you would equally trust the men of that country. This was a mere supposition. I now come to a real example. When you conquered India, what did you yourself do? For how many centuries was there no Hindu in the army list? But when the time of the Mughal family came and mutual trust was established, the Hindus were given very high appointments. Think how many years old is the British rule? How long ago was the Mutiny? And tell me how many years ago Government suffered such grievous troubles, though they arose from the ignorant and not from the gentlemen? Also call to mind that in the Madras Presidency, Government has given permission to the people to enlist as volunteers. I say, too, that this concession was premature, but it is a proof that when trust is established, Government will have no objection to make you also volunteers. And when we shall be qualified, we shall acquire those positions with which our forefathers were honoured. Government has advanced one step. She has also shown a desire to admit us to the civil appointments in the Empire (Cheers). In the time of Lord Ripon I happened to be a member of the Council. Lord Ripon had a very good heart and kind disposition and every qualification for a Governor. But, unfortunately, his hand was weak. His ideas were radical. At that time the Local Board and Municipality Bills were brought forward, and the intention of them was that everybody should be appointed by election. Gentlemen, I am not a Conservative, I am a great Liberal. But to forget the prosperity of one's nation is not a sign of wisdom. The only person who was opposed to the system of election was myself. If I am not bragging too much, I may, I think, say that it was on account of my speech that Lord Ripon changed his opinion and made one-third of the members appointed and two-thirds elected. Now just consider the result of election. In no town are Hindus and Mohammedans equal. Can the Mohammedans suppress the Hindus and become the masters of our 'Self-Government?' In Calcutta an old, bearded Mohammedan of noble family met me and said that a terrible calamity had befallen them. In his town there were eighteen elected members, not one of whom was a Mohammedan; all were Hindus. Now, he wanted Government to appoint some Mohammedans; and he hoped Government would appoint him. This is the state of things in all cities. In Aligarh also, were there not a special rule, it would be impossible for any Mohammedan, except my friend Maulvi Mohammed Yusuf, to be elected; and at last he, too, would have to rely on being appointed by Government. Then how can we walk along a road for which neither we nor the country is prepared?

I am now tired and have no further strength left. I can say no more. But, in conclusion, I have one thing to say, lest my friends should say that I have not told them what is of advantage for our nation and for the country, and by what thing we may attain prosperity. My age is above seventy. Although I cannot live to see my nation attain to such a position as my heart longs for it, yet my friends who are present in this meeting will certainly see the nation attain such honour, prosperity and high rank, if they attend to my advice. But, my friends, do not liken me to that dyer who, only possessing mango-coloured dyer, said mango-coloured dye was the only one I liked. I assure you that the only thing which can raise you to a high rank is high education. Until our nation can give birth to a highly-educated people it will remain degraded; it will be below others, and will not attain such honour as I desire for it. These precepts I have given you from the bottom of my heart. I do not care if any one calls me a mad man or anything else. It was my duty to tell those things which, in my opinion, are necessary for the welfare of my nation, and to cleanse my hands before God the Omnipotent, the Merciful, and the Forgiver of sins.

APPENDIX II

AL-HILAL
OBJECTIVES AND POLITICAL MESSAGE*
by
Abul Kalam Azad
8 September 1912

This week, I had already planned to write an article on this subject, but when I received this note from an esteemed friend, the need to do so became imperative. He wrote:

Even after I had read the seven volumes of *Al-Hilal*, word for word, it was unclear to me what political doctrine you want to preach? A significant fundamental principle that you seem to believe in, and which invokes great respect for you in my heart is that you consider religion and the Quran to be the cure for whatever ails the Muslims, and you want to invoke a true (not merely a formal) spirit of Islam in them. Many others also subscribe to this principle, but the truth is that no one can translate it into practice better than you can. Only a few of your writings have appeared so far, but they reflect your profound understanding of the truths and mysteries of the Quran. But, begging your pardon, you mix politics in religion in a manner such that it becomes difficult to distinguish one from the other. I do believe, that like me, hundreds of readers of *Al-Hilal* must be concerned about this matter. You should, therefore, first explain your policy, and secondly, by separating political doctrine from religious ideas, define the direction in which you want to lead the community?

There is one direction which we have followed so far; the other one is that of the moderate Hindus who, while endorsing the continuance of British imperialism, have submitted the demand for their rights. The third way is that of the Hindu anarchists who want to use grenades and guns to rid *Bharat Mata* of the foreign rule. Tell us, please, which is your way, and with whom do you want us to throw our lot? Once we know, we shall either follow you all the way, or abide with you in religious matters, and disassociate from all others. What I wish to say is, simply, that I don't know what obstacles you must have overcome before you started such a mighty mission. There is no doubt that your interest is genuine. As for your scholarship and erudition, especially in matters of religion, words fail in its praise. These qualities are not always available to our unfortunate community. I hope that all this potential is not wasted (God forbid), and the community is not deprived of the benefit of your wisdom.

*Syeda Saiyidain Hameed, ed., *India's Maulana: Abul Kalam Azad, Centenary Volume II, Selected Speeches and Writings* (New Delhi, 1990), pp. 27-36.

I intend to start with a comprehensive series of articles on the objectives of *Al-Hilal* and codify the goals and objectives of our journey. Certain issues arose, however, on which I felt compelled to write immediately. I had to plunge into the main body of the work, even before writing its preface. I am grateful to my esteemed friend, who brought this matter to the forefront.

The words in which he has extolled my religious views and writings are a reflection of the affection of an elder youth. I must confess that I do not find myself worthy of his words of praise. Perhaps, I am familiar with religious precepts, but the mysteries of the Holy Quran are not accessible to my rudimentary understanding. The words he has used about me in his letter are quite startling. If knowledge of Arabic were needed to understand the truth and mysticism in the Quran, then, I do admit that I know a little Arabic. If religious knowledge were enough, I could try to acquire it. If a study of the commentaries was required, there are several such books in my possession which I would have read. But all this is of no use. The first prerequisite is piety of soul and purity of heart. Alas! I possess neither one of these virtues. A heart which is devoid of the wealth of piety, and a prisoner of sensual pleasures and worldly affairs, cannot, even momentarily, become the repository for the truths and mysteries of the Quran. Scholarship and erudition are of no use, mind and intellect of no value.

Believe my words! A man without piety, even if he has scaled all the degrees of erudition and scholarship, cannot partake of the mysteries and deeper meanings of the Quran. Judge for yourself: if this be the criterion, where do I stand?

A few points in the above letter deserve special attention:

1. Political debates should be separated from religious education.
2. Among the existing political parties in India, which does *Al-Hilal* support?

About the first, I believe that you have questioned the very foundation on which I want to build the structure of *Al-Hilal*. If you had said that an arch was not attractive, perhaps, I could change it. But if you want the girders at the base to be removed, I am afraid I cannot comply with your desire. I view every branch of human activity from the perspective of religion. If I take any guidance, it is from the Holy Quran; save that, I know nothing. My eyes are closed to the rest of the scenery and my ears deaf to all other sounds. If light were needed, believe me, I have the one and only light given to us by the 'source of all light'. Remove it, and I will be struck blind. 'The Quran has been revealed to mankind to bring them from darkness to light.' You say, separate politics from religion; but if I do so what will remain? I have derived my politics from religion. My ideas not only have a religious bias, they are themselves the product of religion. How can I separate them from religion? In my creed, any idea derived from a source other than Quran is outright blasphemous; in this I include politics.

It is unfortunate that you have never seen Islam in its pristine glory. Else, for your political guidance you need neither bow at the doors of the government nor follow the Hindus. You could have derived everything from the Quran, the book which enabled you to teach everything to the world. Islam has brought a comprehensive and perfect system for mankind. There is not a single sphere of human activity for which it does not provide guidance. The Islamic principle of *Tawhid*, or 'Oneness of God' is much too upright; it would never tolerate the fact that one who submits before it, should knock at other doors. Whether it is ethical, educational, political, cultural, religious, or the temporal life of the Muslims; whether the life of the ruler or the ruled, it provides the most perfect system for all. Had it not been so, it could not have ordained the world's final and universal religion. It is the voice of God. Its school is the divine circle of God. The one who gives his hand to God needs no human guide.

It has often been said that the Quranic word is *Noor* or light, and where there is light, darkness is dispelled; whether it is the darkness of religion or of political waywardness.

> Verily, there hath come to you from God a (new) light and a perspicuous Book, wherewith God guideth all who seek His approval, to ways of peace and safety and leadeth them out of darkness, into the light, and guideth them to the path that is straight. (15:5)

Is there any book in the world which has, on its own strength, made such majestic claims? The above verse clearly states that the Holy Quran is light; and thereby, the only means of removing the darkness of human misdeeds. It is further stated that everything in it has been explicitly explained, and there is no branch of human activity for which it does not have a guideline. This thought recurs at another place in the Quran:

> Verily! I gave them the Book and I made it explicit with knowledge; it is a guide and a blessing for those who believe.

The next verse says that the Quran is a guide for the ways of safety, for it leads to the ways of well-being. If you believe that political activity must have a direction, there is no reason why you cannot find it in the Quran. Again, it is stated that it brings men out of the pit of wantonness into the light of guidance. If we find ourselves in political wilderness, it is because we have not allowed ourselves to benefit from the guiding spirit of the Quran. Otherwise, instead of being plunged in darkness there would have been a pool of light all around us. And, finally, it states that it leads to the *Sirat-al-Mustaqueem* or the 'Straight Path'. In the interpretation of the Quran, the 'Straight Path' is all-inclusive and all-comprehensive; it encompasses the entire world.

Unfortunately, this is no occasion for a lengthy discourse, but this discussion has brought hundreds of verses to mind. At one place it has been said:

(Oh! Prophet), I have bestowed upon you a book, wherein everything has been explained explicitly and which is a guide and a blessing for those who believe.

In the last verse of the *Surah-e-Yusuf* (XII), it is stated:

The Quran is not a tale invented, but a confirmation of truths that went before it. It is a detailed exposition of all things, and a Guide and Mercy for those who believe.

At another place it has been proclaimed:

I have given all sorts of examples for men to seek guidance from.

In these verses, the assertion of the Quran is very explicit. It claims to be perfect for all branches of knowledge. Its messages are clean and unambiguous, provided one ponders over them.

Praise be to God who has bestowed the Quran on His servants and has not allowed any ambiguity in it.

How is it possible that its followers seek guidance from other sources when they have the Quran as a command, and an *Imam-i-Mubeen* (guide manifest)?

Everything has been taken account of in this explicit book.

At another place, it has been called the *Quol-e-Faisal*, last word in all matters.

Verily, the Quran is the last word for all divergences and actions; Nothing in it is meaningless or superfluous.

All the miseries of the Muslims are due to their negligence and due to the fact that they have turned from this divine source of guidance, and thought that they needed to look upon it only in regard to religious rituals, like *Roza* and *Namaz*. They did not realise its importance in all aspects, educational, cultural and political. The more they turned away from the Quran, the faster the world slipped away from them. Whichever direction they took they were misled and they fell into the depths of darkness. The Quran had predicted these times:

On the day of judgement the Prophet of God would say, Oh my Lord! My people took the Quran for nonsense and did not act according to it.

I believe that if at the time of the revelation of the Quran the polytheists of Mecca had shunned and overlooked it, they had not committed any greater sin than what the Muslims all over the world, including temporal or religious leaders, have been doing for centuries. If at the time of the recitation of the Quran, those heathens used to put their fingers in their ears, or shouted and clapped in the *Kaaba* so that nobody could hear its verses, the Muslims of today, have done no less. They have closed their hearts if not their ears. And though they are physically quiet, the cacophony of their worldly affairs has created such a din that nobody hears the call of God:

O Prophet, when you recite the Quran, we put between you and those who do not believe in the hereafter an invisible veil; we put coverings over their hearts lest they should understand the Quran; and deafness into their ears lest they should hear.

Thus, if this is the cause of your anxiety, I am sorry, I cannot remove it. If I could not find time to present my objectives in detail, no matter. They can as well be stated briefly. The real purpose of *Al-Hilal* is no more than to invite the Muslims to follow the Quran in their beliefs and actions, and act according to the precedent set by the Prophet. It wants to see the Muslims as true Muslims, whether in the educational, cultural, political or any other sphere of activity. Its only message is, 'Come towards the Book of God which is common between us and which nobody can deny as a basic belief.' In actual fact the situation is different. With their lips they say, 'We believe', but in their hearts they have no faith.

God exalts you before His Word; why do you, then, turn away from it and bow your heads in humiliation before man? Except for this, *Al-Hilal's* education has no other objective:

And whose counsel can be better than one who beckons us towards God, does good deeds and says, 'I am a Muslim'.

Your second question is that there are three streams of political thought in India. Along which one does *Al-Hilal* want to lead the community? You have listed the three, but it is unfortunate that you have completely forgotten the fourth one. These three paths have emerged only now, but the fourth is the one which has delivered thousands to their destinations. When the creator of the earth bestowed upon men eyes with which to see, He also opened before them this path. Adam followed it; and while being pelted with rocks, Noah preached about it. Abraham constructed the sacrificial altar and Ismail laid the bricks, as a momento to its greatness. When a fellow prisoner in Egypt asked Yusuf, he guided him towards this very same path. When Moses became restless for light in the valley of Yemen, the beacon light of this path was shown to him in a green tree. When the Israelite preacher of Galilee climbed the mountain near Jerusalem, his eyes were on this path, and when God's radiance shone on the peaks of Faran, he too, invited the world to follow this path:

God has fixed for your religion the same path which he had ordered Noah to follow. O, Prophet! That very path is revealed to you; and we ordered Abraham, Moses and Jesus to adhere to this path and let no dissensions occur.

This is the path about which Yusuf, imprisoned in Egypt, concluded in his sermon:

This is the right path, but most men do not understand. The Prophet of Islam was ordered to tell the people: "This is my way; I invite you unto God. I and my followers are embarked on this road of faith with our eyes open."

Thank God, we belong to the category of 'my followers'. Therefore, we need have nothing to do with the three ways created by man, we should invite all to walk along the fourth, or the divine path, the straight path shown by the Quran. It is my belief that any Muslim who seeks guidance in matters of faith and action from any group or ideology other than the Quran is not a Muslim. He is an infidel because he creates alternatives for the Quran which amounts to creating alternatives for God.

Muslims have their own political path

You ask, 'The Hindus have two political groups, which of them are you with?' I have to say that I am with neither of them, but only with God. There is too much dignity and grace in Islam, for its votaries to have to follow the Hindus in order to delineate their political policy. Nothing can be more demeaning for the Muslims than having to determine their course by submitting to the political precepts of others. They need not belong to any group; they should be the ones to make the world join their group and guide it along their way; they have done this for centuries. If they stand in the presence of God, the whole world will stand with them. When their path has been clearly defined, why should they knock at others' doors in search of a way? God exalts them, why should they bow their heads? They are God's own *jamaat*. It is inconceivable that heads that bow before Him should bend at other altars as well.

Where does the road lead?

The message of *Al-Hilal* in politics, like in other fields, is not to put one's faith in government, nor follow the precepts of Hindus. Follow only the *Sirat-al-Mustaqueem*, the path shown by Islam.

1. The basic tenet of Islam is *Tawhid*. It teaches us to believe only in God and to submit only before God. One should only ask for His help and rely on His benevolence. *Tawhid* means belief in the oneness of God; and not attributing his qualities to any other being. Except for God there is none whose command is final, none who is worthy of submission and humility, none whose domination and greatness is beyond question, and none worthy of fear.
2. God has made the Muslims *Khairul-ummam*, benefactors of mankind, and bestowed upon them the viceregency on earth. Therefore, every Muslim should realize his status and instead of misery, cowardice and fear should inculcate dignity, self-esteem, courage and steadfastness.

3. God has proclaimed Muslims as the force of justice. He has decreed that all their actions should be based on justice and moderation. Muslims must, therefore, always be balanced in their views and act with moderation.
4. Muslims are the messengers of peace on earth; even if they took to the sword, it was for peace. If miscreancy is forbidden to others, for Muslims it is a deadly sin. The miscreant communities have become the victims of divine wrath.
5. The Quran teaches: 'Help each other in good deeds and acts of piety and not in creating trouble.' God has given Muslims the responsibility to protect goodness and prevent disorder. So they should help all who are engaged in doing good, be it the government or any other organization.
6. The Quran considers it essential for the world order to oppose individual authority and control. It teaches that except for God no one has the right to compel people to follow the rules made for his private reasons.

   No man to whom God has given the Book, Wisdom and Prophethood, has the right to say to people, 'Worship me instead of God'.

No worldly power or government has the right or authority that was even denied to the Prophets. God says that His wisdom lies in the community and the group. 'God's hand is placed over the group'. He regards as legitimate only that government which is not individualistic, but in the hands of a community or nation. That is why He commands that there be mutual consultation:

> He commanded them to do everything by mutual consultation. O Prophet! Accomplish all work and deeds by consultation.

It should be the duty of Muslims to make every effort to achieve Independence and, according to their religious precepts, they should not rest until they have established a parliamentary form of government.

On the above-stated principles we can frame our political policy; we neither need the policy of the moderate Hindus nor that of the extremists. If we form our own, we shall be a moderate but fearless group, from which no party need fear any harm. In accordance with our religious precepts, we shall strive for the progress and independence of our country. Our efforts will have no element of mischief, turmoil, uproar or rebellion. The Quran has taught us:

> Do not create disturbance after peace has been brought on the earth.

Undoubtedly, the British Government has created peaceful conditions, under which we perform our religious duties freely. It should be our creed to dissociate from those who create trouble, be they anarchist Hindus or criminal organizations. If possible, we should try to reform them.

The Government should remember that if we become true Muslims, it will be equally advantageous to it, to ourselves, as well as to our neighbours. If we become true Muslims, we will hold the Quran in our hands, and the hand that holds the Quran cannot hold the bomb. It must be understood that Islam has taught us two lessons, that of giving freedom, as well as of seeking it. When we were the rulers we bestowed liberty and now that we are the ruled, we demand the same. We believe that it is the Will of God that nations and countries should be given the freedom for self-rule. Europe achieved independence only by following this principle. We demand from Britain precisely what, until recently, she had sought for itself.

Undoubtedly, if we have before us the political path shown by Islam, we shall be a powerful group, fearless and uninhibited in speaking the truth, because we fear none but God. But by the same principle of Islam, the law and the government, need have no apprehensions so far as we are concerned. Since our path would be clear and our mind free of doubts, our preaching and our practice will be identical. We may be enraged, but our rage and agitation would be within the limits of good behaviour, because God commands us, 'Do not create trouble'. So far, the leaders of the Muslims tried to keep the community silent and ignorant, and allowed their sores to bleed internally. They tried to hide the flames under a heap of ashes. But if we follow the true path, our lacerations would not be on our hearts, they will be written on our faces. The cancers of our complaints and aspirations will not fester internally and injure the wholesome body of peace. We shall, no doubt, cry out, but no ill feelings will remain in our hearts. We shall complain, but will not nurse the consuming fires. So it is in the interest of the Government to let us become true Muslims, because in that capacity we shall be beneficial for the whole world as well as for ourselves.

This is *Al-Hilal's* policy and this is the call we have to give to the Muslims. This is not the innovation of any human mind nor is it the emulation of any human group. The Lord of the Universe, who has sent his Prophets on earth, the Books and Wisdom, Justice and Fairness, has shown us this path. Provided I have His blessings, I will devote my life to the propagation of this path of righteousness. I expect neither favour nor appreciation. God's command to the Prophet is before me as an example:

> O Prophet! Call them to faith. And stand steadfast as thou art commanded. Nor follow thou their desire; but say, I believe in all the Books which God has sent down. And I am commanded to perform justice on you. God is our Lord and your Lord. For us the responsibility for our deeds, and for you the responsibility for your deeds. There is no contention between us. God has brought us together and towards Him is our final goal. (42:14)

The Muslim League, if it wants to give political leadership to the Muslims, should adopt this path:

> God Almighty's instruction is to follow the *Sirat-al-Mustaqueem* (Straight Path).

APPENDIX III

EXCERPTS FROM MUHAMMAD IQBAL'S PRESIDENTIAL ADDRESS TO THE TWENTY-FIRST SESSION OF THE ALL INDIA MUSLIM LEAGUE, ALLAHABAD, 29 DECEMBER 1930 *

Islam and Nationalism

It cannot be denied that Islam, regarded as an ethical ideal plus a certain kind of polity—by which expression I mean a social structure regulated by a legal system and animated by a specific ethical ideal—has been the chief formative factor in the life-history of the Muslims of India. It has furnished those basic emotions and loyalties which gradually unify scattered individuals and groups, and finally transform them into a well-defined people, possessing a moral consciousness of their own. Indeed it is no exaggeration to say that India is perhaps the only country in the world where Islam, as a people-building force, has worked at its best. In India, as elsewhere, the structure of Islam as a society is almost entirely due to the working of Islam as a culture inspired by a specific ethical ideal. What I mean to say is that Muslim society, with its remarkable homogeneity and inner unity, has grown to be what it is, under the pressure of the laws and institutions associated with the culture of Islam. The ideas set free by European political thinking, however, are now rapidly changing the outlook of the present generation of Muslims, both in India and outside India. Our younger men, inspired by these ideas, are anxious to see them as living forces in their own countries, without any critical appreciation of the facts which have determined their evolution in Europe. In Europe, Christianity was understood to be a purely monastic order which gradually developed into a vast church-organization. The protest of Luther was directed against the church-organization, not against any system of polity of a secular nature, for the obvious reason that there was no such polity associated with Christianity. And Luther was perfectly justified in rising in revolt against this organization; though, I think, he did not realize that, in the peculiar condition which obtained in Europe, his revolt would eventually mean the complete displacement of the universal ethics of Jesus by the growth of a plurality of national and hence narrower systems of ethics. Thus, the upshot of the intellectual movement initiated by men as Rousseau and Luther was the break-

*Syed Sharifuddin Pirzada, ed., *Foundations of Pakistan, All-India Muslim League Documents 1906-1947* (Karachi, 1970), pp. 154-61.

up of the one into a mutually ill-adjusted many, the transformation of a human into a national outlook, requiring a more realistic foundation, such as the notion of country, and finding expression through varying systems of polity evolved on national lines, i.e. on lines which recognize territory as the only principle of political solidarity. If you begin with the conception of religion as complete other-worldliness, then what has happened to Christianity in Europe is perfectly natural. The universal ethics of Jesus is displaced by national systems of ethics and polity. The conclusion to which Europe is consequently driven is that religion is a private affair of the individual and has nothing to do with what is called man's temporal life.

Islam does not bifurcate the unity of man into an irreconcilable duality of spirit and matter. In Islam God and the universe, spirit and matter, church and state, are organic to each other. Man is not the citizen of a profane world to be renounced in the interest of a world of spirit situated elsewhere. To Islam matter is spirit realizing itself in space and time.

Europe uncritically accepted the duality of spirit and matter probably from Mannichaean thought. Her best thinkers are realizing this initial mistake today, but her statesmen are indirectly forcing the world to accept it as an unquestionable dogma. It is, then, this mistaken separation of spiritual and temporal which has largely influenced European religious and political thought, and has resulted practically in the total exclusion of Christianity from the life of European States. The result is a set of mutually ill-adjusted States dominated by interests not human but national. And these mutually ill-adjusted States, after trampling over the moral and religious convictions of Christianity, are today feeling the need of a federated Europe, i.e. the need of a unity which the Christian church-organization originally gave them, but which, instead of reconstructing in the light of Christ's vision of human brotherhood, they considered it fit to destroy under the inspiration of Luther.

A Luther in the world of Islam, however, is an impossible phenomenon; for here there is no Church-organization, similar to that of Christianity in the Middle Ages, inviting a destroyer. In the world of Islam, we have a universal polity whose fundamentals are believed to have been revealed, but whose structure, owing to our legists' want of contact with the modern world, today stands in need of renewed power by adjustments. I do not know what will be the final fate of the national idea in the world of Islam. Whether Islam will assimilate and transform it, as it has before assimilated and transformed many ideas expressive of a different spirit, or follow a radical transformation of its own structure by the force of this idea, is hard to predict. Professor Wensinck of Leiden (Holland) wrote to me the other day: 'it seems to me that Islam is entering upon a crisis through which Christianity has been passing for more than a century. The great difficulty is how to save the foundations of religion when many antiquated notions have to be given up. It seems to me scarcely possible to state what the outcome will be for Christianity, still less what it will be for Islam.' At the present moment, the national idea is racializing the outlook of Muslims, and this is materially counteracting the humanizing work of Islam. And the growth of racial consciousness may mean the growth of standards different and even opposed to the standards of Islam.

I hope you will pardon me for this apparently academic discussion. To address this Session of the All-India Muslim League, you have selected a man who is not despaired of Islam as a living force for freeing the outlook of man from its geographical limitations, who believes that religion is a power of the utmost importance in the life of individuals as well as of states, and finally, who believes that Islam is itself Destiny and will not suffer a destiny! Such a man cannot but look at matters from his own point of view. Do not think that the problem I am indicating is a purely theoretical one. It is a very living and practical problem calculated to affect the very fabric of Islam as a system of life and conduct. On a proper solution of it alone depends your future as a distinct cultural unit in India. Never in our history Islam has had to stand a greater trial than the one which confronts it today. It is open to a people to modify, reinterpret or reject the foundational principles of their social structure; but it is absolutely necessary for them to see clearly what they are doing before they undertake to try a fresh experiment. Nor should the way in which I am approaching this important problem lead any body to think that I intend to quarrel with those who happen to think differently. You are a Muslim assembly and, I suppose, anxious to remain true to the spirit and ideals of Islam. My sole desire, therefore, is to tell you frankly what I honestly believe to be the truth about the present situation. In this way alone it is possible for me to illuminate, according to my light, the avenues of your political action.

Unity Through Harmony of Differences

What, then, is the problem and its implications? Is religion a private affair? Would you like to see Islam, as a moral and political idea, meeting the same fate in the world of Islam as Christianity has already met in Europe? Is it possible to retain Islam as an ethical ideal and to reject it as a polity, in favour of national politics in which the religious attitude is not permitted to play any part? This question becomes of special importance in India where the Muslims happen to be in a minority. The proposition that religion is a private individual experience is not surprising on the lips of a European. In Europe, the conception of Christianity as a monastic order, renouncing the world of matter and fixing its gaze entirely on the world of spirit, led, by a logical process of thought, to the view embodied in this proposition. The nature of the Prophet's religious experience, as disclosed in the Quran, however, is wholly different. It is not mere experience in the sense of a purely biological event, happening inside the experiment and necessitating no reactions on its social environment. It is individual experience creative of a social order. Its immediate outcome is the fundamentals of a polity with implicit legal concepts whose civic significance cannot be belittled merely because their origin is revelational. The religious ideal of Islam, therefore, is organically related to the social order which it has created. The rejection of the one will eventually involve the rejection of the other. Therefore the construction of a polity on national lines, if it means a displacement of the Islamic principle of solidarity, is simply unthinkable to a Muslim. This is a matter which, at the present moment, directly concerns the Muslims of India. 'Man', says Renan, 'is enslaved neither by his race, nor by his religion, nor by the course of rivers, nor by the direction of mountain ranges. A great aggregation of men, sane of mind and warm of heart, creates a moral consciousness which is called a nation.' Such a formation is quite possible, though it involves the long and arduous process of practically remaking men and furnishing [them] with a fresh emotional equipment. It might have been a fact in India, if the teaching of Kabir and 'Divine Faith' of Akbar had seized the imagination of the masses of this country. Experience, however, shows that the various caste units in India have shown no inclination to sink their respective individualities in a larger whole. Each group is intensely jealous of the collective existence. The formation of the kind of moral consciousness which constitutes the essence of a nation in Renan's sense demands a price which the peoples of India are not prepared to pay. The unity of an Indian nation, therefore, must be sought, not in the negation, but in the mutual harmony and cooperation of the many. True statesmanship cannot ignore facts, however unpleasant they may be. The only practical course is not to assume the existence of a state of things which does not exist, but to recognize facts as they are, and to exploit them to our greatest advantage. And it is on the discovery of Indian unity in this direction that the fate of India as well as of Asia really depends. India is Asia in miniature. Part of her people have cultural affinities with nations in the East, and part with nations in the middle and west of Asia. If an effective principle of cooperation is discovered in India, it will bring peace and mutual goodwill to this ancient land which has suffered so long, more because of her situation in historic space than because of any inherent incapacity of her people. And it will at the same time solve the entire political problem of Asia.

It is, however, painful to observe that our attempts to discover such a principle of internal harmony have so far failed. Why have they failed? Perhaps, we suspect each other's intentions, and inwardly aim at dominating each other. Perhaps, in the higher interests of mutual cooperation, we cannot afford to part with the monopolies which circumstances have placed in our hands, and conceal our egoism under the cloak of a nationalism, outwardly simulating a large-hearted patriotism, but inwardly as narrow-minded as a caste or tribe. Perhaps, we are unwilling to recognize that each group has a right to free development according to its own cultural traditions. But whatever may be the causes of our failure, I still feel hopeful. Events seem to be tending in the direction of some sort of internal harmony. And as far as I have been able to read the Muslim mind, I have no hesitation in declaring that, if the principle that the Indian Muslim is entitled to full and free development on the lines of his own culture and tradition in his own Indian homeland, is recognized as the basis of a permanent communal settlement, he will be ready to stake his all for the freedom of India. The principle that each group is entitled to free development on its own lines is not inspired by any feeling of narrow communalism. There are communalisms and communalisms. A community which is inspired by a feeling of ill-will towards other communities is low and ignoble. I entertain the highest respect for the customs, laws, religious and social institutions of other communities. Nay, it is my duty, according to the teaching of the Quran, even to defend their places of worship if need be. Yet I love the communal group which is the source of my life and behaviour; and which has formed me what I am by giving me its religion, its literature, its thought, its culture, and thereby recreating its whole past, as a living operative factor, in my present consciousness. Even the authors of the Nehru Report recognize the value of this higher aspect of communalism. While discussing the separation of Sind, they say : 'To say from the view-point of nationalism that no communal provinces should be created is, in a way, equivalent to saying from the still wider international view-point that there should be no separate nations. Both these statements have a measure of truth in them. But the staunchest internationalist recognizes that without the fullest national autonomy, it is extraordinarily difficult to create the international State. So also, without the fullest cultural autonomy—and communalism in its better aspect is culture—it will be difficult to create a harmonious nation'.

Muslim India within India

Communalism, in its higher aspect, then, is indispensable to the formation of a harmonious whole in a country like India. The units of Indian society are not territorial as in European countries. India is a continent of human groups belonging to different races, speaking different languages, and professing different religions. Their behaviour is not at all determined by a common race-consciousness. Even the Hindus do not form a homogeneous group. The principle of European democracy cannot be applied to India without recognizing the fact of communal groups. The Muslim demand for the creation of a Muslim India within India is, therefore, perfectly justified. The resolution of the All-Parties Muslim Conference at Delhi is to my mind wholly inspired by this noble ideal of a harmonious whole which, instead of stifling the respective individualities of its component whole, affords them chances of fully working out the possibilities that may be latent in them. And I have no doubt that this House will emphatically endorse the Muslim demand embodied in this resolution.

Personally, I would go further than the demands embodied in it. I would like to see the Punjab, the North-West Frontier Province, Sind and Baluchistan amalgamated into a single State. Self-government within the British Empire, or without the British empire, the formation of a consolidated North-West

Indian Muslim State appears to me to be the final destiny of the Muslims, at least of north-west India. The proposal was put forward before the Nehru Committee. They rejected it on the ground that, if carried into effect, it would give a very unwieldy State. This is true insofar as the area is concerned; in point of population, the State contemplated by the proposal would be much smaller than some of present Indian provinces. The exclusion of Ambala Division, and perhaps of some districts where non-Muslims predominate, will make it less extensive and more Muslim in population—so that the exclusion suggested will enable this consolidated State to give a more effective protection to non-Muslim minorities within its area. The idea need not alarm the Hindus or the British. India is the greatest Muslim country in the world. The life of Islam as a cultural force in this living country very largely depends on its centralization in a specified territory. This centralization of the most living portion of the Muslims of India, whose military and police service has, notwithstanding unfair treatment from the British, made the British rule possible in this country, will eventually solve the problem of India as well as of Asia. It will intensify their sense of responsibility and deepen their patriotic feeling. Thus, possessing full opportunity of development within the body-politic of India, the north-west Indian Muslims will prove the best defenders of India against a foreign invasion, be that invasion one of ideas or of bayonets. The Punjab with a 56 per cent Muslim population supplies 54 per cent of total combatant troops in the Indian army; and if the 19,000 Gurkhas recruited from the independent State of Nepal are excluded, the Punjab contingent amounts to 62 per cent of the whole Indian Army. This percentage does not take into account nearly 6,000 combatants supplied to the Indian Army by the north-west Frontier Province and Baluchistan. From this, you can easily calculate the possibilities of north-west Indian Muslims in regard to the defence of India against foreign aggression. The Right Hon'ble Mr. Srinivasa Sastri thinks that the Muslim demand for the creation of autonomous Muslim States along the north-west border is actuated by a desire 'to acquire means of exerting pressure in emergencies on the Government of India'. I may frankly tell him that the Muslim demand is not actuated by the kind of motive he imputes to us; it is actuated by a genuine desire for free development, which is practically impossible under the type of unitary government contemplated by the nationalist Hindu politicians with a view to securing permanent communal dominance in the whole of India.

Nor should the Hindus fear that the creation of autonomous Muslim States will mean the introduction of a kind of religious rule in such States. I have already indicated to you the meaning of the word religion, as applied to Islam. The truth is that Islam is not a church. It is a State, conceived as a contractual organism long, long before Rousseau ever thought of such a thing, and animated by an ethical ideal which regards man not as an earth-rooted creature, defined by this or that portion of the earth, but as a spiritual being understood in terms of a social mechanism, and possessing rights and duties as a living factor in that mechanism. The character of a Muslim State can be judged from what *The Times of India* pointed out sometime ago in a leader on the Indian Banking Inquiry Committee. 'In ancient India', the paper points out, 'the State framed laws regulating the rates of interests; but in Muslim times, although Islam clearly forbids the realization of interest on money loaned, Indian Muslim States imposed no restrictions on such rates'. I therefore demand the formation of a consolidated Muslim State in the best interests of India and Islam. For India, it means security and peace resulting from an internal balance of power; for Islam, an opportunity to rid itself of the stamp that Arabian Imperialism was forced to give it, to mobilize its laws, its education, its culture, and to bring them into closer contact with its own original spirit and with the spirit of modern times.

APPENDIX IV

NOW OR NEVER
ARE WE TO LIVE OR PERISH FOR EVER?*

by

Rahmat Ali and three others

28 January 1933

At this solemn hour in the history of India, when British and Indian statesmen are laying the foundations of a Federal Constitution for that land, we address this appeal to you, in the name of our common heritage, on behalf of our thirty million Muslim brethren who live in PAKSTAN—by which we mean the five Northern units of India, viz.: Punjab, North-West Frontier Province (Afghan Province), Kashmir, Sind and Baluchistan—for your sympathy and support in our grim and fateful struggle against political crucifixion and complete annihilation.

Our brave but voiceless nation is being sacrificed on the altar of Hindu Nationalism not only by the non-Muslims, but to the lasting disgrace of Islam, by our own so-called leaders, with reckless disregard to our future and in utter contempt of the teachings of history.

The Indian Muslim Delegation at the Round Table Conference have committed an inexcusable and prodigious blunder. They have submitted, in the name of Hindu Nationalism, to the perpetual subjection of the ill-starred Muslim nation. These leaders have already agreed, without any protest or demur and without any reservation, to a Constitution based on the principle of an All-India Federation. This, in essence, amounts to nothing less than signing the death-warrant of Islam and its future in India. In doing so, they have taken shelter behind the so-called Mandate from the community. But they forgot that that suicidal Mandate was framed and formulated by their own hands. That Mandate was not the Mandate of the Muslims of India. Nations never give Mandates to their representatives to barter away their very souls; and men of conscience never accept such self-annihilating Mandates, if given—much less execute them. At a time of a crisis of this magnitude, the foremost duty of saving statesmanship is to give a fair, firm and fearless lead,

*India Office Library and Records, L/P & J/8/689; Private Office Papers. Also included in *Complete Works of Rahmat Ali*, I, edited by K.K. Aziz (Islamabad, 1978), pp. 5-10.

which, alas, has been persistently denied to eighty millions of our co-religionists in India by our leaders during the last seventy-five years. These have been the years of false issues, of lost opportunities and of utter blindness to the most essential and urgent needs of the Muslim interests. Their policy has throughout been nerveless in action and subservient in attitude. They have all along been paralysed with fear and doubt, and have deliberately, time and again, sacrificed their political principles for the sake of opportunism and expediency. To do so even at this momentous juncture is a policy of Bedlam. It is idle for us not to look this tragic truth in the face. The tighter we shut our eyes, the harder that truth will hit us.

At this critical moment, when this tragedy is being enacted, permit us to appeal to you for your practical sympathy and active support for the demand of a separate Federation—a matter of life and death for the Muslims of India—as outlined and explained below.

India, constituted as it is at the present moment, is not the name of one single country; nor the home of one single nation. It is, in fact, the designation of a State created for the first time in history, by the British. It includes peoples who have never previously formed part of India at any period of its history; but who have, on the other hand, from the dawn of history till the advent of the British, possessed and retained distinct nationalities of their own.

In the five Northern Provinces of India, out of a total population of about forty millions, we, the Muslims, constitute about thirty millions. Our religion, culture, history, tradition, economic system, laws of inheritance, succession and marriage are basically and fundamentally different from those of the people living in the rest of India. The ideals which move our thirty million brethren-in-faith living in these Provinces to make the highest sacrifices are fundamentally different from those which inspire the Hindus. These differences are not confined to the broad basic principles—far from it. They extend to the minutest details of our lives. We do not inter-dine; we do not inter-marry. Our national customs and calendars, even our diet and dress are different.

It is preposterous to compare, as some superficial observers do, the differences between Muslims and Hindus with those between Roman Catholics and Protestants. Both the Catholics and Protestants are part and parcel of one religious system—Christianity; while the Hindus and Muslims are the followers of two essentially and fundamentally different religious systems. Religion in the case of Muslims and Hindus is not a matter of private opinion as it is in the case of Christians; but on the other hand constitutes a Civic Church which lays down a code of conduct to be observed by their adherents from birth to death.

If we, the Muslims of Pakstan, with our distinct marks of nationality, are deluded into the proposed Indian Federation by friends or foes, we are reduced to a minority of one to four. It is this which sounds the death-knell of the Muslim nation in India for ever. To realise the full magnitude of this impending catastrophe, let us remind you that we thirty millions constitute about one-tenth of the whole Muslim world. The total area of the five units comprising PAKSTAN, which are our homelands, is four times that of Italy, three times that of Germany and twice that of France; and our population seven times that of the Commonwealth of Australia, four times that of the Dominion of Canada, twice that of Spain, and equal to France and Italy considered individually.

These are facts—hard facts and realities—which we challenge any-body to contradict. It is on the basis of these facts that we make bold to assert without the least fear of contradiction that we, Muslims of PAKSTAN, do possess a separate and distinct nationality from the rest of India, where the Hindu nation lives and has every right to live. We, therefore, deserve and must demand the recognition of a separate national status by the grant of a separate Federal Constitution from the rest of India.

In addressing this appeal to the Muslims of India, we are also addressing it to the two other great interests—British and Hindu—involved in the settlement of India's future. They must understand that in our conviction our body and soul are at stake. Our very being and well-being depends upon it. For our five great Northern states to join an All-India Federation would be disastrous, not only to ourselves, but to every other race and interest in India, including the British and the Hindu.

This is more especially true when there is a just and reasonable alternative to the proposed settlement, which will lay the foundations of a peaceful future for this great sub-continent; and should certainly allow for the highest development of each of these two peoples without one being subject to another. This alternative is a separate Federation of these five predominantly Muslim units—Punjab, North-West Frontier Province (Afghan Province), Kashmir, Sind and Baluchistan. The Muslim Federation of north-west India would provide the bulwark of a buffer state against any invasion either of ideas or of arms from outside. The creation of such a federation would not materially disturb the ratio of the Muslim and Hindu populations in the rest of India. It is wholly to the interest of British and Hindu statesmanship to have as an ally a free, powerful and contented Muslim nation having a similar but separate Constitution to that which is being enacted for the rest of India. Nothing but a separate Federation of our homelands would satisfy us. This demand is basically different from the suggestion put forward by Doctor Sir Mohammed Iqbal in his Presidential address to the All-India Muslim League in 1930. While he proposed the amalgamation of these Provinces into a single state forming a unit of the All-India Federation, we propose that these Provinces should have a separate Federation of their own. There can be no peace and tranquillity in the land if we, the Muslims, are duped into a Hindu-dominated Federation where we cannot be the masters of our own destiny and captains of our own souls.

Do the safeguards provided for in the Constitution give us any scope to work for our salvation along our own lines? Not a bit. Safeguard is the magic word which holds our leaders spellbound, and has dulled their consciences. In the ecstasy of their hallucinations they think that the pills of safeguards can cure nation-annihilating earthquakes. Safeguards asked for by these leaders and agreed to by the makers of the Constitution can never be a substitute for the loss of separate nationality. We, the Muslims, shall have to fight that course of suicidal insanity to death. What safeguards can be devised to prevent our minority of one in four in an All-India Federation from being sacrificed on every vital issue to the aims and interests of the majority race, which differs from us in every essential of individual and corporate life? What safeguards can prevent the catastrophe of the Muslim nation smarting and suffering eternally at the frustration of its every social and religious ideal? What safeguards can compensate our nation awakened to its national consciousness for the destruction of its distinct national status? However effective and extensive the safeguards may be, the vital organs and proud symbols of our national life, such as army and navy, foreign relations, trade and commerce, communications, posts and telegraphs, taxation and customs, will not be under our control, but will be in the hands of a Federal Government, which is bound to be overwhelmingly Hindu. With all this, how can we, the Muslims, achieve any of our ideals if those ideals conflict—as they must—with the ideals of Hindus?

The history of the last century, in this respect, is full of unforgettable lessons for us. Even one who runs may read them. To take just one instance: Despite all these safeguards and guarantees we have enjoyed in the past, the very name of our national language—URDU, even now the *lingua franca* of that great sub-continent—has been wiped out of the list of Indian languages. We have just to open the latest census report to verify it. This by itself is a tragic fall. Are we fated to fall farther? But that too is dust in the scales by comparison with the tremendous national issues involving our whole future as a nation and a power not only in India but also in the whole of Asia.

In the face of these incontrovertible facts, we are entitled to ask for what purpose are we being asked to make the supreme sacrifice of surrendering our nationality and submitting ourselves and our posterity to Non-Muslim domination? What good is likely to accrue to Islam and Muslims by going into the Federation is a thing which passes our understanding. Are we to be crucified just to save the faces of our leaders, or to bolster up the preposterous falsehood that India can be a single nation? Is it with a view to achieve [*sic*] a compromise at all costs, or is it to support the illusion that Hindu nationalism is working in the interests of Muslims as well as Hindus? Irony is flattered to death by a mental muddle of such a nature and on such a scale. We have suffered in the past without a murmur and faced dangers without demur. The one thing we would never suffer is our own self-strangulation. We will not crucify ourselves upon the cross of Hindu nationalism in order to make a Hindu holiday.

May we be permitted to ask of all those statesmen—Muslim or British or Hindu—supporting the Federal Constitution, if it is really desirable to make our nation sacrifice all that Islam has given us during the last fourteen hundred years to make India a nation? Does humanity really stand to gain by this stupendous sacrifice? We dare say that still in Islam the ancient fire glows and promises much for the future, if only the leaders would let it live. Whilst in Europe, excluding Russia, in about the same area as that of India and with about the same population, there live and prosper as many as twenty-six nations, with one and the same religion, civilisation and economic system, surely it is not only possible but highly desirable for two fundamentally different and distinct nations, i.e. Muslim and Hindu, to live as friendly neighbours in peace and prosperity in that vast sub-continent. What bitter irony is it that our leaders have not the courage to stand up and demand the minimum for our political salvation.

We are face to face with a first-rate tragedy, the like of which has not been seen even in the long and eventful history of Islam. It is not the question of a sect or of a community going down; but it is the supreme problem which affects the destiny of the whole of Islam and the millions of human beings who, till quite recently, were the custodians of the glory of Islam in India and the defenders of its frontiers. We have a still greater future before us, if only our soul can be saved from the perpetual bondage of slavery forged in an All-India Federation. Let us make no mistake about it. The issue is now or never. Either we live or perish for ever. The future is ours only if we live up to our faith. It does not lie in the lap of the gods, but it rests in our own hands. We can make or mar it. The history of the last century is full of open warnings, and they are as plain as were ever given to any nation. Shall it be said of us that we ignored all these warnings and allowed our ancient heritage to perish in our own hands?

MOHD ASLAM KHAN
(Khattak)
President, Khyber Union

RAHMAT ALI
(Choudhary)

SHEIKH MOHD SADIQ
(Sahibzada)

INAYAT ULLAH KHAN
(of Charsaddah)
Secretary, Khyber Union

Bibliography

PRIMARY SOURCES: MANUSCRIPTS

INDIA OFFICE LIBRARY AND RECORDS (IOR) LONDON

MSS Eu. C. 152, Halifax Collections.
MSS Eu. D. 558, Lansdowne Collection.
MSS Eu. F. 125, Linlithgow Collection.
L/P&J/8/689, Private Office Papers.
MSS Eu. E. 238, Reading Collection.
MSS Eu. E. 240, Templewood Collection.

NATIONAL ARCHIVES OF INDIA

Badruddin Tyabji Papers.

PRINTED MATERIALS: OFFICIAL PUBLICATIONS

Census of India, 1901.
——— 1911.
——— 1921.
Bengal Legislative Assembly Proceedings, 1937, Vol. LI, No. 4.
Report of the Indian Education Commission (Calcutta, 1883).
Indian Education Commission: Report of the North Western Provinces and Oudh (Calcutta, 1884).
Indian Education Commission: Report of the Punjab Provincial Committee (Calcutta, 1884).
Islington Commission Report, 1913 (Calcutta, 1914).
Memorandum Prepared for the use of the Simon Commission by the Government of the Punjab (Lahore, 1928).
Progress of Education in India, 1927-32, Vol. I.
Report of the Indian Statutory Commission (London, 1930), I.
Report of the Joint Select Committee on Indian Constitutional Reform (London, 1934).
Report of the United Provinces Banking Enquiry Committee, 1929-30, Vol. I (Allahabad).

DOCUMENTS RELATING TO SOME MOVEMENTS AND POLITICAL PARTIES

Ahmad, Jamil-ud-Din, ed., *Historical Documents of the Muslim Freedom Movement* (Lahore, 1970).

Aziz, K.K., *Prelude to Pakistan, 1930-1940: Documents and Readings Illustrating the Growth of the Idea of Pakistan*, 2 Vols. (Lahore, 1992).

Government of Bombay, Source Material for a History of the Freedom Movement in India, Vol. II, 1885-1920 (Bombay, 1958).

Indian National Congress, *A History of the Hindu-Muslim Problem in India, Being the Report of the Committee Appointed by the Indian National Congress, Karachi Session, 1931* (Allahabad, 1932).

Muhammad, Shan, ed., *The Aligarh Movement: Basic Documents*, 3 Vols. (Meerut, 1938).

Pirzada, Syed Sharifuddin, *The Foundations of Pakistan: All India Muslim League Documents, 1906-1947*, 2 Vols. (Karachi, 1970).

Zaidi, A.M., ed., *Evolution of Muslim Political Thought in India*, I (New Delhi).

Zaidi, A.M. and S.G. Zaidi, eds., *The Encyclopaedia of the Indian National Congress*, Vols. I-XII (New Delhi, 1981).

WRITINGS OF PROMINENT POETS, THINKERS AND LEADERS

Ahmad, Jamil-ud-Din, ed., *Speeches and Writings of Mr. Jinnah*, 2 Vols. (Lahore, 1968).

Ali, Ameer, *The Spirit of Islam* (London, 1961).

Ali, Rahmat, *Complete Works of Rahmat Ali*, ed. by K.K. Aziz, I (Islamabad, 1978).

Aurobindo, Sri, *Birth Centenary Library*, Vol. I (Pondicherry, 1972).

Azad, Maulana Abul Kalam, *India's Maulana*, Vol. II: *Selected Speeches and Writings*, ed. by Syeda Saiyidain Hameed (New Delhi, 1990).

Bhushan, *Bhushan Granthawali*, ed. by Brajratna Das (Allahabad, 1950).

Bose, Rajnarain, *Old Hindu's Hope or A Proposal for the Establishment of a Hindu National Congress* (Calcutta, 1888).

Dayanand, Swami, *Light of Truth or An English Translation of the Satyartha Prakash*, ed. by Chiranjiv Bhardwaja (New Delhi, 1927).

Derozio, Henry Louis Vivian, *Poems* (Calcutta, 1972).

Golwalkar, M.S., *We Or Our Nationhood Defined* (Nagpur, 1939).

Hali, Altaf Husain, *Musaddas-i-Hali*, tr. by Syeda Saiyidain Hameed (to be published).

Iqbal, Muhammad, *Letters of Iqbal to Jinnah with a Foreword by M.A Jinnah* (Lahore, 1974, 1st pub. 1942).

———, *Reconstruction of Religious Thought in Islam* (London, 1934).

———, *The Secrets of the Self: Alama Iqbal's Asrar-i-Khudi*, tr. by Reynold A. Nicholson (Lahore, 1955).

———, *Thoughts and Reflections of Iqbal*, ed. by Syed Abdul Vahid (Lahore, 1964).

———, *Shikwa* and *Jawab-e-Shikwa*, tr. by Khushwant Singh (Delhi, 1981).

Khan, Hamid Ali, *The Vernacular Controversy* (n.d., but perhaps published in 1900; presented by the author to the British Museum on 8 February 1902).

Khan, Sayyid Ahmad, *The Present State of Indian Politics: Speeches and Letters* (Allahabad, 1888).

———, *Writings and Speeches of Sir Syed Ahmad Khan*, ed. by Shan Muhammad (Bombay, 1972).

———, *Political Profile of Sir Sayyid Ahmad Khan: A Documentary Record*, ed. by Hafeez Malik (Islamabad, 1982).

Lajpat Rai, Lala, *Autobiographical Writings*, ed. by V.C. Joshi (New Delhi, 1965).

———, *Lala Lajpat Rai: Writings and Speeches*, 2 Vols., ed. by V.C. Joshi (Delhi, 1966).

Malaviya, Madan Mohan, *Court Character and Primary Education in the North Western Provinces and Oudh* (Allahabad, 1897).
(No author is mentioned in this publication, running into 65 pages of text and 100 pages of appendices, but the British Museum, which possesses a copy, lists it under the name of Malaviya.)

Mohammed Ali, Maulana, *Select Speeches, Writings and Statements of Maulana Mohammed Ali,* ed. by A. Iqbal (Lahore, 1963).

———, *Selections from Maulana Mohammad Ali's Comrade*, ed. by S.R.A. Jafari (Lahore, 1965).

———, *Mohammed Ali in Politics: Select Writings*, ed. by Mushirul Hasan, 3 Vols. (New Delhi, 1982-6).

Nehru, Jawaharlal, *An Autobiography* (London, 1936).

———, *Discovery of India* (Calcutta, 1946).

Pal, Bipin Chandra, *Memories of My Life and Times*, I (Calcutta, 1932).

Prasad, Rajendra, *India Divided* (Bombay, 1947; 3rd edn).

Ranade, Mahadev Govind, *The Miscellaneous Writings of the late Hon'ble Mr. Justice M.G. Ranade*, ed. by Rambai Ranade (Bombay, 1915).

———, *Rise of Maratha Power* (Delhi, 1961).

Roy, Raja Rammohun, *Selected Works of Raja Rammohan Roy* (Delhi, 1977).

Savarkar, V.D., *Hindu-Pad-Padshahi or Critical Review of the Hindu Empire of Maharashtra* (Madras, 1925).

———, *Hindu Rashtra Darshan* (Bombay, 1945).

Vivekananda, Swami, *Complete Works of Swami Vivekananda*, 8 Vols. (Calcutta, 1956).

———, *Swami Vivekananda: An Anthology*, ed. by Bimal Prasad (New Delhi, 1994).

Waliullah, Shah, *Shah Waliullah Ke Siyasi Maktubat*, ed. by Khaliq Ahmad Nizami (Delhi, 1969).

SECONDARY SOURCES: BOOKS AND ARTICLES

Abbott, Freeland, *Islam and Pakistan* (Ithaka, New York, 1968).

Afzal, M. Rafiq, 'Origin of the Idea of a Separate Muslim State: Nawab Sir Zulfiqar Ali Khan's Lahore Address, 1929', *Journal of the Research Society of Pakistan*, January-April 1966.

Ahmad, A.F. Salahuddin, 'Muslim Thought and Leadership in Bengal in the Nineteenth Century', in Barun De, ed., *Essays in Honour of Professor S.C. Sarkar* (New Delhi, 1976).

Ahmad, Aziz, *Studies in Islamic Culture in the Indian Environment* (Oxford, 1964).

———, *Islamic Modernism in India and Pakistan: 1857-1964* (London, 1967).

Ahmad, Aziz and G.E. Von Grunebaum, eds., *Muslim Self-Statement in India and Pakistan, 1857-1968* (Wiesbaden, 1970).

Ahmad, Qeyamuddin, *The Wahhabi Movement in India* (Calcutta, 1966).

Ahmad, Razi, *Gandhiji aur Musalman* (New Delhi, 1985).

Ahmed, Rafiuddin, *The Bengal Muslims, 1871-1906: A Quest for Identity* (Delhi, 1981).

Ahmed, Sufia, *Muslim Community in Bengal, 1884-1912* (Dacca, 1974).

Alam, Muzaffar, *The Crisis of Empire in Mughal North India: Awadh and the Punjab, 1707-1748* (Delhi, 1986).

Ali, M. Athar, *The Mughal Nobility Under Aurangzeb* (Bombay, 1966).

Allami, Abul-Fazl, *The Ain-i-Akbari*, tr. and ed. by H.S. Jarrett, III (Calcutta, 1978).

Andrews, C.F., *Zaka Ullah of Delhi* (Cambridge, 1929).

Ashraf, Ali, 'Khilafat Movement: A Factor in Muslim Separatism', in Mushirul Hasan, ed., *Communal and Pan-Islamic Trends in Colonial India* (New Delhi, 1981).

Ashraf, Mujeeb, *Muslim Attitudes towards British Rule and Western Culture in India in the First Half of the Nineteenth Century* (Delhi, 1982).

Aziz, K.K., *Britain and Muslim India* (London, 1963).

———, *The Making of Pakistan: A Study in Nationalism* (London, 1967).

———, *A History of the Idea of Pakistan*, 4 Vols. (Lahore, 1987).

Bagal, Jogesh C., 'Rajnarain Bose and Indian Nationalism', *Modern Review*, Vol. LXXV, No. 6, June 1944.

———, *Hindu Melar Itivritta* (Calcutta, 1968).

Bagchi, Amiya Kumar, *Private Investment in India, 1900-1939* (Cambridge, 1972).

Baker, C. and D.A. Washbrook, *South India: Political Institutions and Political Change, 1880-1940* (Delhi, 1975).

Baljon, J.R., J.M.S., *The Reforms and Religious Ideas of Sir Sayyid Ahmad Khan* (Leiden, 1949).
Ball, Charles, *The History of the Indian Mutiny* (New Delhi, 1981, 1st Indian rpt.), Vol. II.
Barrier, Norman Gerald, *The Punjab Alienation of Land Bill of 1900* (Duke University, 1965).
———, *The Punjab in Nineteenth Century Tracts* (East Lansing, Michigan, 1969).
———, 'The Arya Samaj and Congress Politics in the Punjab, 1894-1908', *The Journal of Asian Studies*, Vol. XXVI, No. 3, May 1967.
———, 'The Punjab Government and Communal Politics, 1870-1908', *The Journal of Asian Studies,* Vol. XXVII, No. 3, May 1968.
———, 'Muslim Politics in the Punjab, 1870-1890', *The Punjab Past and Present*, Vol. VI, April 1971, pp. 84-127.
———, ed., *Roots of Communal Politics* (New Delhi, 1976).
Basu, Aparna, *Education and Political Development in India 1898-1920* (Delhi, 1974).
———, 'Growth of Education and Muslim Separatism, 1919-1939', in B.R. Nanda, ed., *Essays in Modern Indian History* (Delhi, 1980).
Basu, Sankri Prasad and Sunil Bihari Ghosh, eds., *Vivekananda in Indian Newspapers, 1893-1902* (Calcutta, 1969).
Bayly, C.A., *The Local Roots of Indian Politics: Allahabad 1880-1920* (Oxford, 1975).
———, *Rulers, Townsmen and Bazars: North Indian Society in the Age of British Expansion* (Cambridge, 1983).
———, 'Patrons and Politics in Northern India', *Modern Asian Studies*, Vol. VII, July 1973.
———, 'The Pre-History of "Communalism"? Religious Conflict in India, 1700-1860', *Modern Asian Studies,* 19, 2 (1985).
Bose, Nemai Sadhan, *The Indian Awakening and Bengal* (Calcutta, 1960).
Bose, Sugata, 'The Roots of "Communal" Violence in Rural Bengal: A Study of the Kishoreganj Riots of 1930', *Modern Asian Studies,* Vol. XVI, No. 3 (1982).
———, *Agrarian Bengal: Economy, Social Structure and Politics, 1919-1947* (Cambridge, 1986).
Brass, Paul, R., *Language, Religion and Politics in North India* (Cambridge, 1974).
Brennan, Lance, 'The Illusion of Security: The Background to Muslim Separatism in the United Provinces', *Modern Asian Studies,* Vol. XVII, No. 1 (1984).
Buchanan, D.H., *Development of Capitalistic Enterprise in India* (Cambridge, 1934).
Chandra, Bipan, *Communalism in Modern India* (New Delhi, 1984).
Chandra, Satish, *Medieval India* (New Delhi, 1982).

———, 'Jizyah and the state in India during the 17th century', *Journal of the Economic and Social History of the Orient*, 1968.

Chandra, Sudhir, 'Communal Consciousness in Late 19th Century Hindi Literature', in Mushirul Hasan, ed., *Communal and Pan-Islamic Trends in Colonial India* (New Delhi, 1981).

———, 'The Cultural Complement of Economic Nationalism: R.C. Dutt's "The Lake of Palm" ', *Indian Historical Review*, XII, 1-2, pp. 106-20.

Chatterjee, Margaret, *Gandhi's Religious Thought* (London, 1983).

Chatterjee, Partha, 'Agrarian Relations and Politics in Bengal: Some Considerations on the Making of the Tenancy Act Amendment 1928', *Occasional Paper No. 30*, Centre for Studies in Social Sciences, Calcutta (September 1980).

———, 'Agrarian Relations and Communalism in Bengal', in Ranajit Guha, ed., *Subaltern Studies,* I (Delhi, 1982).

———, 'Bengal Politics and the Muslim Masses, 1920-1945', *The Journal of Commonwealth and Comparative Politics,* Vol. XX, No. 1, March 1982.

———, *Bengal 1920-1947, I, The Land Question* (Calcutta, 1984).

Chaudhary, Nirad C., *The Autobiography of an Unknown Indian* (London, 1951).

Clark, T.W., 'The Role of Bankim Chandra in the Development of Nationalism', in C.H. Philips, ed., *Historians of India, Pakistan and Ceylon* (London, 1961).

Cromwell, S. Crawford, *Rammohan Roy: His Era and Ethics* (New Delhi, 1984).

Curran Jr., Jean A., *Militant Hinduism in Indian Politics: A Study of R.S.S.* (New York, 1951).

Dale, Stephen Frederic, *Islamic Society on the South Asian Frontier: The Mappilas of Malabar* (Oxford, 1980).

Dar, Bashir Ahmad, *Religious Thought of Sayyid Ahmed Khan* (Lahore, 1971, 2nd edn).

Darling, Malcom Lyall, *The Punjab Peasant in Prosperity and Debt* (London, 1925).

Das, Suranjan, *Communal Riots in Bengal, 1905-1947* (Delhi, 1991).

De, Amalendu, *Roots of Separatism in Nineteenth Century Bengal* (Calcutta, 1974).

De, Barun, 'A Historiographical Critique of Renaissance Analogues for Nineteenth Century India', in Barun De, ed., *Perspectives in Social Sciences,* I (Calcutta, 1977).

Desai, A.R., *Social Background of Indian Nationalism* (Bombay, 1957).

Digby, Simon, 'Abd Al-Quddus Gangohi (1456-1537 A.D.): The Personality and Attitudes of a Medieval Indian Sufi', *Medieval India—A Miscellany*, ed. by S. Nurul Hasan, III, 1975.

Dixit, Prabha, *Communalism: A Struggle for Power* (New Delhi, 1974).

———, 'The Political and Social Dimensions of Vivekananda's Ideology', *The*

Indian Economic and Social History Review, Vol. XXI, No. 3, July-September 1975.

Dungen, P.H.M. Van Den, *The Punjab Tradition* (London, 1972).

Dwivedi, Hazari Prasad, *Granthawali* (New Delhi, 1981).

Dyson, Ketaki Kushari, *A Various Universe: A Study of the Journals and Memories of British Men and Women in the Indian Subcontinent, 1765-1856* (Delhi, 1978).

Elliot, Henry M. and John Dowson, *The History of India as Told by Its Own Historians* (London, 1867).

Faruki, Zahiruddin, *Aurangzeb and His Times* (Delhi, 1972).

Faruqi, Ziaul Hasan, *The Deoband School and the Demand for Pakistan* (Bombay, 1963).

Friedmann, Yohanan, *Shaikh Ahmad Sirhindi: An Outline of His Thought and a Study of His Image in the Eyes of Posterity* (McGill, 1971).

Gadgil, D.R., *The Industrial Evolution of India in Recent Times, 1860-1939* (London, 1971; 5th edn).

Gandhi, M.K., *In Search of the Supreme*, ed. by V.B. Kher, 3 Vols. (Ahmedabad, 1961-2).

Gankovsky, Z.V. and L.R. Gordon-Polonskaya, *A History of Pakistan* (Moscow, 1964).

Ghatak, Kamal Kumar, 'Bankim Chandra Chattopadhyaya (1836-1894) and the Revival of Hinduism in Bengal', *The Calcutta Historical Journal,* Vol. VII, No. 2, January-June 1983.

Gibb, H.A.R., *Modern Trends in Islam* (London, 1945).

———, *Studies in the Civilisation of Islam* (London, 1962).

Gokhale, Balkrishna Govind, 'Hindu Responses to the Muslim Presence in Maharastra', in Yohanan Friedmann, ed., *Islam in Asia,* Vol. I: *South Asia* (Jerusalem, 1984).

Golwalkar, M.S., *We Or Our Nationhood Defined* (Nagpur, 1939).

Gopal, Ram, *Indian Muslims: A Political History, 1858-1947* (Bombay, 1959).

Gopal, S., *British Policy in India, 1858-1905* (Cambridge, 1965).

Gordon, Richard, 'The Hindu Mahasabha and the Indian National Congress, 1915 to 1926', *Modern Asian Studies*, 9:2 (1975).

Goyal, D.R., *Rashtriya Swayamsewak Sangh* (New Delhi, 1979).

Graham, G.F.I., *The Life and Work of Sir Syed Ahmed Khan* (Karachi, 1974; 1st pub. 1885).

Grewal, J.S., *Muslim Rule in India: The Assessments of British Historians* (Oxford, 1970).

Gupta, Ashin Das, 'Trade and Politics in 18th Century India', in D.S. Richards, ed., *Islam and the Trade of Asia: A Colloquium* (Oxford, 1970).

Gupta, S.L., *Pandit Madan Mohan Malviya* (Allahabad, 1978).

Habib, Irfan M., 'The Political Role of Shaikh Ahmad Sirhindi and Shah Waliullah', *Enquiry,* No. 5, 1961.

Habib, Mohammad, *Politics and Society During the Early Medieval Period: Collected Works,* ed. by K.A. Nizami, I (New Delhi, 1974).

——, 'Introduction' in Khaliq Ahmed Nizami, *Some Aspects of Religion and Politics in India during the Thirteenth Century* (Delhi, 1974).

Habibullah, A.B.M., 'Historical Writing in Urdu: A Survey of Tendencies', C.H. Philips, ed., *Historians of India, Pakistan and Ceylon* (London, 1961).

Haldar, M.K., *Renaissance and Reaction in Nineteenth Century Bengal* (Calcutta, 1977).

Haq, Mushir U., *Muslim Politics in Modern India* (Meerut, 1970).

Haq, S. Moinul, *Islamic Thought and Movements in the Subcontinent* (Karachi, 1979).

Hardgrave, Robert L., 'The Mapilla Rebellion, 1921: Peasant Revolt in Malabar', *Modern Asian Studies,* Vol. XI, No. 1 (1977).

Hardy, Peter, *Historians of Medieval India* (London, 1960).

——, 'The Muslim Historians of the Delhi Sultanate: Is What They Say Really What They Mean?', *Journal of the Asiatic Society of Pakistan* (Dacca), Vol. IX, No. 11, June 1964.

——, *Partners in Freedom and True Muslims: The Political Thought of Some Muslim Scholars in British India, 1912-1947* (Lund, 1971).

——, *The Muslims of British India* (Cambridge, 1972).

Hasan, Mushirul, *Nationalism and Communal Politics in India* (New Delhi, 1979).

—— ed., *Communal and Pan-Islamic Trends in Colonial India* (New Delhi, 1981).

Heimsath, Charles H., *Indian Nationalism and Hindu Social Reform* (Princeton, 1964).

Hunter, W.W., *The Indian Mussalmans* (Lahore, 1968, rpt. from the 1871 edn).

Ikram, S.M., *Modern Muslim India and the Birth of Pakistan, 1858-1951* (Lahore, 1965, 2nd edn, 1st pub. 1950).

——, *Muslim Civilisation in India,* ed. by Ainslie T. Embree (New York, 1965; 2nd edn).

Islam, Zafarul and Raymond L. Jansen, 'Indian Muslims and the Public Service', *Journal of the Asiatic Society of Pakistan* (Dacca), Vol. IX, No. 1, June 1965.

Jain, M.S., *The Aligarh Movement* (Agra, 1965).

Jhaveri, Mansukhlal, *History of Gujrati Literature* (New Delhi, 1978).

Johnson, Gordon, *Provincial Politics and Indian Nationalism: Bombay and the Indian National Congress, 1880 to 1915* (Cambridge, 1973).

Jones, Kenneth W., 'Communalism in the Punjab: The Arya Samaj Contribution', *The Journal of Asian Studies*, Vol. XXVIII, No.1, November 1968.

——, *Arya Dharm: Hindu Consciousness in 19th Century Punjab* (Berkeley, 1976).

Jordens, J.T.F., *Dayananda Sarasvati: His Life and Ideas* (Delhi, 1976).

Joshi, P.C., 'The Economic Background of Communalism in India', in B.R. Nanda, ed., *Essays in Modern Indian History* (Delhi, 1980).

Karim, A.K.N., 'The Modern Muslim Political Elite in Bengal', unpublished, Ph.D. thesis, University of London, 1969.
Karmarkar, D.P., *Bal Gangadhar Tilak: A Study* (Bombay, 1956).
Kaura, Uma, *Muslims and Indian Nationalism, 1928-40* (New Delhi, 1977).
Khan, Iktidar Alam, 'The Nobility under Akbar and the Development of His Religious Policy, 1560-80', *Journal of the Royal Asiatic Society,* 1968.
———, 'The Secular State in India: Historical Perspective', in Barun De, ed., *Essays in Honour of Professor S.C. Sarkar* (New Delhi, 1976).
———, 'Shaikh Abdul Quddus Gangohi's Relations with Political Authorities: A Reappraisal', in *Medieval India—A Miscellany,* ed. by S. Nurul Hasan, IV, 1977.
———, 'A Note on the Conception of Akbar's Religious Policy', in Debiprasad Chattopadhyaya, ed., *History and Society* (Calcutta, 1978).
———, 'Medieval Indian Notions of Secular Statecraft in Retrospect', *Social Scientist*, No. 152, January 1986.
Khan, Muinuddin, *The Faraidi Movement* (Karachi, 1965).
Kole, Shrimati Ashru, *Rajnarain Basu: Jivan O Sahitya* (Calcutta, 1975).
Krishna, K.B., *The Problem of Minorities in India* (London, 1939).
Laired, M.A., ed., *Bishop Heber in Northern India: Selections from Heber's Journal* (Cambridge, 1971).
Lelyveld, David, *Aligarh's First Generation: Muslim Solidarity in British India* (Princeton, 1978).
Majumdar, Bimanbehari, 'The Anandmath and Phadke', *Journal of Indian History*, Vol. XLIV, part I (April 1966).
Majumdar, R.C., *The Glimpses of Bengal in the Nineteenth Century* (Calcutta, 1960).
———, 'Nationalist Historians', in C.H. Philips, ed., *Historians of India Pakistan and Ceylon* (London, 1961).
———, *History of the Freedom Movement in India,* I (Calcutta, 1962).
———, 'The National Movement 1833-1905', in N.K. Sinha, ed., *The History of Bengal 1757-1905* (Calcutta, 1961).
———, 'Impact of Islam on Hinduism', in Horst Kruger, ed., *Kunwar Mohammad Ashraf* (Delhi 1969).
———, ed., *The Delhi Sultanate: Being Vol. VI of The History and Culture of the Indian People* (Bombay, 1960).
Mallick, Azizur Rahman, *British Policy and the Muslims in Bengal, 1757-1856* (Dacca, 1961).
Malik, Hafeez, *Moslem Nationalism in India and Pakistan* (Washington D.C., 1963).
———, *Sir Sayyid Ahmed Khan and Muslim Modernism in India and Pakistan* (New York, 1980).
———, ed., *Iqbal: Poet-Philosopher of Pakistan* (New York, 1971).
Malik, Ikram Ali, *Hindu-Muslim Riots in the British Punjab, 1849-1900* (Lahore, 1984).
Manshardt, Clifford, *The Hindu-Muslim Problem in India* (London, 1936).

Marx, Karl, 'The Eighteenth Brumaire of Louis Bonaparte', in Karl Marx and Frederick Angeles, *Selected Works* (Moscow, 1970).

McLane, John R., *Indian Nationalism and the Early Congress* (Princeton, 1977).

Mehrotra, S.R., *The Emergence of the Indian National Congress* (New Delhi, 1971).

Mehta, Asoka and Achyut Patwardhan, *The Communal Triangle in India* (Allahabad, 1942, 2nd edn).

Menon, M. Gangadhar, *Malabar Rebellion, 1921-22* (Allahabad, 1989).

Metcalf, Barbara Daly, *Islamic Revival in British India: Deoband, 1860-1900* (Princeton, 1982).

Metcalf, Thomas R., *The Aftermath of Revolt: India 1857-1870* (Princeton, 1964).

Mill, James, *The History of British India* (London, 1826, 3rd edn) II, Chap. V entitled 'A Comparison of the State of Civilization among the Mahomedan Conquerors of India with the State of Civilization among the Hindus'.

Misra, B.B., *The Central Administration of the East India Company* (Manchester, 1959).

———, *The Indian Middle Classes* (London, 1961).

———, *The Indian Political Parties* (Delhi, 1976).

Moon, Penderel, *Divide and Quit* (London, 1961).

Morison, T., *History of the Muhammadan Anglo-Oriental College* (Allahabad, 1903).

Mujahid, Sharif al, 'Pan-Islamism', in *A History of Freedom Movement,* III (I) (Karachi, 1961).

———, 'Muslim Nationalism: Iqbal's Synthesis of Pan-Islamism and Nationalism', *Journal of Pakistan Studies,* Vol. I, No. I, June 1979.

———, *Allama Iqbal: Poet-Philosopher of the East* (Karachi, 1986).

Mujeeb, M., *Indian Muslims* (London, 1967).

Mukherjee, Rudrangshu, 'The Azamgarh Proclamation and Some Questions on the Revolt of 1857 in the North-Western Provinces', in Barun De, ed., *Essays in Honour of Professor S.C. Sarkar* (New Delhi, 1976).

Muztar, A.D., *Shah Wali Allah* (Islamabad, 1979).

Naidu, Ratna, *The Communal Edge to Plural Societies: India and Malaysia* (Sahibabad, 1980).

Naim, C.M., ed., *Iqbal, Jinnah and Pakistan: The Vision and the Reality* (Syracuse, 1979).

Narain, Sushma, *Bhartiya Rastravad Ke Vikas Ki Hindi Sahitya Me Abhivyakti* (Delhi, 1966).

Narendranath, Raja, 'Punjab Agrarian Laws and their Economic and Constitutional Bearing', *Modern Review,* Vol. LXV, No.1, January 1939.

Nemade, Bhalchandra, 'The Revolt of the Under-Privileged', in Jayant Lele, ed., *Tradition and Modernity in Bhakti Movements* (Leiden, 1981).

Nijami, Azra, 'Socio-Religious Outlook of Abul Fazl', *Medieval India: A Miscellany,* II (1972).

Nivedita, Sister, *The Master as I Saw Him* (Calcutta, 1977).

Nizami, Khaliq Ahmed, 'Shah Waliullah Dehlawi and Indian Politics in the Eighteenth Century', *Islamic Culture*, 1951.

———, 'Socio-Religious Movements in Indian Islam, 1763-1898', in S.T. Lokhandwala, ed., *India and Contemporary Islam* (Simla, 1971).

Nizami, Taufiq Ahmad, *Muslim Political Thought and Activity in India during the Nineteenth Century* (Aligarh, 1969).

Nooruzzaman, A.H.M., 'Rise of the Muslim Middle Classes as a Political Factor in India and Pakistan, 1858-1947', unpublished Ph.D. thesis, University of London, 1964.

Owen, H.F., 'Negotiating the Lucknow Pact', *Journal of Asian Studies,* XXXI, May 1972.

Page, David, *Prelude to Partition: The Indian Muslims and the Imperial System of Control, 1920-1932* (Delhi, 1982).

Pandey, Gyanendra, 'Rallying Round the Cow: Sectarian Strife in the Bhojpuri Region, *c.* 1888-1917', in Ranajit Guha, ed., *Subaltern Studies*, II (Delhi, 1983).

———, *Notes on the Construction of the Hindu Community in 19th Century North India*, Handwritten Notes which Formed the Basis for an Oral presentation to the Seminar on 'The Historical and Contemporary Character of Hinduism' held at the Nehru Memorial Museum and Library (New Delhi) in May 1986.

———, *The Construction of Communalism in Colonial North India* (Delhi, 1990).

Panikkar, K.M., *A Survey of Indian History* (London, 1971, 1st pub. 1947).

Panikkar, K.N., *Against Lord and State: Religion and Peasant Uprisings in Malabar* (Delhi, 1989).

———, ed., *Peasant Protests and Revolts in Malabar* (New Delhi, 1990).

Pathak, Jitram, *Adhunik Hindi Kavya Me Rashtriya Chetna Ka Vikas* (Allahabad, 1976).

Pathik, Devaraj Sharma, *Hindi Ki Rashtriya Kavya Dhara* (Delhi, 1979).

Philips, C.H., ed., *Politics and Society in India* (London, 1962).

Philips, C.H. and B.N. Pandey, eds., *The Evolution of India and Pakistan, 1858-1947: Select Documents* (London, 1962).

Philips, C.H., B.N. Pandey and Mary Doreen Wainwright, eds., *Partition of India: Politics and Perspectives, 1935-1947* (London, 1970).

Pirzada, Syed Sharifuddin, *Evolution of Pakistan* (Lahore, 1963).

Prakash, Indra, *A Review of the History and Work of the Hindu Sangathan Movement* (New Delhi, 1952).

———, *Hindu Mahasabha: Its Contribution to Indian Politics* (New Delhi, 1966).

Prasad, Beni, *The Hindu-Muslim Questions* (Allahabad, 1941).

Prasad, Rajendra, *India Divided* (Bombay, 1947, 3rd edn).
Qureshi, Ishtiaq Husain, *The Muslim Community of the Indo-Pakistan Subcontinent, 610-1947* (The Hague, 1962).
———, *The Struggle for Pakistan* (Karachi, 1969).
Rahman, Akhlaqur, *Partition, Integration and Economic Growth and Interregional Trade, 1948-1959* (Dacca, 1963).
Rahman, M., *From Consultation to Confrontation: A Study of the Muslim League in British Indian Polity (1906-1912)* (London, 1970).
Rai, Satya M., *Partition of the Punjab* (Bombay, 1965).
Ray, Niharranjan, *Nationalism in India* (Aligarh, 1973).
Reeves, P.D., ed., *Sleeman in Oudh* (Cambridge, 1971).
Rizvi, Saiyid Athar Abbas, *Muslim Revivalist Movements in North India in the Sixteenth and Seventeenth Centuries* (Agra, 1965).
———, 'Ideological Background of the Wahhabi Movement in India in the 18th and 19th Centuries', in Bisheshwar Prasad, ed., *Ideas in History* (Bombay, 1968).
———, *Shah Wali-Allah and His Times* (Canberra, 1980).
———, *Shah Abd-Al-Aziz: Puritanism, Sectarian Politics and Jihad* (Canberra, 1980)
Robb, Peter, 'The Challenge of Gau Mata: British Policy and Religious Change in India, 1880-1916', *Modern Asian Studies,* Vol. XX, No. 2.
Robinson, Francis, *Separatism Among Indian Muslims: The Politics of the United Provinces Muslims, 1860-1923* (Cambridge, 1974).
Rungta, Radhe Shyam, *The Rise of Business Corporations in India, 1851-1900* (Cambridge, 1970).
Sachau, Edward C., ed., *Alberuni's India* (Delhi, 1964).
Sadiq, Muhammad, *A History of Urdu Literature* (London, 1964).
Sanjana, J.E., *Studies in Gujarati Literature* (Bombay, 1950).
Sardesai, Govind Sakharam, *New History of the Marathas,* I (Bombay, 1957, 2nd edn).
———, 'Shivaji', in R.C. Majumdar, ed., *The Mughal Empire, being Vol. VII of The History and Culture of the Indian People* (Bombay, 1974).
Sarkar, Jadunath, *History of Aurangzeb*, III and IV (Calcutta, 1919).
———, *Shivaji and His Times* (Calcutta, 1961; 1st pub. 1919).
———, *A Short History of Aurangzeb* (Calcutta, 1962).
Sarkar, Jagdish Narayan, *Hindu-Muslim Relations in Bengal (Medieval Period)* (Delhi, 1985).
Sarkar, Sumit, *The Swadeshi Movement in Bengal, 1903-1908* (New Delhi, 1973).
———, 'Rammohan Roy and the Break with the Past', in V.C. Joshi, ed., *Rammohan Roy and the Process of Modernisation in India* (Delhi, 1975).
Sarkar, Susobhan, 'General President's Address', *Indian History Congress: Proceedings of the Thirty-Third Session: Muzaffarpur 1972* (New Delhi, 1973).
———, *On the Bengal Renaissance* (Calcutta, 1979).

Sarkar, Tanika, 'Communal Riots in Bengal', in Mushirul Hasan, ed., *Communal and Pan-Islamic Trends in Colonial India* (New Delhi, 1981).
Sayeed, Khalid B., *Pakistan: The Formative Phase* (London, 1968, 2nd edn).
Seal, Anil, *The Emergence of Indian Nationalism* (Cambridge, 1968).
Sen, Amit, *Notes on the Bengal Renaissance* (Bombay, 1946).
Sen, Shila, *Muslim Politics in Bengal, 1937-1947* (New Delhi, 1976).
Sen, Sukumar, *History of Bengali Literature* (New Delhi, 1960).
Sen, S.P., *Dictionary of National Biography*, I (Calcutta, 1972).
Sharin, Dharam Paul, *Influence of Political Movement on Hindi Literature* (Chandigarh, 1967).
Sharma, Kranti Kumar, *Hindi Sahitya Me Rashtriya Kabya Ka Vikas* (Bhopal, 1970).
Sharma, S.R., *The Founding of Maratha Freedom* (Bombay, 1964).
———, *The Religious Policy of the Mughal Emperors* (Bombay, 1972).
Shobha, Savitri Chandra, *Social Life and Concepts in Medieval Hindi Bhakti Poetry: A Socio-Cultural Study* (Meerut, 1983).
Shukla, Ram Chandra, *Hindi Sahitya Ka Itihas* (Banaras, n.d.).
Singh, Ganda, 'Development of Sikh Thought upto the End of the Eighteenth Century', in Bisheshwar Prasad, ed., *Ideas in History* (Bombay, 1968).
Singh, Iqbal, *The Ardent Pilgrim: An Introduction to the Life and Work of Mohammed Iqbal* (Delhi, 1997, 2nd edn).
Sinha, N.K., *The Economic History of Bengal from Plassey to the Permanent Settlement*, II (Calcutta, 1962).
Sleeman, W.H., *Rambles and Recollections of an Indian Official* (London, 1844).
Smith, Wilfred Cantwell, *Modern Islam in India* (London, 1946).
———, *Islam in Modern History* (Princeton, 1957).
———, *On Understanding Islam: Selected Studies* (The Hague, 1981).
Sobhan, Rahman, 'Political Dimensions of South Asian Co-operation: The Perspective for Bangladesh', in V. Kanesalingam, ed., *Political Dimensions of South Asian Co-operation* (Delhi, 1991).
Spear, Percival, *India, Pakistan and the West* (London, 1958).
———, *India: A Modern History* (Ann Arbor, 1961).
Strachey, Sir John, *India* (London, 1888).
Subramanian, Lakshmi, 'Capital and Crowd in a Declining Asian Port City: The Anglo-Bania Order and the Surat Riots of 1795', *Modern Asian Studies*, 19, 2 (1985).
Sudesh, *Aadhunik Hindi aur Urdu Kavya Ki Pravritian* (Delhi, 1974).
Tara Chand, *Influence of Islam on Indian Culture* (Allahabad, 1963, 1st pub. 1936).
———, 'India and the West', in Humayun Kabir, ed., *Abul Kalam Azad* (Bombay, 1959).
Thomas, F.W., *Mutual Influence of Muhammedans and Hindus in India* (Cambridge, 1892).

Thorburn, S.S., *Musalmans and Money-Lenders in the Punjab* (Edinburgh, 1886).

Thursby, G.R., *Hindu Muslim Relations in British India: A Study of Controversy, Conflict and Communal Movements in Northern India, 1923-1928* (Leiden, 1975).

Titus, Murray, *Indian Islam* (London, 1930).

Tripathi, Amalas, *The Extremist Challenge* (New Delhi, 1967).

Troll, Christian W., *Sayyid Ahmad Khan: A Restatement of Muslim Theology* (New Delhi, 1978).

Tucker, Richard P., *Ranade and the Roots of Indian Nationalism* (Bombay, 1977).

Vakil, C.N., *Economic Consequences of the Partition* (Bombay, 1948).

Verma, Harish Chandra and Ram Niwas Gupta, *Hindi Sahitya ka Itihas* (Rohtak, 1982).

Varma, Vishwanath Prasad, *The Life and Philosophy of Lokmanya Tilak* (Agra, 1978).

Vidyalankar, Satyaketu, ed., *Arya Samaj ka Itihas*, IV (New Delhi, 1985).

Washbrook, D.A., *The Emergence of Provincial Politics: The Madras Presidency, 1870-1920* (Calcutta, 1976).

Watt, W. Montgomery, *Islam and the Integration of Society* (London, 1970, 4th edn).

Wolpert, Stanley A., *Tilak and Gokhale: Revolution and Reform in the Making of Modern India* (Berkeley, 1961).

Wood, Conrad, *The Moplah Rebellion and Its Genesis* (New Delhi, 1987).

Zakaria, Rafiq, *Rise of Muslims in Indian Politics* (Bombay, 1971, 2nd edn).

———, *Iqbal: The Poet and the Politician* (New Delhi, 1993).

Zbaritel, Dusan, *Bengali Literature* (Wiesbaden, 1976).

Index

Abbott, Freeland 194
Abd Al-Qadir, Shah 137
Abdali, Ahmad Shah 21, 74
Abdul Aziz 144
Abu Hanifia 164
Abul Fazal 59, 70-1
Adi Brahmo Samaj 224
Afzal, M. Rafiq 196
Agarkar, Gopal Ganesh 36, 208
Agrarian relations, in UP and Punjab 87-8
Ahl-i-Hadis 168
Ahmad, A.F. Salahuddin 131
Ahmad, Aziz 48, 75, 92, 93, 95, 96, 135, 191, 192, 194, 195, 256
Ahmad, Jamil-ud-Din 260
Ahmad, Maulvi Nazir 28, 158-9, 177
Ahmad, Mirza Ghulam 256
Ahmad, Qeyamuddin 96, 191
Ahmadiya sect 38
Ahmed, Refiuddin 118, 132, 168, 191, 194
Ahmed, Razi 259
Ahmed, Sufia 131, 132
A'in-i-Akbari 70, 95
Aitchison Commission 105
Akbar 21, 55-6, 59-60, 70-1, 80, 86, 95, 156, 166, 208
Al-Afghani, Jamal al-din 171-2
Al-Faruq 164
Al-Hilal 172-4, 195
Al-Mamun 164
Al Mujahid, Sharif 194, 195
Al-Musta'sim 170
Alam, Muzaffar 87-8, 98
Alberuni 79
Alberuni's India 97
Ali, Karamat 138
Ali, Maulana Inayat 138
Ali, Maulana Muhammad 172, 195
Ali, Maulvi Wilayat 138
Ali, Nadir 186
Ali, Rahmat 32, 189-91, 196, 253, 260
Ali, Sadiq 259
Ali, Syed Ameer 28-9, 112, 114, 116, 163-4, 167, 194, 228
  writings of 163-4
Aligarh Institute Gazette 148
Aligarh movement 140, 150-2, 156-9, 164-6, 176-7
All India Federation 189-90
All India Hindu Mahasabha 40, 228-34
All India Khilafat Conference, Lahore 31, 188
All India Muhammedan Educational Congress 151
All India Muslim Conference 184, 188
All India Muslim League 31, 40, 45, 151, 182, 188, 191, 221, 228-30, 241, 251
Allami, Abul Fazl 95
Allen, George 247
Anandavanabhuvana 85
Anandmath 36, 205-6
Andrews, C.F. 156-7, 193, 194
Aney, M.S. 233
Anjuman-i-Himayat-i-Islam 177
Anjuman-us-Sabha 217
Ansari, M.A. 30, 45, 176
Anti-Partition movement in Bengal (1905-10) 228, 238, 240, 248
Apte, Hari Narayana 36, 209
Arya 228
Arya Samaj 34, 38, 199, 218-19, 236
Ashraf, Ali 195
Ashraf, Mujeeb 96
Asrar-i-Khudi (secrets of self) 181
Aurangzeb 21, 37, 55-6, 60-1, 70-3, 84-7, 95, 136, 158, 166, 207, 211, 237
Aurobindo, Sri 205, 239, 254, 259
Azad, Abul Kalam 30, 93, 172-6
Azamgarh Proclamation of August 1857 91
Aziz, K.K. 48, 93, 195, 196, 247, 260

Aziz, Shah Abdul 22, 75, 137

Babar 61, 68
Badauni 59
Bagal, Jogesh C. 257
Bagchi, Amiya Kumar 133
Bajirao II 209
Baljon, J.M.S. 192
Balkan wars 173
Ball, Charles 98
Banda Bahadur 88
Bande Mataram 36, 205, 227
Bannerjee, Hemchandra 228
Barani, Ziauddin 68
Barelvi, Sayyid Ahmad 22, 75-6
see also Shahid, Sayyid Ahmad
Bari, Maulana Abdul 175
Barni, Ziauddin 20, 69
Barrier, N. Gerald 97, 131, 132, 193, 218, 256, 257, 258
Basu, Aparna 101, 118, 130, 131
Basu, Maladhar 58
Basu, Sankari Prasad 254
Bayly, C.A. 87, 98, 257, 258
Beg, Adam 61
Bengal Banking Enquiry Commission, 1929-30 115
Bengal Renaissance 34
Bengal Tenancy Act, 1885 113-14
Bengal Tenancy (Amendment) Act, 1938 114
Bengal Tenancy Bill 113
Bhagavata Purana 53, 58
Bhakti movement 53-4, 81-3
Bharadwaja, Chiranjiva 254
Bhatt, Balkrishna 36, 207
Bhawani Mandir 239
Bhushan 85
Bilgrami, Muhammad Abdul Qadir 186, 196
Bipan Chandra 131, 259
Birbal 60
Birkenhead 249-51, 260
Birla, G.D. 32
Bombay Mutual Life Assurance Society 127
Bose, Nemai Sadhan 257
Bose, Rajnarain 39-40, 224-7
Bose, Sugata 132
Brahmo Samaj 198, 225
Brass, Paul R. 109, 131, 192, 256
Brennan, Lance 131
British Indian Association of the North Western Provinces and Oudh 148
British Policy, towards Indian nationalism 45, 99-100, 241-53
Buchanan, D.H. 62, 133
Buddhism 28
Bukhari, Shaikh Farid 69
Butterfield, Herbert 49

Caliphate 170-2, 174, 176, 182
Canning 44, 244-5
Chaitanya 54, 81
Chaitanya-mangla 81
Chandra, Sudhir 255
Chatterjee, Bankim Chandra 36, 205-7, 227, 238-9
Chatterjee, Joya 255
Chatterjee, Margaret 259
Chatterjee, Partha 131, 132
Chattopadhyaya, Debiprasad 95
Chaudhury, Nirad C. 254, 255
Chauri-Chaura 30
Chinese Wall theory 53, 55-7, 92
Chintamani temple 60
Chiplunkar, Vishnushastri 36, 209
Christ, Jesus 28, 163-4
Christian missionary propaganda 135-6
Civil Disobedience Movement (1922) 176
Clark, T.W. 255
Communal Award of 1932 45, 233, 250
Community consciousness, among
Hindus 36, 209-34
Muslims 22, 65-7, 77-83, 91, 135
composite culture in India, theory of existence of 50-1
Comrade 172
Congress *see* Indian National Congress
Cornwallis 113
Cow protection movement 38-9, 219-24
Cromwell, S. Crawford 254

Crosthwaite, C.H.T. 257
Curimbhai Cotton Mills 127
Curran, Jean A. 258
Curzon 248

Dadu 23, 54, 83
Dalpatram 36, 208
Dar-ul-Musannifin (Academy of Authors) 165
Dara Shikoh 55, 59, 71-2, 166
Darling, Malcolm Lyall 121, 123, 132, 133
Das, Bashir Ahmad 192
Das, Brajratna 98
Das, C.R. 250
Das, Narayan 215
Das, Suranjan 132
Das Gupta, Ashin 127, 133
Dass, Pundit Bhagwan 216
De, Amalendu 131
De, Barun 253
Dehlavi 252
Delhi Literary Society 216
Deoband, religious seminary 139-40, 168
Derozio Henry Louis Vivian 34, 199, 254
Desai, A.R. 130
Deshmukh, Gopal Hari 36, 208
Devanagari script, movement for use of 37-8 *see also* Hindi language movement
Dhimmi 66, 76
Digby, Simon 95
Din-i-Ilahi 70
Dixit, Prabha 254
Dowson, John 259
Dudu Miyan 22, 76, 138
Dufferin 247-8
Durrani, F.K. Khan 185-6, 196
Dutt, R.C. 255
Dyson, Ketaki Kushari 98 , 259

Education Commission of 1882-3 102
Eknath 82-3
Elliot, Henry M. 43, 242-3, 259
Embree, Ainslie T. 93
Engels, Frederick 93
Ewart, J.M. 196

Faizi 70
Faraizi movement 76, 138
Faruki, Zahiruddin 73, 96
Faruqi, Ziaul Hasan 192, 195
Friedmann, Yohanan 95 , 97, 255

Gadgil, D.R. 129, 133
Ganapati festival 236-7
Gandhi, M.K. 30, 41-2, 45, 176, 186, 240-1, 252, 259
Gandhi-Irwin pact 45
Gangohi, Abd Al-Quddus 67, 70
Gangohi, Rashid Ahmad 139-40
Gankovsky, Z.V. 133
Gardee, Ibrahim 61
Gaurakshini Sabhas 221
Ghatak, Kamal Kumar 255
Ghazali, Imam 96, 164
Ghazee, Abul Muzuffer Serajuddin Bahadur Shah 91
Ghosh, Aurobindo 41
Ghosh, Sunil Bihari 254
Gibb, H.A.R. 95, 176, 195
Gibb, Hamilton 65
Gokhale, Balkrishna Govind 97, 98, 255
Gokhale, Gopal Krishna 238
Golwalkar, Madhavrao Sadashiv 232-3, 258
Gopal, S. 258, 259, 260
Gordon, Richard 258
Gordon-Polonskaya, L.R. 133
Goswami, Radha Charan 36, 207
Government of India Bill, 1935 190
Govind Singh, Guru 87
Graham, G.F.I. 147, 192
Great Hindu Union 226
Greenberger, Allen J. 259
Grewal, J.S. 259
Guha, Ranajit 131, 257
Gujarat Bhasha Pracharini Sabha 215
Gupta, Balmukund 36, 207
Gupta, Maithili Sharan 208, 255
Gupta, Ram Niwas 97
Gupta, S.L. 258
Gurdas, Bhai 83

Guru Purshad, Pandit 216

Habib, Irfan M. 95, 96
Habib, Mohammad 78, 95, 97
Habibullah, A.B.M. 193, 194
Hadith 136, 139, 147
Hailey, Malcolm 31, 187-8, 196
Hajj, institution of 170
Halder, M.K. 205, 253, 254
Hali, Altaf Husain 28, 149, 159-63, 194, 208
Haq, M. Moinul 194
Haq, Mushir U. 193
Hardgrave, Robert L. 133
Hardy, P. 95, 194, 259
Harishchandra, Bharatendu 36, 207
Hasan, Mushirul 132, 195, 255, 258
Heber, Bishop 43, 243
Hedgewar, Keshav Baliram 232
Heimsath, Charles H. 259
Hindi language movement 25-6, 37-8, 124-6, 148-9, 212-19, 224
Hindu(s)
  community consciousness among 22, 36-7, 84-91, 135, 202, 209, 212
  demand for abolition of separate electorates by 23
  education among 101, 109-11, 118-19
  education and employment in
    Bengal 112-20
    Punjab 112, 120-4
    UP 109-11
Hindu Mahasabha 40, 42
Hindu *mela* in Calcutta 39, 225, 228
Hindu-Muslim religio-cultural interaction 47-72, 86-9, 112, 120-4, 220
Hindu-Muslim riots in
  Ahmedabad 89
  Allahabad 89
  Azamgarh 38, 90-1, 220-1
  Ballia 221
  Banaras 90-1
  Bengal 114-16
  Bihar 220-1
  Bombay 38, 124, 220
  Calcutta 88-9
  Delhi 63, 87, 894
  Ghazipur 221
  Junagarh 220
  Kanpur 124
  Kashmir 89
  Malabar 124
  Punjab 38, 62, 87-8, 112, 120-4
  Rangoon 38-9, 220
  Surat 88-9
  Uttar Pradesh 38, 87-8, 220
Hindu nationalism, impact on
  Muslim nationalism 33-40, 178, 197, 212
  British policy towards 241-53
  and cow protection movement 219-41
  demand for replacement of Urdu by Hindi 212-19, 224
  historical roots of 33-40
  ideology of 39-40, 224-34
  in nineteenth century 204-9
Hindu revival and reformation movement in the nineteenth century 33-40, 197-209
  Bankim Chandra Chatterjee 204-7
  Dayanand Saraswati 199-200
  Gujarati literature 208
  Hindi literature 207-9
  Mahadev Govind Ranade 203-4
  Marathi literature 208-9
  Rammohun Roy 198-9
  Vivekananda 200-3
Hindu temples, plundering expeditions against 78, 80
Hindu theism 59
Hinduism, and Islam 19-24, 28, 35, 54, 59
Hirtzel, Arthur 196
Hoare, Samuel 249-50, 252, 260
Hujjat Allah Al-baligha 136
Hunter, W.W. 24, 99-100, 102-3, 116-18, 130, 132, 143, 217, 246
Husain, Fazli 251
Husain, Mohammad Sarfraz 254

Ibn-i-Rashid 96
Ibn-i-Taimiyya 96

Ibn-ul-Vaqt 158
Ijtihad 139, 147
Ikram, S.M. 49, 53-8, 93, 95, 96, 155, 192, 193, 194, 195
Ilbert Bill, 1883 144
Ilm-ul-Kalam 164
Imdadullah 139
Inden, Ronald 259
Indian Councils Act of 1892 220
Indian Councils Act of 1909 45
Indian Economic and Social History Review 196, 254
Indian Education Commission (1882-83) 38, 125, 214-15, 217
Indian Education Commission: Report of the Punjab Provincial Committee 256
Indian Famine Commission, 1880 114
Indian National Congress 23, 28, 36, 40-3, 45, 151, 153-4, 158-9, 164, 221, 226-7, 229, 234-41, 251
Indian national consciousness 36
Indian nationalism
  British policy and 241-53
  Muslims and 45, 99-100
  Congress ideology and 40-3, 234-41
  Ethos of 234-41
  Pan-Islamism and 175
Indian Social Conference 203-4
Indian Statutory Commission *see* Simon Commission
Iqbal, Afzal 195
Iqbal, Allama *see* Iqbal, Muhammad
Iqbal, Muhammad 30-2, 135, 176-85, 189-90, 191, 195, 230
Irwin 45, 196, 249, 251, 260
Islam
  Christianity and 3, 35, 135-6, 143-6, 163-4, 167
  clash with Hinduism 19-24, 28, 35, 54, 59
  glorification of, in works of Muslim elite 167-70
  history of 20-3
  institutions of 170-2, 174, 176
  revival and reformation movements in 21-2, 27, 29, 33, 73-6, 135-91
  rise and growth 65-7
  sense of community and power among Muslims based on 66-7
Islam, Zafarul 105-6, 130
Islamic Anjuman, Dera Ismail Khan 186
Islamic community 65
Izma 147

Jabbar, Abdul 186
Jain, M.S. 193
Jamiyat-ul-Ulama-i-Hind 172, 175
Jansen, Raymond L. 105-6, 130
Jarrett, H.S. 95
Jatiya Mela 225
Jayananda 81
Jayasi 55
Jazirat-ul-Arab 175
Jehangir 55, 60, 68, 86
Jhaveri, Mansukhlal 255
jijya 68 *see jizya*
Jinnah, M.A. 32, 45, 191, 230, 250-3, 260
jizya 55-6, 59-61, 66, 69, 71-3, 80, 86, 158
  abolition of 55, 59, 71
  reimposition 56, 60-1, 71-3, 80, 158
Johnson, Gordon 258
Joint Select Committee on Indian Constitutional Reform (1934) 253
Jones, Kenneth W. 254, 256, 257
Jordens, J.T.F. 254
Joshi, P.C. 101, 130, 133
Joshi, V.C. 253, 256
Kabir 23, 51, 54-5, 59, 70, 82-3
Kabir, Humayun 93
Kafur, Malik 78
Kal 209
Kanesalingam, V. 134
Karim, A.K.N. 131
Karmarkar, D.P. 258
Kaura, Uma 258
Kesari 236-7
Khalifa see Caliphate
Khaliquzzaman, Chaudhry 196
Khalji, Allauddin 58
Khan, Hamid Ali 125, 133

Khan, Hulagu 170
Khan, Iqtidar Alam 95, 97
Khan, Maulvi Ahmed Raza 168
Khan, Muinuddin 96, 191
Khan, Murshid Quli 113
Khan, Nawab Sayyid Sardar Ali 188
Khan, Paragal 58
Khan, Rahim 216
Khan, Syed Ahmad 28, 30, 37, 44, 111-12, 140-65, 171-2, 176, 193, 213, 235, 246-7
Khan, Zafar Ali 172
Khan, Zulfiqar Ali 32, 188, 196
Kher, V.K. 259
Khilafat movement 30, 175-6, 229
Khusro, Amir 53, 59
Kirtilata 80
Kolaskar, M.B. 254
Kole, Ashru 257
Koran 136-7, 143, 146-7, 168, 173
Krishna, K.B. 133
Kruger, Horst 93

Lahore Hindu Sabha 228
Laird, M.A. 259
Land assessments, British policy on 204
Lansdowne 235, 257
Lekh Ram, Pandit 38, 218
Lelyveld, David 193
Linlithgow 251-2, 260
Lokahitwadi *see* Deshmukh, Gopal Hari
Lokhandwalla, S.T. 96, 191
Lyall, J.B. 122
Lytton 144, 150, 246

MacDonnell, A.P. 257
Maclane, John R. 220, 256, 257, 258
Madad-i-maash tenures 87-8
Maha Hindu Samiti 226-7
Mahabharata 53, 58, 158
Mahmud of Ghazni 55, 62, 78-9
Mahratta 237
Maikash, Maulana Murtaza Ahmed Khan 31, 188
Majumdar, Bimanbehari 254
Majumdar, R.C. 37, 49, 51-2, 57, 93, 97, 98, 211, 254, 255, 257
Malaviya, Madan Mohan 40, 228, 233, 256
Malik, Hafeez 47-8, 63, 93, 94, 135, 191, 192, 193, 194, 195
Malik, Ikran Ali 256
Mallick, Azizur Rahman 61, 94, 131
Mamun-ul-Rashid 164
Man Singh 59-60
Mapilla rebellion (also Moplah rebellion) 25, 124, 176
Maqalat-i-Shibli 165
Marathas 37, 210-12
Marx, Karl 47, 93
Masood, Ross 187
Mayo 245-6
Medieval India 95, 97
Meherullah, Munshi 169-70
Mehrotra, S.R. 131
Mehta, Asoka 77, 96, 130
Mehta, M.M. 128
Metcalf, Barbara Daly 191, 192, 194
Metcalf, Thomas R. 104, 130, 259
Middle class in India, rise and growth of, during British rule 26
Militant Hinduism 84
Mill, James 43, 242, 259
Minerva Lodge 178
Minto 23, 45, 248
Mir, Titu 22, 76, 96, 138
Misra, B.B. 97, 133, 258
Misra, Pratap Narain 36, 207
Mitra, Nabagopal 39, 225
Mohammedan Anglo-Oriental College, Aligarh 27, 45, 150, 156, 164-5, 246
Mohsin-ul-Mulk, Nawab 149
Moon, Penderal 133
Morison, T. 193
Motilal Nehru Committee's Report 42
Mubarak, Shaikh 70
Muhammedan Defence Association 152
Muhammedan Educational Conference 151
Muir, William 146, 214
Mujahidin movement 137

Mujeeb, M. 66, 71, 95, 96, 136, 145, 191, 192, 195
Mukherjee, Rudrangshu 98
Musaddas-e-Hali 28, 159-63
Muslim calendar 20
Muslim Chronicle 125
Muslim elite
  abhorrence for idol worship 69, 77-83
  alliance with British authorities 44-5
  caste groups among 63-4
  community consciousness among 22, 65-93, 135
  demand for Muslim majority in Punjab and Bengal Legislative Councils 24
  ideological and emotional environment of 135-91
  sense of insecurity about future of their faith 73-6
  separate electorates and weightage, demand for 12, 15
Muslim-Hindu culture *see* Hindu-Muslim religio-cultural interaction
Muslim League *see* All India Muslim League
Muslim National Homeland 31-2
Muslim National Reformer 152
Muslim nationalism
  British policy and 43-5
  economic explanation of 24-6, 99-130
  emergence of 47
  Hindu nationalism and 33-4, 197
  historical roots of 19-32
  ideological and emotional foundations of 176-85
    in Bengal 24-5, 112-20
    in Punjab 24-5, 112, 120-4
    in Uttar Pradesh 109-11
Muslim peasant movement in Bengal 25, 27
Muslim rulers
  legitimation of rule by *ulama* 20
  Muslim orthodoxy and 21
resentment among Hindus against 22-3
Muslims
  consciousness about education 147-56
  education and employment, in
    Bengal 112-20
    Punjab 112, 120-4
    Uttar Pradesh 109-11
  education among 99-104, 108-11, 118
  government employment among 103-7, 109, 116-17, 120-1
  higher education among 118
  in commerce and industry 110, 123-4, 126-30
  in higher position in Government 105-7, 116-17, 120-1
  in judicial service 105-7, 116-17
  in medical profession 118
  in public service 106, 108
  landlords and peasants 110, 112-13
  middle class 126
  representation in Government 105-7, 116-17
  revival and reformation movement among 21-2, 27, 29, 33, 73-6, 135-91
Mustafa Kamal 182
Muztar, A.D. 96

Nadvat-ul-Ulama 165-6, 168
Nagara, Isana 81
Naidu, Ratna 133
Naim, C.M. 195
Nala-i-Yatim (Orphan's cry) 177
Namadeva 54, 82
Nanak 23, 51, 54, 59, 83
Nanautovi, Muhammad Qasim 139
Nanda, B.R. 130, 131
Naoroji, Dadabhai 234
Narain, Sushma 255
Narendranath, Raja 133
Naramadashankar 36, 208
Nasihat Namas 169
National Muhammadan Association 28, 112, 228
National Paper 39, 225

National Society 39, 225
Nationality Promotion Society 39, 225
Naya Shivala (New Temple) 177
Nehru, Jawaharlal 42, 240-1, 259
Nehru, Motilal 42, 241
Nemade, Bhalchandra 97
Nicholson, Reynold A. 195
Nijami, Azra 95
Nilakanth, Ramachandra 85
Nivedita, Sister 201, 254
Nizami, Khaliq Ahmad 96, 97, 191
Non-cooperation movement 30
Noon, Firoz Khan 251
Nooruzzaman, A.H.M. 131
Norman 246
North-West Frontier Enquiry Committee 186
Now or Never 189-90
Numani, Shibli 28-9, 96, 164-7, 172

Old Hindu's Hope 226, 257
Oriental Government Security Life Insurance Company 127
Ottoman Caliphate 174

Pakistan idea 32
Pakistan National Movement 190
Pakstan 32
Pal, Bipin Chandra 228, 257
Palmerston 244
Pan Indian Hindu political consciousness 86
Pan-Islamic movement 29-30, 45
Pan-Islamism 164-5, 170-6, 182
Pandey, B.N. 193
Pandey, Gyanendra 89, 98, 133, 255, 257
Panikkar, K.M. 49, 58-61, 93, 133
Paramashwar, Kavindra 58
Paranjape, Shivarama Mahadeva 36, 209
Partition of Bengal 173, 178
Partition of India 186-91
Pathak, Jitram 255
Pathik, Devaraj Sharma 255
Patwardhan, Achyut 77, 130
Peasant indebtedness problem 122-4
Peel, Viscount 248
Permanent Settlement (1793) 113
Perpetual Conflict Theory 63
Persian script, objection against use of 37-8
Peshwa, Madhav Rao 87
Philips, C.H. 193, 254, 255
Pilgrim tax 59
Pioneer 154, 247
Pirzada, Syed Sharifuddin 196
Prakash, Indra 257
Prasad, Beni 253
Prasad, Bimal 254
Prasad, Bisheshwar 96, 97
Prasad, Rajendra 130
Prophet Muhammad 27-8, 34, 66, 89, 136, 146, 163-4, 167, 193
Public Service Commission (1886-87) 105, 107
Punjab Alienation of Land Act (1901) 123
Punjab Alienation of Land Bill of 1900 132
Punjab Arya Samaj 218
Punjab Brahmo Samaj 215
Punjab Hindu Sabha 40, 228
purdah system 209

Quran *see* Koran
Qureshi, Ishtiaq Husain 47-8, 93, 155, 193, 196

Rafi-al-Din, Shah 137
Rahim, Abdur 55
Rahman, Akhlaqur 134
Rai, Baboo Navina Chandra 216
Rai, Lala Lajpat 40, 218, 229, 233, 236, 256, 258
Rai, Satya M. 132
Rajatarangini 53, 59
Rajm 146-7
Ram Gopal 130
Ramakrishna 200
Ramayana 53
Ramdas 60, 82, 84
Ranade, Mahadev Govind 35-6, 203-4, 210, 254, 255
Ranade, Ramabai 254
Ranjit Singh 87

Rashtriya Swayamasevak Sangh (RSS) 232-4
Ray, Niharranjan 52, 93
Reading 176, 248, 250, 260
Rebellion of 1857 43-4, 140-3, 244-5
Reeves, P.D. 94
Renan, Earnest 183
Report of Indian Education Commision (1883) 106, 121, 130, 132, 256
Report of the Indian Statutory Commission 260
Report of the Joint Select Committee on Indian Constitutional Reform 260
Report of the Punjab Provincial Committee 133
Report of the United Provices Banking Enquiry Committee 1929-30 133
Richards, D.S. 133
Risail-i-Shibli 64
Rizvi, Saiyid Athar Abbas 89, 95, 96, 98, 191
Robinson, Francis 110-11, 131, 192, 246-7, 259
Round Table Conference 32, 45, 189, 249
Roy, Raja Rammohun 34, 141, 198-9, 204
Roy, Somnath 257
Rumi, Maulana 164
Rungta, Radhe Shyam 133
Russo-Turkish War 144, 171

Sachau, Edward C. 97
Sadiq, Muhammad 193, 194
Sagun Bhakti movement 81
Sanatan Dharma 41
Sangam Lal 228
Sanjana, J.E. 255
Saraswati, Swami Dayanand 34, 199-200, 219
Sardesai, G.S. 37, 98, 212, 255
Sarin, Dharam Pal 255
Sarkar, Jadunath 37, 72, 96, 98, 211, 255
Sarkar, Jagdish Narayan 97
Sarkar, Sumit 132, 253, 258
Sarkar, Susobhan 98, 225, 257
Sarkar, Tanika 132
sati 34, 198
Satish Chandra 73, 96, 97
Sattar, Abdus 186
Satyartha Prakash 34, 200
Savarkar, V.D. 37, 210-11, 229-32, 255, 258
Sayeed, Khalid B. 48, 93
Scientific Society 148
Seal, Anil 94, 132, 193
Secrets of the Self: Allama Iqbal's Asrar-i-Khudi 195
Select Committee of the Anjuman-i-Punjab 216
seminary *see* religious seminary, Deoband
Sen, Amit 255
Sen, Narendra Nath 202
Sen, S.P. 258
Sen, Shila 132
Shafi, Muhammed 251
Shah, Ala-ud-din Husain 81
Shah, Bahadur 91
Shah, Hussain 58
Shah, Nusrat 58
Shah, Sultan Husain 53
Shahid, Sayyid Ahmad 22, 27, 75-6, 137-8 *see also* Barelvi, Sayyid Ahmad
Shahid, Shah Ismail 137
Shahjahan 55, 59-60, 86, 95
Shaikh, Farzana 94
Shakespeare 149
Shams-ud-Din, Mohammad 122
Sharar, Abdul Halim 29, 166-7
Shariah 20, 55, 65-6, 67, 69, 75, 175
Shariatullah, Haji 22, 76, 138
Sharma, Kranti Kumar 255
Sharma, S.R. 95, 97
Shikwa 179, 195
Shikwa-i-Hind 162
Shir-ul-Azam 164
Shivabawani 85
Shivaji 36-7, 60, 82, 84-6, 209-12
as protector of Hinduism 84-6
letter to Aurangzeb 86
Shivaji festival 237-8
Shobha, Savitri Chandra 97

Shukla, Ram Chandra 97, 194
Siddiqi, Majid Hayat 196
Simon Commission 251-2
Singh, Ganda 97
Singh, Khushwant 195
Singh, Raja Ramphal 223
Sinha, N.K. 93, 113, 131
Sirat-ul-Numan 164
Sirat-un-Nabi 164
Sirhindi, Shaikh Ahmad 68, 70-1
Sivaprasad, Raja 37, 149, 213-14
Sleeman, William Henry 43, 62, 73, 96, 242-3, 259
Smith, Vernon 244
Smith, W.C. 24, 66, 76, 95, 100, 126, 130, 133, 192, 193, 194, 195
Sobhan, Rehman 129, 134
Society for the Promotion of National Feeling among the Educated Natives of Bengal 224
Somnath Temple 60
Song of India 227
Spear, Percival 52, 93
Spectator 145
Strachey, John 247, 260
Subramanian, Lakshmi 98
Sudesh 255
Sulh-i-Kul policy of Akbar 86
Sunnah 136-7, 139
Swadeshi movement 212

Tagore, Dwarakanath 34, 92, 199
Tahzib-al-Akhlaq 145-6, 152
Taiyuni movement 138
Tara Chand 50, 70, 77, 93, 95
Tarana-i-Hind 177
Tarana-i-Milli 177
Tarikh-i-Firuzshahi 20, 68
Tarikh-i-Hindusthan 157
Tatler 145
Taubat-un-Nasuh 158
Teg Bahadur, Guru 87
Thomas, F.W. 52, 93
Thompson, A.R. 118
Thorburn, S.S. 62, 94, 121, 132, 133
Tilak, Bal Gangadhar 36, 41-2, 209, 236-9, 241
Time and Tide 260
Time-lag theory 99-101
Timur 158
Titus, Murray 52, 93
Todarmal 60
Tripathi, Amalas 207, 255, 259
Tripoli, Italy's annexation of 172
Troll, Christian W. 192, 193
Tucker, Richard P. 254
Tughlaq, Firoz 58, 69
Tukaram 54
Turkish Rulers, policy of religious toleration of 20, 22
Two-nation theory, 32, 61, 185-91, 230
Tyabji, Badruddin 154, 193

Ulama 67
Umar 164
ummah 65
United India Patriotic Association 152
United Provinces Provincial Banking Enquiry Committee of 1929-30, report of 128-9
Urdu language, movement to replace use of 37-8
Ushahkala 209

Vahid, Syed Abdul 195, 196
Vakil, C.N. 134
Vallabhacharya 81
Van den Dungen P.H.M. 132
Varma, Vishwanath Prasad 258
Verma, Harishchandra 97
Vernacular Press Act (1878) 144
Victoria High School 148
Vidyalankar, Satyaketu 256
Vidyapati 80
Vivekananda, Swami 34-5, 200-3, 238, 254
Von Grunebaum, G.E. 192, 194, 256

Wahhabi movement 22, 27, 44, 75-6, 99, 137-8, 143, 245-6

Waliullah, Shah 21-2, 27, 74-5, 96, 135
7, 139, 146
Wallace Mackenzie 248
Wasiyat Nama 74, 136
Watt, Montgomery 65, 94
Willingdon 249-50, 252, 260
Wolpert, Stanley A. 258, 259

Zaidi, A.M. 193
Zaidi, A. Moin 258
Zaidi, Shabeda 258
Zain-ul-Abidin 53
Zaku Ullah, Munshi 28, 156-7, 166,
193
Zakaria, Rafiq 130, 133, 259
Zakat 55, 68
Zamindar 172
Zbarite, Dusan 254
Zetland 260
Zulqarnain 186